ESSAYS IN
THE LIBERAL INTERPRETATION
OF HISTORY

CLASSIC EUROPEAN HISTORIANS

A SERIES EDITED BY LEONARD KRIEGER

Lord Acton

ESSAYS IN THE
LIBERAL
INTERPRETATION
OF HISTORY

Selected Papers

Edited and with an Introduction
by William H. McNeill

Phoenix Books

THE UNIVERSITY OF CHICAGO PRESS
CHICAGO & LONDON

This book is also available in a clothbound edition from
THE UNIVERSITY OF CHICAGO PRESS

THE UNIVERSITY OF CHICAGO PRESS
CHICAGO & LONDON
The University of Toronto Press, Toronto 5, Canada

First Phoenix Edition 1967

Printed in the United States of America

Series Editor's Preface

To some of our contemporaries, historians are not what they used to be. To others, every day and in every way history gets better and better. But by coincident consent, the works of our forebears that have been winnowed by time have a lasting value, whether as models of historical literature or as milestones in the progress of the profession to its present eminence. To make readily and economically available those histories of this genre that have become difficult of access, the University of Chicago Press herewith inaugurates a series of volumes titled "Classic European Historians."

A "classic," in the context of this series, is defined as a work that satisfies one or both of the following criteria: (*a*) it has opened up or transformed the substantive history of the European field which it treats; (*b*) it is a landmark in the formal development of historical method and understanding. The series is thus designed to serve the purposes of both history and historiography, the former by restoring the broad canvases of a less monographic age, and the latter by supplying crucial documents for the history of history. In the essay which introduces each of these classics, the volume editor correspondingly establishes guidelines for the assessment of both the history and the historian—of the history by distinguishing between the instrumental and the persistent validity of the subject matter, and of the historian by adducing the personal and intellectual factors that converged in his approach to the past. Pursuant to these purposes, the text will cleave as closely to the ideal of complete reproduction as the limits of a single-volume format permit: it is important to know what has as well as what has not been superseded in history, and it is beneficial to watch the parenthetical as well as the essential operations of a great historian at work.

It is fitting that the representative historical essays of Lord Acton help initiate the series. Over and above the longevity of particular pieces and the immortality conferred by a trusting posterity upon his unwritten history of liberty, his assorted lectures and articles conjunctively occupy a central position in the European historical tradition. By virtue of their scope and their very discontinuity, they manifest the broad frame, the manifold tendencies, and the motivating problems of modern European historiography more graphically than the consistency of a single great work would have done. In the introduction which follows, his editor on this occasion, William H. McNeill, whose own monumental *Rise of the West* has realized Acton's proclaimed intention of "extending the scene from Western Europe to the whole world,"* reveals with sympathetic understanding the multiple demands incumbent upon the historian who casts so wide a net, and describes with critical appreciation how their embodiment in Acton's piecemeal history turned a personal failure into a historiographical success. The variety of the influences which Acton incorporated but could not integrate governs the selection of the essays which Professor McNeill has made for republication here. The tensions between power and liberty in history, between persistence and progress through history, between the detailed research and the general interpretation of history, and between the impartial and the moral judgments upon history all find their exemplars in both the narrative and the expository forms that Acton gave them.

The eclectic quality that epitomized Acton's appreciation of both individuality in history and men's incessant urge to transcend it was itself a historical product. It manifested his pivotal position in the history of European history that is the concern of this series. As a member of the post-Rankean generation who

---

* See "Beginning of the Modern State," below.

accommodated the new specialized concern for the verification of particular events to the older but still vital faith in a general, unitary pattern of human history, Acton stands squarely between the century that produced the separate strands of philosophical and scientific history and our own century that has sought to synthesize them. Not only did he articulate the autonomous claims of both truth and meaning in historical theory, but he fertilized the study of European history itself by applying the empirical methods of truth-finding to past politics, and the rational categories of meaning to the history of ideas. He thereby joined the distinguished group of historians who transmitted to the twentieth century the whole range of past European achievement in the knowledge as in the philosophy of history. From him we can work back into the discrete constituents of the achievement and forward into the dialectical and thematic devices through which it has been extended.

LEONARD KRIEGER

Editor's Introduction

JOHN Emerich Edward Dalberg-Acton (1834–1902) steeped himself in paradox. In an age of rising nationalisms, he was an Englishman by choice; but by birth, education, and friendships he remained a cosmopolitan Catholic aristocrat who was as much at home in Germany, Italy, or France as in England. In Acton's youth, Pope Pius IX went to great lengths to draw the line between Catholic truth and Liberal error, and nearly all liberals reciprocated by regarding the Roman Catholic church as the principal obstacle in the path of progress. Yet, to the scandal of fellow Catholics and the surprise of fellow liberals, Acton opted emphatically and in public for both. Then in his later years, he attained a great reputation as a historian, mainly on the strength of a book he never wrote. Nevertheless, Acton's inclusion in this series, not to mention a continued flow of books about him, successive reprints of his essays, and frequent quotation of his aphorisms, all attest to his power of exciting interest (and usually admiration) across the better part of a century—a time sufficient to eclipse the names of many historians far more prolific than he.

Acton's fame rested and continues to rest partly on his social position and personal connections. On his father's side he descended from an English Catholic émigré who had enjoyed a spectacular career in the service of the King of Naples, in which city Acton was born. On his mother's side, he descended from one of the noblest families of southern Germany, the Dalbergs. When Acton was three years old his father died. Three years later his mother remarried, taking as her second husband an

English Whig aristocrat who was only nineteen years older than her son. Acton's stepfather, the second Earl of Granville, inherited a political position in England that allowed him, as a matter of course, to arrange for Acton to occupy a seat in Parliament as soon as his education was finished. Granville himself was a member of almost every Liberal Cabinet formed between 1840 and 1886, and climaxed his career by twice holding the post of Foreign Secretary, in 1870–74 and in 1880–85.

Despite these family connections, no less than three Cambridge colleges refused to admit the young Acton—presumably because the dons of Cambridge feared that his Catholicism might precipitate scandalous conversions to Rome like those with which John Henry, later Cardinal, Newman had recently disturbed the peace of Oxford's quadrangles. As a result, at the age of fifteen, Acton went to Munich to live and study with the Catholic priest and historian, Professor Ignaz Döllinger.

Acton lived in Döllinger's house for seven years. Even when the university was not in session, he continued to enjoy Father Döllinger's company on trips to various cities of Europe, where the two combed archives and second hand bookstores for rare or forgotten materials pertaining to almost every aspect of modern history. Döllinger and his precocious pupil varied their scholarly activity with social calls upon the great and near great of the age, whose doors opened automatically to a brilliant young man with Acton's family connections. The basis for Acton's magnificent private library (60,000 volumes at his death) was laid during these vacation trips; his later fame for knowing everything and everyone of any importance in Europe was based upon this same experience.

From his studies with Döllinger, Acton acquired one preeminent conviction: to wit, that the Church, like other institutions, had undergone and would doubtless continue to undergo important changes across the centuries. German historical scholarship had made it clear that the Church had not always and everywhere remained the same; but this view of ecclesiastical reality was unfamiliar among English Catholics. Upon the completion of his formal education the young Acton therefore resolved to begin a journalistic career in order to communicate this message, together with other fruits of his continental sophistication and learning, to his insular fellow churchmen. He did so as co-editor of, and contributor to, first the *Rambler* and then the *Home and Foreign Review*. By 1864, however, the tone of these journals had aroused the public ire of the Archbishop of Westminster, the Roman Catholic Primate of England. Acton thereupon decided to retire from the fray, and two years later also abandoned his parliamentary career.

As the first six articles here reproduced will suggest, a surprisingly large proportion of Acton's published work dates back to these early years, when weighty essays, polemical reviews, and learned trifles like the study of Charles II's illegitimate son poured easily from his pen. Many of Acton's mature traits were demonstrated in these early essays—in particular, his ability to stand aloof even in dealing with matters like ultramontanism with which he was himself deeply and personally involved. He looked from two perspectives, but both seemed in focus, for the historian's dispassionate and Olympian vision, measuring men and events against the rich tapestry of the past, helped rather than hindered the polemicist's sharp thrust. Acton profoundly believed that, when properly understood, Catholic truth and human liberty did not conflict but were mutually dependent. Without an autonomous and international Church to counterbalance political power, he felt that constitutional liberties could never become genuinely secure. To guard against abuse, rulers had always to be checked and limited, and how better than by a divinely established suprapolitical corporation?

But after his collision with the Archbishop, this happy constellation of circumstances no longer sustained Acton's labors. His effort to mobilize accurate, scientific historical scholarship in the cause of liberal Catholicism having been rejected by his ecclesiastical superiors, Acton fell back upon aimless and desultory journalistic activity for a few years, but he put his main effort into behind-the-scenes negotiations, aimed at galvanizing the liberal forces within the Roman Catholic church into more effective action. Then, after 1870, when the viewpoints Acton had championed were resoundingly repudiated at the Vatican Council, he gave up journalism almost entirely.

Instead, he set himself the task of writing a great book that might deliver his message to a later age more ready to receive it. These, then, were the years when his magnum opus, *The History of Liberty*, was projected but not written. He read voraciously, took endless notes, hastened like a bird dog after every newly opened archive or freshly published work of historical scholarship, and fell, inevitably, farther and farther behind the task of mastering all the available information which might be relevant to his projected history. In 1877 he did sketch the main lines his book might have taken in the two lectures on the history of freedom reprinted here; and in private conversations he often ignited the imaginations of his hearers and amazed them with his erudition as he spoke of how the history of mankind could be understood as a tortuous yet persistent advance towards liberty.

Nevertheless, Acton's total failure to accomplish what he and his friends expected of him is the central fact of his life. His collected writings constitute mere slivers and fragments, occasional pieces and classroom lectures, which were thrown off casually and incidentally in the course of his titanic labor of self-preparation for the great work which he never even started.

Such a catastrophe is not inexplicable. In the first place, Acton's conception of the proper method of historical research made the writing of any large-scale history, dealing with many subjects across long periods of time, an utter impossibility. His extraordinary powers of memory and indefatigable reading habits perhaps allowed him at first to deceive himself about the practicability of realizing his ideal of accuracy in the light of *all* the sources; but by the 1880's such self-deception was no longer possible. Nevertheless, he could not, or at least did not, abandon his naïve notion of how historical truth should be sought.

Let him speak for himself. In the concluding paragraphs of his *Lectures on the French Revolution,* he says:

> Where do we now stand, and what is the elevation that enables us to look down on men who, the other day, were high authorities? We are at the end, or near the end, of the supply of

Memoirs; few are known to exist in manuscript. Apart from Spain, we are advanced in respect of diplomatic and international correspondence; and there is abundant private correspondence. . . . But we are only a little way in the movement for the production of the very acts of the government of revolutionary France.

. . . .One collection is coming out on the Elections for Paris, another on the Paris Electors. . . . Then there is a series of the acts of the Commune, of the several governing committees, of the Jacobins, of the war department, and seven volumes on the Vendée alone.

In a few years all these publications will be completed and *all will be known that ever can be known*. [My italics!] Perhaps someone will then compose a history as far beyond the latest we possess as Sorel, Aulard, Rambaud, Flammermont are in advance of Taine and Sybel. . . . In that golden age our historians will be sincere, and our history certain. The worst will be known, and then sentence need not be deferred. . . . Mendacity depended on concealment of evidence. When that is at an end, fable departs with it, and the margin of legitimate divergence is narrowed.[1]

Thus Truth, the whole Truth, is just around the corner, awaiting the publication of a few more sources. Unaccountably, Acton seems to assume, even at the very end of his life, that there is a definite and forseeable limit to the number of sources that can be found relevant to the study of such a complex reality as the French Revolution, and he dismisses the historian's role as architect, organizer, and interpreter of facts as mere "fable." Yet, at the same time, the "sincere" historian, knowing the truth, will have to judge the crimes and moral failings of the men whose acts he describes; and, knowing all, he must not shrink from pronouncing his magistral, final, and eternal sentence. Acton, in fact, reserves for the historian roles which Christian doctrine assigned to God himself: omniscience and final judgment. No wonder, then, that he concluded with a tacit confession of the vanity of his own ideal:

We might wait long if we watched for the man who knows the whole truth and has the courage to speak it, who is careful of

---

[1] *Lectures on the French Revolution* (London: Macmillan & Co., 1925), pp. 372–73.

other interests besides his own, and labours to satisfy opponents, who can be liberal towards those who have erred, who
have sinned, who have failed, and deal evenly with friend and
foe—assuming that it would be possible for an honest historian
to have a friend.[2]

Yet this explanation of Acton's failure is insufficient. Many
solid and learned tomes were written by his contemporaries and
successors who shared nearly the same view of historical
method. If universal history was impossible, topical histories
were not; and Acton had notes for a dozen or more such works,
any one of which, if executed, would have found a valued place
in the European historiographical tradition. Moreover, even if
the task he set himself exceeded human powers, Acton might
have started to write his great *History of Liberty* and ended his
life with the first volumes behind and some untold number
ahead—a fate which has befallen many historians before and
since.

Because he did neither of these things, something more than
mere methodological folly is needed to explain his inability to
write the book he projected. Indeed, it seems to me that behind
his frantic effort to master all the sources we can discern a
pervasive and paralysing conflict between his moral and his
intellectual judgments.

Morally, Acton was deeply committed all through his life to
the enhancement of liberty for individuals and for small groups.
He found the tyranny of the majority no less than the tyranny of
kings and of prelates utterly repugnant. As a result, all the great
men of history who had to smash their way through obstacles
and overcome vested interests became evildoers. Virtue rested
only with the defeated, who, Acton recognized, usually wished
nothing more than to do to their conquerors what their conquerors had done to them. Nevertheless, facts were facts, and crimes
uncommitted from want of opportunity were less heinous than
those which were committed. Acton's strikingly a-historical
preoccupation with the historian's role as a "hanging judge,"
redressing the injustices of the past by measuring the deeds of

[2] *Ibid.*

rulers and mighty men against the universal yardstick of justice, was a tangible expression of his belief in an absolute morality and in the liberty which, he thought, that morality required.

But intellectually, Acton could not really persuade himself that the actual course of history fitted into the sort of liberal mold his moral principles demanded. Mankind's record, far from being a history of liberty, seemed rather to be a long history of the denial of liberty by any group strong enough to impose its will. In his early years, for example, Acton hailed the American Revolution and the Constitution which emerged in 1789 as the wisest and most perfect expression of liberal principles yet manifest on earth; but the upshot of the American Civil War destroyed the federal principle as he understood it, opening a way for tyrannical democratic majorities to override all opposition just as in revolutionary and post-revolutionary France. If this were the upshot of the wisest statesmanship the world had yet seen, what hope could there be for Acton's brand of liberty? Indeed, he must often have doubted whether the British Constitution itself was the apex of political wisdom and a practicable model for all mankind. Knowing the history of Europe as intimately as he did, British liberty seemed more like an insular oddity which had been able to come into existence and survive because the salt water of the English Channel reduced the exigencies of war and lessened the need for standing armies.

Acton saw quite clearly whence would come the main challenge to liberty as domesticated in late Victorian Britain.

That which arose in Northern Europe about the time of our revolution settlement [that is, 1689] was a new form of practical absolutism. Theological monarchy had done its time, and was now followed by military monarchy. Church and State had oppressed mankind together; henceforth the State oppressed for its own sake. And this was the genuine idea that came in with the Renaissance, according to which the State alone governs, and all other things obey. Reformation had pushed religion to the front: but after two centuries the original theory, that government must be undivided and uncontrolled, began to prevail. It is a new type, not to be confounded with that of Henry VIII, Philip II or Lewis XIV, and better adapted to a more rational and economic age. Government so understood is the intellectual guide of the nation, the promoter of wealth, the teacher of knowledge, the guardian of morality, the mainspring of the ascending movement of man. That is the tremendous power, supported by millions of bayonets, which grew up in the days of which I have been speaking at Petersburg, and was developed, by much abler minds, chiefly at Berlin; and it is the greatest danger that remains to be encountered by the Anglo-Saxon race.[3]

In such an encounter, could liberty, defined as respect for individual rights and for minority privilege, hope to prevail?

Acton, I think, was far from sure that history did not, in fact, march with the big battalions and with the absolute, concentrated power which, according to his most famous aphorism, corrupts absolutely. But he never had to meet his problem squarely because there was always another document to consult before the great *History of Liberty* could begin. Indeed, he may—half consciously—have become a virtuoso of bibliographical erudition in order to avoid having to confront the dilemma between power and virtue that his innermost values—his vision of truth and of morality—presented to him.

Essentially the same problem haunts anyone today who inherits western individualistic values and reflects upon our advancing capacity to control and manipulate one another. It is therefore possible in reading Lord Acton's pages—amid much that seems ponderous, dull, or outmoded—suddenly to come across a brief passage or pithy saying in which one's own half-formulated thoughts or feelings seem to attain a sharper definition or wider ranging expression than before. This capacity for occasional scintillation, surely, constitutes the basis of Action's claim to rank among the great historians of Europe.

There was, however, another aspect of Acton's experience that probably had as much to do with paralyzing his literary activity as any mere intellectual dilemma. For Acton had an unusual emotional life. The early death of his father and his mother's remarriage led to a polite and relaxed but pervasive lack of

---

[3] *Lectures on Modern History* (London: Macmillan & Co., 1906), p. 289.

sympathy between stepfather and stepson. This prepared the young aristocrat to transfer a store of filial feeling to Father Döllinger, the Munich professor who took him into his house. And on the other side, a man of Döllinger's bourgeois origin must have been deeply flattered by Acton's ardor for learning and delight in his modest company. Then, in Acton's middle age, after thirty years of close association, climaxing in the period of the Vatican Council (1869–70) when he and Döllinger had stood together in trying to prevent the declaration of papal infallibility, he went out of his way to pick a quarrel with his friend and mentor. Wishes of the family long prevented the publication of Acton's correspondence with Döllinger,[4] but odd notes that Acton left behind amid his enormous collection of papers make it clear that this break was, for him, fraught with the greatest emotion. Acton's reaction, indeed, was altogether out of proportion to the ostensible issue between the two men, for the point of difference was whether a historian should judge everyone, prince or pauper, guilty of murder if he had ever ordered or contrived a murder![5]

In later years, to be sure, Acton recovered his balance and began once more to write a few articles. From 1886 he became a contributor to the newly established *English Historical Review,* and on the occasion of Döllinger's death was even able to analyze learnedly and dispassionately the historical work of the man he had quarreled with and yet revered. This is perhaps the most remarkable example of Acton's ability to disguise his personal feelings when writing as a historian.

Acton's learning and liberalism led in 1895 to his appointment as Regius Professor of History at Cambridge. This position required him to deliver a famous inaugural lecture—the ripest and most explicit statement he ever made of his views of historical scholarship. He also prepared two series of public lectures, one

---

[4] The first of four projected volumes of this correspondence recently appeared. See Victor Conzemius (ed.), *Ignaz von Döllinger Briefwecksel mit Lord Acton, 1850–1869* (Munich: C. N. Beck Verlagsbuchhandlung, 1963).

[5] Cf. Gertrude Himmelfarb, *Lord Acton: A Study in Conscience and Politics* (Chicago: University of Chicago Press, 1952), pp. 147 ff.

on modern history and the other on the French Revolution, which were published after his death. But his greatest impact upon the historical profession was the result of an invitation issued by the Cambridge University Press to plan and execute a modern history. In Acton's hands this invitation turned into a vast collaborative effort, *The Cambridge Modern History*. Paradigmatically he died (1902) when the first volume was in press, and before he had himself written a projected introductory chapter.

Acton's influence, nevertheless, was far greater than might be expected. More than any other single man, he transplanted German thoroughness and historical method across the Channel. As a result, in the English universities writing history from anything but primary sources became unprofessional after Acton's time, as it had been in German academic circles from Ranke's days. In addition, so far as I can discover, Lord Acton was the first Englishman to view British, American, and Continental European history as a common whole, and to imprint upon this synthesis what Herbert Butterfield has aptly termed the Whig interpretation of history, that is, the notion that all mankind has been toiling onward and upward through time toward the pinnacle of English (and/or American) constitutional liberty. Acton presented this view in his public lectures on modern history and—at least implicitly—in his plan for *The Cambridge Modern History*. Thereby he set the mold within which the English-speaking world has tended to view modern times ever since.

The longevity of such a view is not really to be wondered at. Cross-fertilization of nineteenth-century German academic standards of historical research with the native English Whig view (which before Acton's time had been applied mainly within the parochial frame of British constitutional development) obviously created an interpretation of modern history which was both persuasive—"scientific"—and enormously flattering to the self-esteem of the entire English-speaking world. Moreover, the prestige first of Britain and more recently of the United States in international affairs assured that other peoples and men of deeply alien culture would learn their history from schoolbooks shaped into this mold as much by Acton as by any other single man.

Yet, with a final paradox, such a smugly certain, simple view of the past was precisely what Acton himself had never unambiguously enunciated or really been able to believe. His university lectures and his editorial planning lent themselves to this interpretation; his own essays never went so far, and his great masterpiece testified, by the fact that it remained unwritten, to Acton's inability to subscribe to the lessons of history which his students and admirers so readily drew.

World War I and the multiple disillusionments of the interwar years did much to discredit smug confidence in the progress of liberty and justice. Instead, the idea that history moves in cycles and that the heyday of liberalism was perhaps drawing ineluctably toward an end gained plausibility. Oswald Spengler in Germany proclaimed this view with relish; Arnold J. Toynbee in England concurred, but with reluctance. Yet these and similarly systematic schemata never won more than marginal and grudging acceptance among professional historians. Too many details did not fit. The result, therefore, of the dethronement of Whiggish history in the twentieth century has been to introduce a general confusion and intellectual uncertainty among historians. Contemporary historians lack the homogeneity of outlook that seems (at least in retrospect) to characterize those who wrote in Queen Victoria's day, for we are aware as our predecessors scarcely were of the historical reality and complexity of the non-Western world, and are committed viscerally if not always intellectually to the virtues of democratic government and liberal institutions, but remain at least as unsure as Acton ever was of whether history is a record of the advance of human freedom, of human power, of both freedom and power, or of power at the expense of freedom.

And because, like Acton himself, we have begun to doubt the adequacy of the Whiggish history inherited from Acton's age, his enigmatic, paradoxical, subtle, and erudite reputation has serenely survived. During his lifetime Acton became accustomed to survival amid the ruins of his own ambition; since his death his reputation appears to be equally invulnerable to the collapse of the view of modern history erected by his disciples and admirers. His greatness is perhaps sufficiently authenticated by these facts.

WILLIAM H. McNEILL

Contents

ESSAYS IN
THE LIBERAL INTERPRETATION
OF HISTORY

I

Mr. Buckle's Thesis and Method

MR. BUCKLE is a gentleman who has had the rare fortune of jumping to celebrity at a bound, by the publication of an elaborate book on a profound subject. The success of the published portion of his *History of Civilisation in England* has been hitherto far above that which usually attends such efforts; and it must be conceded, that a work which could thus seize on the public ear must be, at any rate, a remarkable production. It must have powerfully appealed to something or other in the public mind, or tell something or other very important, which people wanted to know, in order to have won so rapid a popularity.

The object which he proposes to himself is, to prove that history may be reduced to a science. To comprehend the full meaning of this proposition we must ask, what is "history," and what is "science"? History is a generalised account of the personal actions of men united in bodies for any public purposes whatever; and science is the combination of a great mass of similar facts into the unity of a generalisation, a principle, or a law, which principle or law will enable us to predict with certainty the recurrence of like events under given conditions. Now, then, can there be a science of history? Can we ever arrive at such a complete knowledge of all the motives and laws of human conduct as to be able to predict with certainty of any bodies of men what their conduct in given circumstances will be? Mr. Buckle

Review of H. T. Buckle, *History of Civilisation in England* (London: J. W. Parker). First printed in the *Rambler*, 1858. Reprinted from Acton, *Historical Essays and Studies* (London: Macmillan, 1907).

thinks we can. Not that he ever hopes to be able to predict the actions of individual men; but for men in masses, for humanity in general, for large races, for nations, he supposes that pretty close approximations may be arrived at.

The "history" which Mr. Buckle proposed to write is not history in general, nor history of such kind as biography, or accounts of families, but the special history of civilisation. Now, what is civilisation? It is the progress of mankind measured by "the triumph of mind over external agents." It is the conquest of nature by man. In thought, it is the gradual weaning of the mind from a superstitious veneration for, and deification of, nature; in action, it is the use of nature, the making matter and its forces obedient to our behests, and using them for our needs and convenience.

It is important to settle that this is *all* that Mr. Buckle means by civilisation; for on this definition depends the whole logical value and consistency of his book. Among many passages that might be selected, the following, from p. 205, where he announces the plan of his future volumes, includes all that we want to show:—

In a great and comprehensive view, the *changes* in every civilised people are in their aggregate dependent solely on three things: first, on the amount of knowledge possessed by their ablest men; secondly, on the direction which that knowledge takes, that is to say, the sort of subjects to which it refers; thirdly, and above all, on the extent to which the knowledge is diffused and the freedom with which it pervades all classes of society.

The word *changes* indicates that the fundamental idea in the writer's mind is that of *progress*. The *knowledge* which he requires for this progress must be either religious, moral, or scientific. He proves, with great care, that it is neither of the two former; it must, therefore, be the last. Not that he denies the power of religious and moral convictions, but he says that their action ceases with individuals, and leaves no permanent result on society. Vices and virtues, like plus and minus quantities in an equation, eliminate each other, and leave the residuum to be attributed to some other cause; they are equivalent opposing forces, neutralising each other, therefore contributing nothing to *progress*, therefore not to be considered in the history of civilisation, according to the terms of the definition. The following passage immediately succeeds that quoted above:—

These are the three great movers of every civilised country; and although their operation is frequently disturbed by vices or the virtues of powerful individuals, *such moral feelings correct each other*, and the average of long periods remains unaffected. Owing to causes of which we are ignorant, the moral qualities do, no doubt, constantly vary; so that in one man, or perhaps even in one generation, there will be an excess of good intentions, in another an excess of bad ones. But we have no reason to think that any permanent change has been effected in the proportion which those who naturally possess good intentions bear to those in whom bad ones seem to be inherent. *In what may be called the innate and original morals of mankind, there is, so far as we are aware, no progress.* Of the different passions with which we are born, some are more prevalent at one time, some at another; but experience teaches us that, as they are always antagonistic, they are held in balance by the force of their own opposition. The activity of one motive is corrected by the activity of another. For to every vice there is a corresponding virtue. Cruelty is counteracted by benevolence, sympathy is excited by suffering, the injustice of some provokes the charity of others, new evils are met by new remedies, and even the most enormous offences that have ever been known have left behind them no permanent impression. The desolation of countries and the slaughter of men are losses which never fail to be repaired, and at the distance of a few centuries every vestige of them is effaced. This is the ebb and flow of history, the perpetual flux to which, by the laws of our nature, we are subject. Above all this, there is a far higher movement; and as the tide rolls on, now advancing, now receding, there is, amid its endless fluctuations, one thing, and one alone, which endures for ever. The actions of bad men produce only temporary evil, the actions of good men only temporary good; and eventually the good and the evil together subside, are neutralised by subsequent generations, absorbed by the incessant movement of future ages. But the discoveries of great men never leave us; they are immortal, they contain those eternal truths which survive the shock of empires, outlive the struggles of rival creeds, and witness the decay of successive religions.

5

All these have their different measures and their different standards; one set of opinions for one age, another set for another. They pass away like a dream; they are as the fabric of a vision, which leaves not a rack behind. The discoveries of genius alone remain: it is to them we owe all that we now have, they are for all ages and all times; never young and never old, they bear the seeds of their own life; they flow on in a perennial and undying stream; they are essentially cumulative, and, giving birth to the additions which they subsequently receive, they thus influence the most distant posterity, and after the lapse of centuries produce more effect than they were able to do even at the moment of their promulgation.

Let us not allow the emotions stirred up by Mr. Buckle's eloquence to blind us to the real meaning of his grand words. We must note that the "eternal truths" do not concern morality, or that "flux and reflux" of human action which neutralises itself and forms no element of progress. They have still less to do with religion; for they "outlive the struggles of rival creeds, and witness the decay of successive religions," but they are "the discoveries of genius"—not barren truths regarding intellect and will, and such-like metaphysical matters, which yield no fruit, but truths which teach man how to conquer and make use of nature, which tell him what he may do with water, and steam, and electricity, and wood, and coal, and iron, and gas, and skins, and horns. They are "essentially cumulative": one man begins where the last ended, and adds improvement on improvement—not as in morals, where all men begin afresh, and no real advance is made. Again, it is evident that individual happiness or misery forms no element in Mr. Buckle's computation: he eliminates both vice and virtue, not only because they balance one another, but because, after a century or two, no vestiges are left of the greatest crimes or most splendid acts of goodness. Mr. Buckle, therefore, does not contemplate the action, but the result; not the life or thinking of the man, but the work he has done, or the theory he has thought out. Where no trace remains of the work, nothing was done worth speaking of.

Having thus made the individual soul of no account in his investigations on the history of human progress, it is clear that only one manner of looking at mankind remains: if they are not to be viewed as persons in detail, they must be considered as bodies in mass. Hence not individual acts, but their statistics engage his attention. It is not personal doings, but sums total, that he seeks. But here we will let him speak for himself:—

The actions of individuals are greatly affected by their moral feelings and by their passions, but these being antagonistic to the passions and feelings of other individuals, are balanced by them. So that their effect is, in the great average of human affairs, nowhere to be seen, and the total actions of mankind, considered as a whole, are left to be regulated by the total knowledge of which mankind is possessed. And of the way in which individual feeling and individual caprice are thus absorbed and neutralised, we find a clear illustration in the history of crime. For the amount of crime committed in a country is, year after year, reproduced with the most startling uniformity, not being in the least affected by those capricious and personal feelings to which human actions are too often referred. But if, instead of examining the history of crime year by year, we were to examine it month by month, we should find less regularity, and if we were to examine it hour by hour, we should find no regularity at all; neither would its regularity be seen if, instead of the criminal records of a whole country, we only knew those of a single street, or of a single family. This is because the great social laws by which crime is governed can only be perceived after observing great numbers of long periods; but *in a small number, and a short period, the individual moral principle triumphs, and disturbs the operation of the larger and intellectual law.* While, therefore, the moral feelings by which a man is urged to commit a crime, or to abstain from it, will produce an immense effect on the amount of his own crimes, they will produce no effect on the amount of crimes committed by the society to which he belongs; because, in the long-run, they are sure to be neutralised by opposite moral feelings, which cause in other men an opposite conduct. Just in the same way, *we are all sensible that moral principles do affect nearly the whole of our actions,* but we have incontrovertible proof that they produce not the least effect on mankind in the aggregate, or even in men in very large masses, provided that we take the precaution of studying social phenomena for a period sufficiently long, and on a scale sufficiently great to enable the superior laws to come into uncontrolled operation.

7

The doings of individual men, of families, of the inhabitants of single streets, are nothing to Mr. Buckle; they must be divested of all personality, of all reminiscences of personality, before they are of use to him. That is to say, in his view of civilisation, he looks at men not as persons, but as machines; and the result he contemplates is not the action of these machines, but their productions. This is all that Mr. Buckle's design includes, all that logically he has any right to pretend to discuss. Defining, as he does, civilisation to be that mass of ideas, knowledge, and production which remains over and above when you have abstracted all transitory actions, all the results of politics, war, or religion, of course his history of civilisation ought to be confined to the genesis of this product, and the rules on which he proceeds to such as are applicable only to such a history. For instance, as virtues, vices, and all transitory actions are excluded from his view, of course he has nothing to do with the question of the force on which they depend; hence he is quite right in eliminating free-will from his laws of civilisation. Man's knowledge depends not on his will, but on his intellect; now it is his will, not his intellect, that is free. A man cannot refuse to see that which he does see, nor force himself to disbelieve that which is demonstratively proved. It is only when he has to decide whether he will open his eyes to see, or whether he will act on that which is proved to him, that he is free to do as he chooses. Again, it is only to men as persons that free-will belongs: look at them in masses, and they become machines; with their personality you abstract their freedom. Looking, therefore, at mankind as Mr. Buckle does, not as individual persons but as masses of producers, he could not allow free-will to come into his calculations. So again with Providence. Providence dealing with the world is that creative and preservative force which conducts the universe according to "a law which shall not be broken"; the expression of Providence is this law, wherein no personality can be proved. But Providence dealing with persons is the action of a Personal God upon his personal creatures; warning them, teaching them, judging them. Eliminate personality from your science, and of course your science has nothing to do with the personal providence. Nothing can be clearer.

But then, again, nothing can be clearer than this, that when you have cut off a part from anything, the thing is no longer a whole. This very clear truth Mr. Buckle, with the most charming simplicity, not only forgets, but tries to make his readers forget also. Having arbitrarily settled the limit of his history; having, in so many words, recognised that things do exist outside of these limits, which, however, do not require his attention, as they do not influence the precise matter on hand; having confessed that the constant variation of moral qualities in men is "owing to causes of which we are ignorant"; that to individuals, or a small number of persons his rules will not apply, because there "the individual moral principle triumphs, and disturbs the operation of the larger and intellectual law," and that "we are all sensible that moral principles do affect nearly the whole of our actions,"—yet he goes on to treat his science as exhaustive, as including every possible kind of human actions, and as furnishing the true key to the only real "history" of the human race. Let us see how Mr. Buckle manages to turn this wonderful intellectual somersault. We must suppose that the man who has written so remarkable a book had the whole plan of it in his mind. He knew that he was to write about men, not as individuals, but in masses. He knew that all his proofs were to be statistical, that is, winnowed from all personal detail, lumped together, averaged, and reduced to mathematical symbols. Yet, for all this, he pretends to begin from persons. The fundamental question of his book is thus stated: "Are the actions of men, *and therefore of societies*, governed by fixed laws, or are they the result either of chance or supernatural interference?" [1] He discusses these latter alternatives, not mathematically, or metaphysically, or logically, but by means of a fanciful theory, illustrated by an apologue. He imagines man to have been originally a wild and savage hunter, sometimes finding game, sometimes starving, and attributing his

[1] P. 8.

9

good or ill success only to chance; next the savage becomes agricultural, and seeing that seasons succeed regularly, and that the crop answers to the seed, the first notion of "uniform sequence" arises, and ripens into that of "law of nature" and "necessary connection." These doctrines of the people give rise, among the men of leisure, or thinkers, to two corresponding doctrines of the learned—free-will and predestination; founded one on a metaphysical, the other on a theological hypothesis. Mr. Buckle rejects both doctrines: the second, as unproved, and if proved only a barren hypothesis; the first, free-will, as "in reality resting on the metaphysical dogma of the supremacy of the human consciousness. Every man, it is alleged, feels and knows that he is a free agent; nor can any subtleties of argument do away with our consciousness of possessing a free-will." This *supremacy* of consciousness he denies: first, because we cannot prove that consciousness is a faculty; secondly, because if a faculty it is fallible, or, as he explains in a note, infallible as to the *fact*, but fallible as to the *truth;* infallible in testifying the presence of a phenomenon to the mind, fallible in affirming the substantial reality of the phenomenon. Now the consciousness is often deceived in affirming the existence of ghosts and the like, therefore it may be deceived in affirming the existence of free-will. This is literally the whole proof which Mr. Buckle deigns to give us of the premiss of the fundamental proposition of his book.

It is almost too absurd to controvert. He foists the unnecessary word *supremacy* into his adversary's statement, in order that he may object that, consciousness not being a faculty, there is no supremacy. Possibly not. Yet consciousness being the mind's knowledge of its own acts, and of the motives upon which it acts, either consciousness is true, or all our knowledge of our own thoughts is possibly false—*i.e.,* possibly I am thinking exactly the contrary of that which I know I am thinking. Next, the mind may be infallibly conscious of its acts and motives, and, among the rest, of its own freedom. Put the case of every imaginable motive of interest and pleasure, temporal and eternal, being offered me to determine me to a certain act: I know that if I choose, I may do exactly the reverse, simply to prove my freedom. I am conscious not only of my freedom to act, but also that the assertion of this freedom may be a motive outweighing all other motives together. We are all conscious that we often will not do what we ought, simply because we are commanded: "If you tell me I may, I won't; if you tell me I must, I will see you hanged first,"—that is, egotistical freedom asserts itself by not brooking permission, and by defying command. Mr. Buckle has no right to object to this, that our consciousness may be wrong, for he himself appeals to it in a passage quoted above: "We are all *sensible* that moral principles do affect nearly the whole of our actions." *Sensible* means *conscious;* he therefore puts himself out of court by producing in his own behalf the witness whose truth he had before impeached. To compare our *consciousness* of ghosts with our *consciousness* of our own freedom, is to confound the mind's *self-consciousness* of itself with its *consciousness* of a false sensation, or false nervous impression; one is outward, the other inward. It is to argue that because a blind man cannot *see* colours, therefore he cannot *see* the validity of a syllogism. So that Mr. Buckle utterly fails to establish the premiss of his fundamental proposition: "the actions of men, and therefore of societies, are governed by fixed laws, and not by will."

Again, why make an "alternative" between fixed laws and free-will? God is absolutely free and absolutely immutable. Freedom is not instability. The liberty of the children of God does not consist in holding an even balance between obeying and disobeying God, now inclining to one side, now to the other. True liberty is a self-determined, self-chosen perseverance in the way we deliberately think the best. Fixedness, then, is not really opposed to freedom. But further; let us assume as an hypothesis the existence of an immaterial soul, having perfect and even capricious freedom,—such that there is no fixity in its intentions, no possibility of predicting the changes of its self-determination. Yet as soon as this soul is united with body, as soon as it manifests its acts in time and space, it must follow the laws of time and space. It must work "in number, measure, and weight." It cannot enclose a space with two straight lines; it cannot find a shorter way of joining two points than by a straight line. So also in moral acts; it cannot do anything that may not be referred to the seven virtues, or the seven sins; nay, there must be an average in its sins or virtues; it must either attach itself to all equally, or it must now prefer one, now another. Its acts must be capable of numeration; and every thing that is numerable becomes at once a subject of statistics,—it has its average, its maximum, and its minimum, and is ticketed as belonging to a "fixed law." Yet, by the hypothesis, it was perfectly free. Therefore perfect freedom, and subjection to a fixed law, are quite compatible even in the individual soul, working in space and time. In its inner self-determination it may be perfectly free; yet in the manifestations or results of its free action it is bound by the fixed laws of number, space, and time. Again, these results, before they become appreciable, are done; they have become facts, and as such are removed from the influence of free-will. Not even God, says the poet, can make a fact not a fact, can render undone what is done. That which is done is become a material external product, altogether independent of the interior determination, or free-will, which motived or gave the first occasion of its existence. Hence no examination of the facts, apart from the consciousness of the doers of them, free possibly give us the element of freedom; they are mere material external facts, as subject to numeration and measurement as a crop of wheat, or the velocity of a bullet.

And if this is true of the acts of an individual, how much more true will it be of the acts of a mass of men? The laws of number are capable of a much more varied manifestation in large than in small numbers. There is no regularity in throws of dice taken ten and ten together; but in 10,000 throws we can predict with great confidence how many times sixes will be thrown. There is no possible certainty that any given individual will commit murder; but take a population of 100,000 and in a given time some one or other is sure to be found committing murder. All double things are done at intervals; and though there is the greatest uncertainty when they will be done, yet give laxity enough, allow a thousand, a hundred, or fifty years, and it may be confidently predicted that the thing will be done in that time; and this by no quality inherent in the thing or the doer, but by the law of numeration. Hence we cannot say, as Emerson somewhere says, that "if one man in thirty thousand eats shoes, or marries his grandmother, then one man in every thirty thousand must eat shoes, or marry his grandmother," for there is no necessity in the case. Take the dice. The mathematician will tell you exactly how often he will throw aces in 10,000 throws. But suppose by some very possible accident you had made 9990 throws without turning aces the average number of times, are you in any conceivable way surer of having aces in the last ten throws than if you were only just beginning the game? Not a bit. The former throws have nothing to do with the latter. The law is a law of numbers, a law of chances applicable to numbers and *on the average* applicable to all numerable things; but not implying any force, or cause, or reason why the things themselves should be thus rather than otherwise. Hence, in the first place, we should never be surprised if facts, the origin of which is free-will, are numbered; nor, secondly, if they are found capable of being averaged, so that a given number of them take place in a given time, but from this to make the third step, and to say, because they are numerable, because they can be averaged, therefore they happened by necessity, by a fixed law, is absurd in any man, and in Mr. Buckle dishonest.

It is dishonest in Mr. Buckle, because he must be aware that he is using the words *law* and *necessity* in a sense quite different from that intended by ordinary mortals. When we say "law," we always think of some force, or command, which is the cause of the thing being done. But Mr. Buckle, by *law*, only means *numerical average*. Now it is clear that when a thing has an average, it has an average; you may call this a *fixed law* if you please; but use your terms in such a way that we may not be led into the mistake of concluding that *fixed law* means a necessity inherent in the essence of the thing, and that therefore whatever has an average is necessary, and could not be otherwise. So, again, the word *necessary*. Common thinkers mean

13

by it that which cannot be thought to be otherwise without self-contradiction; thus it is necessary that two and two make four, that the three angles of a triangle equal two right angles, and the like. Now, is there any *necessity* of this kind in averages? Clearly not, or they would not be averages, but identical numbers. If there were any fixed law, or necessity of murder, the annual number of murders would not be merely approximate, but identical, or varying directly as the population. As they are not thus identical, there clearly is no fixed law in the usual sense, no necessary average of murder; and Mr. Buckle has no right to mislead his readers by using the word in his sense.

And now let us see what Mr. Buckle says on these points.

> Rejecting the metaphysical doctrine of free-will, and the theological dogma of predestined events, we are driven to the conclusion that the actions of men, being determined solely by their antecedents, must have a character of uniformity, that is to say, must, under precisely the same circumstances, always issue in precisely the same results.

Here, we observe, Mr. Buckle contradicts himself; for though he expresses so confidently that the law of individual action is, that it is "necessarily determined by antecedents," he concedes in another place that the variation in human conduct is "owing to causes of which we are ignorant." But let us proceed:—

> To state some of the most decisive proofs we now possess of the regularity with which mental phenomena succeed each other, . . . murder, one of the most arbitrary and irregular of crimes, is committed with as much regularity, and bears as uniform a relation to certain known circumstances as do the movements of the tides and the rotations of the seasons.

The great authority for this statement, and for the theory he derives from it, is M. Quételet. Now although he conceives that because he calls M. Quételet "confessedly the first statistician in Europe" his conclusions will therefore pass unchallenged, we must observe that a very different opinion of him prevails among those who are more competent judges than either Mr. Buckle or ourselves. His way of applying the theory of probabilities to statistics is rejected even by the French writers; and the following observations made with reference to him by one of the most celebrated political economists of the age, show the estimation in which his method is held in Germany:—

> Of late years an opinion has been gaining ground that statistics have only to deal with political and social facts expressed in figures, without being confined to any particular time. Calculations are made with tables, etc.; and meanwhile the signification of the figures virtually disappears from the mind, which becomes conscious of it only when the result is obtained. Now for all those facts which are susceptible of it, the mathematical form of expression is undoubtedly the most perfect, and we must endeavour, therefore, to make the mathematical branch of statistics as comprehensive as possible. But one branch of a science is not the science itself. Just as there is no special science in natural philosophy called *Microscopia,* which combines all observations made through the microscope, so the principle of a science ought never to be deduced from the character of its principal instrument. This restriction would deprive statistics of all scientific unity and interior coherence.[1]

But to return to Mr. Buckle—

> "This," says he, "will appear strange to those who believe that human actions depend more on the peculiarities of each individual than on the general state of society."

So suicide; the number of suicides in every year is about the same, therefore—

> . . . in a given state of society a certain number of persons must put an end to their own life. This is the general law; and the special question as to who shall commit the crime depends of course upon special law; which, however, in their total action, must obey the large irresistible social law to which they are all subordinate.

Alas, then, if one person in our village is to commit suicide, if nobody else will, I must! And why? Simply because one person has committed suicide there yearly for several years past. Noth-

---

[1] Roscher, *System der Volkswirthschaft,* i. 29.

ing can withstand the simple rules of arithmetic! But fortunately this "irresistible social law" allows of a considerable *laxum* in its operation; *about* two hundred and forty persons a year must kill themselves in London, but the special number may vary between two hundred and sixty-six and two hundred and thirteen. Our readers, too, may take comfort from hearing that "suicide is more frequent among Protestants than among Catholics."

> Nor is it merely the crimes of men which are marked by this uniformity of sequence. . . . In England the experience of a century has proved that marriages, *instead of having any connection with personal feelings,* are simply regulated by the average earnings of the great mass of the people. . . . Year after year the same proportion of letter-writers forget to direct their letters, so that we can actually foretell how many will do it next year.

The chief things we note here are, the utter worthlessness of the reasoning itself, and its formal contradiction by the author's admissions previously quoted. What can we think of the judgment of a man who allows statistics to make him believe that marriages *have no connection* with personal feelings! or that can use a few imperfect returns about murders, suicides, and undirected letters, to upset all the affirmations of personal consciousness, the whole common sense of the world, as expressed in human language, and his own common sense to boot! For we do not forget, that though at p. 26 he tells us that the question who, what individual, shall commit suicide "depends upon special laws, which in their total action must obey the large social law to which they are subordinate," at p. 208 he tells us that this is only true for great numbers of men, and long periods of time; for "in a small number, and a short period, the individual moral principle triumphs, and disturbs the operation of the larger and intellectual law": we must study "social phenomena for a period sufficiently long, and on a scale sufficiently great, to enable the superior laws to come into uncontrolled operation."

Now this very contradiction should have taught Mr. Buckle that he was involved in a fallacy. In nature totals are made up of parts similar to the whole. A block of stone is made up of stony molecules; a kidney of several little kidneys; a wave is an accumulation of little waves. Every chip of wood has the same construction as the block. Yet Mr. Buckle pretends to show us a long period and a great number made up of a quantity of short periods and small numbers, which are ruled by principles contradictory in their action to the principle which rules the total. In other words, the repetition of an individual law destroys that law! Individual moral principle manifests itself so often that it is never seen! A thing, by being multiplied, is annihilated! Addition, instead of increasing, diminishes the sum!

Mr. Buckle's fallacy consists mainly in this: that whereas his whole conception of the object of his work required him to abstract his consideration entirely from all persons, and to consider man only in the mass, as so much productive machinery, oiled indeed, and kept in working order by a due amount of virtue, but intended only to produce intellectual truths capable of teaching how more and more to subdue nature,—he has chosen to apply the rules, applicable exclusively to man under this aspect, to man as a person, as an individual; though he knows and confesses that they are not so applicable. We are sorry that we are thus reduced to defend either Mr. Buckle's understanding at the expense of his honesty, or his honesty at the expense of his understanding. In fact, man, as person, cannot be added to man; soul cannot be mixed with soul; each individual stands apart, or loses his individuality by addition.

History, therefore, on Mr. Buckle's plan, is impossible. For as soon as we seek simply statistics and averages, we have lost sight of man, and are contemplating only his works, his products. The true historian takes the individual for his centre; he describes the typical man, whom all others more or less resemble; he recounts the adventures of the ruler, to whose will multitudes bow. If he treats of mobs, or armies, or bodies of men, he invests this multitude with a kind of personality of its own,—its own wishes, passions, character, will, and conscience. Mr. Buckle's history, if he *could* write a history according to his programme, would be the reverse of all this: he would merge the individual in the company, the person in the body; wishes, passions, character, conscience, all would be abstracted; for those things either balance, and so neutralise each other, or else are transient in their effects, and so immaterial to the total. History would consist in tabular views of births, deaths, marriages, diseases, prices, commerce, and the like; and the historian would be chiefly useful in providing grocers with cheap paper to wrap up butter in. But Mr. Buckle knows better than to reduce history to such dry chaff; when he writes history he makes persons his centres, and reduces it to what it must always be, an intricate and interlacing tissue of biographies, so far as men advanced some particular movement on which the historian is writing. Thus Louis XIV., Richelieu, and Burke crop out in Mr. Buckle's volume as the centres of his political speculations.

Mr. Buckle's practice herein is utterly contrary to his theory. History can only be reduced to a science by excluding individualism and personality. Persons act, if not by free-will, at least by unknown laws, which are in opposition, as Mr. Buckle owns, to the great statistical laws on which he would found historical science. The reason of this opposition is manifest; and an explanation will clearly show why it is, and always will be, impossible to write a history upon Mr. Buckle's programme, and why he must be disappointed in his expectation of reducing history to a science.

All sciences are either inductive or deductive. We need not waste time in arguing with Mr. Buckle that history is not a deductive science, for he himself spends several pages in proving this proposition. It must, therefore, be a science depending upon induction. Now what is induction? Though essentially the same as of old, this act of reason is differently conducted now. Formerly, if two or three instances suggested a principle or a generalisation to the mind, this principle was said to be gained by induction. Or if a mere guess or fancy could be strengthened by a few instances or analogies, this might readily be turned into an inductive argument: "It is the case in this, and a second and third instance, therefore in all." But this loose unscientific induction is now changed; the instances have to be well manipulated before they can be used for a true induction; and not only similarities but dissimilarities have to be investigated. We must abstract all points of difference before adding the various elements; induction therefore is not only addition but subtraction also. Before we can include two things under a general law, we must subtract all that makes them different from one another; otherwise we should include contradictions in a pretended unity.

Now, if we submit men and human actions to the crucible of induction, they must be "prepared," like everything else, for the process. The unlike must first be abstracted. Take any two men: what is the first element that constitutes their difference? Clearly their personality; John is not Robert; not because they have a different nature, but because they have a different personality. If we wish to include John and Robert under a single generalisation, the first thing we must divest them of is personality, with all its distinctive characteristics, the chief of which is usually said to be freedom of the will. Man, then, in this induction is not real man; he is no longer a personal free agent, but a machine, subject in his movements to those laws of action which remain after personality and free-will have been subtracted.

Thus, if free-will is the source of action in men, it will be impossible ever to reduce all the sources of human action to an inductive generalisation, such as will enable us to predict how men will act. Free-will refuses the inductive process. The only chance is, to prove that free-will does not exist, or is not such a source of action. This Mr. Buckle has attempted to do in various ways. In his first chapter he tries to prove that "the actions of men, *and therefore of societies,* are governed by fixed laws"; how weakly, we have shown above. We reproduce the thesis here to show that even Mr. Buckle allows that individuals are the primary elements of societies, and that the laws of society may be deduced from the laws that govern individuals. In other places, before quoted, Mr. Buckle asserts that the moral actions of men depend on particular laws, to him unknown, which laws are in their operation *antagonistic* to the great laws that govern society. And elsewhere he says that the laws of society are the rule for the individual, the actions of men are regular because "they

19

are *governed* by the state of the society in which they occur."

Here, then, we see that there is a fundamental impossibility, because a self-contradiction, in Mr. Buckle's method and system, when applied to anything beyond the limits to which he himself is conscious it should be confined. If he would really eliminate all the moral actions of men, all the "flux and reflux" of society, all war and politics, from his speculations, and apply his theory to the "discoveries of genius" and to the progressive knowledge and subjugation of nature alone, he would escape all contradiction. But if he insists on applying his method to history, in the usual acceptation of the word, we are forced to tell him that his pretensions are untenable. These pretensions may perhaps be traced to that characteristic which Socrates holds up to such ridicule in his speech in the *Apologia*. Every artisan, he says, because he is expert in his own art, thinks he knows every other art. The tendency of the intellect is to complete its own circle; whatever gaps a man finds in his knowledge are filled up by an unwarrantable stretching of the next subject which he knows. The whole system of positive philosophy is the work of under-educated, or half-educated men, adepts in physical science, but ignorant of the principles of any other, who insist that all science must have the same method as theirs, and that metaphysical realities must be measured and explained by physical laws. We state this to show that Mr. Buckle's absurdities and dishonesties are not his own, but those of his school.

We are quite conscious that in this article our criticism does not reach over the whole extent of the work under review; but as the limits of a monthly journal are so narrow, we thought it better to confine our remarks to one or two points, rather than to dissipate our attention over the multitude of subjects that ought to be discussed. We have, however, attempted to discover the fundamental and leading idea of the book, which we have proved to be untenable. We do not deny all merit to the work; we only say that the mass of information, collected with immense labour, and put together with great acuteness, a boldness fearless of consequences, and in a captivating style, does not exactly prove that which he undertakes to prove; for nothing can prove a proposition that contradicts itself.

We shall have to return to the book, to make observations on Mr. Buckle's detailed proofs. Hitherto we have only attacked his general thesis, the conclusion which he proposes as the end of his induction; we shall hereafter have to examine some specimens of the terms of his inductive argument, and to inquire into the validity of his claims to respect for the extent and accuracy of his learning.

21

II

Mr. Buckle's Philosophy of History

In our last Number we explained the theory which Mr. Buckle's book is written to prove, and estimated his merits as a philosopher. We have now to consider his attainments as a scholar. We have to examine his competency for the task he has undertaken, and the degree of success with which he has executed it. This is the more imperatively necessary, that it would be very unfair to Mr. Buckle to judge him by the merits of his system only; for the system is not his own. We may praise him or blame him for his judgment in adopting it, certainly not for his skill in devising it. His view of "the principles which govern the character and destiny of nations" is borrowed partly from Comte and partly from Quételet, and has already been applied, not indeed by historians, but by natural philosophers. We find it stated, for instance, by the celebrated physiologist Valentin, as follows (*Grundriss der Physiologie,* 1855, p. 10):—

> Chance, to which we ascribe the event of an isolated case, must make way for a definite law as soon as we include a greater number of cases in our observation. No fixed rule appears to regulate the proportion of the sexes to each other, or the relative number of twins that are born, or the kind of crimes committed within a given period. But if we extend our range of observation over millions of cases, certain regular quantities constantly recur. Where this is not the case, the causes of the fluctuation can often be ascertained by the rule of probabilities. Here, as everywhere, chance vanishes as a phantom of superstition,—as a result of that short-sightedness which

First printed in the *Rambler,* 1858. Reprinted from Acton, *Historical Essays and Studies* (London: Macmillan, 1907).

has burdened the history of human opinion with so many apparently higher, but in reality degrading and erroneous, ideas.

This nearly describes the theory which Mr. Buckle has transferred from the history of nature to the history of man. He can hardly be said to challenge inquiry into its truth. He is at small pains to recommend it to those who are not predisposed in its favour. He is more inclined to dogmatise than to argue; and treats with placid scorn all who may not agree with him, and who are attached to one or other of the creeds and systems which have subsisted amongst men. It is a characteristic of certain diminutive parties to make up by the confidence and doggedness of their language for the small support they are able to command in public opinion. It is the same spirit in which Coleridge used to be worshipped at Highgate, and Jeremy Bentham at Westminster.

Taking a survey of literature from the pinnacle of his self-esteem, Mr. Buckle repeatedly affirms that history has been generally written by very incapable men; that before his time there was no science of history; that "the most celebrated historians are manifestly inferior to the cultivators of physical science" (p. 7), and much more to the same purpose *passim*. He gives us, moreover, to understand that he is as much at home in ethical as in historical literature; and delivers the valuable opinion, "that a man, after reading everything that has been written on moral conduct and moral philosophy, will find himself nearly as much in the dark as when his studies first began" (p. 22). Having thus cleared the way for his own appearance on the neglected fields of history and philosophy, he leaves us to infer that there are very few people capable of appreciating his performance, or for whose judgment he cares a pin. He writes for a school; and uttering its oracles to the world, he may question the competency of any tribunal which does not in some degree admit his premises and consents to judge him out of his own mouth. But if we are unworthy to judge his theories, his facts at least are common property, and are accessible to all men; and it is important to see what they are worth, and how much Mr.

Buckle knew about the matter when he endeavoured to make history subservient to his philosophy.

The attempt to reconcile philosophical speculation with the experience of history, and to harmonise their teachings, is perfectly natural, and, at a certain stage, inevitable. Both are unbounded in their range, and in some sense they may be said to include each other. Neither science is perfect till it obtains the confirmation of the other. "Man," says Jacobi, "requires not only a truth whose creator he is, but a truth also of which he is the creature." Yet the comparison could take place only at an advanced period of the progress of philosophy and of the knowledge of history. Philosophy must be seen by the light of history that the laws of its progress may be understood; and history, which records the thoughts as well as the actions of men, cannot overlook the vicissitudes of philosophic schools. Thus the history of philosophy is a postulate of either science. At the same time, history, unless considered in its philosophic aspect, is devoid of connection and instruction; and philosophy, which naturally tends to embrace all the sciences, necessarily seeks to subject history, amongst the rest, to its law. Hence arose the philosophy of history. "In history," says Krug, "philosophy beholds itself reflected. It is the text to which history supplies the commentary." [1] Both sciences had attained a certain maturity of development before they sought each other. "Philosophy," said Schelling, "ought not to precede the particular sciences, but to follow after them." [2] Generalisation in history was not possible until a great part of its course was run, and the knowledge of its details tolerably complete. Nor could the history of philosophy be written before it had passed through many phases, or before it had attained a considerable development. Thus it naturally happened that the philosophy of history and the history of philosophy, as they proceeded from the same causes, began to be cultivated about the same time. They are scarcely a century old.

The mediaeval philosophy had taken no cognisance of the

---

[1] *Handwörterbuch der philosophischen Wissenschaften,* ii. 217.
[2] Salat, *Schelling in München,* i. 60.

external world until, in the sixteenth century, a reaction took place. As theology had predominated in the Middle Ages, now physiology prevailed in its stead. The study of nature became the first of sciences, and in the age of the supremacy of the Baconian system, Kepler and Galileo and Newton were considered philosophers. To the philosophic investigation of nature was added, in the eighteenth century, the philosophic contemplation of history. The method by which Bacon had revolutionised natural science "ab experientia ad axiomata, et ab axiomatibus ad nova inventa," [3] came to be tried on history. Since that time a philosophy of history has been attempted upon the principles of almost every system. The result has not always been to the advantage of history, or to the credit of the philosophers. "When things are known and found out, then they can descant upon them; they can knit them into certain causes, they can reduce them to their principles. If any instance of experience stands against them, they can range it in order by some distinctions. But all this is but a web of the wit; it can work nothing." [4]

The first attempt to give unity to universal history by the application of a philosophic system was made by Lessing, in his celebrated fragment on the *Education of the Human Race*. It was his last work, "and must be considered the foundation of all modern philosophy, of religion, and the beginning of a more profound appreciation of history." [5] He employs the ideas of Leibniz's *Théodicée* to explain the government of the world. Condorcet's *Sketch of the Progress of the Human Mind* is inspired, in like manner, by the sensualist doctrines of Condillac. Kant, though perfectly ignorant of the subject, was incited by the French Revolution to draw up a scheme of universal history in unison with his system. It was the entire inadequacy of Kant's philosophy to explain the phenomena of history which led Hegel, "for whom the philosophical problem had converted itself

---

[3] *De Augmentis,* iii. 3: "From experiment to axioms, from axioms to new discoveries."

[4] Bacon, "In Praise of Knowledge," *Works,* ed. Bohn, i. 216.

[5] Schwarz, *Lessing als Theologe,* p. 79.

into an historical one," [6] to break with the system altogether. Thirty years later, when the supremacy of Kant had long passed away, and Hegel was reigning in his stead, he too set up his philosophy of history as the crown and end of his own philosophy, and as the test of its absolute truth. [7] "It is for historical science," says his latest biographer, "to enjoy the inheritance of Hegel's philosophy." [8] In like manner, the transcendental system of Schelling resulted in a Christian philosophy of history, of which a late able writer says that by it "the antagonism of philosophy and history, proceeding from a defective notion of the first, and an utterly inadequate view of the latter, was removed." [9] So, again, the system of Krause presents a combination of philosophy and history in which their respective methods are blended together. [10] Especially since the publication of Hegel's *Lectures*, history has been generally considered by philosophers as belonging to their legitimate domain. And their dominion is such, that even a moderate acquaintance with the events of the past has ceased to be deemed a necessary or even a useful ingredient in the preparation of a philosophy of history. No system will confess itself so poor that it cannot reconstruct the history of the world without the help of empirical knowledge. A Pole, Cieszkowski (*Prolegomena zur Historiosophie*, 1838), has a physical scheme for the arrangement of historical phenomena. According to him, light is the type of Persia, mechanism of China, Athens represents dynamic electricity, Sparta static electricity. The electro-magnetic system answers to Macedon, the

---

[6] Haym, *Hegel und seine Zeit*, p. 45.

[7] "Gewissermassen, die Probe des ganzen Systems" (Michelet, *Entwickelungsgeschichte der neuesten deutschen Philos.*, p. 304). "Die Wahrhafte Theodicee, die Probe von der Wahrheit des ganzen Systems" (Huber, *Deutsche Vierteljahrs Schrift*, 1853, ii. 50). "Die unwidersprichlichste Bewährung des Systems" (Haym, *Allgem. Encyclop.*, art. "Philosophie," sect. iii. vol. xxiv. p. 176).

[8] Haym, *Hegel und seine Zeit*, p. 466.

[9] Schaarschmidt, *Entwickelungsgang der neuesten Speculation*, p. 194; and Schelling, *Werke*, i. 480, 481.

[10] According to his disciples, "der harmonische Haupttheil," "die Blüthenknospe," of the system (Erdmann, *Entwickelung der Speculation seit Kant*, ii. 676).

expansive force of heat to the Roman Empire. The dualism of Church and State in the Middle Ages corresponds to the antithesis of acid and alkali, etc., etc. The same ingenious person argues from the analogy of the natural sciences, in which, with the help of an old tooth, you can reconstruct an antediluvian monster, that history has to deal with the future, and cannot submit to be confined to the knowledge of the past. Twenty years ago, the well-known novelist Gutzkow was in prison, and not having books at hand to help him in writing a novel, beguiled the time by writing and publishing a philosophy of history.

These recent examples may serve to show us that it is not to be wondered at that an attempt should be made to obtain for a new system the sanction of history; or that, having been made, it should have produced a ludicrous result, and should have furnished the most complete confutation of the system it was meant to confirm. But we have already said that the theory is not the most remarkable part about Mr. Buckle's book. It is by his portentous display of reading that he will impose upon many in whom the principles in their naked deformity would simply excite abhorrence. The theoretical portion is completely overgrown and hidden by the mass of matter which is collected to support it, and on which Mr. Buckle has brought to bear all the reading of a lifetime. The wonderful accumulation of details and extravagance of quotation have the manifest purpose of dazzling and blinding his readers by the mere mass of apparent erudition. "So learned a man cannot be mistaken in his conclusions," is no doubt what they are expected to say. We cannot, therefore, consider the success of Mr. Buckle's work as a fair indication of the extent to which the peculiar form of infidelity which he holds prevails in this country. To accept his conclusions, we must be prepared to say, *Credo quia impium;* but in order to be overawed by his learning, it is enough to have less of it than Mr. Buckle himself.

It is for this reason worth while to inquire briefly whether Mr. Buckle is in this respect so great an authority as he professes to be, and as it is commonly taken for granted he is—whether he really possesses that knowledge of his subject which justifies him in writing upon it, or whether, in a word, he is an impostor.

Apart from the historical excursions of modern philosophers which we have spoken of, and with which Mr. Buckle has not thought fit to make himself acquainted, the great problems of civilisation which he tries to solve have been discussed within the last few years by three eminent men, whose works have some points of similarity with his own. In 1853 a French diplomatist, M. de Gobineau, published the first portion of a work which he has since completed in four volumes, *Essai sur l'Inégalité des Races humaines.* Familiar with all the latest researches of French and German writers, he investigates in great detail the laws which regulate the progress and the decline of civilisation. He finds that it depends entirely on purity of blood. The deterioration produced by the mixture of races is the sole cause of decline: "A people would never die if it remained eternally composed of the same national elements" (i. 53). The fate of nations is unconnected with the land they inhabit; it depends in nothing on good government or purity of morals. Even Christianity has no permanent influence on civilisation: "Le Christianisme n'est pas civilisateur, et il a grandement raison de ne pas l'être" (p. 124). Whether we admit or reject these conclusions, it is unquestionable that they are founded on most various and conscientious research, and an abundance of appropriate learning, strongly contrasting with the dishonest affectation of knowledge by which Mr. Buckle deludes his readers. There is, moreover, a learned appendage to Gobineau's book, in the shape of a pamphlet of 275 pages, by Professor Pott. About the same time an anonymous work appeared at Marburg, in three volumes, bearing the somewhat obscure title, *Anthropognosie, Ethnognosie und Polignosie,* in which also the laws which influence the political and social progress of mankind are explained with uncommon erudition. It was by a well-known political writer, Dr. Vollgraff; and, though disfigured by endless subdivisions and an obscure arrangement, it is undoubtedly one of the most comprehensive and instructive works that have appeared in our time. All the principal points of Mr. Buckle's theory are here discussed and illustrated with infinitely greater fulness of knowledge than in the work of our English author; and although the conclusions to which the German philosopher would lead us are not much better, at least there is much more to be learnt on the road.

The third work to which we allude is very different in style and spirit, and bears a motto which at once deprives it of any considerable resemblance to Mr. Buckle's work: *Lo bueno, si breve, dos vezes bueno.* It is the work of the most eloquent and accomplished philosopher in Germany,[11] and passes in review, in 168 pages, all the great questions which constitute the philosophy of history. The wisest sayings of the ancients, and the latest discoveries of the moderns, are brought together with incomparable taste and learning; since Schlegel, so brilliant a work had not appeared on the same field.

We have drawn attention to these works because they treat of exactly the same questions as Mr. Buckle's *History of Civilisation,* and are all written by men of distinguished abilities—the last by one of the greatest modern scholars; because, moreover, they are the only works which, during the last ten years, have really advanced the study of the philosophy of history, and are therefore the first books to which anybody would naturally turn who is employed upon the subject. None of them, we may add, are written from a specifically Catholic point of view, yet Mr. Buckle has never once alluded to any of them.

We may attribute this monstrous neglect of what has been done and is doing in the field which he is cultivating, either to simple ignorance of the present state of learning, or to a wary dislike of whatever might not help to support his own views. There is no other alternative, and either supposition is equally fatal to his credit.

As Mr. Buckle despises the historians, and knows nothing of the principal philosophers, it may be asked, where, then, are his authorities? The answer is given in a note (p. 5), where we are

---

[11] Ernst von Lasaulx, *Neuer Versuch einer Alten auf die Wahrheit der Thatsachen gegründeten Philosophie der Geschichte.*

told that Comte is the "writer who has done more than any other to raise the standard of history." This is the key to the whole book, and in general to Mr. Buckle's state of mind. His view seldom extends beyond the bounds of the system of that philosopher, and he has not sought enlightenment in the study of the great metaphysicians of other schools. The limits of his knowledge in this respect are curious. Of Aristotle, though he frequently mentions him, and in one place even places him on a level with the French physician Bichât (p. 812), there is no proof that he knows anything at all. He tells us, for instance, that the chief writers on the influence of climate are Hume, Montesquieu, Guizot, and Comte. It never occurs to him that his favourite theory on this point is to be found in Aristotle (*Problemata,* xiv), or that Hippocrates wrote a work on the subject. Plato, though sometimes quoted, seems hardly better known. Nobody familiar with his works and life would venture upon the statement that it is doubtful whether he ever visited Egypt (p. 81); still less would a scholar with any self-respect have cited Bunsen as an authority on the matter. In reality, the only question is how long he remained there.

This is a fair instance of our author's habit of going to the wrong place for information, and ignoring the obvious authorities. Altogether Mr. Buckle, who does not commonly put his light under a bushel, exhibits acquaintance with scarcely four or five of the most common writers of antiquity.

It is not to be expected that the Christian writers should come off better; there is a good deal said about them, but it is borrowed at second-hand, generally from Neander, sometimes from Mosheim or Milman. For it makes no difference to Mr. Buckle whether a thing is true, or whether somebody has said that it is true. It is enough that it should answer some particular purpose of the moment. Indeed, although his reading appears excessively promiscuous, it is in reality selected with great discrimination. So far as we have observed, the standard work which is the real and acknowledged authority on each particular subject is never by any chance or oversight consulted for the purpose. We have shown how the case stands relatively to the general subject of civilisation. For the history of philosophy we have continual references in Tennemann, who was greatly esteemed at the time of Kant's supremacy in the schools. The progress of learning has long since displaced his works, as well as those which immediately succeeded him. Sometimes we find reference to Ritter's *Ancient Philosophy*, the most antiquated portion of his highly unsatisfactory work. The vast literature on this subject which has arisen within the last few years is never noticed. So, for the history of medicine we have Sprengel and Renouard, whose books were long since superseded by the works of Hecker, Häser, and others. On India, again, we are referred to a number of obsolete publications, and the great work of Lassen is never mentioned. The same ignorance prevails upon almost every branch of learning that is ostentatiously brought forward; but we should be following Mr. Buckle's very bad example if we were to go on giving lists of books which he ought to have consulted.

The title of the sixth chapter, "Origin of History, and State of Historical Literature during the Middle Ages," excited our expectations. To a man of Mr. Buckle's industry, the hundreds of folios in which the historical works of the Middle Ages are contained offer a splendid and inexhaustible field for the exhibition of his powers of research. Here was to be found, in the history of European civilisation for a thousand years, the secret of its subsequent progress. But Mr. Buckle's method is the same here as elsewhere. He shows himself acquainted with just half a dozen of the commonest mediaeval historians; and these, if we remember rightly, with only one exception, all English. On the other hand, whatever is to be found about them in the most ordinary books—Hallam, Warton, Turner, Palgrave, Wright, etc.,—is diligently repeated. The vulgar practice of reading the books one is to write about was beneath so great a philosopher. He has read about them, but very little in them. They could not greatly attract him; for the Middle Ages must be a mere blank to one who writes the history of modern civilisation without taking into account the two elements of which it is chiefly composed—the civilisation of antiquity, and the Christian religion. Having to utter a few generalities upon the subject, it was obviously more convenient to know nothing about it, and to take counsel of a few writers who knew very little about it, than to run the risk of finding an imprudent curiosity rewarded by the unexpected discovery of unpalatable and inflexible facts. This safe and timely ignorance, which he has discreetly cherished and preserved, has made him fully competent to declare "that not only was no history written before the end of the sixteenth century, but that the state of society was such as to make it impossible for one to be written" (p. 299).

Agreeably to the materialistic character of his philosophy, Mr. Buckle examines with special predilection the physical causes which influence mankind. His second chapter, which is devoted to this inquiry, is the most interesting and elaborate part of the volume. In these regions he is somewhat more at home. It is but an act of justice, therefore, to give some attention to this chapter. Nowhere do the ignorance and incapacity of the author more visibly appear.

The subject here treated has very recently been raised to the dignity of a separate and distinct science; and it has been cultivated on the Continent with extraordinary zeal and success. In no department was so much assistance to be derived from contemporary writers. Ritter, the founder of the science of comparative geography, began forty years ago the great work of which he has not yet finished even the Asiatic portion. He was the first among the moderns to determine in detail the connection of the material world with the history of man. In his footsteps a numerous school of writers have followed— Rougemont, Mendelssohn, Knapp, etc.,—and a variety of able writers have made it a popular study.

As Ritter first established a bridge between history and geography, the link between geology and history was discovered by the Saxon geologist Cotta. Another branch of the same subject—the connection between the vegetable world and the civilisation of man—has been treated by the celebrated botanist,

Unger of Vienna.[12] Finally, Professor Volz [13] has produced a most learned work on the influence of the domestic animals and plants on the progress of civilisation. Yet Mr. Buckle is totally ignorant of the writings and discoveries of these men; and he has therefore written a dissertation which not only does not exhaust the subject, but is of no value whatever at the present day.

The proposition that out of Europe civilisation is dependent chiefly upon physical causes, and man subordinate to nature, is proved, among other examples, by that of Egypt (p. 44). The instance is infelicitous, inasmuch as it is cited by Ritter in support of precisely the contrary view.[14] The original inhabitants of the valley of the Nile were not better off or more civilised than their neighbours in the deserts of Libya and Arabia.

It was by the intelligence of the remarkable people who settled there that Egypt became the richest granary of the ancient world. The inundation of the Nile was rendered a source of fertility by the skill of those who made use of it. But when the vigour of the nation died away under the wretched government which succeeded upon the fall of Rome, that fertile valley relapsed in great measure into its old sterility; the Thebais became a desert, and the Mareotis a marsh. Instead of proving Mr. Buckle's case, Egypt is the best instance of the subordination of nature to the intellect and will of man.

Pursuing his idea of the influence of the aspect of nature on man, Mr. Buckle, who has a theory for everything, discovers that the cause of Catholicism lies in earthquakes:—

> "The peculiar province of the imagination," he informs us, "being to deal with the unknown, every event which is unexplained as well as important, is a direct stimulus to our imaginative faculties. . . . Earthquakes and volcanic eruptions are more frequent and more destructive in Italy and in the Spanish and Portuguese Peninsula than in any other of the great countries, and it is precisely there that superstition is most rife, and the superstitious classes most powerful. Those were the coun-

---

[12] *Botanische Streifzüge auf dem Gebiete der Culturgeschichte.*
[13] *Beiträge zur Culturgeschichte.*
[14] "Ueber das historische Element in der geographischen Wissenschaft," 1833, in his *Abhandlungen*, p. 165.

tries where the clergy first established their authority, where the worst corruptions of Christianity took place, and where superstition has during the longest period retained the firmest hold."

In other words, sequence is cause, as Hume proves; whence *post hoc, ergo propter hoc,* the great logical principle of the positivists. But increase of Popery follows increase of earthquakes; therefore, the consequence is clear. And not only is Christianity extracted out of earthquakes, but also, by a similar chemistry, Providence is derived from the plague.

Our ignorance about another life, he says, is complete:—

> On this subject the reason is perfectly silent; the imagination, therefore, is uncontrolled. . . . The vulgar universally ascribe to the intervention of the Deity those diseases which are peculiarly fatal. The opinion that pestilence is a manifestation of the Divine anger, though it has long been dying away, is by no means extinct, even in the most civilised countries. Superstitions of this kind will, of course, be strongest either where medical knowledge is most backward, or where disease is most abundant.

It is in tropical climates that nature is most terrible; and here, says our author, "imagination runs riot, and religion is founded on fear; while in Europe nature is subject to man, and reason rules supreme." This theme he illustrates by the extreme instances of India and Greece; and he generalises his conclusions into the statement that "the tendency of Asiatic civilisation was to widen the distance between men and their deities; the tendency of Greek civilisation was to diminish it." Hence "in Greece we for the first time meet with hero-worship, that is, the deification of mortals"; this could not take place in tropical countries. "It is therefore natural that it should form no part of the ancient Indian religion; neither was it known to the Egyptians, nor to the Persians, nor, so far as I am aware, to the Arabians"; but it was part of the national religion of Greece, and has been found so natural to Europeans, that "the same custom was afterwards renewed with eminent success by the Romish Church."

Perhaps no writer of pretension ever made a more disgraceful exhibition of ignorance and unreason than Mr. Buckle in these passages. Unreason: for if the Catholic cultus of saints is to be identified with the Greek deification of heroes, then certainly this deification is not simply European; it is as natural to the Indian Catholic as to the Italian or German, not to mention the Orientals. Exactly the same thing is found in Mahometanism, wherever it spreads. If Allah alone receives divine honours, anyhow the chief cultus is paid to the tomb of the prophet, and to the graves of the various holy personages with which Moslem countries are so thickly studded. But if this cultus is not what Mr. Buckle meant by the Greek hero-worship, then his mention of the Catholic practice is invidious, impertinent, and utterly irrelevant to his argument. Ignorance: for the "deification of mortals," so far from forming no part of the ancient Indian and Egyptian religions, was their very central idea and foundation. The fearful, terrible gods that Mr. Buckle's imagination is so full of, were only elemental deities, rising and falling with the world, destined to be annihilated; while the human soul was to last for ever, and was in its essence superior to all those beings that kept it in a tedious but temporary thraldom. The whole idea of the Vedas is the power of the Brahmin over the elemental deities, exerted by means of the sacrifice. The deities in question, though vast in power and wonderfully large, are by themselves undefined and vague; they want personality, and therefore require personal direction; though they are in some sense universal intellect and soul, yet they are formless and void; they are mere blunderers till they are directed by the more sure intelligence of minds akin to those of man. Hence, in the Vedantic genesis of things, the elemental deities are the matter of forces which compose the universe; while the intelligent agents who conduct the creative process are the seven primeval sages, Rishis, or Manus, whose very name attests their human nature.[15] It is by the sacrifice of these Rishis, and by the metres they chanted, that the mundane deities received their place and office in the world; and, what is more, the sacrifices of the Vedantic religion are all identified with this primitive creative offering.

---

[15] See the fable of Purusha, *Rig Veda*, lib. viii. cap. iv., hymns 17, 18, 19; and *Yadjur Veda*, cap. xxxi.

The seven priests who offer the Soma sacrifice, so often mentioned in the hymns, are only the successors of the primitive Rishis or Angiras, whose work they carry on. The Sama Veda was their ritual; and they pretended that this ceremonial was necessary for the preservation of the universe, by continuing the action of the seven creative forces which first formed the world. In the more modern system of the Puranas the same agency is found. The world is successively destroyed and reconstructed; there are seven such revolutions each day of Brahma, and each time the world is restored by a Manu and seven attendant Rishis. Here, instead of the subserviency of man to nature, we have the inferiority of nature to man, and the deification of men in as exaggerated a form as can possibly be conceived. The same may be said of the Buddhist system; the seven human Buddhas are successively the great rulers of the universe. And here the facts are so directly contrary to Mr. Buckle's crude speculations, that in the very country where nature is most intractable, and where natural forces exert the most terrific influence on man—in the great frozen plateau of Thibet—there the deification of man is carried to the farthest extent, and the Grand Lama, or living Buddha, is actually identified with the Supreme God. With regard to the Egyptians, Mr. Buckle founds a hasty conclusion on a few words of Herodotus, and cares nothing for the universal and most ancient worship of Osiris, the human god, with whom every man is identified at death in the ritual. In Egypt the human soul, or man, was superior to the elemental deities. "I am your lord," says the soul to the mundane gods in a monumental inscription: [16] "Come and do homage to me; for you belong to me in right of my divine father." The same doctrine may be found in the Egypto-Gnostic lucubrations of the pseudo-Hermes Trismegistus. In the Persian system, Mithra seems to have held a place somewhat similar to that of Osiris in Egypt. At any rate, so far from its being true that the deification of mortals was unknown, the fact is, that the king assumed successively the insignia of each of the seven planets, and was adored

---

[16] Champollion, *Grammaire*, p. 285.

by the people as the incarnate presence of each.[17] Of the ancient Arabian religion, Mr. Buckle professes his ignorance; the name, therefore, is only inserted to swell his catalogue to the eye, without any corresponding increase in the value of his induction. As we have shown each of his other assertions to be exactly the contrary of the truth, we need not trouble ourselves with disproving one that he owns to be a mere guess. In a later page he says, that in Central America, as in India, the national religion was "a system of complete and unmitigated terror. Neither there, nor in Mexico, nor in Peru, nor in Egypt, did the people desire to represent their deities in human forms, or ascribe to them human attributes." On the contrary, we can prove, in all these countries, the gods—at least the human-formed gods—are in sculptures only distinguishable from men by the addition of their respective symbols; while, on the other hand, the Egyptian kings and queens are continually represented by the characters of the various gods and goddesses whom they patronised. As to human attributes being ascribed to these gods, it is more difficult to prove this point against Mr. Buckle from the scarcity of poetical legends. But he will find his negative still harder to prove against us. In Mexico, the progenitors of our race, Cihuacohuatl (the woman-serpent, or mother of our flesh) and her husband, are placed among the thirteen great gods; and, as such, take precedence of all the elemental deities, coming next after Tezatlipoca, the creator, and Ometeuctli and his wife, the progenitors of the heroes. In Peru the Aztec sovereign was, as in Egypt, worshipped as the sun. Again, Mr. Buckle's principle is as false as his facts. Religious terrorism is in direct proportion to the humanitarianism of a religion. As among men, according to Mr. Mill, and therefore according to Mr. Buckle, cruelty is in proportion to inequality—as the despot sheds more blood than the constitutional sovereign, and as the despot by divine right, who claims not only the civil homage but the religious veneration of his people, is obliged to be more severe than the mere military adventurer; so, when we go a step further, and raise a

---

[17] Dabistan, p. 42.

living man, or a caste, into the place of God, we are obliged to hedge them round with a fence of the most bloody rites and laws. The real cause of Brahmin and Mexican cruelty was not because the Divine nature was so separated from mankind, but because it was so identified with a certain class of men, that this class was obliged to maintain its position by a system of unmitigated terrorism. The farther we remove God from humanity, the less we care about Him. We could not fancy an Epicurean fighting in defence of his indolent deities. As a general rule, those who persecute are willing to suffer persecution; we cannot fancy anybody willing to suffer in defence of an abstract divinity: hence we suppose that the more abstract, intangible, and unreal a religion is, the less cruelty will be perpetrated in its name. This, it appears to us, is the true account of the cruelties of the religions Mr. Buckle enumerates, and not the mere influence of climate and the aspects of nature.

The origin of Mr. Buckle's mistakes here, as in other subjects, is his learned ignorance. He never goes to the best authorities; he scarcely ever consults the originals. If he had given himself the trouble to read and understand the Vedas, which he so ostentatiously quotes at second-hand, the Puranas, the collections of Egyptian monumental inscriptions, the Zendavesta, and to understand the documents about America by M'Culloch, he might have given a rather more rational account of the religions which he pretends to philosophise upon.

In the same unlucky chapter Mr. Buckle declares, what on his principles was inevitable, that "original distinctions of race are altogether hypothetical" (p. 36); in support of which view that eminent positivist Mr. Mill is very properly quoted. As we have to deal now with Mr. Buckle's false learning rather than with his false theories, we can only glance at this great absurdity. For the same race of men preserves its character, not only in every region of the world, but in every period of history, in spite of moral as well as physical influences. Were not the Semitic races everywhere and always monotheists; whilst Japhetic nations, from Hindostan to Scandinavia, were originally pantheists or polytheists. Epic poetry, again, is distinctive of the Indo-Germanic race alone. The most amusing example of a nation's fidelity to the character which it obtained on its first appearance in history is afforded by France. Lasaulx has collected the judgments of the ancients upon the Gauls: "Gallia," said Cato, "duas res industriosissime persequitur, rem militarem et argute loqui. Mobilitate et levitate animi novis imperiis studebant" (*Caesar, B. G.* ii. 1). "Omnes fere Gallos novis rebus studere et ad bellum mobiliter celeriterque excitari" (*Ibid.* iii. 10). "Sunt in consiliis capiendis mobiles, et novis plerumque rebus student" (*Ibid.* iv. 5). "Galli quibus insitum est esse leves" (*Trebellius Pollio Galien.* 4). "Gens hominum inquietissima et avida semper vel faciendi principis vel imperii" (*Flavius Vopiscus Saturninus,* 7).[18]

But we must conclude. We have said quite enough to show that Mr. Buckle's learning is as false as his theory, and that the ostentation of his slovenly erudition is but an artifice of ignorance. In his laborious endeavor to degrade the history of mankind, and of the dealings of God with man, to the level of one of the natural sciences, he has stripped it of its philosophical, of its divine, and even of its human character and interest.

When an able and learned work appears, proclaiming new light and increase of knowledge to the world, the first question is not so much whether it was written in the service of religion, as whether it contains any elements which may be made to serve religion. A book is not necessarily either dangerous or contemptible because it is inspired by hatred of the Church. "Nemo inveniret, quia nemo discuteret, nisi pulsantibus calumniatoribus. Cum enim haeretici calumniantur, parvuli perturbantur. . . . Negligentius enim veritas quaereretur, si mendaces adversarios non haberet"[19] (Augustine, *Sermones ad Populum,*

---

[18] "Gaul pursues two things with immense industry,—military matters and neat speaking." "Through instability and levity of mind they were meditating the overthrow of the government." "Almost all men of Gaul are revolutionists, and are easily and quickly excited to war." "In council they are unstable, and generally revolutionary." "The French, to whom levity is natural. A most restless kind of men, always wanting to set up a king or an empire."

[19] "No one would discover, for no one would discuss, unless roused by the blows of misrepresentation. For while heretics misrepresent, the little ones are scandalised. . . . Truth would not be sought so industriously, if it had no enemies to tell lies of it."

lib. xi). Theodore of Mopsuestia, Julian of Eclanum, Calvin, and Strauss, have not been without their usefulness. An able adversary, sincere in his error and skilful in maintaining it, is in the long-run a boon to the cause of religion. The greatness of the error is the measure of the triumph of truth. The intellectual armour with which the doctrine of the Church is assailed becomes the trophy of her victory. All her battles are defensive, but they all terminate in conquest.

The mental lethargy of the last generation of English Catholics was due perhaps not a little to the very feebleness of their adversaries. When a formidable assailant arose at Oxford, he found an adversary amongst us who was equal to the argument. In like manner, when the Duke of Wellington was the no-popery champion of Toryism, a very sufficient opponent appeared in the person of O'Connell. And now that Mr. Spooner is the representative of anti-Catholic politics, by a similar admirable dispensation and fitness of things he too finds among Catholic statesmen foemen who are worthy of his steel.

It is not, however, on such grounds as these that Mr. Buckle had a claim on our attention. He is neither wise himself, nor likely to be the cause of wisdom in others; and with him

Bella geri placuit nullos habitura triumphos.[20]

for we could not allow a book to pass without notice into general circulation and popularity which is written in an impious and degrading spirit, redeemed by no superiority or modesty of learning, by no earnest love of truth, and by no open dealing with opponents.

We may rejoice that the true character of an infidel philosophy has been brought to light by the monstrous and absurd results to which it has led this writer, who has succeeded in extending its principles to the history of civilisation only at the sacrifice of every quality which makes a history great.

---

[20] "We understand a war where victory is no triumph."

III

Political Causes of the American Revolution

AT the time of the utmost degradation of the Athenian democracy, when the commanders at Arginusae were condemned by an unconstitutional decree, and Socrates alone upheld the sanctity of the law, the people, says Xenophon, cried out that it was monstrous to prevent them from doing whatever they pleased.[1] A few years later the archonship of Euclides witnessed the restoration of the old constitution, by which the liberty, though not the power, of Athens was revived and prolonged for ages; and the palladium of the new settlement was the provision that no decree of the council or of the people should be permitted to overrule any existing law.[2]

The fate of every democracy, of every government based on the sovereignty of the people, depends on the choice it makes between these opposite principles, absolute power on the one hand, and on the other the restraints of legality and the authority of tradition. It must stand or fall according to its choice, whether to give the supremacy to the law or to the will of the people; whether to constitute a moral association maintained by

First printed in the *Rambler*, May, 1861. Reprinted from Acton, *Essays on Church and State*, edited by Douglas Woodruff (London: Hollis and Carter, 1952).

[1] τὸ δὲ πλῆθος ἐβόα δεινὸν εἶναι εἰ μή τις ἐάσει τὸν δῆμον πράττειν ὃ ἂν βούληται. *Hellen*, i, 7, 12.

[2] ψήφισμα δὲ μηδὲν μήτε βουλῆς μήτε δήμου νόμου κυριώτερον εἶναι. Andocides, *de Myst.* (Or. *Atl.*, ed. Dobson, i, 259.)

duty, or a physical one kept together by force. Republics offer, in this respect, a strict analogy with monarchies which are also either absolute or organic, either governed by law, and therefore constitutional, or by a will which, being the source, cannot be the object of laws, and is therefore despotic. But in their mode of growth, in the direction in which they gravitate, they are directly contrary to each other. Democracy tends naturally to realize its principle, the sovereignty of the people, and to remove all limits and conditions of its exercise; whilst monarchy tends to surround itself with such conditions. In one instance force yields to right; in the other might prevails over law. The resistance of the king is gradually overcome by those who resist and seek to share his power; in a democracy the power is already in the hands of those who seek to subvert and to abolish the law. The process of subversion is consequently irresistible, and far more rapid.

They differ, therefore, not only in the direction, but in the principle of their development. The organization of a constitutional monarchy is the work of opposing powers, interests, and opinions, by which the monarch is deprived of his exclusive authority, and the throne is surrounded with, and guarded by, political institutions. In a purely popular government this antagonism of forces does not exist, for all power is united in the same sovereign; subject and citizen are one, and there is no external power that can enforce the surrender of a part of the supreme authority, or establish a security against its abuse. The elements of organization are wanting. If not obtained at starting they will not naturally spring up. They have no germs in the system. Hence monarchy grows more free, in obedience to the laws of its existence, whilst democracy becomes more arbitrary. The people is induced less easily than the king to abdicate the plenitude of its power, because it has not only the right of might on its side, but that which comes from possession, and the absence of a prior claimant. The only antagonism that can arise is that of contending parties and interests in the sovereign community, the condition of whose existence is that it should be homogeneous. These separate interests can protect themselves only by setting bounds to the power of the majority; and to this the majority cannot be compelled, or consistently persuaded, to consent. It would be a surrender of the direct authority of the people, and of the principle that in every political community authority must be commensurate with power.

Infirma minoris
Vox cedat numeri, parvaque in parte quiescat.

"La pluralité," says Pascal, "est la meilleure voie, parce-qu'elle est visible, et qu'elle a la force pour se faire obéir; cependant c'est l'avis des moins habiles." The minority can have no permanent security against the oppression of preponderating numbers, or against the government which these numbers control, and the moment will inevitably come when separation will be preferred to submission. When the classes which compose the majority and the minority are not defined with local distinctness, but are mingled together throughout the country, the remedy is found in emigration; and it was thus that many of the ancient Mediterranean states, and some of the chief American colonies, took their rise. But when the opposite interests are grouped together, so as to be separated not only politically, but geographically, there will ensue a territorial disruption of the state, developed with a rapidity and certainty proportioned to the degree of local corporate organization that exists in the community. It cannot, in the long run, be prevented by the majority, which is made up of many future, contingent minorities, all secretly sympathizing with the seceders, and unwilling to compel them to remain, because they dread to perpetuate the tyranny of majorities. The strict principle of popular sovereignty must therefore lead to the destruction of the state that adopts it, unless it sacrifices itself by concession.

The greatest of all modern republics has given the most complete example of the truth of this law. The dispute between absolute and limited power, between centralization and self-government, has been, like that between privilege and prerogative in England, the substance of the constitutional history of the United States. This is the argument which confers on the whole period that intervenes between the convention of 1787 and the election of Mr Davis in 1861 an almost epic unity. It is this problem that has supplied the impulse to the political progress of the United States, that underlies all the great questions that have agitated the Union, and bestows on them all their constitutional importance. It has recurred in many forms, but on each occasion the solution has failed, and the decision has been avoided. Hence the American government is justly termed a system of compromises, that is to say, an inconsistent system. It is not founded, like the old governments of Europe, on tradition, nor on principles, like those which have followed the French Revolution; but on a series of mutual concessions, and momentary suspensions of war between opposite principles, neither of which could prevail. Necessarily, as the country grew more populous, and the population more extended, as the various interests grew in importance, and the various parties in internal strength, as new regions contrasting with each other in all things in which the influence of nature and the condition of society bear upon political life were formed into states, the conflict grew into vaster proportions and greater intensity, each opinion became more stubborn and unyielding, compromise was more difficult, and the peril to the Union increased.

Viewed in the light of recent events, the history of the American Republic is intelligible and singularly instructive. For the dissolution of the Union is no accidental or hasty or violent proceeding, but the normal and inevitable result of a long course of events, which trace their origin to the constitution itself. There we find the germs of the disunion that have taken seventy years to ripen, the beginning of an antagonism which constantly asserted itself and could never be reconciled, until the differences widened into a breach.

The convention which sat at Philadelphia in 1787, for the purpose of substituting a permanent constitution in the place of the confederacy, which had been formed to resist the arms of England, but which had broken down in the first years of peace, was not a very numerous body, but it included the most eminent men of America. It is astounding to observe the political wisdom, and still more the political foresight, which their deliberations exhibit. Franklin, indeed, appears to have been the only very foolish man among them, and his colleagues seem to have been aware of it. Washington presided, but he exercised very little influence upon the assembly, in which there were men who far exceeded him in intellectual power. Adams and Jefferson were in Europe, and the absence of the latter is conspicuous in the debates and in the remarkable work which issued from them. For it is a most striking thing that the views of pure democracy, which we are accustomed to associate with American politics, were almost entirely unrepresented in that convention. Far from being the product of a democratic revolution, and of an opposition to English institutions, the constitution of the United States was the result of a powerful reaction against democracy, and in favour of the traditions of the mother country. On this point nearly all the leading statesmen were agreed, and no contradiction was given to such speeches as the following. Madison said: "In all cases where a majority are united by a common interest or passion, the rights of the minority are in danger. What motives are to restrain them? A prudent regard to the maxim, that honesty is the best policy, is found by experience to be as little regarded by bodies of men as by individuals. Respect for character is always diminished in proportion to the number among whom the blame or praise is to be divided. Conscience, the only remaining tie, is known to be inadequate in individuals; in large numbers little is to be expected from it." [3]

Mr Sherman opposed the election by the people, "insisting that it ought to be by the State legislatures. The people immediately should have as little to do as may be about the government."

Mr Gerry said: "The evils we experience flow from the excess of democracy. The people do not want virtue, but are the dupes of pretended patriots. . . . He had been too republican heretofore; he was still, however, republican, but had been taught by experience the danger of the levelling spirit." Mr Mason "admit-

---

[3] Madison's *Reports,* 162.

ted that we had been too democratic, but was afraid we should incautiously run into the opposite extreme." Mr Randolph observed "that the general object was to provide a cure for the evils under which the United States laboured; that, in tracing these evils to their origin, every man had found it in the turbulence and follies of democracy: that some check, therefore, was to be sought for against this tendency of our government." [4]

Mr Wilson, speaking in 1787, as if with the experience of the seventy years that followed, said: "Despotism comes on mankind in different shapes; sometimes in an executive, sometimes in a military one. Is there no danger of a legislative despotism? Theory and practice both proclaim it. If the legislative authority be not restrained, there can be neither liberty nor stability." [5] "However the legislative power may be formed," said Gouverneur Morris, the most conservative man in the convention, "it will, if disposed, be able to ruin the country." [6]

Still stronger was the language of Alexander Hamilton: "If government is in the hands of the few, they will tyrannize over the many; if in the hands of the many, they will tyrannize over the few. It ought to be in the hands of both, and they should be separated. This separation must be permanent. Representation alone will not do; demagogues will generally prevail; and, if separated, they will need a mutual check. This check is a monarch. . . . The Monarch must have proportional strength. He ought to be hereditary, and to have so much power that it will not be his interest to risk much to acquire more. . . . Those who mean to form a solid republican government ought to proceed to the confines of another government. . . . But if we incline too much to democracy, we shall soon shoot into a monarchy." [7] "He acknowledged himself not to think favourably of republican government, but addressed his remarks to those who did think favourably of it, in order to prevail on them to tone

---

[4] *Ibid.*, 135, 138.
[5] *Ibid.*, 196.
[6] *Ibid.*, 433.
[7] Hamilton's *Works*, ii, 413–417.

their government as high as possible." [8] Soon after, in the New York convention for the adoption of the constitution, he said: "It has been observed that a pure democracy, if it were practicable, would be the most perfect government. Experience has proved that no position in politics is more false than this. The ancient democracies, in which the people themselves deliberated, never possessed one feature of good government. Their very character was tyranny." [9]

Hamilton's opinions were in favour of monarchy, though he despaired of introducing it into America. He constantly held up the British constitution as the only guide and model; and Jefferson has recorded his conversations, which show how strong his convictions were. Adams had said that the English government might, if reformed, be made excellent; Hamilton paused and said: "Purge it of its corruption, and give to its popular branch equality of representation, and it would become an impracticable government; as it stands at present, with all its supposed defects, it is the most perfect government which ever existed." And on another occasion he declared to Jefferson: "I own it is my own opinion . . . that the present government is not that which will answer the ends of society, by giving stability and protection to its rights; and that it will probably be found expedient to go into the British form." [10]

In his great speech on the constitution, he spoke with equal decision: "He had no scruple in declaring, supported as he was by the opinion of so many of the wise and good, that the British government was the best in the world, and that he doubted much whether anything short of it would do in America. . . . As to the executive, it seemed to be admitted that no good one could be established on republican principles. Was not this giving up the merits of the question? For can there be a good government without a good executive? The English model was the only good one on this subject. . . . We ought to go as far,

---

[8] Madison's *Reports*, 244.
[9] Hamilton's *Works*, ii, 440.
[10] Rayner's *Life of Jefferson*, 268.

in order to attain stability and permanency, as republican principles will admit." [11]

Mr Dickinson "wished the Senate to consist of the most distinguished characters—distinguished for their rank in life and their weight of property, and bearing as strong a likeness to the British House of Lords as possible." [12]

Mr Pinckney, of South Carolina, said: "Much has been said of the constitution of Great Britain. I will confess that I believe it to be the best constitution in existence; but, at the same time, I am confident that it is one that will not or cannot be introduced into this country for many centuries." [13]

The question on which the founders of the constitution really differed, and which has ever since divided, and at last dissolved the Union, was to determine how far the rights of the States were merged in the federal power, and how far they retained their independence. The problem arose chiefly upon the mode in which the central Congress was to be elected. If the people voted by numbers or by electoral districts, the less populous States must entirely disappear. If the States, and not the population, were represented, the necessary unity could never be obtained, and all the evils of the old confederation would be perpetuated. "The knot," wrote Madison in 1831, "felt as the Gordian one, was the question between the larger and the smaller States, on the rule of voting."

There was a general apprehension on the part of the smaller States that they would be reduced to subjection by the rest. Not that any great specific differences separated the different States; for though the question of the regulation of commerce and of slavery afterwards renewed the dispute, yet interests were so different from what they have since become, and so differently distributed, that there is little analogy, excepting in principle, with later contests; what was then a dispute on a general principle has since been envenomed by the great interests and great passions which have become involved in it. South Carolina,

[11] Madison's *Reports*, 202.
[12] *Ibid.*, 166.
[13] *Ibid.*, 234.

which at that time looked forward to a rapid increase by immigration, took part with the larger States on behalf of the central power; and Charles Pinckney presented a plan of a constitution which nearly resembled that which was ultimately adopted. The chief subject of discussion was the Virginia plan, presented by Edmund Randolph, in opposition to which the small State of New Jersey introduced another plan founded on the centrifugal or State-rights principle. The object of this party was to confirm the sovereignty of the several States, and to surrender as little as possible to the federal government. This feeling was expressed by Mr Bedford: "Is there no difference of interests, no rivalship of commerce, of manufacturers? Will not these large States crush the small ones, whenever they stand in the way of their ambitions or interested views?" [14]

"The State legislatures," said Colonel Mason, "ought to have some means of defending themselves against encroachments of the national government. In every other department we have studiously endeavoured to provide for its self-defence. Shall we leave the States alone unprovided with means for this purpose?" [15]

These speakers may have been good or bad politicians, they were certainly good prophets. They were nearly balanced in numbers, and surpassed in ability, by the centralizing party. Madison, at that time under the powerful influence of Hamilton, and a federalist, but who afterwards was carried by Jefferson into the democratic camp, occupied an uncertain intermediate position. A note preserved in Washington's handwriting records: "Mr Madison thinks an individual independence of the States utterly irreconcilable with their aggregate sovereignty, and that a consolidation of the whole into a simple republic would be as inexpedient as it is unattainable." [16]

In convention he said: "Any government for the United States formed on the supposed practicability of using force against the

---

[14] Madison's *Reports,* 173.
[15] *Ibid.,* 170.
[16] William's *Statesman's Manual,* 268.

unconstitutional proceedings of the States would prove as visionary and fallacious as the government of Congress." [17]

The consistent Federalists went farther: "Too much attachment," said Mr Read, "is betrayed to the State governments. We must look beyond their continuance; a national government must soon, of necessity, swallow them all up." [18]

Two years before the meeting of the convention, in 1785, Jay, the very type of a Federalist, wrote: "It is my first wish to see the United States assume and merit the character of one great nation, whose territory is divided into different States merely for more convenient government."

Alexander Hamilton went farther than all his colleagues. He had taken no part in the early debates, when he brought forward an elaborate plan of his own; the most characteristic features of which are, that the State governments are to be altogether superseded; their governors to be appointed by the general government, with a veto on all State laws, and the president is to hold office on good behaviour. An executive, elected for life, but personally responsible, made the nearest possible approach to an elective monarchy; and it was with a view to this all but monarchical constitution that he designed to destroy the independence of the States. This scheme was not adopted as the basis of discussion. "He has been praised," said Mr Johnson, "by all, but supported by none." Hamilton's speech is very imperfectly reported, but his own sketch, the notes from which he spoke, are preserved, and outweigh, in depth and in originality of thought, all that we have ever heard or read of American oratory. He left Philadelphia shortly after, and continued absent many weeks; but there can be no doubt that the spirit of his speech greatly influenced the subsequent deliberations. "He was convinced," he said, "that no amendment of the confederation, leaving the States in possession of their sovereignty, could answer the purpose. . . . The general power, whatever be its form, if it preserves itself, must swallow up the State powers. . . . They are

---

[17] Madison's *Reports,* 171.
[18] Madison's *Reports,* 163.

not necessary for any of the great purposes of commerce, revenue or agriculture. Subordinate authorities, he was aware, would
be necessary. There must be distinct tribunals; corporations for
local purposes. . . . By an abolition of the States, he meant that
no boundary could be drawn between the national and State
legislatures; that the former must therefore have indefinite authority. If it were limited at all, the rivalship of the States would
gradually subvert it. . . . As States, he thought they ought to be
abolished. But he admitted the necessity of leaving in them
subordinate jurisdictions." [19]

This policy could be justified only on the presumption that
when all State authorities should disappear before a great central power, the democratic principles, against which the founders of the constitution were contending, would be entirely overcome. But in this Hamilton's hopes were not fulfilled. The
democratic principles acquired new force, the spirit of the convention did not long survive, and then a strong federal authority
became the greatest of all dangers to the opinions and institutions which he advocated. It became the institute of the popular
will instead of its barrier; the organ of arbitrary power instead of
a security against it. There was a fundamental error and contradiction in Hamilton's system. The end at which he aimed was
the best, but he sought it by means radically wrong, and necessarily ruinous to the cause they were meant to serve. In order to
give to the Union the best government it could enjoy, it was
necessary to destroy, or rather to ignore, the existing authorities.
The people was compelled to return to a political state of
nature, irrespective of the government it already possessed, and
to assume to itself powers of which there were constitutional
administrators. No adaptation of existing facts to the ideal was
possible. They required to be entirely sacrificed to the new
design. All political rights, authorities and powers must be restored to the masses, before such a scheme could be carried into
effect. For the most conservative and anti-democratic government the most revolutionary basis was sought. These objections

---

[19] Madison's *Reports*, 201, 212.

were urged against all plans inconsistent with the independence of the several States by Luther Martin, Attorney General for Maryland.

"He conceived," he said, "that the people of the States, having already vested their powers in their respective legislatures, could not resume them without a dissolution of their governments. . . . To resort to the citizens at large for their sanction to a new government will be throwing them back into a state of nature; the dissolution of the State governments is involved in the nature of the process; the people have no right to do this without the consent of those to whom they have delegated their power for State purposes."[20] And in his report to the convention of Maryland of the proceedings out of which the constitution arose, he said:

> If we, contrary to the purpose for which we were intrusted, considering ourselves as master-builders, too proud to amend our original government, should demolish it entirely, and erect a new system of our own, a short time might show the new system as defective as the old, perhaps more so. Should a convention be found necessary again, if the members thereof, acting upon the same principles, instead of amending and correcting its defects, should demolish that entirely, and bring forward a third system, that also might soon be found no better than either of the former; and thus we might always remain young in government, and always suffering the inconveniences of an incorrect imperfect system.[21]

It is very remarkable that, while the Federalists, headed by Hamilton and Madison, advocated, for the soundest and wisest object, opinions which have since been fatal to the Union, by furnishing the democratic party with an irresistible instrument and consequently an irresistible temptation, Martin supported a policy in reality far more conservative, although his opinions were more revolutionary, and although he quoted as political authorities writers such as Price and Priestley. The controversy, although identical in substance with that which has at last destroyed the Union, was so different in form, and consequently

---

[20] *Ibid.*, 218, 248.
[21] Elliot's *Debates*, i, 350.

in its bearings, that the position of the contending parties became inverted as their interests or their principles predominated. The result of this great constitutional debate was that the States were represented as units in the Senate, and the people according to numbers in the House. This was the first of the three great compromises. The others were the laws by which the regulation of commerce was made over to the central power, and the slave-trade was tolerated for only twenty years. On these two questions, the regulation of commerce and the extension of slavery, the interests afterwards grew more divided, and it is by them that the preservation of the Union has been constantly called in question. This was not felt at first, when Jay wrote that "Providence has been pleased to give this one connected country to one united people; a people descended from the same ancestors, speaking the same language, professing the same religion, attached to the same principles of government, very similar in their manners and customs." [22] The weakening of all these bonds of union gradually brought on the calamities which are described by Madison in another number of the same publication:

A landed interest, a manufacturing interest, a mercantile interest, a moneyed interest with many lesser interests, grow up of necessity in civilized nations, and divide them into different classes, actuated by different sentiments and views. The regulation of these varying and interfering interests forms the principal task of modern legislation, and involves the spirit of party and faction in the necessary and ordinary operations of the government. . . . When a majority is included in a faction, the form of popular government enables it to sacrifice to its ruling passion or interest both the public good and the rights of other citizens. . . . It is of great importance in a republic not only to guard the society against the oppression of its rulers, but to guard one part of the society against the injustice of the other part. Different interests necessarily exist in different classes of citizens. If a majority be united by common interests, the rights of the minority will be insecure. There are but two methods of providing against this evil: the one by creating a

---

[22] *Federalist*, 2.

will in the community independent of the majority, that is, of the society itself; the other, by comprehending in the society so many separate descriptions of citizens as will render one unjust combination of a majority of the whole very improbable, if not impracticable. . . . In a free government, the security for civil rights must be the same as that for religious rights. It consists, in the one case, in the multiplicity of interests, and in the other in the multiplicity of sects.[23]

That Madison should have given so absurd a reason for security in the new constitution can be explained only by the fact that he was writing to recommend it as it was, and had to make the best of his case. It had been Hamilton's earnest endeavour to establish that security for right which Madison considers peculiar to monarchy, an authority which should not be the organ of the majority. " 'Tis essential there should be a permanent will in a community. . . . The principle chiefly to be established is this, that there must be a permanent will. . . . There ought to be a principle in government capable of resisting the popular current." [24]

This is precisely what Judge Story means when he says: "I would say in a republican government the fundamental truth is, that the minority have indisputable and inalienable rights; that the majority are not every thing, and the minority nothing; that the people may not do what they please."

Webster thought the same, but he took a sanguine view of actual facts when he said: "It is another principle, equally true and certain, and, according to my judgment of things, equally important, that the people often limit themselves. They set bounds to their own power. They have chosen to secure the institutions which they establish against the sudden impulses of mere majorities." [25]

Channing was nearer the truth when he wrote: "The doctrine that the majority ought to govern passes with the multitude as an intuition, and they have never thought how far it is to be

---

[23] *Federalist*, 10, 51.
[24] *Works*, ii, 414, 415.
[25] *Works*, vi, 225.

modified in practice, and how far the application of it ought to be controlled by other principles." [26]

In reality, the total absence of a provision of this kind, which should raise up a law above the arbitrary will of the people, and prevent it from being sovereign, led the greatest of the statesmen who sat in the convention to despair of the success and permanence of their work. Jefferson informs us that it was so with Washington: "Washington had not a firm confidence in the durability of our government. Washington was influenced by the belief that we must at length end in something like a British constitution."

Hamilton, who by his writing contributed more than any other man to the adoption of the constitution, declared in the convention that "no man's ideas were more remote from the plan than his own," and he explained what he thought of the kind of security that had been obtained: "Gentlemen say that we need to be rescued from the democracy. But what the means proposed? A democratic Assembly is to be checked by a democratic Senate, and both these by a democratic chief magistrate." [27]

"A large and well organized republic," he said, "can scarcely lose its liberty from any other cause than that of anarchy, to which a contempt of the laws is the high-road. . . . A sacred respect for the constitutional law is the vital principle, the sustaining energy of a free government. . . . The instruments by which it must act are either the authority of the laws, or force. If the first be destroyed, the last must be substituted; and when this becomes the ordinary instrument of government, there is an end to liberty." [28]

His anticipations may be gathered from the following passages:

A good administration will conciliate the confidence and affection of the people, and perhaps enable the government to acquire more consistency than the proposed constitution seems

[26] *Memoir*, 417.
[27] *Works*, ii, 415.
[28] *Works*, vii, 164.

to promise for so great a country. It may then triumph altogether over the State governments, and reduce them to an entire subordination, dividing the larger States into smaller districts. . . . If this should not be the case, in the course of a few years it is probable that the contests about the boundaries of power between the particular governments and the general government, and the momentum of the larger States in such contests, will produce a dissolution of the Union. This, after all, seems to be the most likely result. . . . The probable evil is, that the general government will be too dependent on the State legislatures, too much governed by their prejudices, and too obsequious to their humours; that the States, with every power in their hands, will make encroachments on the national authority, till the Union is weakened and dissolved.[29]

The result has justified the fears of Hamilton, and the course of events has been that which he predicted. Democratic opinions, which he had so earnestly combated, gained ground rapidly during the French revolutionary period. Jefferson, who, even at the time of the Declaration of Independence, which was his work, entertained views resembling those of Rousseau and Paine, and sought the source of freedom in the abstract rights of man, returned from France with his mind full of the doctrines of equality and popular sovereignty. By the defeat of Adams in the contest for the presidency, he carried these principles to power, and altered the nature of the American government. As the Federalists interpreted and administered the constitution, under Washington and Adams, the executive was, what Hamilton intended it to be, supreme in great measure over the popular will. Against this predominance the State legislatures were the only counterpoise, and accordingly the democratic party, which was the creature of Jefferson, vehemently defended their rights as a means of giving power to the people. In apparent contradiction, but in real accordance with this, and upon the same theory of the direct sovereignty of the people, Jefferson, when he was elected, denied the right of the States to control the action of the executive. Regarding the President as the representative of a power wholly arbitrary, he admitted no limits to its exercise. He

---

[29] *Ibid.*, ii, 421, 450.

held himself bound to obey the popular will even against his own opinions, and to allow of no resistance to it. He acted as the helpless tool of the majority, and the absolute ruler of the minority, as endowed with despotic power, but without free will.

It is of this principle of the revolution that Tocqueville says: "Les gouvernements qu'elle a fondées sont plus fragiles, il est vrai, mais cent fois plus puissants qu'aucun de ceux qu'elle a renversés; fragiles et puissants par les mêmes causes." [30]

Hence Jefferson's determined aversion to every authority which could oppose or restrain the will of the sovereign people, especially to the State legislatures and to the judiciary. Speaking of an occasion in which the judges had acted with independence, Hildreth says: "Jefferson was not a little vexed at this proceeding, which served, indeed, to confirm his strong prejudices against judges and courts. To him, indeed, they were doubly objects of hatred, as instruments of tyranny in the hands of the Federalists, and as obstacles to himself in exercises of power." [31]

His views of government are contained in a paper which is printed in Rayner's life [32] of him.

Governments are republican only in proportion as they embody the will of their people, and execute it. . . . Each generation is as independent of the one preceding as that was of all which had gone before. It has, then, like them, a right to choose for itself the form of government it believes most promotive of its own happiness . . . it is for the peace and good of mankind, that a solemn opportunity of doing this, every nineteen or twenty years, should be provided by the constitution. . . . The dead have no rights. . . . This corporeal globe and everything upon it belongs to its present corporeal inhabitants during their generation. . . . That majority, then, has a right to depute representatives to a convention, and to make the constitution which they think will be best for themselves. . . . Independence can be trusted nowhere but with the people in mass.

---

[30] *L'ancien Régime et la Révolution,* p. 13.
[31] *History of the U.S.,* vi, 70.
[32] *Life of Jefferson,* 378.

With these doctrines Jefferson subverted the republicanism of America, and consequently the Republic itself.

Hildreth describes as follows the contest between the two systems, at the time of the accession of Jefferson to power, in 1801:

> From the first moment that party lines had been distinctly drawn, the opposition has possessed a numerical majority, against which nothing but the superior energy, intelligence and practical skill of the Federalists, backed by the great and venerable name and towering influence of Washington, had enabled them to maintain for eight years past an arduous and doubtful struggle. The Federal party, with Washington and Hamilton at its head, represented the experience, the prudence, the practical wisdom, the discipline, the conservative reason and instincts of the country. The opposition, headed by Jefferson, expressed its hopes, wishes, theories, many of them enthusiastic and impracticable, more especially its passions, its sympathies and antipathies, its impatience of restraint. The Federalists had their strength in those narrow districts where a concentrated population had produced and contributed to maintain that complexity of institutions, and that reverence for social order, which, in proportion as men are brought into contiguity, become more absolutely necessaries of existence. The ultra-democratical ideas of the opposition prevailed in all that more extensive region in which the dispersion of population, and the despotic authority vested in individuals over families of slaves, kept society in a state of immaturity.[33]

Upon the principle that the majority have no duties, and the minority no rights, that it is lawful to do whatever it is possible to do, measures were to be expected which would oppress most tyrannically the rights and interests of portions of the Union, for whom there was no security and no redress. The apprehension was so great among the Federalists that Hamilton wrote in 1804: "The ill opinion of Jefferson, and jealousy of the ambition of Virginia, is no inconsiderable prop of good principles in that country [New England]. But these causes are leading to an opinion that the dismemberment of the Union is expedient."[34]

[33] *History of the U.S.*, v, 414.
[34] *Works*, vii, 852.

Jefferson had given the example of such threats, and owed his election to them during his contest for the presidency with Colonel Burr. He wrote to Monroe, February 15, 1801: "If they could have been permitted to pass a law for putting the government into the hands of an officer, they would certainly have prevented the election. But we thought it best to declare openly and firmly, one and all, that the day such an act passed the middle States would, and that no such usurpation, even for a single day, should be submitted to."

Shortly afterwards a conjunction arose in which Jefferson put his principles into practice in such a way as greatly to increase the alarm of the North-Eastern States. In consequence of Napoleon's Berlin decree and of the British orders in council, he determined to lay an embargo on all American vessels. He sent a pressing message to Congress, and the Senate passed the measure after a four-hours' debate with closed doors. In the House the debate was also secret, but it lasted several days, and was often prolonged far into the night, in the hope of obtaining a division. The Bill was passed December 22, 1807. The public had no voice in the matter; those whom the measure touched most nearly were taken by surprise, and a conspicuous example was given of secrecy and promptitude in a species of government which is not commonly remarkable for these qualities.

The embargo was a heavy blow to the ship-owning States of New England. The others were less affected by it. "The natural situation of this country," says Hamilton, "seems to divide its interests into different classes. There are navigating and non-navigating States. The Northern are properly the navigating States; the Southern appear to possess neither the means nor the spirit of navigation. This difference in situation naturally produces a dissimilarity of interests and views respecting foreign commerce." [35]

Accordingly the law was received in those States with a storm of indignation. Quincy, of Massachusetts, declared in the House: "It would be as unreasonable to undertake to stop the

---

[35] *Works*, ii, 433.

rivers from running into the sea, as to keep the people of New England from the ocean. They did not believe in the constitutionality of any such law. He might be told that the courts had already settled that question. But it was one thing to decide a question before a court of law, and another to decide it before the people." [36]

Even in a juridical point of view the right to make such a law was very doubtful. Story, who first took part in public affairs on this occasion, says: "I have ever considered the embargo a measure which went to the extreme limit of constructive power under the constitution. It stands upon the supreme verge of the constitution." [37]

The doctrine of State-rights, or nullification, which afterwards became so prominent in the hands of the Southern party, was distinctly enunciated on behalf of the North on this occasion. Governor Trumbull, of Connecticut, summoned the legislature to meet, and in his opening address to them he took the ground that, in great emergencies, when the national legislature had been led to overstep its constitutional power, it became the right and duty of the State legislatures "to interpose their protecting shield between the rights and liberties of the people, and the assumed power of the general government." [38]

They went farther and prepared to secede from the Union, and thus gave the example which has been followed, on exactly analogous grounds, by the opposite party. Randolph warned the administration that they were treading fast in the fatal footsteps of Lord North.[39]

John Quincy Adams declared in Congress that there was a determination to secede. "He urged that a continuance of the embargo much longer would certainly be met by forcible resistance, supported by the legislature, and probably by the judiciary of the State. . . . Their object was, and had been for

---

[36] Hildreth, *History of the U.S.*, vi, 100.

[37] *Life*, i, 185.

[38] *History of the U.S.*, vi, 120.

[39] *Ibid.*, vi, 117.

several years, a dissolution of the Union, and the establishment of a separate confederation." Twenty years later, when Adams was President, the truth of this statement was impugned. At that time the tables had been turned, and the South was deny-ing the right of Congress to legislate for the exclusive benefit of the North-Eastern States, whilst these were vigorously and prof-itably supporting the Federal authorities. It was important that they should not be convicted out of their own mouths, and that the doctrine they were opposing should not be shown to have been inaugurated by themselves. Adams therefore published a statement, October 21, 1828, reiterating his original declaration: "The people were constantly instigated to forcible resistance against it, and juries after juries acquitted the violators of it, upon the ground that it was unconstitutional, assumed in the face of a solemn decision of the district court of the United States. A Separation of the Union was openly stimulated in the public prints, and a convention of delegates of the New Eng-land States, to meet at New Haven, was intended and pro-posed." That this was true is proved by the letters of Story, written at the time: "I was well satisfied," he says, "that such a course would not and could not be borne by New England, and would bring on a direct rebellion. . . . The stories here of rebel-lion in Massachusetts are continually circulating. My own impressions are, that the Junto would awaken it, if they dared; but it will not do. . . . A division of the States has been medi-tated, but I suspect that the public pulse was not sufficiently inflamed. . . . I am sorry to perceive the spirit of disaffection in Massachusetts increasing to so high a degree; and I fear that it is stimulated by a desire in a very few ambitious men to dissolve the Union. . . . I have my fears when I perceive that the public prints openly advocate a resort to arms to sweep away the present embarrassments of commerce." [40]

It was chiefly due to the influence of Story that the embargo was at length removed, with great reluctance and disgust on the part of the President. "I ascribe all this," he says, "to one

---

[40] *Life*, i, 187.

pseudo-republican Story." [41] On which Story, who was justly proud of his achievement, remarks, "Pseudo-republican of course I must be, as every one was, in Mr Jefferson's opinion, who dared to venture upon a doubt of his infallibility." [42] In reality Jefferson meant that a man was not a republican who made the interests of the minority prevail against the wish of the majority. His enthusiastic admirer, Professor Tucker, describes very justly and openly his policy in this affair. "If his perseverance in the embargo policy so long, against the wishes and interests of New England, and the mercantile community generally, may seem to afford some contradiction to the self-denying merit here claimed, the answer is, that he therein fulfilled the wishes of a large majority of the people. . . . A portion of the community here suffered an evil necessarily incident to the great merit of a republican government, that the will of the majority must prevail." [43]

We have seen that in the case of the embargo, as soon as this democratic theory was acted upon, it called up a corresponding claim of the right of the minority to secede, and that the democratic principle was forced to yield. But secession was not a theory of the constitution, but a remedy against a vicious theory of the constitution. A sounder theory would have avoided the absolutism of the democrats and the necessity for secession. The next great controversy was fought upon this ground. It exhibits an attempt to set up a law against the arbitrary will of the government, and to escape the tyranny of the majority, and the remedy, which was worse than the disease. An ideal of this kind had already been sketched by Hamilton. "This balance between the national and state governments ought to be dwelt on with peculiar attention, as it is of the utmost importance. It forms a double security to the people. If one encroaches on their rights, they will find a powerful protection in the other. Indeed, they will both be prevented from overpassing their constitutional limits, by a certain rivalship which will ever subsist between

---

[41] *Correspondence*, iv, 148.

[42] *Life*, i, 185.

[43] *Life of Jefferson*, 322.

them." [44] This was also what Mr Dickinson looked forward to when he said in the Convention of 1787: "One source of stability is the double branch of the legislature. The division of the country into distinct States forms the other principal source of stability." [45]

The war with England, and the long suspension of commerce which preceded it, laid the foundations of a manufacturing interest in the United States. Manufactories began to spring up in Pennsylvania, and more slowly in New England. In 1816 a tariff was introduced, bearing a slightly protective character, as it was necessary to accommodate the war prohibitions to peaceful times. It was rather intended to facilitate the period of transition than to protect the new industry; and that interest was still so feeble, and so little affected by the tariff, that Webster, who was already a representative of Massachusetts in Congress, voted against it. It was carried by the coalition of Clay with the South Carolina statesmen, Lowndes and Calhoun, against whom this vote was afterwards a favourite weapon of attack. In the following years the increasing importance of the cultivation of cotton, and the growth of manufactures, placed the Northern and Southern interests in a new position of great divergency. Hamilton had said long before: "The difference of property is already great amongst us. Commerce and industry will still increase the disparity. Your government must meet this state of things, or combinations will, in process of time, undermine your system." [46]

The New England manufacturers were awakened to the advantage of protection for their wares. In the memorial of the merchants of Salem, written by Story in 1820, he says: "Nothing can be more obvious than that many of the manufacturers and their friends are attempting, by fallacious statements, founded on an interested policy, or a misguided zeal, or very short-sighted views, to uproot some of the fundamental principles of our revenue policy. . . . If we are unwilling to receive foreign manu-

[44] *Works*, ii, 444.
[45] Madison's *Debates*, 148.
[46] Elliot's *Debates*, i, 450.

factures, we cannot reasonably suppose that foreign nations will receive our raw materials. . . . We cannot force them to become buyers when they are not sellers, or to consume our cotton when they cannot pay the price in their own fabrics. We may compel them to use the cotton of the West Indies, or of the Brazils, or of the East Indies." About the same time, May 20, 1820, he writes to Lord Stowell on the same subject: "We are beginning also to become a manufacturing nation; but I am not so much pleased, I am free to confess, with the efforts made to give an artificial stimulus to those establishments in our country. . . . The example of your great manufacturing cities, apparently the seats of great vices, and great political fermentations, affords no very agreeable contemplation to the statesman or the patriot, or the friend of liberty." [47]

The manufacturers obtained a new tariff in 1824, another was carried by great majorities in 1828, and another in 1832 by a majority of two to one. It is the measure of 1828, which raised the duties on an average to nearly fifty per cent on the value of the imports, that possesses the greatest importance in a constitutional point of view. "To it," says the biographer of Mr Calhoun, "may be traced almost every important incident in our political history since that time, as far as our internal affairs are concerned." [48]

At this time the interests of North and South were perfectly distinct. The South was teeming with agricultural produce, for which there was a great European demand; whilst the industry of the North, unable to compete with European manufacturers, tried to secure the monopoly of the home market. Unlike the course of the same controversy in England, the agriculturists (at least the cotton-growers) desired free trade, because they were exporters; the manufacturers protection, because they could not meet competition. "The question," said Calhoun, "is in reality one between the exporting and non-exporting interests of the country." The exporting interest required the utmost freedom of

<hr>

[47] *Life*, i, 385.
[48] *Life of Calhoun*, p. 34.

imports, in order not to barter at a disadvantage. "He must be ignorant of the first principles of commerce, and the policy of Europe, particularly England, who does not see that it is impossible to carry on a trade of such vast extent on any other basis than barter; and that if it were not so carried on, it would not long be tolerated. . . . The last remains of our great and once flourishing agriculture must be annihilated in the conflict. In the first place, we will be thrown on the home market, which cannot consume a fourth of our products; and instead of supplying the world, as we would with a free trade, we should be compelled to abandon the cultivation of three-fourths of what we now raise, and receive for the residue whatever the manufacturers—who would then have their policy consummated by the entire possession of our market—might choose to give." [49] It seemed a fulfilment of the prophecy of Mr Lowndes, who, in resisting the adoption of the constitution in South Carolina forty years before, declared that "when this new constitution should be adopted, the sun of the Southern States would set, never to rise again. . . . The interest of the Northern States would so predominate as to divest us of any pretensions to the title of a republic." [50] Cobbett, who knew America better than any Englishman of that day, described in his *Political Register* for 1833 the position of these hostile interests in a way which is very much to the point. "All these Southern and Western States are, commercially speaking, closely connected with Birmingham, Sheffield, Manchester, and Leeds . . . they have no such connection with the Northern States, and there is no tie whatsoever to bind them together, except that which is of a mere political nature. . . . Here is a natural division of interests, and of interests so powerful, too, as not to be counteracted by any thing that man can do. The heavy duties imposed by the Congress upon British manufactured goods is neither more nor less than so many millions a year taken from the Southern and Western States, and given to the Northern States." [51]

---

[49] Calhoun's *Works*, vi, 12.
[50] Elliot's *Debates*, iv, 272.
[51] *Political Works*, vi, 662.

Whilst in England protection benefited one class of the population at the expense of another, in America it was for the advantage of one part of the country at the expense of another. "Government," said Calhoun, "is to descend from its high appointed duty, and become the agent of a portion of the community to extort, under the guise of protection, tribute from the rest of the community." [52]

Where such a controversy is carried on between opposite classes in the same State, the violence of factions may endanger the government, but they cannot divide the State. But the violence is much greater, the wrong is more keenly felt, the means of resistance are more legitimate and constitutional, where the oppressed party is a sovereign State.

The South had every reason to resist to the utmost a measure which would be so injurious to them. It was opposed to their political as well as to their financial interests. For the tariff, while it impoverished them, enriched the government, and filled the treasury with superfluous gold. Now the Southern statesmen were always opposed to the predominance of the central authority, especially since it lent itself to a policy by which they suffered. They had practical and theoretical objections to it. The increase of the revenue beyond the ordinary wants of the government placed in its hands a tempting and dangerous instrument of influence. Means must be devised for the disposal of these sums, and the means adopted by the advocates of restriction was the execution of public works, by which the people of the different States were bribed to favour the central power. A protective tariff therefore, and international improvement, were the chief points in the policy of the party, which, headed by Henry Clay, sought to strengthen the Union at the expense of the States, and which the South opposed, as both hostile to their interests and as unconstitutional. "It would be in vain to attempt to conceal," wrote Calhoun of the tariff in 1831, "that it has divided the country into two great geographical divisions, and arrayed them against each other, in opinion at least, if not

---

[52] *Works,* iv, 181.

interests also, on some of the most vital of political subjects—on its finance, its commerce, and its industry. . . . Nor has the effect of this dangerous conflict ended here. It has not only divided the two sections on the important point already stated, but on the deeper and more dangerous questions, the constitutionality of a protective tariff, and the general principles and theory of the constitution itself: the stronger, in order to maintain their superiority, giving a construction to the instrument which the other believes would convert the general government, with the total destruction of liberty." [53] "On the great and vital point—the industry of the country, which comprehends almost every interest—the interest of the two great sections is opposed. We want free trade, they restrictions; we want moderate taxes, frugality in the government, economy, accountability, and a rigid application of the public money to the payment of the debt, and to the objects authorized by the constitution. In all these particulars, if we may judge by experience, their views of their interest are precisely the opposite." [54] In 1828 he said of the protective system: "No system can be more efficient to rear up a moneyed aristocracy"; wherein he is again supported by Cobbett, in the well-known saying, uttered five years later, concerning the United States: "It is there the aristocracy of money, the most damned of all aristocracies." South Carolina took the lead in resisting the introduction of the protective system, and being defeated by many votes on the question itself, took its stand on the constitutional right of each sovereign State to arrest by its veto any general legislation of a kind which would be injurious to its particular interests. "The country," said Calhoun, "is now more divided than in 1824, and then more than in 1816. The majority may have increased, but the opposite sides are, beyond dispute, more determined and excited than at any preceding period. Formerly the system was resisted mainly as inexpedient, but now as unconstitutional, unequal, unjust, and oppressive. Then relief was sought exclusively from the general government;

[53] *Works*, vi, 77, 78.
[54] *Ibid.*, vi, 31.

but now many, driven to despair, are raising their eyes to the reserved sovereignty of the States as the only refuge." [55] Calhoun was at that time Vice-President of the United States, and without a seat in Congress. The defence of the theory of the constitution devolved therefore upon the senator from South Carolina, General Hayne; and a debate ensued between Hayne and Webster, in January 1830, which is reckoned by Americans the most memorable in the parliamentary history of their country. Hayne declared that he did not contend for the mere right of revolution, but for the right of constitutional resistance; and in reply to Webster's defence of the supreme power, he said: "This I know is a popular notion, and it is founded on the idea that as all the States are represented here, nothing can prevail which is not in conformity with the will of the majority; and it is supposed to be a republican maxim, 'that the majority must govern.' . . . If the will of a majority of Congress is to be the supreme law of the land, it is clear that the constitution is a dead letter, and has utterly failed of the very object for which it was designed—the protection of the rights of the minority. . . . The whole difference between us consists in this—the gentlemen would make force the only arbiter in all cases of collision between the States and the federal government; I would resort to a peaceful remedy." [56]

Two years later Mr Calhoun succeeded Hayne as senator for South Carolina, and the contest was renewed. After the tariff of 1828 Virginia, Georgia, and North Carolina joined in the recognition of the principle of nullification. When the tariff of 1832 was carried, South Carolina announced that the levying of dues would be resisted in the State. Calhoun defended the nullifying ordinance in the Senate, and in speeches and writings, with arguments which are the very perfection of political truth, and which combine with the realities of modern democracy the theory and the securities of medieval freedom. "The essence of liberty," he said,

---

[55] *Ibid.*, vi, 80.
[56] Elliot's *Debates*, iv, 498.

comprehends the idea of comprehensible power—that those who make and execute the laws should be controlled by those on whom they operate—that the governed should govern. . . . No government based on the naked principle that the majority ought to govern, however true the maxim in its proper sense, and under proper restrictions, can preserve its liberty even for a single generation. This history of all has been the same—violence, injustice, and anarchy, succeeded by the government of one, or a few, under which the people seek refuge from the more oppressive despotism of the many. . . . Stripped of all its covering the naked question is, whether ours is a federal or a consolidated government; a constitutional or absolute one; a government resting ultimately on the solid basis of the sovereignty of the States, or on the unrestrained will of a majority; a form of government, as in all other unlimited ones, in which injustice and violence and force must finally prevail. Let it never be forgotten that, when the majority rules without restriction, the minority is the subject. . . . Nor is the right of suffrage more indispensable to enforce the responsibility of the rulers to the ruled, than a federal organization to compel the parts to respect the rights of each other. It requires the united action of both to prevent the abuse of power and oppression, and to constitute really and truly a constitutional government. To supersede either is to convert it in fact, whatever may be its theory, into an absolute government.[57]

In his disquisition on government Calhoun has expounded his theory of a constitution in a manner so profound and so extremely applicable to the politics of the present day, that we regret we can only give a very feeble notion of the argument by the few extracts for which we can make room.

The powers which it is necessary for government to possess, in order to repress violence and preserve order, cannot execute themselves. They must be administered by men in whom, like others, the individual are stronger than the social feelings. And hence the powers vested in them to prevent injustice, and oppression on the part of others, will, if left unguarded, be by them converted into instruments to oppress the rest of the community. That by which this is prevented, by whatever name called, is what is meant by constitution, in its most

---

[57] *Works,* vi, 32.

comprehensive sense, when applied to government. Having its origin in the same principle of our nature, constitution stands to government as government stands to society; as the end for which government is ordained would be defeated without government, so that for which government is ordained would, in a great measure, be defeated without constitution. . . . Constitution is the contrivance of man, while government is of divine ordination. . . . Power can only be resisted by power, and tendency by tendency. . . . I call the right of suffrage the indispensable and primary principle; for it would be a great and dangerous mistake to suppose, as many do, that it is of itself sufficient to form constitutional governments. To this erroneous opinion may be traced one of the causes why so few attempts to form constitutional governments have succeeded; and why, of the few which have, so small a number had durable existence. . . . So far from being of itself sufficient—however well guarded it might be, and however enlightened the people—it would, unaided by other provisions, leave the government as absolute as it would be in the hands of irresponsible rulers, and with a tendency at least as strong towards oppression and abuse of its powers. . . . The process may be slow, and much time may be required before a compact, organized majority can be formed; but formed it will be in time, even without preconcert or design, by the sure workings of that principle or constitution of our nature in which government itself originates. . . . The dominant majority, for the time, would have the same tendency to oppression and abuse of power which, without the right of suffrage, irresponsible rulers would have. No reason, indeed, can be assigned why the latter would abuse their power, which would not apply with equal force to the former. . . . The minority, for the time, will be as much the governed or subject portion as are the people in an aristocracy, or the subject in a monarchy. . . . The duration or uncertainty of the tenure by which power is held cannot of itself counteract the tendency inherent in government to oppression and abuse of power. On the contrary, the very uncertainty of the tenure, combined with the violent party warfare which must ever precede a change of parties under such governments, would rather tend to increase than diminish the tendency to oppression. . . . It is manifest that this provision must be of character calculated to prevent any one interest, or combination of interests, from using the powers of government to aggrandize itself at the expense of others. . . . This too can be accomplished in only one way, and that is, by such an organism of the government—and, if necessary for the purpose, of the community also—as will, by dividing and distributing the powers of government, give to each division or interest, through its appropriate organ, either a concurrent voice in making and executing the laws, or a veto on their execution. . . . Such an organism as this, combined with the right of suffrage, constitutes, in fact, the elements of constitutional government. The one, by rendering those who make and execute the laws responsible to those on whom they operate, prevents the rulers from oppressing the ruled, and the other, by making it impossible for any one interest or combination of interests, or class, or order, or portion of the community, to obtain exclusive control, prevents any one of them from oppressing the other. . . . It is this negative power—the power of preventing or arresting the action of the government—be it called by what term it may, veto, interposition, nullification, check, or balance of power—which in fact forms the constitution. . . . It is indeed the negative power which makes the constitution, and the positive which makes the government. . . . It follows necessarily that where the numerical majority has the sole control of the government, there can be no constitution; as constitution implies limitation or restriction; . . . and hence, the numerical, unmixed with the concurrent majority, necessarily forms in all cases absolute government. . . . Constitutional governments, of whatever form, are, indeed, much more similar to each other in their structure and character than they are, respectively, to the absolute governments even of their own class; . . . and hence the great and broad distinction between governments is—not that of the one, the few, the many—but of the constitutional and the absolute. . . . Among the other advantages which governments of the concurrent have over those of the numerical majority—and which strongly illustrates their more popular character—is that they admit, with safety, a much greater extension of the right of suffrage. It may be safely extended in such governments to universal suffrage, that is, to every male citizen of mature age, with few ordinary exceptions; but it cannot be so far extended in those of the numerical majority, without placing them ultimately under the control of the more ignorant and dependent portions of the community. For, as the community becomes populous, wealthy, refined, and highly civilized, the difference between the rich and the poor will become more strongly marked, and the number of the ignorant and dependent greater in proportion to the rest of the community. . . . The tendency of the concurrent government is to unite the community, let its interests be ever so diversified or opposed; while that of the numerical is to divide it into two conflicting portions, let its interest be naturally ever so united and identified. . . . The numerical majority, by regarding the community as a unit, and having as such the same interests throughout all its parts, must, by its necessary operation, divide it into two hostile parts, waging, under the forms of law, incessant hostility against each other. . . . To make equality of condition essential to liberty, would be to destroy liberty and progress. The reason is both that inequality of condition, while it is a necessary consequence of liberty, is at the same time indispensable to progress. . . . It is, indeed, this inequality of condition between the front and rear ranks, in the march of progress, which gives so strong an impulse to the former to maintain their position, and to the latter to press forward into their files. . . . This gives to progress its greatest impulse. . . . These great and dangerous errors have their origin in the prevalent opinion, that all men are born free and equal, than which nothing can be more unfounded and false. . . . In an absolute democracy party conflicts between the majority and the minority . . . can hardly ever terminate in compromise. The object of the opposing minority is to expel the majority from power, and of the majority to maintain their hold upon it. It is on both sides a struggle for the whole; a struggle that must determine which shall be the governing and which the subject party. . . . Hence, among other reasons, aristocracies and monarchies more readily assume the constitutional form than absolute popular government.[58]

This was written in the last years of Calhoun's life, and published after his death; but the ideas, though he matured them in the subsequent contest on slavery, guided him in the earlier stage of the dispute which developed nullification into secession, during the tariff controversy of the years 1828 to 1833. Many of those who differed from him most widely deemed that his resistance was justified by the selfish and unscrupulous policy of the North. Legaré, the most accomplished scholar among American statesmen, afterwards Attorney General, made a Fourth-of-July oration in South Carolina, during the height of the excitement of 1831, in which he said:

---

[58] *Works*, i, 7–83.

The authors of this policy are indirectly responsible for this deplorable state of things, and for all the consequences that may grow out of it. They have been guilty of an inexpiable offence against the country. They found us a united, they have made us a distracted people. They found the union of these States an object of fervent love and religious veneration; they have made even its utility a subject of controversy among very enlightened men. . . . I do not wonder at the indignation which the imposition of such a burden of taxation has excited in our people, in the present unprosperous state of their affairs. . . . Great nations cannot be held together under a united government by any thing short of despotic power, if any one part of the country is to be arrayed against another in a perpetual scramble for privilege and protection, under any system of protection.[59]

Brownson, at that time the most influential journalist of America, and a strong partisan of Calhoun, advocated in 1844 his claims to the presidency, and would, we believe, have held office in his cabinet if he had been elected. In one of his earliest numbers of his well-known *Review* he wrote:

Even Mr Calhoun's theory, though unquestionably the true theory of the federal constitution, is yet insufficient. . . . It does not, as a matter of fact, arrest the unequal, unjust and oppressive measures of the federal government. South Carolina in 1833 forced a compromise; but in 1842 the obnoxious policy was revived, is pursued now successfully, and there is no State to attempt again the virtue of State interposition. . . . The State, if she judged proper, had the sovereign right to set aside this obnoxious tariff enactment in her own dominions, and prohibit her subjects or citizens from obeying it. . . . The parties to the compact being equal, and there being no common umpire, each, as a matter of course, is its own judge of the infraction of the compact, and of the mode and measure of redress.[60]

The President, General Jackson, had a strong aversion for the theory and for the person of Calhoun. He swore that he would have him impeached for treason, and that he should hang on a gallows higher than Haman's. One of the nullifying declarations

---

[59] *Writings of Legaré*, i, 272.
[60] *Quarterly Review*, ii, 522.

of his Vice-President reached him late at night; in a fit of exultation he had the law officers of the government called out of their beds to say whether at last here was not hanging matter. He issued a manifesto condemning the doctrine of nullification and the acts of South Carolina, which was very ably drawn up by Livingston, the Secretary for State, famous in the history of legislation as the author of the Louisiana code. Webster, the first orator of the day, though not a supporter of the administration, undertook to answer Calhoun in the Senate, and he was fetched from his lodging, when the time came, in the President's carriage. His speech, considered the greatest he ever delivered, was regarded by the friends of the Union as conclusive against State-rights. Madison, who was approaching the term of his long career, wrote to congratulate the speaker in words which ought to have been a warning: "It crushes nullification, and must hasten an abandonment of secession. But this dodges the blow by confounding the claim of secede at will with the right of seceding from intolerable oppression."

Secession is but the alternative of interposition. The defeat of the latter doctrine on the ground of the constitution, deprived the South of the only possible protection from the increasing tyranny of the majority, for the defeat of nullification coincided in time with the final triumph of the pure democratic views; and at the same time that it was resolved that the rights of the minority had no security, it was established that the power of the majority had no bounds. Calhoun's elaborate theory was an earnest attempt to save the Union from the defects of its constitution. It is useless to inquire whether it is legally right, according to the letter of the constitution, for it is certain that it is in contradiction with its spirit as it has grown up since Jefferson. Webster may have been the truest interpreter of the law; Calhoun was the real defender of the Union. Even the Unionists made the dangerous admission, that there were cases in which, as there was no redress known to the law, secession was fully justified. Livingston gave the opinion that "if the act be one of the few which, in its operation, cannot be submitted to the Supreme Court, and be one that will, in the opinion of the State,

74

justify the risk of a withdrawal from the Union, this last extremity may at once be resorted to." [61]

The intimate connection between nullification and secession is shown by the biographer of Clay, though he fails to see that one is not the consequence, but the surrogate, of the other: "The first idea of nullification was doubtless limited to the action of a State in making null and void a federal law or laws within the circle of its own jurisdiction, without contemplating the absolute independence of a secession. Seeing, however, that nullification, in its practical operation, could hardly stop short of secession, the propounders of the doctrine in its first and limited signification afterwards came boldly up to the claim of the right of secession." [62]

Practically, South Carolina triumphed, though her claims were repudiated. The tariff was withdrawn, and a measure of compromise was introduced by Clay, the leading protectionist, which was felt so great a concession that Calhoun accepted, whilst Webster opposed it, and it was carried. But the evil day, the final crisis, was only postponed. The spirit of the country had taken a course in which it could not be permanently checked; and it was certain that new opportunities would be made to assert the omnipotence of the popular will, and to exhibit the total subservience of the executive to it.[63] Already a new controversy had begun, which has since overshadowed that which shook the Union from 1828 to 1833. The commercial question was not settled; the economical antagonism, and the determination on the part of the North to extend its advantages, did not slumber from Clay's Compromise Act to the Morill Tariff in 1861; and in his farewell address, in 1837, Jackson drew a gloomy and desponding picture of the period which is filled with his name.

---

[61] Elliot's *Debates,* iv, 519.

[62] Colton's *Life of Clay,* v, 392.

[63] ὁ γὰρ δῆμος οὐ βούλεται εὐνομουμένης τῆς πόλεως αὐτὸς δουλεύειν, ἀλλ' ἐλεύθερος εἶναι καὶ ἄρχειν, τῆς δὲ κακονομίας αὐτῷ ὀλίγον μέλει· ὃ γὰρ σὺ νομίζεις οὐκ εὐνομεῖσθαι, αὐτὸς ἀπὸ τούτου ἰσχύει ὁ δῆμος καὶ ἐλεύθερός ἐστιν· Xenophon, *Athen. Repub.,* i, 8.

Many powerful interests are continually at work to procure heavy duties on commerce, and to swell the revenue beyond the real necessities of the public service; and the country has already felt the injurious effects of their combined influence. They succeeded in obtaining a tariff of duties bearing most oppressively on the agricultural and labouring classes of society, and producing a revenue that could not be usefully employed within the range of the powers conferred upon Congress; and in order to fasten upon the people this unjust and unequal system of taxation, extravagant schemes of internal improvement were got up in various quarters to squander the money and to purchase support. . . . Rely upon it, the design to collect an extravagant revenue, and to burden you with taxes beyond the economical wants of the government, is not yet abandoned. The various interests which have combined together to impose a heavy tariff and to produce an overflowing treasury, are too strong, and have too much at stake, to surrender the contest. The corporations and wealthy individuals who are engaged in large manufacturing establishments desire a high tariff to increase their gains. Designing politicians will support it to conciliate their favour, and to obtain the means of profuse expenditure, for the purpose of purchasing influence in other quarters. . . . It is from within, among yourselves—from cupidity, from corruption, from disappointed ambition, and inordinate thirst for power—that factions will be formed and liberty endangered.[64]

Jackson was himself answerable for much of what was most deplorable in the political state of the country. The democratic tendency, which began under Jefferson, attained in Jackson's presidency its culminating point. The immense change in this respect may be shown in a single example. Pure democracy demands quick rotation of office; as all men have an equal claim to official power and profit, and must be supposed nearly equally qualified for it, and require no long experience (so that at Athens offices were distributed by lot), the greatest possible number of citizens should successively take part in the administration. It diminishes the distinction between the rulers and the ruled, between the State and the community, and increases the dependence of the first upon the last. At first such changes are

---

[64] *Statesman's Manual,* 953–960.

not contemplated. Washington dismissed only nine officials in eight years, Adams removed only ten, Madison five, Monroe nine, John Quincy Adams only two, both on specific disqualifying grounds. Jefferson was naturally in favour of rotation in office, and caused a storm of anger when he displaced thirty-nine official men in order to supply vacancies for supporters. Jackson, on succeeding the younger Adams, instantly made 176 alterations, and in the course of the first year 491 postmasters lost their places. Mr Everett says very truly: "It may be stated as the general characteristic of the political tendencies of this period that there was a decided weakening of respect for constitutional restraint. Vague ideas of executive discretion prevailed on the one hand in the interpretation of the constitution, and of popular sovereignty on the other, as represented by a President elevated to office on overwhelming majorities of the people." [65]

This was the period of Tocqueville's visit to America, when he passed the following judgment: "When a man, or a party, suffers an injustice in the United States, to whom can he have recourse? To public opinion? It is that which forms the majority. To the legislative body? It represents the majority, and obeys it blindly. To the executive power? It is appointed by the majority, and serves as its passive instrument. To public force? It is nothing but the majority under arms. To the jury? It is the majority invested with the right of finding verdicts. The judges themselves, in some States, are elected by the majority. However iniquitous, therefore, or unreasonable the measure from which you suffer, you must submit." [66] Very eminent Americans [67] quite agreed with him in his censure of the course things had taken, and which had been seen long beforehand. In 1818 Story writes: "A new race of men is springing up to govern the nation; they

---

[65] *Memoir of Webster*, p. 101.

[66] Vol. ii, cap. vii.

[67] There is a remarkable passage in Story's letters on Tocqueville's celebrated book; "The work of De Tocqueville has had great reputation abroad, partly founded on their ignorance that he has borrowed the greater part of his reflections from American work, and little from his own observation. The main body of his materials will be found in the *Federalist*, and in Story's *Commentaries*" (*Life of Story*, ii, 330).

are the hunters after popularity; men ambitious, not of the honour so much as of the profits of office—the demagogues whose principles hang laxly upon them, and who follow not so much what is right as what leads to a temporary vulgar applause. There is great, very great, danger that these men will usurp so much of popular favour that they will rule the nation; and if so, we may yet live to see many of our best institutions crumble in the dust." [68]

The following passages are from the conclusion of his *Commentary on the Constitution:* "The influence of the disturbing causes, which more than once in the convention were on the point of breaking up the Union, have since immeasurably increased in concentration and vigour. . . . If, under these circumstances, the Union should once be broken up, it is impossible that a new constitution should ever be formed, embracing the whole territory. We shall be divided into several nations or confederacies, rivals in power and interest, too proud to brook injury, and too close to make retaliation distant or ineffectual." On February 18, 1834, he writes of Jackson's administration: "I feel humiliated at the truth, which cannot be disguised, that though we live under a republic, we are in fact under the absolute rule of a single man." And a few years later, November 3, 1837, he tells Miss Martineau that she has judged too favourably of his country: "You have overlooked the terrible influence of a corrupting patronage, and the system of exclusiveness in official appointments, which have already wrought such extensive mischiefs among us, and threaten to destroy all the safeguards of our civil liberties. . . . You would have learned, I think, that there may be a despotism exercised in a republic, as irresistible and as ruinous as in any form of monarchy."

The foremost of the Southern statesmen thought exactly like the New England judge. "I care not," said Calhoun, "what the form of the government is; it is nothing, if the government be despotic, whether it be in the hands of one, or of a few, or of many men, without limitation. . . . While these measures were

---

[68] *Life*, i, 311.

destroying the equilibrium between the two sections, the action of the government was leading to a radical change in its character, by concentrating all the power of the system in itself. . . . What was once a constitutional federal republic is now converted, in reality, into one as absolute as that of the autocrat of Russia, and as despotic in its tendency as any absolute government that ever existed. . . . The increasing power of this government, and of the control of the Northern section over all its departments, furnished the cause. It was this which made an impression on the minds of many, that there was little or no restraint to prevent the government from doing whatever it might choose to do." [69] At the same period, though reverting to a much earlier date, Cobbett wrote: "I lived eight years under the republican government of Pennsylvania; and I believe that to have been the most corrupt and tyrannical government that the world ever knew. . . . I have seen enough of republican government to convince me that the mere name is not worth a straw." [70] Channing touches on a very important point, the influence of European liberalism on the republicanism of America: "Ever since our revolution we have had a number of men who have wanted faith in our free institutions, and have seen in our almost unlimited extension of the elective franchise the germ of convulsion and ruin. When the demagogues succeed in influencing the ignorant multitude, and get office and power, this anti-popular party increases; in better times it declines. It has been built up in a measure by the errors and crimes of the liberals of Europe. . . . I have endeavoured on all occasions to disprove the notion that the labouring classes are unfit depositaries of political power. I owe it, however, to truth to say that I believe that the elective franchise is extended too far in this country." [71]

In 1841 he described very accurately the perils which have since proved fatal: "The great danger to our institutions, which alarms our conservatives most, has not perhaps entered Mr

[69] *Works,* iv, 351, 550, 553.
[70] *Works,* vi, 683.
[71] *Memoir of Channing,* 418, 419.

Smith's mind. It is the danger of a party organization, so subtle and strong as to make the government the monopoly of a few leaders and to insure the transmission of the executive power from hand to hand almost as regularly as in a monarchy. . . . That this danger is real cannot be doubted. So that we have to watch against despotism as well as, or more than, anarchy." [72] On this topic it is impossible to speak more strongly, and nobody could speak with greater authority than Dr Brownson: "Our own government, in its origin and constitutional form, is not a democracy, but, if we may use the expression, a limited elective aristocracy. . . . But practically the government framed by our fathers no longer exists, save in name. Its original character has disappeared or is rapidly disappearing. The constitution is a dead letter, except in so far as it serves to prescribe the modes of election, the rule of the majority, the distribution and tenure of offices, and the union and separation of the functions of government. Since 1828 it has been becoming in practice, and is now substantially, a pure democracy, with no effective constitution but the will of the majority for the time being. . . . The constitution is practically abolished, and our government is virtually, to all intents and purposes, as we have said, a pure democracy, with nothing to prevent it from obeying the interest or interests which for the time being can succeed in commanding it." [73] Shortly before his conversion he wrote: "Looking at what we were in the beginning, and what we now are, it may well be doubted whether another country in Christendom has so rapidly declined as we have, in the stern and rigid virtues, in the high-toned and manly principles of conduct essential to the stability and wise administration of popular government. . . . The established political order in this country is not the democratic; and every attempt to apply the democratic theory as the principle of its interpretation is an attempt at revolution, and to be resisted. By a democracy I understand a political order—if that may be called order which is none—in which the people, primarily and without reference to any au-

[72] *Ibid.*, 421.
[73] Brownson's *Quarterly Review*, 1844, ii, 515, 523.

thority constituting them a body politic, are held to be the source of all the legitimate power in the state." [74]

The partisans of democratic absolutism who opposed State-rights in the affair of the tariff, and led to the unhappy consequences and lamentations we have seen, were already supplied with another topic to test the power of their principle. The question of abolition, subordinate at first, though auxiliary to the question of protection, came into the front when the other had lost its interest, and had been suspended for a season by the Compromise Act. It served to enlist higher sympathies on the side of revolution than could be won by considerations of mere profit. It adorned cupidity with the appearance of philanthropy, but the two motives were not quite distinct, and one is something of a pretext, and serves to disguise the other. They were equally available as means of establishing the supremacy of the absolute democracy, only one was its own reward; the other was not so clearly a matter of pecuniary interest, but of not inferior political advantage. A power which is questioned, however real it may be, must assert and manifest itself if it is to last. When the right of the States to resist the Union was rejected, although the question which occasioned the dispute was amicably arranged, it was certain to be succeeded by another, in order that so doubtful a victory might be commemorated by a trophy.

The question of slavery first exhibited itself as a constitutional difficulty about 1820, in the dispute which was settled by the Missouri compromise. Even at this early period the whole gravity of its consequences was understood by discerning men. Jefferson wrote: "This momentous question, like a fire-ball in the night, awakened and filled me with terror. I considered it at once as the knell of the Union. It is hushed, indeed, for the moment. But this is a reprieve only, not a final sentence."

In 1828, when South Carolina was proclaiming the right of veto, and was followed by several of the Southern States, abolition was taken up in the North as a means of coercion against them, by way of reprisal, and as a very powerful instrument of

---

[74] *Ibid.*, i, 84, 19.

party warfare. Channing writes to Webster, May 14, 1828: "A little while ago, Mr Lundy of Baltimore, the editor of a paper called *The Genius of Universal Emancipation,* visited this part of the country, to stir us up to the work of abolishing slavery in the South; and the intention is to organize societies for this purpose. . . . My fear in regard to our efforts against slavery is, that we shall make the case worse by rousing sectional pride and passion for its support, and that we shall only break the country into two great parties, which may shake the foundations of government."

In the heart of the great controversies of Jackson's administration, on the Bank question and the Veto question, slavery was not brought prominently forward; but when the democratic central power had triumphed, when the Bank question was settled, and there was no longer an immediate occasion for discussing State-rights, the party whose opinion had prevailed in the constitution resolved to make use of their predominance for its extinction. Thenceforward, from about the year 1835, it became the leading question, and the form in which the antagonism between the principles of arbitrary power and self-government displayed itself. At every acquisition of territory, at the formation of new States, the same question caused a crisis; then in the Fugitive-Slave Act, and finally in the formation of the republican party, and its triumph in 1860. The first effect of making abolition a political party question, and embodying in it the great constitutional quarrel which had already threatened the existence of the Union in the question of taxation, was to verify the prophecy of Channing. Webster, who had been the foremost antagonist of nullification in the affair of the tariff, lived to acknowledge that even secession was being provoked by the insane aggression of the North. In one of his latest speeches, in that which is known as his speech for the Union, March 7, 1850, he denounced the policy of the abolitionists: "I do not mean to impute gross motives even to the leaders of these societies, but I am not blind to the consequences of their proceedings. I cannot but see what mischief their interference with the South has produced. And is it not plain to every man? Let any gentleman who entertains doubts on this point recur to the debates in the Virginia House of Delegates in 1832, and he will see with what freedom a proposition made by Mr J. Randolph for the gradual abolition of slavery was discussed in that body. . . . Public opinion, which in Virginia had begun to be exhibited against slavery, and was opening out for the discussion of the question, drew back and shut itself up in its castle. . . . We all know the fact, and we all know the cause; and everything that these agitating people have done has been not to enlarge, but to restrain, not to set free, but to bind faster, the slave-population of the South." [75]

Howe, the Virginian historian, in principle though not in policy an abolitionist, says: "That a question so vitally important would have been renewed with more success at an early subsequent period, seems more than probable, if the current opinions of the day can be relied on; but there were obvious causes in operation which paralysed the friends of abolition, and have had the effects of silencing all agitation on the subject. The abolitionists in the Northern and Eastern States, gradually increasing their strength as a party, became louder in their denunciation of slavery, and more and more reckless in the means adopted for assailing the constitutional rights in the South." [76]

Story writes, January 19, 1839: "The question of slavery is becoming more and more an absorbing one, and will, if it continues to extend its influence, lead to a dissolution of the Union. At least there are many of our soundest statesmen who look to this as a highly probable event." [77]

At that time the abolitionist party was yet in its infancy, and had not succeeded in combining together in a single party all the interests that were hostile to the slave States. Lord Carlisle, describing a conversation he had in 1841 with the present Secretary of State, Mr Seward, says: "I find that I noted at the time that he was the first person I had met who did not speak

[75] *Works*, v, 357.
[76] *Historical Collections of Virginia*, 128.
[77] *Life*, ii, 307.

slightingly of the abolitionists; he thought they were gradually gaining ground." [78]

But in the following year the abolitionist policy rapidly grew up into a great danger to the Union, which the great rivals, Webster and Calhoun, united to resist at the close of their lives. Commercially speaking, it is not certain that the North would gain by the abolition of slavery. It would increase the Southern market by encouraging white emigration from the North; but the commerce of New England depends largely on the cotton crop, and the New England merchants are not for abolition. Calhoun did not attribute the movement to a desire of gain: "The crusade against our domestic institution does not originate in hostility of interests. . . . The rabid fanatics regard slavery as a sin, and thus regarding it deem it their highest duty to destroy it, even should it involve the destruction of the constitution and the Union." [79]

In this view he is fully supported by Webster: "Under the cry of universal freedom, and that other cry that there is a rule for the government of public men and private men which is of superior obligation to the constitution of the country, several of the States have enacted laws to hinder, obstruct, and defeat the enactments in this act of Congress to the utmost of their power. . . . I suspect all this to be the effect of that wandering and vagrant philanthropy which disturbs and annoys all that is present, in time or place, by heating the imagination on subjects distant, remote, and uncertain." [80]

Webster justly considered that the real enemies of the constitution were the abolitionists, not the slave-owners, who threatened to secede. To appeal from the constitution to a higher law, to denounce as sinful and contrary to natural right an institution expressly recognized by it, is manifestly an assault upon the Union itself. The South have the letter and the spirit of the law in their favour. The consistent abolitionists must be ready to sacrifice the Union to their theory. If the objection to slavery is

[78] *Lectures on America,* p. 27.
[79] *Works,* iv, 386.
[80] *Works,* vi, 556, 561.

on moral grounds, paramount to all political rights and interests, abolition is a peremptory duty, to which the Union itself,
whose law is opposed to compulsory abolition, must succumb. It
was therefore perfectly just to remind Mr Seward that in attacking slavery, and denying that it could be tolerated, he was
assailing the law to which he owed his seat in Congress. "No
man," said Webster, "is at liberty to set up, or affect to set up,
his own conscience as above the law, in a matter which respects
the rights of others, and the obligations, civil, social and political, due to others from him." [81]

Dr Brownson says with great truth, as only a Catholic can:
"No civil government can exist, none is conceivable even, where
every individual is free to disobey its orders, whenever they do
not happen to square with his private convictions of what is the
law of God. . . . To appeal from the government to private
judgment, is to place private judgment above public authority,
the individual above the state." [82]

Calhoun was entirely justified in saying that, in the presence
of these tendencies, "the conservative power is in the slave-
holding States. They are the conservative portion of the country." [83]

His own political doctrines, as we have described them, fully
bear out this view. But the conservative anti-revolutionary character of the South depended on other causes than the influence
of its master mind. Slavery is itself in contradiction with the
equal rights of man, as they are laid down in the Declaration of
Independence. Slave-owners are incapacitated from interpreting
that instrument with literal consistency, for it would contradict
both their interests and their daily experience. But as there are
advanced democrats at the South as well as at the North, and
as, indeed, they have succeeded in resisting so long the Northern
politicians, by using the jealousy of the Northern people against
the wealthy capitalists, and the appearance of aristocracy, they
find means of escaping from this dilemma. This is supplied by

[81] *Ibid.*, vi, 578.
[82] *Essays and Reviews*, pp. 357, 359.
[83] *Works*, iv, 360.

the theory of the original inferiority of the African race to the rest of mankind, for which the authority of the greatest naturalist in America is quoted. "The result of my researches," says Agassiz, "is, that Negroes are intellectually children; physically one of the lowest races; inclining with the other blacks, especially the South Sea Negroes, most of all to the monkey type, though with a tendency, even in the extremes, towards the real human form. This opinion I have repeatedly expressed, without drawing from it any objectionable consequence, unless, perhaps, that no coloured race, least of all the Negroes, can have a common origin with ourselves." If this theory were not the property of the infidel science of Europe, one would suppose it must have been invented for the Americans, whom it suits so well.

Webster spoke with great power against the projects of the North:

> There is kept up a general cry of one party against the other, that its rights are invaded, its honour insulted, its character assailed, and its just participation in political power denied. Sagacious men cannot but suspect from all this, that more is intended than is avowed; and that there lies at the bottom a purpose of the separation of the States, for reasons avowed or disavowed, or for grievances redressed or unredressed.
>
> In the South, the separation of the States is openly professed, discussed, and recommended, absolutely or conditionally, in legislative halls, and in conventions called together by the authority of the law.
>
> In the North, the State governments have not run into such excess, and the purpose of overturning the government shows itself more clearly in resolutions agreed to in voluntary assemblies of individuals, denouncing the laws of the land, and declaring a fixed intent to disobey them. . . . It is evident that, if this spirit be not checked, it will endanger the government; if it spread far and wide, it will overthrow the government.[84]

The language of Calhoun about the same period is almost identical with Webster's: "The danger is of a character—

---

[84] *Works*, vi, 567, 582.

whether we regard our safety or the preservation of the Union—which cannot be safely tampered with. If not met promptly and decidedly, the two portions of the Union will become thoroughly alienated, when no alternative will be left to us, as the weaker of the two, but to sever all political ties, or sink down into abject submission." [85]

His last great speech, delivered March 4, 1850, a few days before his death, opened with the words: "I have believed from the first that the agitation of the subject of slavery would, if not prevented by some timely and effective measure, end in disunion." And he went on to say: "If something is not done to avert it, the South will be forced to choose between abolition and secession. Indeed, as events are now moving, it will not require the South to secede in order to dissolve the Union." [86]

The calamity which these eminent men agreed in apprehending and in endeavouring to avert, was brought on after their death by the rise of the republican party—a party in its aims and principles quite revolutionary, and not only inconsistent with the existence of the Union, but ready from the first to give it up. "I do not see," said the New England philosopher Emerson, "how a barbarous community and a civilized community can constitute one State." In order to estimate the extravagance of this party declaration, we will only quote two unexceptionable witnesses, who visited the South at an interval of about forty years from each other; one a Boston divine, the other an eager abolitionist. "How different from our Northern manners! There, avarice and ceremony, at the age of twenty, graft the coldness and unfeelingness of age on the disinterested ardour of youth. I blush for my own people when I compare the selfish prudence of the Yankee with the generous confidence of a Virginian. Here I find great vices, but greater virtues than I left behind me. There is one single trait which attaches me to the people I live with more than all the virtues of New England—they love money less than we do." [87] Lord Carlisle says, in the lecture already referred

---

[85] *Works*, iv, 395.
[86] *Ibid.*, 542, 556.
[87] *Memoir of Channing*, p. 43.

to: "It would be uncandid to deny that the planter in the Southern States has much more in his manner and mode of intercourse that resembles the English country gentleman than any other class of his countrymen." [88]

Emerson's saying is a sign of the extent to which rabid abolitionists were ready to go. Declaring that the Federal Government was devoted to Southern interests, against Northern doctrines, they openly defied it. Disunion societies started up at the North for the purpose of bringing about separation. Several States passed laws against the South and against the constitution, and there were loud demands for separation. This was the disposition of the North at the presidential election of a successor to Pierce. The North threatened to part company, and if it carried its candidate, it threatened the Southern institutions. The South proclaimed the intention of seceding if Fremont should be elected, and threatened to march upon Washington and burn the archives of the Union. Buchanan's election pacified the South; but it was evident from the growing strength of the republican party, that it was their last victory. They accordingly made use of their friends in office to take advantage of the time that remained to them to be in readiness when the next election came. Secession was resolved upon and prepared from the time when the strength of the republicans was exhibited in 1856. In spite of all the horrors of American slavery, it is impossible for us to have any sympathy with the party of which Mr Seward is the chief. His politics are not only revolutionary, but aggressive; he is not only for absolutism but for annexation. In a speech on January 26, 1853, he spoke as follows: "The tendency of commercial and political events invites the United States to assume and exercise a paramount influence in the affairs of the nations situated in this hemisphere; that is, to become and remain a great Western continental power, balancing itself against the possible combinations of Europe. The advance of the country towards that position constitutes what, in the lan-

[88] *Lectures on America,* 35.

guage of many, is called 'progress' and the position itself is what, by the same class, is called 'manifest destiny.' " [89]

When Cass moved a resolution affirming the Monroe doctrine with regard to Cuba, Seward supported it, together with another resolution perfectly consistent with it, of which he said: "It is not well expressed but it implies the same policy in regard to Canada which the main resolutions assert concerning Cuba." [90] Nor is this the limit of his ambition. "You are already," he says to his countrymen, "the great continental power of America. But does that content you? I trust it does not. You want the commerce of the world, which is the empire of the world." [91]

When Kossuth was received in the Senate, he was introduced by Mr Seward, whose European policy is as definite and about as respectable as his American. Speaking of Hungary, he writes, in December 1851: "I trust that some measure may be adopted by the government which, while it will not at all hazard the peace and the prosperity of the country, may serve to promote a cause that appeals so strongly to our interests and our sympathies, viz. the establishment of republicanism, in the countries prepared for it, in Europe." [92] And again, two days later: "Every nation may, and every nation ought to make its position distinctly known in every case of conflict between despots and States struggling for the inalienable and indefeasible rights of independence and self-government, that when despots combine, free States may lawfully unite."

It is impossible to sympathize on religious grounds with the categorical prohibition of slavery as, on political grounds, with the opinions of the abolitionists. In this, as in all other things, they exhibit the same abstract, ideal absolutism, which is equally hostile with the Catholic and with the English spirit. Their democratic system poisons everything it touches. All constitutional questions are referred to the one fundamental principle of

[89] *Works,* iii, 609.
[90] *Ibid.,* 609.
[91] *Ibid.,* 618.
[92] *Ibid.,* 505.

popular sovereignty, without consideration of policy or expediency. In the Massachusetts convention of 1853, it was argued by one of the most famous Americans, that the election of the judiciary could not be discussed on the grounds of its influence on the administration of justice, as it was clearly consonant with the constitutional theory. "What greater right," says the *North American Review*,[93] "has government to deprive people of their representation in the executive and judicial, than in the legislative department?" In claiming absolute freedom, they have created absolute power, whilst we have inherited from the Middle Ages the notion that both liberty and authority must be subject to limits and conditions. The same intolerance of restraints and obligations, the same aversion to recognize the existence of popular duty, and of the divine right which is its correlative, disturb their notions of government and of freedom. The influence of these habits of abstract reasoning, to which we owe the revolution in Europe, is to make all things questions of principle and of abstract law. A principle is always appealed to in all cases, either of interest or necessity, and the consequence is that a false and arbitrary political system produces a false and arbitrary code of ethics, and the theory of abolition is as erroneous as the theory of freedom.

Very different is the mode in which the Church labours to reform mankind by assimilating realities with ideals, and accommodating herself to times and circumstances. Her system of Christian liberty is essentially incompatible with slavery and the power of masters over their slaves was one of the bulwarks of corruption and vice which most seriously impeded her progress. Yet the Apostles never condemned slavery even within the Christian fold. The sort of civil liberty which came with Christianity into the world, and was one of her postulates, did not require the abolition of slavery. If men were being free by virtue of their being formed after the image of God, the proportion in which they realized that image would be the measure of their freedom.

---

[93] Vol. lxxxvi, 477.

Accordingly, St Paul prescribed to the Christian slave to remain content with his condition.[94]

We have gone at inordinate length into the causes and peculiarities of the revolution in the United States, because of the constant analogy they present to the theories and the events which are at the same time disturbing Europe. It is too late to touch upon more than one further point, which is extremely suggestive. The Secession movement was not provoked merely by the alarm of the slave-owners for their property, when the election of Lincoln sent down the price of slaves from 25 to 50 per cent, but by the political danger of Northern preponderance; and the mean whites of the Southern States are just as eager for separation as those who have property in slaves. For they fear lest the republicans, in carrying emancipation, should abolish the barriers which separate the negroes from their own caste. At the same time, the slaves show no disposition to help the republicans, and be raised to the level of the whites. There is a just reason for this fear, which lies in the simple fact that the United States are a republic. The population of a republic must be homogeneous. Civil equality must be founded on social equality, and on national and physiological unity. This has been the strength of the American republic. Pure democracy is that form of government in which the community is sovereign, in which, therefore, the State is most nearly identified with society. But society exists for the protection of interests; the State for the realization of right—"concilia coetusque hominum *jure* sociati, quae civitates appellantur." [95] The State sets up a moral, objective law, and pursues a common object distinct from the ends and purposes of society. This is essentially repugnant to democracy, which recognizes only the interests and rights of the community, and is therefore inconsistent with the consolidation of authority which is implied in the notion of the State. It resists

---

[94] I Cor. vii, 21. The opposite interpretation, common among Protestant commentators, is inconsistent with verses 20 and 24, and with the tradition of the Greek Fathers.

[95] Cicero, *Somnium Scipionis*, 3.

the development of the social into the moral community. If, therefore, a democracy includes persons with separate interests or an inferior nature, it tyrannizes over them. There is no mediator between the part and the whole; there is no room, therefore, for differences of class, of wealth, of race; equality is necessary to the liberty which is sought by a pure democracy.

Where society is constituted without equality of condition or unity of race, where there are different classes and national varieties, they require a protector in a form of government which shall be distinct from, and superior to, every class, and not the instrument of one of them, in an authority representing the State, not any portion of society. This can be supplied only by monarchy; and in this sense it is fair to say that constitutional government, that is, the authority of law as distinguished from interest, can exist only under a king. This is also the reason why even absolute monarchies have been better governors of dependencies than popular governments. In one case they are governed for the benefit of a ruling class; in the other, there is no ruling class, and they are governed in the name of the State. Rome under the Republic and under the Empire is the most striking instance of this contrast. But the tyranny of republics is greatest when differences of races are combined with distinctions of class. Hence South America was a prospering and flourishing country so long as the Spanish Crown served as moderator between the various races, and is still prosperous where monarchy has been retained; whilst the establishment of republics in countries with classes divided by blood has led to hopeless misery and disorder, and constant recourse to dictatorships as a refuge from anarchy and tyranny. Democracy inevitably takes the tone of the lower portions of society, and, if there are great diversities, degrades the higher. Slavery is the only protection that has ever been known against this tendency, and it is so far true that slavery is essential to democracy. For where there are great incongruities in the constitution of society, if the Americans were to admit the Indians, the Chinese, the Negroes, to the rights to which they are justly jealous of admitting European emigrants, the country would be thrown into disorder, and if not, would be degraded to the level of the barbarous races. Accordingly, the Know-nothings rose up as the reaction of the democratic principle against the influx of an alien population. The Red Indian is gradually retreating before the pioneer, and will perish before many generations, or dwindle away in the desert. The Chinese in California inspire great alarm for the same reason, and plans have been proposed of shipping them all off again. This is a good argument too, in the interest of all parties, against the emancipation of the blacks.

This necessity for social equality and national unity has been felt in all democracies where the mass as a unit governs itself. Above all it is felt as a necessity in France, since the downfall of the old society, and the recognition, under republic, charter, and despotism, of the sovereignty of the people. Those principles with which France revolutionizes Europe are perfectly right in her own case. They are detestable in other countries where they cause revolutions, but they are a true and just consequence of the French Revolution. Men easily lose sight of the substance in the form, and suppose that because France is not a republic she is not a democracy, and that her principles therefore will apply elsewhere. This is the reason of the power of the national principle in Europe. It is essential as a consequence of equality to the notion of the people as the source of power. Where there is an aristocracy it has generally more sympathy and connection with foreign aristocracies than with the rest of the nation. The bonds of class are stronger than those of nationality. A democracy, in abolishing classes, renders national unity imperative.

These are some of the political lessons we have learned from the consideration of the vast process of which we are witnessing the consummation. We may consult the history of the American Union to understand the true history of republicanism, and the danger of mistaking it. It is simply the spurious democracy of the French Revolution that has destroyed the Union, by disintegrating the remnants of English traditions and institutions. All the great controversies—on the embargo, restriction, internal improvement, the Bank-Charter Act, the formation of new States, the acquisition of new territory, abolition—are phases of this mighty change, steps in the passage from a constitution framed on an English model to a system imitating that of France. The secession of the Southern States—pregnant with infinite consequences to the African race, by altering the condition of slavery, to America by awakening an intenser thirst for conquest, to Europe by its reaction on European democracy, to England, above all, by threatening for a moment one of the pillars of her social existence, but still more by the enormous augmentation of her power, on which the United States were always a most formidable restraint—is chiefly important in a political light as a protest and reaction against revolutionary doctrines, and as a move in the opposite direction to that which prevails in Europe.

IV

Secret History of Charles II

IN the register of the House of Novices of the Jesuits at Rome there is the following entry: *Jacobus de la Cloche ingressus 11 Aprilis 1668*. From another list, which is signed by the novice himself, we learn that he came from the island of Jersey, and was a subject of the King of England; that his age was about twenty-four; and that he presented himself for admission in the dress of an ecclesiastic, with scarcely any luggage but the clothes he wore. This youth, whose name occurs no more in the books of the Order, and has never yet been pronounced by history, was the eldest of the sons of Charles the Second, the elder brother of Monmouth, and destined to be for a moment his rival in the fanciful schemes of his father. So well was the secret of his birth preserved that throughout the long intrigue to save the Protestant succession, and to supplant the Duke of York by the son of Lucy Walters, no man ever discovered that there was another who, by his age and by his mother's rank, had a better claim than the popular favourite, and who had voluntarily renounced the dazzling fortunes which were once within his grasp. The obscurity which he preferred has endured for nearly two hundred years, and even now is not entirely dispelled; but the facts which I have to relate add a new and interesting episode to the chequered history of the Stuarts, and clear up whatever remained uncertain as to the attachment of Charles II. to the Catholic Church.

This attachment, which excited so keenly the curiosity of the

First printed in the *Home and Foreign Review*, July, 1862. Reprinted from Acton, *Historical Essays and Studies* (London: Macmillan, 1907).

world, and influenced so many of the actions of his reign, has been admitted with greater unanimity by recent historians than by those who spoke from personal observation, and whom Charles succeeded in partially misleading. "It was not," says the ablest of the statesmen who approached him, "the least skilful part of his concealing himself to make the world think he leaned towards an indifference in religion." [1] That belief was long since found to be untenable. Mr. Fox, and the author of the *Annals of England,* believe that he had been actually reconciled to the Catholic Church; and Mackintosh fixes the date of that event in the year 1658. Hallam justly rejects this opinion, but is certain that the king had imbibed during the period of his banishment a persuasion that if any scheme of Christianity was true, it could only be found in the bosom of an infallible Church. Dr. Vaughan believes that, so far as he could be said to have any religion, he was a Catholic; and Macaulay exactly agrees with Dr. Vaughan. Lingard, who declares his early professions of regard for Catholicism a pretence, supplies no psychological explanation of the discrepancy between the scene at his death and his previous insincerity; while Dod more reasonably considers the reconciliation at the last moment a proof that he had inwardly espoused the Catholic doctrines before.

Many things contributed during the life of Charles to spread and to keep alive the report of his conversion. His mother's sincerity and zeal in religion were well known. She had attempted to instil the sentiments of her faith into her eldest daughter Mary, afterwards Princess of Orange, and although this was prevented by the king, she obtained his consent in her exile that their youngest child Henrietta should be educated a Catholic. At Paris Henrietta Maria exerted herself to induce the Duke of Gloucester to change his religion; and when the exhortations of Charles, the influence of Ormond, and the memory of the last solemn parting with his father prevailed against her efforts, she drove him from her presence. Charles I. had feared that the

---

[1] Halifax, *Character of Charles II.,* p. 11.

religion of his queen would injure the cause of his son, and sent earnest warnings to both when the prince joined his mother in France. To the former he wrote from Oxford, 22nd March 1646: "I command you, upon my blessing, to be constant to your religion; neither hearkening to Roman superstitions, nor the seditious and schismatical doctrines of the Presbyterians and Independents; for know that a persecuted church is not thereby less pure, though less fortunate. For all other things I command you to be totally directed by your mother." [2] Shortly after, he wrote to the queen from Newcastle: "In God's name, let him stay with thee till it is seen what ply my business will take; and, for my sake, let the world see that the queen seeks not to alter his conscience." [3] Clarendon entertained the same fears, and endeavoured to keep the prince at Jersey, away from his mother's influence. But he bears testimony that, for six years, down to 1652, when the fortunes of the Stuarts seemed desperate, and the motives for prudence had disappeared with the hope of success, Henrietta Maria was sensible of the impolicy of a step which, more than any other act, must have alienated the English people from their king.[4] That she recognised it at first we may conclude from the failure of the match between Charles and Mademoiselle de Montpensier, the cousin of Lewis XIV. That princess insisted that the difference of religion was an insurmountable obstacle; and Jermyn, who was conducting the business, and must have spoken the thoughts of the queen-mother, thereupon replied that the king could not change his religion for her sake without forfeiting for ever the crown of his kingdom.[5]

When, at length, it appeared certain that no chance of recovering the throne remained, except through the support of the Catholic Powers, the exiled courtiers began to debate whether some sacrifice might not be made for the purpose of obtaining

---

[2] Clarendon, *History of the Rebellion*, x. 8.
[3] *Clarendon Papers*, ii. 239.
[4] *History*, xiii. 131.
[5] *Mémoires de Mademoiselle*, 57, ed. Michaud.

their assistance. "The Protestant religion was found to be very unagreeable to their fortune, and very many exercised their thoughts most how to get handsomely from it. . . . Many made little doubt but that it would shortly be very manifest to the king that his restoration depended wholly upon a conjunction of Catholic princes, who could never be united but on the behalf of Catholic religion."[6] Digby, Clifford, and Bennet became Catholics, and proved their sincerity at their deaths; but they all agreed that it would be dangerous for Charles to imitate them. Clarendon, whose purpose it was to divert from his master the suspicion of popery, wished it to be believed that no religious scruples, no doubts in the orthodoxy of the Anglican Church, had ever invaded the exiled court, and that the Catholic inclinations or professions of some of its members were the effects of political design. He had argued with great force that even though Charles should give no cause for suspicion, the fact of his residence in a Catholic country would be a pretext for his enemies to accuse him. It would not be hard, he wrote to Jermyn, to persuade them who believed the king a papist when he was seen every day at church in England, to believe the prince a papist when he had no church in France to go to.[7] But the other advisers, who were less sturdy Protestants than the Chancellor, knew that nothing was to be expected for their cause from a change of religion. In the period of the administration of Mazarin and the peace of Westphalia, no reasonable man could believe that any State would incur the expense and the risk of war for the establishment of a Catholic dynasty in England; and even those who believed that Charles leaned from conviction towards Rome, and whose sympathies were on the same side, were careful to conceal the fact.[8]

---

[6] *Clarendon,* xvi. 74.

[7] Lister, *Life of Clarendon,* i. 284. He would not allow the prince to attend the service of the French Calvinists at Charenton (*History,* xiii. 133).

[8] The testimony of Ormond and Burnet, and the worthless reports to the same effect in Kennet and Echard, are collected in the *Biographia Britannica,* ii. 177D, 2d ed.

A rumour reached their friends in England, and caused an extreme alarm. "There is a report," wrote Mordaunt to Ormond, in November 1659, "so hot of your master's being turned papist, that unless it be suddenly contradicted, and the world disabused by something coming expressly from him, it is likely, in this extraordinary conjuncture, to do him very great injury amongst his friends both in city and country, in both which his constancy all this while hath rendered him many considerable proselytes." [9] This letter justly represents the position of affairs, and the state of public feeling; and Clarendon took his measures to undeceive his party and to silence their enemies.

Yet, although political interest forbade a public declaration, there was truth in the reports circulated in England, and so stoutly contradicted by the royalists. It is certain that Charles had, during the last years of his exile, secretly adopted the Catholic faith, although the fear of detection prevented a formal abjuration of Protestantism. Burnet says he was received before he left Paris, and that Cardinal de Retz and Aubigny had a hand in it. This information he had obtained from two sources, and indirectly, he affirms, from Retz himself. When Charles was at Paris, after the flight from Worcester, he received instruction in religion from Olier, the celebrated founder of the seminary of St. Sulpice. His conferences were no secret, for Olier had informed his friends of his hopes, and entreated their prayers. They probably gave occasion to the exaggerated report of Burnet. Charles, it is true, wrote from Paris to the Pope to ask for assistance in recovering his dominions. Innocent would have been satisfied, under the circumstances, with a private abjuration; but this was refused, and the king could not even obtain an answer to his application.[10] But although he was not received into the Church, he had advanced so far in his opinions that he might, as Thurloe affirmed, in his communications with the Spanish Government have declared himself in private to them to be a Catholic.[11] Neither France nor Spain had any inducement

---

[9] Carte's *Collection*, ii. 264.
[10] *Vie de M. Olier*, ii. 489, from the French Archives.
[11] Carte's *Collection*, ii. 102.

to publish what would diminish the chances of monarchy in England, and strengthen a Government they feared and hated. The story that Ormond discovered Charles on his knees hearing mass in a church at Brussels comes to us through two independent channels, Carte and Echard. The latter supposes the ceremony of abjuration to have occurred when the king was at Fuentarabia, at the time of the treaty of the Pyrenees. There is much reason in a remark which is made by Welwood: "The truth is, King Charles was neither bigot enough to any religion, nor loved his ease so little, as to embark in a business that must at least have disturbed his quiet, if not hazarded his crown." [12]

Ludovick Stuart, Lord Aubigny, to whom Burnet attributes the conversion of Charles, appeared at Whitehall immediately after the Restoration. In France, where he was educated and ordained, he had joined the party of Cardinal de Retz and the Jansenists, and had been made a canon of Notre Dame. As a relative of the royal family, and at one time an inmate of St. Sulpice, he was probably aware of the conferences which Olier, and perhaps others,[13] held with Charles during his residence at Paris. In April 1661, he officiated at the private marriage of Charles with Catherine of Braganza, and became almoner to the queen. His royal descent, and the position he had already attained in the Church, pointed him out as a suitable person to conduct the projected intercourse between the English court and the Holy See. In order to obtain that office, he sought the aid of a more powerful negotiator.

His friend Cardinal de Retz had taken the foremost part in the troubles which distracted both Church and State in France in the days of the Fronde, and after balancing for a season the power of Mazarin, had been deserted by fortune, and suffered in banishment the disgrace both of the French and of the Roman court. Upon the death of Cromwell Ormond had recourse to him in the name of the king, who promised, if the Cardinal

---

[12] *Memoirs*, p. 131.

[13] Charles is reported to have said that though many persons had discoursed with him on religion, none had affected him so much as Olier (*Vie de M. Olier*, ii. 490).

would obtain for him some assistance from the Pope, to protect the Catholics after his restoration. Retz, hoping that the merit of having secured a promise of indulgence for the Catholic subjects of the King of England would powerfully assist his own cause, undertook the negotiation, and sent one of his adherents, the Abbé Charier, to Rome. The envoy could not, however, obtain an audience of the Pope; and he was assured by one of the Cardinals that the promises of Charles had made no impression, and that the prospect of relief to the oppressed Catholics would never induce Alexander VII. to furnish him with money.[14] The Restoration soon altered the position of affairs, and improved the prospects of the Cardinal. He came to London in 1660, and received not only promises of support from the king, but large sums of money, on condition that he would promote the objects which Charles was pursuing in the court of Rome. These objects were of such importance that the notion of a marriage with one of the nieces of Mazarin was entertained for a moment by Charles as a means of securing them,[15] and was eagerly adopted by Retz for the purpose of recovering his favour at Paris. Mazarin despatched a special envoy to England charged with the mission of promoting the match. He found an auxiliary in Aubigny, who represented to Charles the beauty of the Cardinal's nieces, but more particularly their virtue, of which, says the envoy, the king was much pleased to hear. Together with this futile intrigue, Retz was pleading at Whitehall for the Catholics, and at Rome for the settlement of that important affair to which the alliance with Mazarin and the elevation of Aubigny were expected to contribute. The first of these subsidiary negotiations was speedily abandoned; the other was pursued with a strange pertinacity for several years.

---

[14] *Mémoires de Guy Joly,* p. 140, ed. Michaud.

[15] "Aujourd'hui la reine a reçu une lettre du roy son fils, où il parle positivement, et dit qu'après avoir considéré toutes les raisons de son mariage, il se conformoit à son sentiment pour vostre nièce, en vue du grand dessein à quoi il estoit porté de jour en jour avec plus de faveur" (Lionne to Mazarin, 7th July 1660, in Champollion, *Complément des Mémoires de Retz,* p. 589, ed. Michaud).

At first Charles desired a mitre for his kinsman,[16] but he soon raised his demands, and insisted on having him created a cardinal. Clarendon, who was ignorant of the real design of which this was to be the prelude, entered into the idea, and drew up the instructions with which, in October 1662, the queen's secretary, Sir Richard Bellings, was sent to Rome. In the following year the Chancellor's share in these transactions was made a part of the abortive charge preferred against him by Bristol; and it appears from the articles that the great importance which was given to this negotiation, and the correspondence with the Roman cardinals, were generally known at the time. Retz advised Charles to secure the compliance of the Pope by sending a squadron to cruise off Civita Vecchia, and then proceeded to Hamburg to obtain the powerful intervention of the Queen of Sweden. He was charged at the same time with the distribution of a sum of fifteen thousand pounds, which Charles had determined to devote to the interests of Aubigny.[17] Letters were written by both the Queens of England to Cardinal Orsini, Protector of Portugal, urging him to press the suit, and assuring him that if the promotion should be refused, lamentable consequences might be apprehended from the disappointment of the king. Orsini, after an interview with Bellings, warmly took up the cause, and declared in a letter to the famous Cardinal Pallavicini, that he might, by assisting him, render a great service to religion. They also wrote to the two most influential men in Rome, Cardinals Chigi and Azzolini, the latter of whom was an active promoter of the design. His letter to the king, of 8th April 1663, advising the continuation of his efforts, and that of Cardinal Chigi, written on the following day, are in the State Paper Office.[18]

The question was maturely debated at Rome, and an opinion was drawn up in favour of Aubigny, founded partly on the statements of Bellings, and partly on the elaborate memorials of Retz, in which the services of the king were set forth. This

---

[16] Dod, *Church History of England,* iii. 239.
[17] *Mémoires de Guy Joly,* p. 149.
[18] Italian States, Bundle No. 24.

opinion was to the following effect: the Restoration had improved the condition of the Catholics, and whatever relief they enjoyed was due to the influence of Charles himself, and was disliked by the Parliament and the country. The abolition of the penal laws could not be expected, for the royal authority was competent only to suspend them. Indeed, it might be considered almost more advantageous, under the circumstances, that the laws should be suspended than toleration proclaimed. For the same disabilities from which the Catholics suffered extended in great part to the Presbyterians, and the other sects who were hostile to the monarchy. They could not therefore be abrogated without depriving the king of the weapons the law gave him to defend the crown against the Nonconformists, while a partial abolition would excite fresh envy against the Catholics, and add to the number of their enemies. Legislative toleration, inasmuch as its benefits would be shared by the Dissenters, was not to be desired, even if it could be obtained. It was necessary to rely solely on the power and the favour of the king. For his authority might be trusted not only as a security against the heretics, but also against that portion of the Catholics who were in opposition to the Jesuits. To his salutary influence was to be attributed the suppression of the measure for Catholic relief which had been brought forward in July 1662, in answer to the petition presented by that party, who had offered to swear that they did not hold the doctrine of the temporal authority of the Holy See, and that they would "oppose with their lives and fortunes the Pontiff himself, if he should ever attempt to execute that pretended power." [19] Again, when the Irish protestation of allegiance, which many leading Catholics had signed, was found in like manner to be very far removed from the obedience due to the Apostolic See, Charles had refused to countenance it, and had exhibited an unvarying respect for the Pope. Queen Henrietta Maria, who was now supporting the cause of Aubigny, had formerly obtained the same dignity for Conne, and only his death had prevented him from enjoying it. The state of the

---

[19] Lingard, ix. 35.

Catholics was more satisfactory and more hopeful than when the favour now asked for had been granted before, and the new king had in several ways shown that he was favourably disposed. Before leaving the Low Countries to ascend his throne, he had sent a rich present to the English nuns at Ghent. He had given audience to several Jesuits, and among others to two successive provincials, to whom he had promised his protection in case of need. He had been seen in a posture of adoration at high mass in the queen's chapel.

These were the views at that time entertained at Rome concerning the religious character of Charles II., and the arguments advanced in support of the promotion of Aubigny. Nevertheless the demand was rejected. The Pope's answer was conveyed in such terms that Charles was not offended, and accepted the explanation. The refusal, indeed, was only temporary. The solicitations of the English Court were soon after renewed, and they were at last successful. In November 1665, Aubigny, who was then at Paris, received his nomination, and died almost immediately after.[20] His name does not appear in the list of the cardinals created by Alexander VII., but his elevation, and the influence by which it had been obtained, were known, and had excited hopes for the Catholic Church in this country, which caused his death to be regarded as a serious calamity. The general of the Jesuits, on hearing of it, wrote to one of his correspondents: "The clouds which are gathering over Holland, Poland, and Constantinople are so dense, that every prudent man must see reason to apprehend enormous catastrophes, and storms that will not be ended without irreparable disasters. But in my mind all these coming evils are overshadowed by the death of the Abbé Aubigny, which deprives the Church, for a time at least, of the joy of beholding an English cardinal of such illustrious blood, created at the public instances of two queens, and at the secret request of a king: a prodigy which would without doubt have confounded heresy, and inaugurated bright fortunes to the unhappy Catholics."

---

[20] Moréri, *Dictionnaire Historique,* ix. 597; his epitaph in Douglas, *Peerage of Scotland,* ii. 101.

The affair of the cardinal's hat was not the principal object of the mission of Sir Richard Bellings. It was intended as a preliminary to that more important negotiation which the envoy was instructed to reserve if the first should fail, and inspired Queen Catherine with so much anxiety, and Cardinal Orsini with such sanguine hopes of the advancement of religion. The two queens knew that Charles was at heart a Catholic, and they pressed him to declare himself. He was now firmly seated on his throne; the Established Church had recovered its supremacy, and was not only profoundly loyal, but still strongly impregnated with those Catholic tendencies which had hastened its fall; the Puritans and Independents were yet prostrate beneath the ruins of their political system, and the great body that reverenced Baxter as their chief was comparatively tolerant. Charles, believing that the step which would have prevented his return might now be taken without involving the risk of a new revolution, resolved to feel his way towards a reconciliation with the Holy See. In addition to the instructions drawn up by Clarendon, Sir Richard Bellings carried to Rome proposals for the submission of the three kingdoms to the Church, and presented to Alexander VII. the king's profession of faith.[21] Charles declared that he was willing to accept the creed of Pius IV., the decrees of the Council of Trent and of all general Councils on faith and morals, and the decisions of the two last Pontiffs in the affair of the Jansenists, saving the particular rights and customs of the nation, as is the practice in France and in other countries, and provided always no new laws should be imposed upon his realm, and he should be free to complete in his own way the work of reconciliation. He declared that he renounced and detested all the heresies which had involved his country in ecclesiastical and civil troubles, and made England the most distracted State in the world. He undertook to restore the hierarchy as it was under Henry VIII.; and added that the Protes-

---

[21] Oblatio ex parte Caroli II. Magnae Brittanniae Regis pro optatissima trium suorum Regnorum Angliae, Scotiae et Hiberniae cum Sede Apostolica Romana reunione.

tants should have toleration as long as they did not disturb the peace.

In this very remarkable document, Charles, who believed that many of his subjects would follow his example, gave one of the earliest instances of what has since been constantly witnessed,—that princes who, as head of the Protestant Church in their dominions, enjoy an almost unlimited authority, cannot view without jealousy the ecclesiastical liberty which is claimed by Catholicism. He carefully restricted the papal jurisdiction both of doctrine and discipline, and reserved to himself the rights which the Gallican system attributed to the secular power. He even proposed that the Church should abandon her essential function of judging and defining matters of faith as occasion should arise. Although this is a condition contrary to the nature of the Catholic Church, the document proposing it, which is followed by twenty-four articles on particular points, exhibits so much familiarity with ecclesiastical forms that it must have been drawn up by a Catholic hand. It is not probable that many persons were admitted on this occasion into the confidence of Charles. The whole scheme was not discussed beyond the door of the royal closet. It betrays the hand of a layman, for no priest could have expected the Church to discontinue her dogmatic progress; and Aubigny, the only priest likely to be consulted, was not likely to introduce the clause against Jansenism. Now we know that the secret was imparted to one lay Catholic, the agent who was charged with the negotiation. No man was more likely to be chosen for that important mission than he to whom the affair had been confided from the first, or who could discuss the proposals better than he who had helped to devise them. Bellings was a man of note and distinction among the Catholics in both islands, and was often employed by the court in confidential missions. His father had been one of the leaders in the opposition to the nuncio Rinuccini, and was the author of that protestation of allegiance which had been adopted by a large party in Ireland, and which was so badly received at Rome. The son was, therefore, not unlikely to suggest those limitations of ecclesiastical authority which he undertook to defend, and which corresponded with the views of his father and of those who, in the language of Bristol, were Catholics of the Church of Rome, not of the court of Rome.

The answer of Alexander was probably not very encouraging, for the negotiation was broken off. A suspicion was awakened that the king was in correspondence with the Pope, and Charles, in his alarm, took measures to prove his aversion of Catholicism. He opened Parliament on the 18th of February 1663 with a demand for new laws to restrain the progress of popery, and gave his assent to a proclamation ordering all priests to quit the kingdom under pain of death. He explained, five years later, in a letter to which I shall presently return, the failure of his negotiation, and the inconsistency of his subsequent conduct: "Quoy qu'elle nous fust présentée avec touttes les circonstances necessaires, et par personne catholique, touttefois ce ne peut estre avec tant de prudence que nous ne fussions soupçonnés d'intelligence avec le pape par les plus clairvoyants de nostre cour; mais ayant trouvé le moyen d'étouffer le soubçon que l'on començoit d'avoir que nous fussions catholique, nous fusmes obligé, crainte de ne le faire renaistre dans les esprits, de consentir aux occasions à plusieurs choses tournant au desavantage de plusieurs catholiques de nostre royaume d'Hybernie, ce qui est cause encore que bien que nous eussions escry assez secrettement à sa saincteté pour nostre rangement à l'église catholique, au mesme temps que nous prions sa saincteté de faire cardinal nostre très cher cousin le Milord d'Aubigny, dont nous fumes refusés pour bonnes raisons, nous n'avons peu poursuyvre nostre pointe." The scheme was not resumed for several years. Times were not propitious. The Dutch war, the Plague, the Fire, the Triple Alliance, intervened. Public animosity was inflamed against the Catholics; and Charles had no confidential agent whom he could employ without danger to propose, if not the reconciliation of the country, for which he was not disposed to make great efforts or great sacrifices, at least his own submission to the Catholic Church. During this interval, Jacques de la Cloche made his appearance for the first time in England.

In the spring 1646, during his first residence in Jersey, Charles fell in love with a young lady of high rank, who became the mother of a child, who enjoyed the prerogative, denied to all the other natural children of the king, of bearing his father's name. He was called James Stuart, and was brought up in the Protestant religion on the Continent. "Il nous est né lorsque nous n'avions guères plus de seize ou 17 ans, d'une jeune dame des plus qualifiées de nos royaumes, plustost par fragilité de nostre première jeunesse que par malice." The last words appear to indicate Charles's respect for the mother and the care with which he protected her fame. Unlike the Clevelands and Portsmouths who afterwards disgraced his court, the lady who was the object of his earliest attachment obtained of her royal lover the concealment of her fault, and her name has never been divulged. She is nowhere mentioned in the correspondence relating to her son; and if she died before his arrival in England, the reputation of her family may have induced the king to conceal his birth. After the Restoration he allowed him to remain abroad unnoticed, and under the disguise of an assumed name, until the year 1665. In that year he sent for him to England, supplied him with money, and gave him a certificate in which he recognised him as his son, but which he commanded him to show to nobody whilst his father lived. This document, written and signed by Charles's own hand, and sealed with his private seal, is dated Whitehall, 27th September 1665,—a time at which the plague was at its height, and the court was not in London. For greater security he obliged his son once more to change his name. That which he had borne till then is not known. He was now called James de la Cloche du Bourg. It is not easy to say whether the last of these names may afford some clue to the discovery of his mother's family among the three thousand royalists who took refuge in Jersey at the same time as the Prince of Wales.[22] The former name had been made popular in that island when Charles arrived there by the spirit with which Mr. de la Cloche, a clergyman, had resisted the authority of Government.[23] After

---

[22] R. Augier to the Speaker, in Cary, *Memorials of the Civil War*, i. 7.
[23] Le Quesne, *Constitutional History of Jersey*, p. 325.

lying nearly a year in prison, he was released upon the arrival of the Prince, and then left the island. Had his release anything to do with Charles's private affairs? Was the boy christened by him, or afterwards committed to his charge?

James was unwilling to remain in England. It was not his country; he did not speak the language; he had no career and no recognised station; and his position was not to his taste. He had made great proficiency in his studies abroad, and he desired to continue them in the Dutch universities. His father did not know what to do with him in England, and allowed him to go. Eighteen months later, on the 7th of February 1667, he sent him another document, recognising his birth, and directing his successor to give him £500 a year. A condition was attached to the grant of this pension, that it could be enjoyed only while the claimant resided in London, and remained faithful to the religion of his fathers and to the Anglican liturgy. Six months after receiving this letter, on the 29th of July 1667, James Stuart became a Catholic at Hamburg.

The Queen of Sweden, who filled Europe with the fame of her abdication, her abjuration, her talents, and her eccentricities, was for the second time residing at Hamburg, and appears again on the scene of the secret history of Charles. She signed a paper for his son, certifying that he had been received into the Church at that particular place and time, in order that he might be able, in case of need, to satisfy his confessor of the identity of the convert of Hamburg with the Protestant whom the King of Great Britain had privately recognised as his son. This was now necessary, because he had determined, immediately after his conversion, to enter the novitiate of the Jesuits. Christine knew who he was, probably because he had been compelled to apply to her chaplains, or at least for her protection, in order to be received. The Senate of Hamburg exercised with extreme severity the right which the Treaties of Westphalia gave to each Government of exacting religious conformity; and the neighbouring town of Altona, peopled by the Catholics, Anabaptists, and Jews whom the Lutherans had expelled, grew up a monument of the intolerance of the Free City. The queen had attempted, some years before, to obtain freedom of conscience for her own religion through the intervention of the Catholic Powers; but the Emperor, whose rights were derived from the same treaty by which the senate justified its rigour, and who was not disposed to surrender them, refused to disturb the settlement of Münster. At the very time when James was converted, the town had been thrown into confusion by the uproar caused by a fête which Christine gave, in the midst of a Protestant population, to celebrate the election of Clement IX. Charles was much annoyed to learn that she was in his son's confidence. "She is prudent and wise," he said; "but she is a woman, and that is enough to make us doubt whether she is able to keep a secret."

James de la Cloche was hardly settled at Rome when his father determined to have him about his court. That vast intrigue had just commenced which was to raise France to the pinnacle of power, and which, by a timely subservience, promised to emancipate the princes of the House of Stuart from the control of Parliament, and from the terrors which had postponed the king's design of reconciliation with Rome. In that conspiracy the motives of religious belief and political ambition were strangely blended. Turenne, who was destined to be the foremost actor in the execution of the design, was a sincere Calvinist. He had shortly before refused the great dignity of Constable of France, when it was tendered as the reward of his conversion. On the 23rd of October 1668 Turenne became a Catholic. He was shortly after followed by his old lieutenant, a confederate in the new scheme, the Duke of York. James had applied to the Provincial of the Jesuits, and then to the Pope, for permission to conceal his religion, and had been told that it was impossible. With this answer he caught the conscience of the king. On the feast of the conversion of St. Paul, 1669, Charles summoned his Catholic counsellors, declared with tears how uneasy he was not to profess the faith which he believed, and consulted them as to the best mode of carrying out his resolutions. They concluded that the only way was to do it in conjunction with France.[24] A few months before this resolution was

---

[24] Clarke, *Life of James II.,* i. 441.

finally taken, in August 1668, Charles had written to the General
of the Jesuits to send him his son, whose presence he needed for
the good of his soul.

He had long sought in vain, the king said to Oliva, for a
person with whom he could confer on spiritual matters without
creating suspicion. The priests who lived in London were so well
known that no disguise could conceal them; [25] but the conversion of his son, and his entrance into Orders, at length gave him
an opportunity of receiving the sacraments without alarming the
Protestant zeal of his subjects. His son might remain unknown,
as the queens alone were aware of his existence; but before long
he should be publicly acknowledged. "Plusieurs raisons considérables, et concernantes la paix de nos royaumes, nous ont
empesché jusques à présent de le reconnestre publiquement pour
notre fils; mais ce sera pour peu de temps, parceque nous
sommes maintenant en dessein de faire en sorte de le reconnestre
publiquement devant peu d'années." In case he was not a priest,
and could not be ordained before starting, Charles directed that
he should go to Paris, and address himself either to the king or
to the Duchess of Orleans, who knew of his own design, and
would have James ordained without betraying his rank; or, if he
preferred it, the two queens would find an opportunity for his
ordination in England. As soon as he had received his father into
the Church, he would be free either to return to Rome or to live
in England, so as to be within call; but not in London, lest
people should suspect that the king's son was a Jesuit. This was
written on the 3rd of August. On the 29th, Charles, having
heard that the Queen of Sweden was on her way to Rome, wrote
again to hasten the departure of his son; for he feared that
Christine, if she saw him, would discover the purpose of his
intended journey. If that should become known in England, he
said, it would infallibly cost him his life. He therefore desired
that his son, instead of stopping at Paris, should come with all
speed to London, and there make himself known to the
queen-mother by delivering to her a sealed letter in the form of
a petition. This letter was scarcely sealed, when he wrote a third

---

[25] We know, from the account of his death, that none of the Portuguese
chaplains of the queen could speak either English or French.

time to the General. It had occurred to his mother and his wife that a novice is not allowed among the Jesuits to travel alone. Charles hoped that this regulation would be dispensed with, and that his son would be permitted to set out by himself in the dress of a layman. Secret warning had already been given at the southern ports that a foreign prince, whose appearance was described as near that of James as possible, was about to seek refuge in England, and would arrive without any companion. The presence of a Jesuit father would have spoilt this plan. The better to meet the arrangements which had been made, the novice was to call himself Henry de Rohan, a name well known as that of one of the great Huguenot families of France. Charles declared on his royal word, *en foy de roy,* that the sole object of his letters was the salvation of his soul, and the good of his son and of the Order, and that he would either induce the Pope to make him a cardinal, or allow him, if he should prefer it, to remain a simple religious.

In the middle of October 1668 the young ecclesiastic started for England, disguised as a French cavalier. Together with his letters to Oliva, Charles had written to him in terms of the warmest affection. The temper of Parliament, he said, had hitherto made it necessary to defer the public acknowledgment of his birth, but the time was approaching when it would be possible for him to assume the rank which belonged to him. It behoved him, therefore, to reflect maturely on his altered prospects before entering irrevocably into sacred orders. His title was better than that of the Duke of Monmouth, and he had a right of precedence over him, "par touttes raisons, et à cause de la qualité de votre mère." The queen was childless, and the children of the Duke of York were delicate; and if the Catholic religion should be restored in England he would have a claim to the crown: "Nous pouvons vous asseurer que si Dieu permet que nous et notre très honoré frère le duc d'Yorck mourons sans enfans, les royaumes vous apartient, et le parlement ne peut pas legitimement s'y opposer; si ce n'est qu'en matière d'estre catholique vous en soyez exclus. . . . Croyez que nous vous avons toujours eu une affection particulière non seulement à cause que vous nous este né dans nostre plus tendre ieunesse, lorsque nous n'avions guères plus de 16 ou 17 ans, que particulièrement à cause de l'excelent naturel que nous avons toujours remarqué en vous."

Prince James Stuart, as the king now calls him, remained scarcely a fortnight in England. On the 18th of November he was sent back to Rome on a secret mission to the General of the Jesuits, with directions to return as soon as he had obtained what the king desired. It does not appear what that was. It is probable that Charles wished, like his brother, to be allowed to keep his change of religion a secret; and the application which James says that he made to the Pope at this time may have been conveyed, on the part of both brothers, by the youth whom Charles had already selected to be the medium of communication with the Holy See. The Duke of York's letter to the Pope required secrecy, and we know that no messenger was trusted by Charles but the young Stuart himself. This was not, however, the only condition he desired to exact in making his submission to the Holy See. We have seen the tenor of his demands in 1662. In his letters to his sister, published by Dalrymple, he mentions other points, which on the former occasion were probably included in the clause allowing him to carry out the details of the restoration of Catholicism in his own way. "He talks," says Hallam, who has investigated the history of this period more carefully than any other writer, "of a negotiation with the court of Rome to obtain the permission of having mass in the vulgar tongue, and communion in both kinds, as terms that would render his conversion agreeable to his subjects." [26] Before departing for Rome, James must have assured his father that his resolution was fixed, and that he would live and die a Jesuit. Charles, who had promised not to interfere with his vocation, gave him a large subsidy for the new novitiate at St. Andrea on the Quirinal, which Oliva was then erecting, in addition to the old building of St. Francis Borgia. He also desired that on this second journey his son should be accompanied by a Jesuit; for,

---

[26] *Constitutional History*, ii. 387.

as he was not a priest, he was unable to receive his father into the Church, or to administer the sacraments to him. With these instructions James left England. From that day he disappears from history; and after his arrival in Rome, in November or December 1668, the name of De la Cloche, by which he was known in the novitiate, figures no more in the books of the society.

Towards the close of the year a young gentleman, who passed for an Englishman, and travelled with a servant and a well-stored purse, took up his abode at a very humble inn at Naples. The host had a daughter, Teresa Corona, whose extraordinary beauty won the heart of the guest. After he had satisfied the ecclesiastical authorities that he was a Catholic, they were married on the 19th of February 1669. It was not long before the attention of the neighbours was roused by their manner of life. Gold was observed to be suspiciously plentiful in the household of the poor innkeeper, and it began to be whispered that his English son-in-law was related to the King of Great Britain. Rumours came to the ear of the Spanish viceroy, who, in his solicitude for the honour of royalty, caused the stranger to be arrested. Letters were found in his possession bearing the title of Highness, together with many jewels and heaps of pistoles. He declared that he was Prince James Stuart, a son of the King of England, born in Jersey; and he sent for the English consul in order to obtain his release. But he could neither speak English nor give any satisfactory evidence in support of his statement. The viceroy wrote to England to ascertain the truth of the story, and in the meantime treated his captive as a prisoner of State, and sent him to the fortress of Gaeta, whilst he shut up his wife in a convent. Nobody knew what to believe. "Which," writes the English agent, Kent, to Williamson, on the 30th of March, "whether will end in prince or cheat I shall endeavour to inform you hereafter." The bewildered governor allowed his prisoner fifty crowns a month for his maintenance, and permitted his wife's family to visit him. Early in June came the answer of King Charles to the viceroy, who thereupon proclaimed the mysterious personage an impostor, removed him from his honourable confinement at Gaeta to the dungeons for common malefactors at Naples, and condemned him to be whipped through the city. Teresa Corona was taken from her convent on the discovery of her husband's real character; and the story, which was believed at the time, goes on to say that instead of being punished he was released at her intercession, and allowed to go to France, on a visit, as he affirmed, to his mother. Two months later he was again at Naples, asserting that his mother was dead. He called her the Lady Mary Stuart, of the house of the Barons of St. Mars, as it is in the contemporary English translation, or of San Marzo, as it stands in the Italian copy of his will; and said that it was in consequence of her relationship with the royal family that the king was unwilling to acknowledge him. The will is dated 24th August 1669, and two days later the testator died, reiterating his statements in the same breath in which he recommended his soul to the mercy of God and the intercession of Our Lady, in terms of the deepest piety and resignation. He appointed his cousin, Lewis XIV., his executor; demanded of Charles, for his unborn child, either the principality of Wales or Monmouth, or a royal dukedom, with an income of a hundred thousand crowns, besides his mother's fortune, amounting to £16,000 a year; and left enormous legacies to his wife's relations and to the Church. "And this," says Kent, "is the end of that princely cheat, or whatever he was." The cautious agent did not venture to determine the adventurer's quality; and in the manuscript letter of news sent weekly to the English Government, called the *Gazzetta di Roma,* from which most of his information was derived, the Englishman is constantly called the English prince.

Yet none of these contemporaries knew that there was actually at that time a son of King Charles born at Jersey of a lady of high rank, privately addressed as Highness, provided with money, and speaking French as his native tongue. Had they known it, and could they have discovered that the illegitimate prince was really called James Stuart; that though a novice he was not ordained; and that all authentic traces of him were at an end from the moment of his arrival in Italy, at the very time when the English traveller put up at the inn of Corona,—if, in short, their knowledge had extended generally as far as ours, and had stopped where ours stops, it is probable that they would not have hesitated to believe in the claims of the prisoner at Gaeta. The king's denial, and what followed, would not have shaken their conviction. Charles was always careful to conceal the existence of his son, and he was particularly tender of the mother's name. When informed that the young Jesuit who had refused his favour, and had gone forth to prepare the way for his father's conversion, was the husband of a publican's daughter at Naples, and had been thrown into prison after apprising the people of his rank and wealth, he would certainly not have responded to the appeal of the viceroy by a public acknowledgment. It was necessary, in order to shield the father, that the son should be proclaimed an impostor, and sentenced to condign punishment. But it was not necessary that he should be actually punished. Charles's interests were satisfied by his removal to the felons' prison, his sentence, and his immediate pardon. If the accusation had been true, the pardon could not have followed instantly on the discovery; the culprit, after leaving the scene of his disgrace, would not voluntarily have returned so soon; and he would not have mingled with his dying prayers the solemn repetition of a lie, which could serve no further purpose but to bring down disappointment and notoriety on his widow. The claims which he prefers for his child, though inconsistent with his own disinterested conduct, might have proceeded from a natural anxiety to provide for his posterity.

This is the case for the prisoner. It falls to the ground in cross-examination. The tenor of the will itself is fatal to it. The real James Stuart, who was sure of being able to obtain every just demand, would not have compromised the reasonable prospects of his family by the falsehoods and the extravagance of this document. He had, moreover, in his possession papers which proved his claim, and would have delivered him from the rigours of the Spanish governor. There was no reason for his sudden appearance at Naples at the very moment when he was charged with a negotiation of the greatest moment to his father,

his Church, and himself. Nor would he have called his mother
by a name and title which are unquestionably fictitious. And yet
in that imaginary name and title there may perhaps be found a
key to the mystery of the birth of the young James Stuart. For
though the Neapolitan adventurer was an impostor, he enjoyed
good sources of information, and possessed, though imperfectly,
the secrets of King Charles's son. He knew that he was born at
Jersey, and that his birth had been recognised by his father, and
he had secured some of his papers and some of his property. All
the wealth he showed at Naples did not come from that source,
for the young novice was not so rich, and the impostor must
have robbed other people. But he had certainly either accompanied, as his servant, the man he represented, or stolen his letters.
Whatever be the secret of this strange adventure, it is so certain
that it was not the real James Stuart who died at Naples in
August 1669, that it is worth while to institute a further inquiry
as to the probable events of his subsequent career.[27]

He must have returned almost immediately to his father's
court; but here too he was compelled to lay aside the name
which he had borne on his former journey. The same Henry de
Rohan could not twice in two months seek an asylum in England without awakening the suspicions of that suspicious age.
The name which he finally assumed is unknown, and we are
unable with certainty to trace him further. But it can hardly be
doubted that among the French Jesuits of that period the eldest
son of Charles II. may yet be identified. He was by speech and
education a Frenchman, and it is likely that he again took a
French name, and completed his novitiate in France or in
Flanders. Had he quitted the Order, he would have taken with
him the grant of his pension, which lies at Rome. Had he
returned to Rome, he would have resumed his former name.
Had he remained in England, it is hard to believe that he could

---

[27] The papers from which this account is given are in the State Paper
Office, "Italian States," Bundle 32; *Letters of Kent*, March 30, 1669,
June 16, August 31, and September 7; *News Letters*, or *Gazzette di
Roma*, of March 23, April 6, April 13, April 20, June 11, September 7. The
will is in the Domestic Papers, Bundle for August 1669.

have escaped discovery at the time of the Popish Plot, or among the clergy who frequented the palace. He did not succeed in effecting the actual reconciliation of his father with the Church, for it is certain that that event did not occur before the eve of Charles's death. When Charles feared that his brother would expose himself to danger by bringing a priest, and when James declared he would do it at the risk of his life, they could only allude to the law which made it penal to receive a convert. The mere administration of the Sacrament to one already Catholic could get no one into trouble. Huddlestone says that the king declared "that he was most heartily sorry for all the sins of his past life, and particularly for that he had defferred his reconciliation so long." This is implicitly confirmed by what he told Aprice, another priest, who wrote ten days later: "As Mr. Huddlestone himself has told me, by a particular instance of God's grace, the king was as ready and apt in making his confession, and all other things, as if he had been brought up a Catholic all his lifetime." [28] If we had not these proofs that Charles had not been received into the Church before his last illness, still there could be no doubt upon the subject, as the application of James for leave to conceal his religion was rejected, and the publication would also, in the case of the king, have been the necessary condition of his admission into the Church.

James Stuart's ministrations to his father must therefore have been confined to the discussion of the Catholic doctrines. It is possible that a memorial of these discussions and exhortations may still be extant. Manuscript copies of the two papers on religion, in the handwriting of Charles, which were found in his cabinet and published by his brother, were sent to Rome by Father Giudici, the confessor of Mary Beatrice. These copies, attested by King James's own signature, are in French. That which was printed in England was a translation. It would have been useless to publish a French text in England, where an immediate and general effect was required. There could be no object in sending a copy of the translation to Rome, where the

---

[28] Harris, *Life of Charles II.*, ii. 391.

original could be understood and interpreted. The title of the copies in Rome proves that the publication had already taken place. If the originals were printed, it would have been enough to send a printed copy, which would have possessed greater authenticity than a manuscript translation. It is impossible to compare the French and the English versions without perceiving that the latter is a translation of the former—inelegant, somewhat abridged, and not entirely faithful. The word *apogrifes*, which occurs in the French for *apocryphes*, shows that the papers were in the writing of a person who did not know theology. Father Giudici would not have allowed it to stand in the copy if it were not in the original manuscript of the king; but in the English edition the word was altogether omitted, probably because it would not be understood by Protestants in the sense in which the writer used it.

These papers, though in the handwriting of Charles II., were not composed by him. They are in the form of an argument, addressed by one person to another. For this he had no occasion, and he had no reason to write them in French. On the same ground, they cannot have been written by Bristol or Aubigny, to whom Burnet is inclined to attribute them. Bristol did not converse with the king in French. Aubigny, it is true, had spent most of his life in France, but he had not forgotten his native language. Little is known concerning him, but it is on record that his knowledge of English once saved his life. He was attacked at night by two English bloodhounds, who were kept in the garden of the Jacobins, and he pacified them by speaking to them in English.[29] Tallemant, who tells the tale, adds, that a thief who, being a Frenchman, had no means of making himself intelligible to the foreign dogs, was seized by them in getting over the wall, and soon despatched.

An ecclesiastic who conferred with Charles concerning his conversion after he had ascended the throne, and who knew French better than English, must have been the author of these compositions. This would bring the evidence to bear on the

---

[29] *Historiettes de Tallemant des Reaux*, vii. 293.

French priests about the queen-mother or the Duke of York, such as Mansuète or La Colombière. But the tone of these writings is not that which would be adopted by a foreign priest addressing the king. They are written with confidence, frankness, and even familiarity, and they must have been written by one who, though he could not write in English, might consider himself an Englishman. England is more than once spoken of as "nostre Angleterre." There is reason, therefore, to suspect that we have in these letters a record of the religious earnestness and filial piety of the Stuart who preferred a cloister to the steps of his father's throne.

Two years after the day when we lose sight of James Stuart, the question of the reconciliation of Charles II. with the Catholic Church had become a part of European politics, and an element in confederations and treaties. Lewis XIV. proposed that D'Estrées, then Bishop of Laon, and afterwards cardinal, the most successful negotiator in his kingdom, should be employed to bring the matter before the Holy See. Charles received the proposal coldly. He told the French ambassador that he had already made choice of an English priest to treat with the Pope for his conversion, and that instructions were being prepared for him.[30] Arlington undertook to hasten his departure; but he was then at St. Omers, and the illness of Clement IX. made the king anxious to wait, as he did not wish, he said, to confide his secret to a dying man. It is most probable that the English priest at St. Omers, whom Charles had already arranged to send to Rome, was the same through whom he had previously opened the business. On his return from Rome at the end of the year 1668, Prince James Stuart found that the king had resolved to discuss his design with the ministers, and that the great interests involved, and the choice of the mode, and the time of declaring himself, would necessarily postpone the event. The negotiation with France for the dissolution of the Triple Alliance, on which it depended, required time, both on account of the secrecy which had to be preserved, and of the vast

---

[30] Mignet, *Négociations relatives à la Succession d'Espagne,* iii. 232.

preparations which were made for the war, which was to be the signal for the change. James must have perceived that his time had not arrived, and he was doubtless anxious to finish his novitiate and to receive ordination. It is natural to conclude that he would retire to some house of the Society where he could satisfy this desire, and still be at hand whenever his father's plans were ripe, and he should be summoned to be the instrument for their accomplishment. The college of St. Omers, or the neighbouring English novitiate at Watten, would be the fittest and likeliest place for him to inhabit.

We have no other probable record of his life. Once more, in the midst of the excitement of the Popish Plot, the mysterious figure of a foreign priest crosses the life of Charles. A gentleman told Welwood that he was employed to bring over privately a Romish priest, then beyond sea, by whose means the king had some secret matters to manage. The king and the priest were a considerable time together alone in the closet. At last the priest came out, with all the marks of fright and astonishment in his face. Charles had been seized with a fit, and the priest would have called for help; but the king, who feared that their interview should become known, had strength and resolution to hold him till he had recovered his speech.[31] Was this priest, with whom Charles was in correspondence, whom he caused to be fetched secretly from foreign parts, and the discovery of whose presence he so passionately dreaded, his own son?

Among the letters of Oliva there is one that bears no date, addressed to a king who is not named, respecting a certain Jesuit, whose name is also concealed. This father, it appears, had received from the king an important office, which he used for the purpose of interfering in affairs of State, and had not only made enemies by his imprudence, but had injured the interests of the king, and had alienated, by the acrimony and disrespect of his language, persons who belonged to the royal party. He was accused of bearing himself more like a prince than a religious, and his superiors feared that when the king,

---

[31] Welwood's *Memoirs*, p. 146.

who was the protector of the society, should be no more, they would incur great dangers through the animosity he had provoked. The General, therefore, asked leave to summon the father to Rome, promising that he should be treated with kindness. Of the seven kings then living in Europe, two, those of Sweden and Denmark, could not have been in friendly communication with the Jesuits, and neither of them in any way deserved to be called their protector. In France, in Spain, and in Portugal, it is difficult to understand what could be meant by the royal party, or by the fear of great calamities on the death of the king. Poland and England alone remain. Now there are in the collection other letters of Oliva to the King of Poland, and no secret is made about his name. The position of this father must have been quite peculiar. It is clear that he was not the king's confessor, and that he was not, like Father Petre, officially employed in political affairs; yet he had received from the king such a position that he could not be recalled like an ordinary Jesuit, and that the General was obliged to use elaborate precautions in order to obtain the king's consent, and to make the measure appear in his eyes as gentle as possible. This suggests a suspicion of some mystery. The General of the Jesuits writes to a sovereign, whose name he does not venture to publish, for permission to summon to Rome a father of the society, who, though neither the confessor of the king nor a member of the Council, possesses considerable influence, and enjoys so much of the royal favour that, although his imprudence has injured the court, a pledge must be given in removing him that he will be treated well. If we imagine the Jesuit James Stuart established in England exercising some influence over his father and the men of his confidence, and led astray, partly by zeal, partly by the presumption engendered by his royal descent, to commit some acts of imprudence, such as those which were so soon after so greatly exaggerated by popular rumour, and so cruelly punished by the popular fanaticism, it would exactly answer all the conditions of the case. These letters of Oliva were prepared for publication by himself. Everything that is omitted is therefore designedly omitted, and the same caution which obliged him to conceal the name of the sovereign whom he addressed would have prohibited any more distinct allusion by which the position of the offending Jesuit might be betrayed.

These grounds, however, are far from sufficient to justify us in believing that James Stuart, who began life with so much discretion and reserve, afterwards became an ambitious and intriguing politician, and put in jeopardy his father's crown and the fortunes of his Order. That Order occupied in Poland a position in which great influence at court was combined with great unpopularity with his party among the nobles. At the election of 1668, a cry was raised that the new king should be forbidden to have a Jesuit for his confessor; and, at the same time, the grand Hetman, Sobieski, was taking a Jesuit confessor with him to bless his arms in the Turkish war. To him, in the year 1673, Oliva sent his congratulations on his election. He tells him that the Jesuits whom he may place over his conscience or his chapel must be faithful to their rule, and abstain from politics; and in speaking of the new king's affection for the society he uses a word, *svisceratamente*, that occurs in the same connection in the letter which is not directed. It may therefore refer to a father to whom Sobieski had committed some important functions in his court, and the name of the patron may be omitted lest the name of the offender should be surmised. Long after the probable date of this letter, John sent a bitter complaint to Oliva of the faults of the brethren in Poland. "I feel bound," he said, "both by interest and affection, to advise you to seek a remedy for the growing evils, and to remove from the Jesuits in Poland the too visible contagion of ambition and cupidity." [32] Between his predecessor and Oliva there had also been a friendly correspondence. Michael Korybuth was afflicted with a fabulous voracity. The stories told of the classical gluttons of antiquity are eclipsed by his horrible achievements. Once, it is related, the burghers of Dantzig presented him with a thousand China apples, and before night he had devoured them all. Oliva, like a prudent general, attacked this monarch at his weak point. A

---

[32] Salvandy, *Histoire de Jean Sobieski*, ii. 97.

quantity of the finest chocolate has been sent to him from Mexico, and he straightway despatches one of his fathers to lay it at the feet of the King of Poland, "impelled," he says, "by a reverent solicitude to minister as well as I can to the weakness of your stomach, which has already been fortified by drugs of this kind." On the whole, then, it is most probable that James Stuart is not the subject of the General's letter to the nameless correspondent; and comparing his letters written to the two kings it is more likely to have been sent to John Sobieski than to his respected but inglorious predecessor.

The manuscripts I have quoted, most of which I owe to the industry and kindness of Father Boero, librarian of the Gesù,[33] by whose care they have been brought to light and transcribed, reveal the influence actually exerted by religious sentiment in those transactions between Charles and Lewis XIV., which, as the occasion of the Popish Plot, and the commencement of that policy which terminated in the Revolution of 1688, occupy so important a place in our history. The intention of declaring himself a Catholic manifested by the king in the early part of his reign, and checked by the attitude of Parliament, was revived, as we have seen, in the summer of 1668. In the month of April Charles first expressed to the ambassador of Lewis the

---

[33] I subjoin a list of the documents for which I am indebted to Father Boero. They are manifestly too long to be published *in extenso* in a Review.

1. Lettre de la Reine Mère (Henrietta) an Card. Orsini. De Londres, October 30, 1662.

2. Lettre de la Reine Catherine au même. De Londres, October 25, 1662.

3. Voto in favore della promozione al Cardinalato del Signor d'Aubigny.

4. Favori e benefizi fatti ai cattolici d'Inghilterra dal Re presente (in sixteen articles).

5. Bellings to Father Thomas Courtenay, October 22, 1662.

6. Lettera dal Card. Orsini al Card. Sforza Pallavicino. 24 gennaio 1663.

7. Oblatio ex parte Caroli II. Magnae Britanniae Regis pro optatissima trium suorum regnorum Angliae, Scotiae et Hiberniae cum Sede Apostolica Romana reunione.

8. Certificate of Charles II. in favour of Sieur James Stuart, his natural son.

wish to form an alliance with his master.[34] As he had lately joined a league of Protestant Powers, whose purpose it was to arrest the ambition of that monarch, he desired that the understanding between them might be private. He said that he wished to treat as between gentlemen, and that he preferred the word of Lewis to all the parchments in the world. At first Lewis received these advances with reserve, and Charles and his brother were unwilling to trust to the ambassador the secret object of their overtures. But early in 1669 Lord Arundel was sent to Paris, accompanied by Sir Richard Bellings,[35] who was instructed to draw up the articles of the treaty by which England was to join France against the Dutch; while Lewis undertook to support Charles with money, that he might be able to declare himself a Catholic without having a parliament to fear. Of the two leading ministers of the Cabal, the Catholic Arlington was friendly to the Dutch alliance, whilst Buckingham, a Protestant, was a partisan of France. Though the latter encouraged the notion of a French alliance, he knew nothing of his master's design relative to the Catholic religion. It was confided to Arlington, and at length overcame his political scruples, but he was never reconciled to the war with Holland, and he

---

9. Another certificate of the king to the same.

10. Certificate of Christine Queen of Sweden concerning the same, on his conversion at Hamburg.

11. Letter of Charles II. to the General of the Jesuits, Oliva, at Rome. Whitehall, August 3, 1668.

12. Letter of Charles II. to his son James Stuart at Rome. Whitehall, August 4, 1668.

13. Letter of Charles II. to Oliva, General of the Jesuits, at Rome. Whitehall, August 29, 1668.

14. Letter of the same to the same, without date.

15. Reply of Oliva to the king's three letters. Livorno, October 14, 1668.

16. Certificate of Charles that he will pay the expenses of his son's voyage. November 18, 1668.

17. Letter of Charles to Oliva. Whitehall, November 18, 1668.

18 and 19. Two Memoirs written by Charles II. on the Catholic religion.

[34] See the Despatches of the French ambassadors Colbert and Ruvigny, in Mignet, iii. 10 sq., and iv. 42 sq.

[35] Clarke, i. 442.

endeavoured to postpone hostilities until the change of religion
had been declared. The French envoy suspected that he wished
to delude Lewis into supplying the means by which the king's
conversion could be published without danger, and when that
was done, to avoid quarrelling with the Dutch. The confidential
envoys of Charles at Paris evidently entertained the same idea,[36]
and the scheme was near succeeding.

Charles opened his mind to the French ambassador, the
brother of the great Colbert, on the 12th of November 1669. It
was, he said, the most important secret of his life, and he would
probably be considered mad, and all those with him who were
undertaking to restore Catholicism in England. Nevertheless he
hoped, with the help of Lewis, to succeed in that great work.
The sects hated the Established Church more than the Catholic
religion, and would make no resistance if they obtained the
freedom they desired. The great fortresses were in the hands of
trusty men, and the Irish army might be relied upon, for Lord
Orrery, who was at heart a Catholic, would take the lead if
Ormond should refuse. On this point Charles was mistaken, for
Orrery was sent for, and had an interview with the king, in
which he was informed of the design, and refused to take part
in it.[37] "He ended by saying that he was urged by his conscience, and by the confusion he saw increasing daily in his
kingdom, to the diminution of his authority, to declare himself a
Catholic; and that, besides the spiritual advantage he would
derive from it, he considered also that it was the only way of
restoring the monarchy." Lewis applauded the intention, but
advised that it should be postponed until after the war; for he
feared that he might be deprived of the assistance of England
by the internal dissensions which that measure would be sure to
provoke. These two influences contended for a while in the

---

[36] "Il m'a paru que l'affaire de religion étant ce qui tient le premier lieu
dans l'esprit de M. le Comte d'Arondel, il n'y a que le retardement de la
déclaration qui le touche; et comme il croit que la guerre contre les
Hollandais produiroit cet effet-là, c'est la seule raison pour laquelle il s'y
oppose" (Turenne to Ruvigny: *Mémoires de Turenne*, i. 669).

[37] Morrice, *Life of Orrery*, p. 86.

mind of Charles, but he had not strength of purpose to resist the
pressure that came from France.

Arlington said of him, that he saw at once what was to be
done in every affair that was submitted to him, and supported
his opinion with good reasons, but that he did not take the
trouble to go into the objections that were made, and, if he was
spoken to again, often allowed himself to be carried away by
the opinions of others.[38] This description was now verified.
Charles shrank from the incongruity of the life he was then
leading with a conversion which would be an arduous political
undertaking. "The danger," says Colbert, "greatly alarms all
who are in the secret, yet it has no effect on the mind of the
king. But his mode of life—un peu de libertinage, si j'ose parler
ainsi—makes him put it off as long as he can." The famous
journey of Henrietta, Duchess of Orleans, to Dover, in May
1670, settled the question in favour of France. The treaty which
was then signed by the four Catholic counsellors of Charles was
first published from the English copy by Lingard. Mignet gives
it from the French archives, and the texts do not entirely correspond.

Henrietta was in the secret of the whole scheme from the
beginning, and we learn through her that Charles was at that
time in direct communication with the Holy See. There was a
French prelate whom she patronised, Daniel de Cosnac, Bishop
of Valence and afterwards Archbishop of Aix, a clever, witty,
and extravagant man, highly ambitious of a cardinal's hat. A
year before the treaty was signed she wrote to him that, among
a variety of affairs which were being treated between France
and England, this country would soon have one with Rome of
such consequence, and on account of which the Pope would be
so happy to oblige the king her brother, that she was persuaded
he would refuse him nothing. She had already taken her measures with him to make him ask for a cardinal's hat, without
saying for whom; Charles had promised, and it was to be for
Cosnac.[39] After her return from Dover, but a few days before

---

[38] *Mémoires de Gourville*, p. 566, ed. Michaud.
[39] *Mémoires de Cosnac*, i. 383.

that tragic death scene which Bossuet has made memorable by the most striking of his orations, she informed the Bishop that she had succeeded in her mission, and that her brother had given her his word once more. Cosnac was not satisfied with these assurances. The influence of a Protestant king appeared to him a poor security for his elevation. But the Duchess told him that she not only had her brother's promise, but that the Pope had already granted his request, and she informed him, he says, of all that had passed between Pope Clement IX. and the Kings of France and England.[40] This statement is not, however, supported by any of her letters that have been preserved; and we must bear in mind the judgment of his biographer, the Abbé de Choisy, on the character of Cosnac: "He is a man of surprising vivacity, and of such eloquence that it is impossible to doubt his words, although their number is so great that they cannot all be true." The agent on this occasion appears to have been the Lady Diana Digby, daughter of the Earl of Bristol, who had been so eager, six years before, to bring home to Clarendon a charge of corresponding with the Pope and cardinals. In June 1669, she arrived at Rome, in the coach of Cardinal Rospigliosi, the Pope's nephew, and lived for a time in one of his palaces so privately that her own cousin, James Russell, was not allowed to see her. But she was in correspondence with the English priests, and it was believed in Rome that the nomination of Archbishop Plunket to the See of Armagh, which was much opposed by Spain, had been obtained by her influence.[41]

Before anything could be done, the design was again betrayed, and once more, and for the last time, Parliament intervened. It was generally believed that the object of the war against Holland was the establishment of the Catholic faith. It is said that Arlington divulged the secret, partly in order to ruin Clifford, and partly to dissolve the French alliance. Even Protestant statesmen, talking in private with the king, spoke of it as

---

[40] *Ibid.*, ii. 81. "Retardabant eum voluptates blandissimae dominae, et quaedam iners et pene somniculosa natura, quam tamen plura animi ingeniique bona comitabantur. Huic quidem stimulos admovisse suspicor Clementem per occultos homines" (Fabroni, *Vitae Italorum*, ii. 107).

[41] State Paper Office, "Italian States," Letters of Kent, June 29, July 6, August 10, 1669.

a thing about which there was neither doubt nor concealment. Temple, before returning to the Hague in 1674, had an interview with Charles. He went, as he expresses it, to the bottom of the matter, showing how difficult, if not impossible, it was to set up here the same religion and government that was in France, and assuring him that even those who were indifferent to religion would not consent to have it changed by force of an army.[42] Charles relinquished his design, and recalled the warning which his father on the scaffold had intended to impress on his son, as well as on Juxon, by the famous word "Remember,"—that if ever he came to the crown, he should so govern his subjects as not to force them to extremities. He declared that he was too old to go abroad again, and that he left that to his brother, if he had a mind to try it. For the ten remaining years of that reign, James took the lead in all the schemes for the restoration of the Church. It was of him that Coleman wrote in his fatal letter to La Chaise: "If he could gain any considerable new addition of power, all would come over to him as the only centre of our government, and nobody could contend with him further. Then would Catholicks be at ease, and His Most Christian Majesty's interest secured with us in England, beyond all apprehensions whatsoever." But the most Christian king, as he had prevented the declaration of religion before the Dutch war, endeavoured afterwards to have the design abandoned. He found that the English Parliament was not averse to the French alliance provided it was not used for the promotion of Popery and arbitrary power in England; and Lewis was quite willing that religion should be sacrificed in order to save his popularity with the English Protestants. Finding that the supposed connection of the king's conversion with the French alliance had brought suspicion on his ambassador, he replaced him by Ruvigny, who was a Calvinist. The new laws which were made against the Catholics, for the purpose of diverting suspicion, received his approbation; and he acted upon the hint given him by Bristol, that the House of Commons would be favourable to the French alliance if the belief in the existence of the secret

---

[42] Courtenay, *Memoirs of Sir W. Temple*, i. 425.

treaty for the restoration of Catholicism could be removed. That unhappy scheme defiled all that it touched, and neither those who shared in it nor those who condemned it came out of the transaction with honour.

If in the seventeenth century, which achieved so much for civil liberty, freedom of conscience was not established in England, the fault lay with the oppressed communities as much as with the crown or the dominant church. The Catholics and the Protestant sects were alike intolerant. The latter deserved what they received, and justified by their theories and their acts the penal laws by which they suffered. They were ready to do to others what was done to them. No religious party in the country admitted the right of minorities to the protection of the law. Religious liberty grew up in England as the fruit of civil liberty, of which it is a part, and in conjunction with which it has yet much way to make. But if the Protestants were not sincere in arguing for toleration, the Catholics were not honest in the means by which they endeavoured to obtain it. They sought as a concession that which was a right; they wished for privilege instead of liberty; and they defended an exception and not a principle. The Catholics of that age had degenerated from the old mediaeval spirit, which stood by the right and respected the law, but did not stoop to power. In the great constitutional struggle they disregarded the impending absolutism and the outraged laws, and gave to the royal cause, when it was most in fault, a support which, by prolonging the contest, drove the parliamentary opposition into lawless extremes, and postponed for half a century the establishment of freedom. After the Restoration they again trusted their interests to the favour of the court, and were willing to purchase advantages for their religion by political guilt, and to gain private ends at the price of a common servitude. That criminal and short-sighted policy brought quick retribution upon them, and explains how the party which saved the constitution in 1688 imposed disabilities on those who, by similar inconsistency, had been the declared adversaries of that freedom which their church had helped to institute.

V

Nationality

WHENEVER great intellectual cultivation has been combined with that suffering which is inseparable from extensive changes in the condition of the people, men of speculative or imaginative genius have sought in the contemplation of an ideal society a remedy, or at least a consolation, for evils which they were practically unable to remove. Poetry has always preserved the idea, that at some distant time or place, in the Western islands or the Arcadian region, an innocent and contented people, free from the corruption and restraint of civilised life, have realised the legends of the golden age. The office of the poets is always nearly the same, and there is little variation in the features of their ideal world; but when philosophers attempt to admonish or reform mankind by devising an imaginary state, their motive is more definite and immediate, and their commonwealth is a satire as well as a model. Plato and Plotinus, More and Campanella, constructed their fanciful societies with those materials which were omitted from the fabric of the actual communities, by the defects of which they were inspired. The Republic, the Utopia, and the City of the Sun were protests against a state of things which the experience of their authors taught them to condemn, and from the faults of which they took refuge in the opposite extremes. They remained without influence, and have never passed from literary into political history, because something more than discontent and speculative ingenuity is needed

First printed in the *Home and Foreign Review,* July, 1862. Reprinted from Acton, *History of Freedom and Other Essays* (London: Macmillan, 1907).

in order to invest a political idea with power over the masses of mankind. The scheme of a philosopher can command the practical allegiance of fanatics only, not of nations; and though oppression may give rise to violent and repeated outbreaks, like the convulsions of a man in pain, it cannot mature a settled purpose and plan of regeneration, unless a new notion of happiness is joined to the sense of present evil.

The history of religion furnishes a complete illustration. Between the later mediaeval sects and Protestantism there is an essential difference, that outweighs the points of analogy found in those systems which are regarded as heralds of the Reformation, and is enough to explain the vitality of the last in comparison with the others. Whilst Wycliffe and Hus contradicted certain particulars of the Catholic teaching, Luther rejected the authority of the Church, and gave to the individual conscience an independence which was sure to lead to an incessant resistance. There is a similar difference between the Revolt of the Netherlands, the Great Rebellion, the War of Independence, or the rising of Brabant, on the one hand, and the French Revolution on the other. Before 1789, insurrections were provoked by particular wrongs, and were justified by definite complaints and by an appeal to principles which all men acknowledged. New theories were sometimes advanced in the cause of controversy, but they were accidental, and the great argument against tyranny was fidelity to the ancient laws. Since the change produced by the French Revolution, those aspirations which are awakened by the evils and defects of the social state have come to act as permanent and energetic forces throughout the civilised world. They are spontaneous and aggressive, needing no prophet to proclaim, no champion to defend them, but popular, unreasoning, and almost irresistible. The Revolution effected this change, partly by its doctrines, partly by the indirect influence of events. It taught the people to regard their wishes and wants as the supreme criterion of right. The rapid vicissitudes of power, in which each party successively appealed to the favour of the masses as the arbiter of success, accustomed the masses to be arbitrary as well as insubordinate. The fall of many governments, and the frequent redistribution of territory, deprived all settlements of the dignity of permanence. Tradition and prescription ceased to be guardians of authority; and the arrangements which proceeded from revolutions, from the triumphs of war, and from treaties of peace, were equally regardless of established rights. Duty cannot be dissociated from right, and nations refuse to be controlled by laws which are no protection.

In this condition of the world, theory and action follow close upon each other, and practical evils easily give birth to opposite systems. In the realms of free-will, the regularity of natural progress is preserved by the conflict of extremes. The impulse of the reaction carries men from one extremity towards another. The pursuit of a remote and ideal object, which captivates the imagination by its splendour and the reason by its simplicity, evokes an energy which would not be inspired by a rational, possible end, limited by many antagonistic claims, and confined to what is reasonable, practicable, and just. One excess or exaggeration is the corrective of the other, and error promotes truth, where the masses are concerned, by counterbalancing a contrary error. The few have not strength to achieve great changes unaided; the many have not wisdom to be moved by truth unmixed. Where the disease is various, no particular definite remedy can meet the wants of all. Only the attraction of an abstract idea, or of an ideal state, can unite in a common action multitudes who seek a universal cure for many special evils, and a common restorative applicable to many different conditions. And hence false principles, which correspond with the bad as well as with the just aspirations of mankind, are a normal and necessary element in the social life of nations.

Theories of this kind are just, inasmuch as they are provoked by definite ascertained evils, and undertake their removal. They are useful in opposition, as a warning or a threat, to modify existing things, and keep awake the consciousness of wrong. They cannot serve as a basis for the reconstruction of civil society, as medicine cannot serve for food; but they may influence it with advantage, because they point out the direction, though not the measure, in which reform is needed. They oppose an order of things which is the result of a selfish and violent abuse of power by the ruling classes, and of artificial restriction on the natural progress of the world, destitute of an ideal element or a moral purpose. Practical extremes differ from the theoretical extremes they provoke, because the first are both arbitrary and violent, whilst the last, though also revolutionary, are at the same time remedial. In one case the wrong is voluntary, in the other it is inevitable. This is the general character of the contest between the existing order and the subversive theories that deny its legitimacy. There are three principal theories of this kind, impugning the present distribution of power, of property, and of territory, and attacking respectively the aristocracy, the middle class, and the sovereignty. They are the theories of equality, communism, and nationality. Though sprung from a common origin, opposing cognate evils, and connected by many links, they did not appear simultaneously. Rousseau proclaimed the first, Baboeuf the second, Mazzini the third; and the third is the most recent in its appearance, the most attractive at the present time, and the richest in promise of future power.

In the old European system, the rights of nationalities were neither recognised by governments nor asserted by the people. The interest of the reigning families, not those of the nations, regulated the frontiers; and the administration was conducted generally without any reference to popular desires. Where all liberties were suppressed, the claims of national independence were necessarily ignored, and a princess, in the words of Fénelon, carried a monarchy in her wedding portion. The eighteenth century acquiesced in this oblivion of corporate rights on the Continent, for the absolutists cared only for the State, and the liberals only for the individual. The Church, the nobles, and the nation had no place in the popular theories of the age; and they devised none in their own defence, for they were not openly attacked. The aristocracy retained its privileges, and the Church her property; and the dynastic interest, which overruled the natural inclination of the nations and destroyed their independence, nevertheless maintained their integrity. The national sentiment was not wounded in its most sensitive part. To dispossess a sovereign of his hereditary crown, and to annex his dominions, would have been held to inflict an injury upon all monarchies, and to furnish their subjects with a dangerous example, by depriving royalty of its inviolable character. In time of war, as there was no national cause at stake, there was no attempt to rouse national feeling. The courtesy of the rulers towards each other was proportionate to the contempt for the lower orders. Compliments passed between the commanders of hostile armies; there was no bitterness, and no excitement; battles were fought with the pomp and pride of a parade. The art of war became a slow and learned game. The monarchies were united not only by a natural community of interests, but by family alliances. A marriage contract sometimes became the signal for an interminable war, whilst family connections often set a barrier to ambition. After the wars of religion came to an end in 1648, the only wars were those which were waged for an inheritance or a dependency, or against countries whose system of government exempted them from the common law of dynastic States, and made them not only unprotected but obnoxious. These countries were England and Holland, until Holland ceased to be a republic, and until, in England, the defeat of the Jacobites in the forty-five terminated the struggle for the crown. There was one country, however, which still continued to be an exception; one monarch whose place was not admitted in the comity of kings.

Poland did not possess those securities for stability which were supplied by dynastic connections and the theory of legitimacy, wherever a crown could be obtained by marriage or inheritance. A monarch without royal blood, a crown bestowed by the nation, were an anomaly and an outrage in that age of dynastic absolutism. The country was excluded from the European system by the nature of its institutions. It excited a cupidity which could not be satisfied. It gave the reigning families of Europe no hope of permanently strengthening themselves by intermarriage with its rulers, or of obtaining it by bequest or by inheritance. The Habsburgs had contested the possession of Spain and the Indies with the French Bourbons, of Italy with the Spanish Bourbons, of the empire with the house of Wittelsbach, of

Silesia with the house of Hohenzollern. There had been wars between rival houses for half the territories of Italy and Germany. But none could hope to redeem their losses or increase their power in a country to which marriage and descent gave no claim. Where they could not permanently inherit they endeavoured, by intrigues, to prevail at each election, and after contending in support of candidates who were their partisans, the neighbours at last appointed an instrument for the final demolition of the Polish State. Till then no nation had been deprived of its political existence by the Christian Powers, and whatever disregard had been shown for national interests and sympathies, some care had been taken to conceal the wrong by a hypocritical perversion of law. But the partition of Poland was an act of wanton violence, committed in open defiance not only of popular feeling but of public law. For the first time in modern history a great State was suppressed, and a whole nation divided among its enemies.

This famous measure, the most revolutionary act of the old absolutism, awakened the theory of nationality in Europe, converting a dormant right into an aspiration, and a sentiment into a political claim. "No wise or honest man," wrote Edmund Burke, "can approve of that partition, or can contemplate it without prognosticating great mischief from it to all countries at some future time." [1] Thenceforward there was a nation demanding to be united in a State,—a soul, as it were, wandering in search of a body in which to begin life over again; and, for the first time, a cry was heard that the arrangement of States was unjust—that their limits were unnatural, and that a whole people was deprived of its right to constitute an independent community. Before that claim could be efficiently asserted against the overwhelming power of its opponents,—before it gained energy, after the last partition, to overcome the influence of long habits of submission, and of the contempt which previous disorders had brought upon Poland,—the ancient European system was in ruins, and a new world was rising in its place.

---

[1] "Observations on the Conduct of the Minority," *Works*, v. 112.

The old despotic policy which made the Poles its prey had two adversaries,—the spirit of English liberty, and the doctrines of that revolution which destroyed the French monarchy with its own weapons; and these two contradicted in contrary ways the theory that nations have no collective rights. At the present day, the theory of nationality is not only the most powerful auxiliary of revolution, but its actual substance in the movements of the last three years. This, however, is a recent alliance, unknown to the first French Revolution. The modern theory of nationality arose partly as a legitimate consequence, partly as a reaction against it. As the system which overlooked national division was opposed by liberalism in two forms, the French and the English, so the system which insists upon them proceeds from two distinct sources, and exhibits the character either of 1688 or of 1789. When the French people abolished the authorities under which it lived, and became its own master, France was in danger of dissolution: for the common will is difficult to ascertain, and does not readily agree. "The laws," said Vergniaud, in the debate on the sentence of the king, "are obligatory only as the presumptive will of the people, which retains the right of approving or condemning them. The instant it manifests its wish the work of the national representation, the law, must disappear." This doctrine resolved society into its natural elements, and threatened to break up the country into as many republics as there were communes. For true republicanism is the principle of self-government in the whole and in all the parts. In an extensive country, it can prevail only by the union of several independent communities in a single confederacy, as in Greece, in Switzerland, in the Netherlands, and in America; so that a large republic not founded on the federal principle must result in the government of a single city, like Rome and Paris, and, in a less degree, Athens, Berne, and Amsterdam; or, in other words, a great democracy must either sacrifice self-government to unity, or preserve it by federalism.

The France of history fell together with the French State, which was the growth of centuries. The old sovereignty was destroyed. The local authorities were looked upon with aversion and alarm. The new central authority needed to be established on a new principle of unity. The state of nature, which was the ideal of society, was made the basis of the nation; descent was put in the place of tradition, and the French people was regarded as a physical product: an ethnological, not historic, unit. It was assumed that a unity existed separate from the representation and the government, wholly independent of the past, and capable at any moment of expressing or of changing its mind. In the words of Sieyès, it was no longer France, but some unknown country to which the nation was transported. The central power possessed authority, inasmuch as it obeyed the whole, and no divergence was permitted from the universal sentiment. This power, endowed with volition, was personified in the Republic One and Indivisible. The title signified that a part could not speak or act for the whole,—that there was a power supreme over the State, distinct from, and independent of, its members; and it expressed, for the first time in history, the notion of an abstract nationality. In this manner the idea of the sovereignty of the people, uncontrolled by the past, gave birth to the idea of nationality independent of the political influence of history. It sprang from the rejection of the two authorities,—of the State and of the past. The kingdom of France was, geographically as well as politically, the product of a long series of events, and the same influences which built up the State formed the territory. The Revolution repudiated alike the agencies to which France owed her boundaries and those to which she owed her government. Every effaceable trace and relic of national history was carefully wiped away,—the system of administration, the physical divisions of the country, the classes of society, the corporations, the weights and measures, the calendar. France was no longer bounded by the limits she had received from the condemned influence of her history; she could recognise only those which were set by nature. The definition of the nation was borrowed from the material world, and, in order to avoid a loss of territory, it became not only an abstraction but a fiction.

There was a principle of nationality in the ethnological character of the movement, which is the source of the common

observation that revolution is more frequent in Catholic than in
Protestant countries. It is, in fact, more frequent in the Latin
than in the Teutonic world, because it depends partly on a
national impulse, which is only awakened where there is an
alien element, the vestige of a foreign dominion, to expel. Western Europe has undergone two conquests—one by the Romans
and one by the Germans, and twice received laws from the
invaders. Each time it rose again against the victorious race; and
the two great reactions, while they differ according to the different characters of the two conquests, have the phenomenon of
imperialism in common. The Roman republic laboured to crush
the subjugated nations into a homogeneous and obedient mass;
but the increase which the proconsular authority obtained in the
process subverted the republican government, and the reaction
of the provinces against Rome assisted in establishing the empire. The Caesarean system gave an unprecedented freedom to
the dependencies, and raised them to a civil equality which put
an end to the dominion of race over race and of class over class.
The monarchy was hailed as a refuge from the pride and cupidity of the Roman people; and the love of equality, the hatred of
nobility, and the tolerance of despotism implanted by Rome
became, at least in Gaul, the chief feature of the national
character. But among the nations whose vitality had been broken down by the stern republic, not one retained the materials
necessary to enjoy independence, or to develop a new history.
The political faculty which organises states and finds society in
a moral order was exhausted, and the Christian doctors looked
in vain over the waste of ruins for a people by whose aid the
Church might survive the decay of Rome. A new element of
national life was brought to that declining world by the enemies
who destroyed it. The flood of barbarians settled over it for a
season, and then subsided; and when the landmarks of civilisation appeared once more, it was found that the soil had been
impregnated with a fertilising and regenerating influence, and
that the inundation had laid the germs of future states and of a
new society. The political sense and energy came with the new
blood, and was exhibited in the power exercised by the younger

race upon the old, and in the establishment of a graduated freedom. Instead of universal equal rights, the actual enjoyment of which is necessarily contingent on, and commensurate with, power, the rights of the people were made dependent on a variety of conditions, the first of which was the distribution of property. Civil society became a classified organism instead of a formless combination of atoms, and the feudal system gradually arose.

Roman Gaul had so thoroughly adopted the ideas of absolute authority and undistinguished equality during the five centuries between Caesar and Clovis, that the people could never be reconciled to the new system. Feudalism remained a foreign importation, and the feudal aristocracy an alien race, and the common people of France sought protection against both in the Roman jurisprudence and the power of the crown. The development of absolute monarchy by the help of democracy is the one constant character of French history. The royal power, feudal at first, and limited by the immunities and the great vassals, became more popular as it grew more absolute; while the suppression of aristocracy, the removal of the intermediate authorities, was so particularly the object of the nation, that it was more energetically accomplished after the fall of the throne. The monarchy which had been engaged from the thirteenth century in curbing the nobles, was at last thrust aside by the democracy, because it was too dilatory in the work, and was unable to deny its own origin and effectually ruin the class from which it sprang. All those things which constitute the peculiar character of the French Revolution,—the demand for equality, the hatred of nobility and feudalism, and of the Church which was connected with them, the constant reference to pagan examples, the suppression of monarchy, the new code of law, the breach with tradition, and the substitution of an ideal system for everything that had proceeded from the mixture and mutual action of the races,—all these exhibit the common type of a reaction against the effects of the Frankish invasion. The hatred of royalty was less than the hatred of aristocracy; privileges were more detested than tyranny; and the king perished because of the origin of his authority rather than because of its abuse. Monarchy unconnected with aristocracy became popular in France, even when most uncontrolled; whilst the attempt to reconstitute the throne, and to limit and fence it with its peers, broke down, because the old Teutonic elements on which it relied—hereditary nobility, primogeniture, and privilege—were no longer tolerated. The substance of the ideas of 1789 is not the limitation of the sovereign power, but the abrogation of intermediate powers. These powers, and the classes which enjoyed them, come in Latin Europe from a barbarian origin; and the movement which calls itself liberal is essentially national. If liberty were its object, its means would be the establishment of great independent authorities not derived from the State, and its model would be England. But its object is equality; and it seeks, like France in 1789, to cast out the elements of inequality which were introduced by the Teutonic race. This is the object which Italy and Spain have had in common with France, and herein consists the natural league of the Latin nations.

This national element in the movement was not understood by the revolutionary leaders. At first, their doctrine appeared entirely contrary to the idea of nationality. They taught that certain general principles of government were absolutely right in all States; and they asserted in theory the unrestricted freedom of the individual, and the supremacy of the will over every external necessity or obligation. This is in apparent contradiction to the national theory, that certain natural forces ought to determine the character, the form, and the policy of the State, by which a kind of fate is put in the place of freedom. Accordingly the national sentiment was not developed directly out of the revolution in which it was involved, but was exhibited first in resistance to it, when the attempt to emancipate had been absorbed in the desire to subjugate, and the republic had been succeeded by the empire. Napoleon called a new power into existence by attacking nationality in Russia, by delivering it in Italy, by governing in defiance of it in Germany and Spain. The sovereigns of these countries were deposed or degraded; and a system of administration was introduced which was French in its origin, its spirit, and its instruments. The people resisted the change. The movement against it was popular and spontaneous, because the rulers were absent or helpless; and it was national, because it was directed against foreign institutions. In Tyrol, in Spain, and afterwards in Prussia, the people did not receive the impulse from the government, but undertook of their own accord to cast out the armies and the ideas of revolutionised France. Men were made conscious of the national element of the revolution by its conquests, not in its rise. The three things which the Empire most openly oppressed—religion, national independence, and political liberty—united in a short-lived league to animate the great uprising by which Napoleon fell. Under the influence of that memorable alliance a political spirit was called forth on the Continent, which clung to freedom and abhorred revolution, and sought to restore, to develop, and to reform the decayed national institutions. The men who proclaimed these ideas, Stein and Görres, Humboldt, Müller, and de Maistre,[2] were as hostile to Bonapartism as to the absolutism of the old governments, and insisted on the national rights, which had been invaded equally by both, and which they hoped to restore by the destruction of the French supremacy. With the

---

[2] There are some remarkable thoughts on nationality in the State Papers of the Count de Maistre: "En premier lieu les nations sont quelque chose dans le monde, il n'est pas permis de les compter pour rien, de les affliger dans leurs convenances, dans leurs affections, dans leurs intérêts les plus chers. . . . Or le traité du 30 mai anéantit complétement la Savoie; il divise l'indivisible; il partage en trois portions une malheureuse nation de 400,000 hommes, une par la langue, une par la religion, une par le caractère, une par l'habitude invétérée, une enfin par les limites naturelles. . . . L'union des nations ne souffre pas de difficultés sur la carte géographique; mais dans la réalité, c'est autre chose; il y a des nations *immiscibles*. . . . Je lui parlai par occasion de l'esprit italien qui s'agite dans ce moment; il [Count Nesselrode] me répondit: 'Oui, Monsieur; mais cet esprit est un grand mal, car il peut gêner les arrangements de l'Italie' " (*Correspondance Diplomatique de J. de Maistre*, ii. 7, 8, 21, 25). In the same year, 1815, Görres wrote: "In Italien wie allerwärts ist das Volk gewecht; es will etwas grossartiges, es will Ideen haben, die, wenn es sie auch nicht ganz begreift, doch einen freien unendlichen Gesichtskreis seiner Einbildung eröffnen. . . . Es ist reiner Naturtrieb, dass ein Volk, also scharf und deutlich in seine natürlichen Gränzen eingeschlossen, aus der Zerstreuung in die Einheit sich zu sammeln sucht" (*Werke*, ii. 20).

cause that triumphed at Waterloo the friends of the Revolution had no sympathy, for they had learned to identify their doctrine with the cause of France. The Holland House Whigs in England, the Afrancesados in Spain, the Muratists in Italy, and the partisans of the Confederation of the Rhine, merging patriotism in their revolutionary affections, regretted the fall of the French power, and looked with alarm at those new and unknown forces which the War of Deliverance had evoked, and which were as menacing to French liberalism as to French supremacy.

But the new aspirations for national and popular rights were crushed at the restoration. The liberals of those days cared for freedom, not in the shape of national independence, but of French institutions; and they combined against the nations with the ambition of the governments. They were as ready to sacrifice nationality to their ideal as the Holy Alliance was to the interests of absolutism. Talleyrand indeed declared at Vienna that the Polish question ought to have precedence over all other questions, because the partition of Poland had been one of the first and greatest causes of the evils which Europe had suffered; but dynastic interests prevailed. All the sovereigns represented at Vienna recovered their dominions, except the King of Saxony, who was punished for his fidelity to Napoleon; but the States that were unrepresented in the reigning families— Poland, Venice, and Genoa—were not revived, and even the Pope had great difficulty in recovering the Legations from the grasp of Austria. Nationality, which the old *régime* had ignored, which had been outraged by the revolution and the empire, received, after its first open demonstration, the hardest blow at the Congress of Vienna. The principle which the first partition had generated, to which the revolution had given a basis of theory, which had been lashed by the empire into a momentary convulsive effort, was matured by the long error of the restoration into a consistent doctrine, nourished and justified by the situation of Europe.

The governments of the Holy Alliance devoted themselves to suppress with equal care the revolutionary spirit by which they had been threatened, and the national spirit by which they had been restored. Austria, which owed nothing to the national movement, and had prevented its revival after 1809, naturally took the lead in repressing it. Every disturbance of the final settlements of 1815, every aspiration for changes or reforms, was condemned as sedition. This system repressed the good with the evil tendencies of the age; and the resistance which it provoked, during the generation that passed away from the restoration to the fall of Metternich, and again under the reaction which commenced with Schwarzenberg and ended with the administrations of Bach and Manteuffel, proceeded from various combinations of the opposite forms of liberalism. In the successive phases of that struggle, the idea that national claims are above all other rights gradually rose to the supremacy which it now possesses among the revolutionary agencies.

The first liberal movement, that of the Carbonari in the south of Europe, had no specific national character, but was supported by the Bonapartists both in Spain and Italy. In the following years the opposite ideas of 1813 came to the front, and a revolutionary movement, in many respects hostile to the principles of revolution, began in defence of liberty, religion, and nationality. All these causes were united in the Irish agitation, and in the Greek, Belgian, and Polish revolutions. Those sentiments which had been insulted by Napoleon, and had risen against him, rose against the governments of the restoration. They had been oppressed by the sword, and then by the treaties. The national principle added force, but not justice, to this movement, which, in every case but Poland, was successful. A period followed in which it degenerated into a purely national idea, as the agitation for repeal succeeded emancipation, and Panslavism and Panhellenism arose under the auspices of the Eastern Church. This was the third phase of the resistance to the settlement of Vienna, which was weak, because it failed to satisfy national or constitutional aspirations, either of which would have been a safeguard against the other, by a moral if not by a popular justification. At first, in 1813, the people rose against their conquerors, in defence of their legitimate rulers. They refused to be governed by usurpers. In the period between 1825 and 1831, they resolved that they would not be misgoverned by strangers. The French administration was often better than that which it displaced, but there were prior claimants for the authority exercised by the French, and at first the national contest was a contest for legitimacy. In the second period this element was wanting. No dispossessed princes led the Greeks, the Belgians, or the Poles. The Turks, the Dutch, and the Russians were attacked, not as usurpers, but as oppressors,—because they misgoverned, not because they were of a different race. Then began a time when the text simply was, that nations would not be governed by foreigners. Power legitimately obtained, and exercised with moderation, was declared invalid. National rights, like religion, had borne part in the previous combinations, and had been auxiliaries in the struggles for freedom, but now nationality became a paramount claim, which was to assert itself alone, which might put forward as pretexts the rights of rulers, the liberties of the people, the safety of religion, but which, if no such union could be formed, was to prevail at the expense of every other cause for which nations make sacrifices.

Metternich is, next to Napoleon, the chief promoter of this theory; for the anti-national character of the restoration was most distinct in Austria, and it is in opposition to the Austrian Government that nationality grew into a system. Napoleon, who, trusting to his armies, despised moral forces in politics, was overthrown by their rising. Austria committed the same fault in the government of her Italian provinces. The kingdom of Italy had united all the northern part of the Peninsula in a single State; and the national feelings, which the French repressed elsewhere, were encouraged as a safeguard of their power in Italy and in Poland. When the tide of victory turned, Austria invoked against the French the aid of the new sentiment they had fostered. Nugent announced, in his proclamation to the Italians, that they should become an independent nation. The same spirit served different masters, and contributed first to the destruction of the old States, then to the expulsion of the French, and again, under Charles Albert, to a new revolution. It

was appealed to in the name of the most contradictory principles of government, and served all parties in succession, because it was one in which all could unite. Beginning by a
protest against the dominion of race over race, its mildest and
least-developed form, it grew into a condemnation of every
State that included different races, and finally became the complete and consistent theory, that the State and the nation must
be co-extensive. "It is," says Mr. Mill, "in general a necessary
condition of free institutions, that the boundaries of governments should coincide in the main with those of nationalities." [3]
The outward historical progress of this idea from an indefinite aspiration to be the keystone of a political system, may be
traced in the life of the man who gave to it the element in which
its strength resides,—Giuseppe Mazzini. He found Carbonarism
impotent against the measures of the governments, and resolved
to give new life to the liberal movement by transferring it to the
ground of nationality. Exile is the nursery of nationality, as
oppression is the school of liberalism; and Mazzini conceived
the idea of Young Italy when he was a refugee at Marseilles. In
the same way, the Polish exiles are the champions of every
national movement; for to them all political rights are absorbed
in the idea of independence, which, however they may differ
with each other, is the one aspiration common to them all.
Towards the year 1830 literature also contributed to the national idea. "It was the time," says Mazzini, "of the great conflict
between the romantic and the classical school, which might
with equal truth be called a conflict between the partisans of
freedom and of authority." The romantic school was infidel in
Italy, and Catholic in Germany; but in both it had the common
effect of encouraging national history and literature, and Dante
was as great an authority with the Italian democrats as with the
leaders of the mediaeval revival at Vienna, Munich, and Berlin.
But neither the influence of the exiles, nor that of the poets and
critics of the new party, extended over the masses. It was a sect
without popular sympathy or encouragement, a conspiracy

---

[3] *Considerations on Representative Government,* p. 298.

founded not on a grievance, but on a doctrine; and when the attempt to rise was made in Savoy, in 1834, under a banner with the motto "Unity, Independence, God and Humanity," the people were puzzled at its object, and indifferent to its failure. But Mazzini continued his propaganda, developed his *Giovine Italia* into a *Giovine Europa,* and established in 1847 the international league of nations. "The people," he said, in his opening address, "is penetrated with only one idea, that of unity and nationality. . . . There is no international question as to forms of government, but only a national question."

The revolution of 1848, unsuccessful in its national purpose, prepared the subsequent victories of nationality in two ways. The first of these was the restoration of the Austrian power in Italy, with a new and more energetic centralisation, which gave no promise of freedom. Whilst that system prevailed, the right was on the side of the national aspirations, and they were revived in a more complete and cultivated form by Manin. The policy of the Austrian Government, which failed during the ten years of the reaction to convert the tenure by force into a tenure by right, and to establish with free institutions the condition of allegiance, gave a negative encouragement to the theory. It deprived Francis Joseph of all active support and sympathy in 1859, for he was more clearly wrong in his conduct than his enemies in their doctrines. The real cause of the energy which the national theory has acquired is, however, the triumph of the democratic principle in France, and its recognition by the European Powers. The theory of nationality is involved in the democratic theory of the sovereignty of the general will. "One hardly knows what any division of the human race should be free to do, if not to determine with which of the various collective bodies of human beings they choose to associate themselves." [4] It is by this act that a nation constitutes itself. To have a collective will, unity is necessary, and independence is requisite in order to assert it. Unity and nationality are still more essential to the notion of the sovereignty of the people than the

[4] Mill's *Considerations,* p. 296.

147

cashiering of monarchs, or the revocation of laws. Arbitrary acts of this kind may be prevented by the happiness of the people or the popularity of the king, but a nation inspired by the democratic idea cannot with consistency allow a part of itself to belong to a foreign State, or the whole to be divided into several native States. The theory of nationality therefore proceeds from both the principles which divide the political world,—from legitimacy, which ignores its claims, and from the revolution, which assumes them; and for the same reason it is the chief weapon of the last against the first.

In pursuing the outward and visible growth of the national theory we are prepared for an examination of its political character and value. The absolutism which has created it denies equally that absolute right of national unity which is a product of democracy, and that claim of national liberty which belongs to the theory of freedom. These two views of nationality, corresponding to the French and to the English systems, are connected in name only, and are in reality the opposite extremes of political thought. In one case, nationality is founded on the perpetual supremacy of the collective will, of which the unity of the nation is the necessary condition, to which every other influence must defer, and against which no obligation enjoys authority, and all resistance is tyrannical. The nation is here an ideal unit founded on the race, in defiance of the modifying action of external causes, of tradition, and of existing rights. It overrules the rights and wishes of the inhabitants, absorbing their divergent interests in a fictitious unity; sacrifices their several inclinations and duties to the higher claim of nationality, and crushes all natural rights and all established liberties for the purpose of vindicating itself.[5] Whenever a single definite object is made the supreme end of the State, be it the advantage of a

---

[5] "Le sentiment d'indépendance nationale est encore plus général et plus profondément gravé dans le cœur des peuples que l'amour d'une liberté constitutionnelle. Les nations les plus soumises au despotisme éprouvent ce sentiment avec autant de vivacité que les nations libres; les peuples les plus barbares le sentent même encore plus vivement que les nations policées" (*L'Italie au Dix-neuvième Siècle*, p. 148, Paris, 1821).

class, the safety or the power of the country, the greatest happiness of the greatest number, or the support of any speculative idea, the State becomes for the time inevitably absolute. Liberty alone demands for its realisation the limitation of the public authority, for liberty is the only object which benefits all alike, and provokes no sincere opposition. In supporting the claims of national unity, governments must be subverted in whose title there is no flaw, and whose policy is beneficent and equitable, and subjects must be compelled to transfer their allegiance to an authority for which they have no attachment, and which may be practically a foreign domination. Connected with this theory in nothing except in the common enmity of the absolute state, is the theory which represents nationality as an essential, but not a supreme element in determining the forms of the State. It is distinguished from the other, because it tends to diversity and not to uniformity, to harmony and not to unity; because it aims not at an arbitrary change, but at careful respect for the existing conditions of political life, and because it obeys the laws and results of history, not the aspirations of an ideal future. While the theory of unity makes the nation a source of despotism and revolution, the theory of liberty regards it as the bulwark of self-government, and the foremost limit to the excessive power of the State. Private rights, which are sacrificed to the unity, are preserved by the union of nations. No power can so efficiently resist the tendencies of centralisation, of corruption, and of absolutism, as that community which is the vastest that can be included in a State, which imposes on its members a consistent similarity of character, interest, and opinion, and which arrests the action of the sovereign by the influence of a divided patriotism. The presence of different nations under the same sovereignty is similar in its effect to the independence of the Church in the State. It provides against the servility which flourishes under the shadow of a single authority, by balancing interests, multiplying associations, and giving to the subject the restraint and support of a combined opinion. In the same way it promotes independence by forming definite groups of public opinion, and by affording a great source and centre of political sentiments, and of notions of duty not derived from the sovereign will. Liberty provokes diversity, and diversity preserves liberty by supplying the means of organisation. All those portions of law which govern the relations of men with each other, and regulate social life, are the varying result of national custom and the creation of private society. In these things, therefore, the several nations will differ from each other; for they themselves have produced them, and they do not owe them to the State which rules them all. This diversity in the same State is a firm barrier against the intrusion of the government beyond the political sphere which is common to all into the social department which escapes legislation and is ruled by spontaneous laws. This sort of interference is characteristic of an absolute government, and is sure to provoke a reaction, and finally a remedy. That intolerance of social freedom which is natural to absolutism is sure to find a corrective in the national diversities, which no other force could so efficiently provide. The coexistence of several nations under the same State is a test, as well as the best security of its freedom. It is also one of the chief instruments of civilisation; and, as such, it is in the natural and providential order, and indicates a state of greater advancement than the national unity which is the ideal of modern liberalism.

The combination of different nations in one State is as necessary a condition of civilised life as the combination of men in society. Inferior races are raised by living in political union with races intellectually superior. Exhausted and decaying nations are revived by the contact of a younger vitality. Nations in which the elements of organisation and the capacity for government have been lost, either through the demoralising influence of despotism, or the disintegrating action of democracy, are restored and educated anew under the discipline of a stronger and less corrupted race. This fertilising and regenerating process can only be obtained by living under one government. It is in the cauldron of the State that the fusion takes place by which the vigour, the knowledge, and the capacity of one portion of mankind may be communicated to another. Where political and national boundaries coincide, society ceases to advance, and nations relapse into a condition corresponding to that of men who renounce intercourse with their fellow-men. The difference between the two unites mankind not only by the benefits it confers on those who live together, but because it connects society either by a political or a national bond, gives to every people an interest in its neighbours, either because they are under the same government or because they are of the same race, and thus promotes the interests of humanity, of civilisation, and of religion.

Christianity rejoices at the mixture of races, as paganism identifies itself with their differences, because truth is universal, and errors various and particular. In the ancient world idolatry and nationality went together, and the same term is applied in Scripture to both. It was the mission of the Church to overcome national differences. The period of her undisputed supremacy was that in which all Western Europe obeyed the same laws, all literature was contained in one language, and the political unity of Christendom was personified in a single potentate, while its intellectual unity was represented in one university. As the ancient Romans concluded their conquests by carrying away the gods of the conquered people, Charlemagne overcame the national resistance of the Saxons only by the forcible destruction of their pagan rites. Out of the mediaeval period, and the combined action of the German race and the Church, came forth a new system of nations and a new conception of nationality. Nature was overcome in the nation as well as in the individual. In pagan and uncultivated times, nations were distinguished from each other by the widest diversity, not only in religion, but in customs, language, and character. Under the new law they had many things in common; the old barriers which separated them were removed, and the new principle of self-government, which Christianity imposed, enabled them to live together under the same authority, without necessarily losing their cherished habits, their customs, or their laws. The new idea of freedom made room for different races in one State. A nation was no longer what it had been to the ancient world,—the progeny of a common ancestor, or the aboriginal product of a particular region,—a result of merely physical and material causes,—but a moral and political being; not the creation of geographical or physiological unity, but developed in the course of history by the action of the State. It is derived from the State, not supreme over it. A State may in course of time produce a nationality; but that a nationality should constitute a State is contrary to the nature of modern civilisation. The nation derives its rights and its power from the memory of a former independence.

The Church has agreed in this respect with the tendency of political progress, and discouraged wherever she could the isolation of nations; admonishing them of their duties to each other, and regarding conquest and feudal investiture as the natural means of raising barbarous or sunken nations to a higher level. But though she has never attributed to national independence an immunity from the accidental consequences of feudal law, of hereditary claims, or of testamentary arrangements, she defends national liberty against uniformity and centralisation with an energy inspired by perfect community of interests. For the same enemy threatens both; and the State which is reluctant to tolerate differences, and to do justice to the peculiar character of various races, must from the same cause interfere in the internal government of religion. The connection of religious liberty with the emancipation of Poland or Ireland is not merely the accidental result of local causes; and the failure of the Concordat to unite the subjects of Austria is the natural consequence of a policy which did not desire to protect the provinces in their diversity and autonomy, and sought to bribe the Church by favours instead of strengthening her by independence. From this influence of religion in modern history has proceeded a new definition of patriotism.

The difference between nationality and the State is exhibited in the nature of patriotic attachment. Our connection with the race is merely natural or physical, whilst our duties to the political nation are ethical. One is a community of affections and instincts infinitely important and powerful in savage life, but pertaining more to the animal than to the civilised man; the other is an authority governing by laws, imposing obligations, and giving a moral sanction and character to the natural relations of society. Patriotism is in political life what faith is in religion, and it stands to the domestic feelings and to homesickness as faith to fanaticism and to superstition. It has one aspect derived from private life and nature, for it is an extension of the family affections, as the tribe is an extension of the family. But in its real political character, patriotism consists in the development of the instinct of self-preservation into a moral duty which may involve self-sacrifice. Self-preservation is both an instinct and a duty, natural and involuntary in one respect, and at the same time a moral obligation. By the first it produces the family; by the last the State. If the nation could exist without the State, subject only to the instinct of self-preservation, it would be incapable of denying, controlling, or sacrificing itself; it would be an end and a rule to itself. But in the political order moral purposes are realised and public ends are pursued to which private interests and even existence must be sacrificed. The great sign of true patriotism, the development of selfishness into sacrifice, is the product of political life. That sense of duty which is supplied by race is not entirely separated from its selfish and instinctive basis; and the love of country, like married love, stands at the same time on a material and a moral foundation. The patriot must distinguish between the two causes or objects of his devotion. The attachment which is given only to the country is like obedience given only to the State—a submission to physical influences. The man who prefers his country before every other duty shows the same spirit as the man who surrenders every right to the State. They both deny that right is superior to authority.

There is a moral and political country, in the language of Burke, distinct from the geographical, which may be possibly in collision with it. The Frenchmen who bore arms against the Convention were as patriotic as the Englishmen who bore arms against King Charles, for they recognised a higher duty than that of obedience to the actual sovereign. "In an address to France," said Burke, "in an attempt to treat with it, or in considering any scheme at all relative to it, it is impossible we should mean the geographical, we must always mean the moral and political, country. . . . The truth is, that France is out of itself—the moral France is separated from the geographical. The master of the house is expelled, and the robbers are in possession. If we look for the corporate people of France, existing as corporate in the eye and intention of public law (that corporate people, I mean, who are free to deliberate and to decide, and who have a capacity to treat and conclude), they are in Flanders and Germany, in Switzerland, Spain, Italy, and England. There are all the princes of the blood, there are all the orders of the State, there are all the parliaments of the kingdom. . . . I am sure that if half that number of the same description were taken out of this country, it would leave hardly anything that I should call the people of England." [6] Rousseau draws nearly the same distinction between the country to which we happen to belong and that which fulfils towards us the political functions of the State. In the *Emile* he has a sentence of which it is not easy in a translation to convey the point: "Qui n'a pas une patrie a du moins un pays." And in his tract on Political Economy he writes: "How shall men love their country if it is nothing more for them than for strangers, and bestows on them only that which it can refuse to none?" It is in the same sense he says, further on, "La patrie ne peut subsister sans la liberté." [7]

The nationality formed by the State, then, is the only one to which we owe political duties, and it is, therefore, the only one which has political rights. The Swiss are ethnologically either French, Italian, or German; but no nationality has the slightest

---

[6] Burke's "Remarks on the Policy of the Allies" (*Works*, v. 26, 29, 30).

[7] *Œuvres*, i. 593, 595, ii. 717. Bossuet, in a passage of great beauty on the love of country, does not attain to the political definition of the word: "La société humaine demande qu'on aime la terre où l'on habite ensemble, ou la regarde comme une mère et une nourrice commune. . . . Les hommes en effet se sentent liés par quelque chose de fort, lorsqu'ils songent, que la même terre qui les a portés et nourris étant vivants, les recevra dans son sein quand ils seront morts" ("Politique tirée de l'Ecriture Sainte," *Œuvres*, x. 317).

claim upon them, except the purely political nationality of Switzerland. The Tuscan or the Neapolitan State has formed a nationality, but the citizens of Florence and of Naples have no political community with each other. There are other States which have neither succeeded in absorbing distinct races in a political nationality, nor in separating a particular district from a larger nation. Austria and Mexico are instances on the one hand, Parma and Baden on the other. The progress of civilisation deals hardly with the last description of States. In order to maintain their integrity they must attach themselves by confederations, or family alliances, to greater Powers, and thus lose something of their independence. Their tendency is to isolate and shut off their inhabitants, to narrow the horizon of their views, and to dwarf in some degree the proportions of their ideas. Public opinion cannot maintain its liberty and purity in such small dimensions, and the currents that come from larger communities sweep over a contracted territory. In a small and homogeneous population there is hardly room for a natural classification of society, or for inner groups of interests that set bounds to sovereign power. The government and the subjects contend with borrowed weapons. The resources of the one and the aspirations of the other are derived from some external source, and the consequence is that the country becomes the instrument and the scene of contests in which it is not interested. These States, like the minuter communities of the Middle Ages, serve a purpose, by constituting partitions and securities of self-government in the larger States; but they are impediments to the progress of society, which depends on the mixture of races under the same governments.

The vanity and peril of national claims founded on no political tradition, but on race alone, appear in Mexico. There the races are divided by blood, without being grouped together in different regions. It is, therefore, neither possible to unite them nor to convert them into the elements of an organised State. They are fluid, shapeless, and unconnected, and cannot be precipitated, or formed into the basis of political institutions. As they cannot be used by the State, they cannot be recognised by it; and their peculiar qualities, capabilities, passions, and attachments are of no service, and therefore obtain no regard. They are necessarily ignored, and are therefore perpetually outraged. From this difficulty of races with political pretensions, but without political position, the Eastern world escaped by the institution of castes. Where there are only two races there is the resource of slavery; but when different races inhabit the different territories of one Empire composed of several smaller States, it is of all possible combinations the most favourable to the establishment of a highly developed system of freedom. In Austria there are two circumstances which add to the difficulty of the problem, but also increase its importance. The several nationalities are at very unequal degrees of advancement, and there is no single nation which is so predominant as to overwhelm or absorb the others. These are the conditions necessary for the very highest degree of organisation which government is capable of receiving. They supply the greatest variety of intellectual resource; the perpetual incentive to progress, which is afforded not merely by competition, but by the spectacle of a more advanced people; the most abundant elements of self-government, combined with the impossibility for the State to rule all by its own will; and the fullest security for the preservation of local customs and ancient rights. In such a country as this, liberty would achieve its most glorious results, while centralisation and absolutism would be destruction.

The problem presented to the government of Austria is higher than that which is solved in England, because of the necessity of admitting the national claims. The parliamentary system fails to provide for them, as it presupposes the unity of the people. Hence in those countries in which different races dwell together, it has not satisfied their desires, and is regarded as an imperfect form of freedom. It brings out more clearly than before the differences it does not recognise, and thus continues the work of the old absolutism, and appears as a new phase of centralisation. In those countries, therefore, the power of the imperial parliament must be limited as jealously as the power of the crown, and many of its functions must be discharged by provincial diets, and a descending series of local authorities.

The great importance of nationality in the State consists in the fact that it is the basis of political capacity. The character of a nation determines in great measure the form and vitality of the State. Certain political habits and ideas belong to particular nations, and they vary with the course of the national history. A people just emerging from barbarism, a people effete from the excesses of a luxurious civilisation, cannot possess the means of governing itself; a people devoted to equality, or to absolute monarchy, is incapable of producing an aristocracy; a people averse to the institution of private property is without the first element of freedom. Each of these can be converted into efficient members of a free community only by the contact of a superior race, in whose power will lie the future prospects of the State. A system which ignores these things, and does not rely for its support on the character and aptitude of the people, does not intend that they should administer their own affairs, but that they should simply be obedient to the supreme command. The denial of nationality, therefore, implies the denial of political liberty.

The greatest adversary of the rights of nationality is the modern theory of nationality. By making the State and the nation commensurate with each other in theory, it reduces practically to a subject condition all other nationalities that may be within the boundary. It cannot admit them to an equality with the ruling nation which constitutes the State, because the State would then cease to be national, which would be a contradiction of the principle of its existence. According, therefore, to the degree of humanity and civilisation in that dominant body which claims all the rights of the community, the inferior races are exterminated, or reduced to servitude, or outlawed, or put in a condition of dependence.

If we take the establishment of liberty for the realisation of moral duties to be the end of civil society, we must conclude that those states are substantially the most perfect which, like the British and Austrian Empires, include various distinct nationalities without oppressing them. Those in which no mixture of races has occurred are imperfect; and those in which its effects have disappeared are decrepit. A State which is incompetent to satisfy different races condemns itself; a State which labours to neutralise, to absorb, or to expel them, destroys its own vitality; a State which does not include them is destitute of the chief basis of self-government. The theory of nationality, therefore, is a retrograde step in history. It is the most advanced form of the revolution, and must retain its power to the end of the revolutionary period, of which it announces the approach. Its great historical importance depends on two chief causes.

First, it is a chimera. The settlement at which it aims is impossible. As it can never be satisfied and exhausted, and always continues to assert itself, it prevents the government from ever relapsing into the condition which provoked its rise. The danger is too threatening, and the power over men's minds too great, to allow any system to endure which justifies the resistance of nationality. It must contribute, therefore, to obtain that which in theory it condemns,—the liberty of different nationalities as members of one sovereign community. This is a service which no other force could accomplish; for it is a corrective alike of absolute monarchy, of democracy, and of constitutionalism, as well as of the centralisation which is common to all three. Neither the monarchical, nor the revolutionary, nor the parliamentary system can do this; and all the ideas which have excited enthusiasm in past times are impotent for the purpose except nationality alone.

And secondly, the national theory marks the end of the revolutionary doctrine and its logical exhaustion. In proclaiming the supremacy of the rights of nationality, the system of democratic equality goes beyond its own extreme boundary, and falls into contradiction with itself. Between the democratic and the national phase of the revolution, socialism had intervened, and had already carried the consequences of the principle to an absurdity. But that phase was passed. The revolution survived its offspring, and produced another further result. Nationality is more advanced than socialism, because it is a more arbitrary system. The social theory endeavours to provide for the existence of the individual beneath the terrible burdens which modern society heaps upon labour. It is not merely a development of the notion of equality, but a refuge from real misery and starvation. However false the solution, it was a reasonable demand that the poor should be saved from destruction; and if the freedom of the State was sacrificed to the safety of the individual, the more immediate object was, at least in theory, attained. But nationality does not aim either at liberty or prosperity, both of which it sacrifices to the imperative necessity of making the nation the mould and measure of the State. Its course will be marked with material as well as moral ruin, in order that a new invention may prevail over the works of God and the interests of mankind. There is no principle of change, no phase of political speculation conceivable, more comprehensive, more subversive, or more arbitrary than this. It is a confutation of democracy, because it sets limits to the exercise of the popular will, and substitutes for it a higher principle. It prevents not only the division, but the extension of the State, and forbids to terminate war by conquest, and to obtain a security for peace. Thus, after surrendering the individual to the collective will, the revolutionary system makes the collective will subject to conditions which are independent of it, and rejects all law, only to be controlled by an accident.

Although, therefore, the theory of nationality is more absurd and more criminal than the theory of socialism, it has an important mission in the world, and marks the final conflict, and therefore the end, of two forces which are the worst enemies of civil freedom,—the absolute monarchy and the revolution.

VI

Ultramontanism

KNOWLEDGE is treated by the Christian Church not merely as a means, but much more as an end, because it is the only atmosphere in which her progress is unwavering and subject to no relapse. When in successive ages she defines or surveys anew the system it is her mission to teach, she has always to record some advance upon the past. Though amongst the units of mankind the boundary of her dominion may waver or recede, yet, in the order of truth, she works out a law of inevitable and invariable advance. She must teach all nations; but she has no special promise that any one will listen to her. She must watch over those within her fold, but she knows not whether her vigilance will avail. No divine protection insures her against losses by persecution, dogged unbelief, neglect of her law, or apostasy from her creed; and there is no assurance that the means of grace which she dispenses will effect by degrees the moral improvement of our race, or that sanctity will gain in intensity or in extent as time goes on. There may be diminution in the area of Christendom, and decline in the virtue of Christians. But there must be some exception to the possibility of retrogression, or Christianity would be inferior to Judaism; nay, if stagnation could paralyse every function of the Church of Christ, His works would be less perfect than the works of men. The divine nature of the institution which He founded must therefore be manifest in some element which is secured against

First printed in the *Home and Foreign Review,* July, 1863. Reprinted from Acton, *Essays on Church and State,* edited by Douglas Woodruff (London: Hollis and Carter, 1952).

loss or deterioration by the assurance of a constant growth. To refuse to the Church this character of progress is to deny the divinity of her Founder; and if we seek it anywhere else than in that order of truth which is subject to the immediate guidance of the Holy Ghost, we are contradicted alike by the holiness of the early ages, and by the most memorable lessons of later religious history.

In this growth the Church does not yield to the action of eternal forces, or simply consent to a change which she cannot impede. Progress is a necessity of her existence, and a law of her nature. She does not passively suffer it, but actively imposes it upon society. Whilst she continually and continuously develops her doctrines, and evolves truth from the inexhaustible tradition of the teaching of our Lord, her action is the ever-present impulse, pattern and guide of society in the formation of law, and in the advancement of learning.

How great is the influence thus exercised by the example of the Church on civil government, and how close is the parallel between her method and the principles of political science, we do not here inquire. Her more direct and necessary action is on human knowledge. For the full exposition of truth is the great object for which the existence of mankind is prolonged on earth. It may be that individual goodness is not greater, or the proportion of the saved larger, than in earlier times; but Almighty God is more fully known, the articles of faith are multiplied, and the certainty of knowledge is increased. This growth in knowledge is not by new revelations or by a continuance of inspiration, but it is a conquest of the Christian mind in its conflict with the phases of untruth. It is earned by exertion; it is not simply given by faith itself. The development of doctrine is essential to the preservation of its purity; hence its preservation implies its development; and the intellectual act which accompanies belief is the agent of the progress of the Church in religious knowledge. In the course of this process she lays under contribution all human learning, which she exacts and sanctifies by using it. As she does not possess at once the fulness of all knowledge, and as her authority leaves many things uncertain, she must rely on other resources for that which is not hers by inheritance; and her demand must necessarily promote the supply of that on which she so much depends. Therefore, by the side of the progressive study of revealed truth a vast intellectual labour continues incessantly, carried on in the presence of authority, on the basis of faith, and within the sphere of unity and charity, in order that all science may become tributary to religion, and that God may be worshipped in the harmony of His words, His works, and His ways.

This duty has been discharged in all ages, except the intervals of corruption and decline, with a zeal commensurate with its importance; and the bitter anxiety which has accompanied each rising doubt and division has equalled that excited by assaults on the faith itself. For in disputes with a hostile religion there is the certainty of belief to guide, and confidence in authority to sustain the combatant. He confesses himself inferior to the cause; he dares not degrade it by the introduction of personal motives or emotions, or allow it to be desecrated by the conditions of human controversy; and he is not tempted to do so, for neither fear nor doubt mingles with his feelings. But in discussions confined within the sphere of religious unity, which do not directly involve fundamental truths, and where private judgement occupies the place of faith and obedience, the antagonism is necessarily more personal, there is more selfishness in opinion and less assurance of victory, and the purest motives may become tainted by ignorance, interest or pride. Disputes which authority cannot decide are an excitement to those for whom its restraint is irksome, and an indulgence for those who are weary of acquiescing in silent unity. The lines of separation are most distinctly marked because the chasm is less wide.

Hence arise two phenomena which vex the Catholic and perplex the Protestant—the number of parties within the Church, and the heat of their dissensions. It is not always easy for a stranger to reconcile these things with the notion of unity, or for a friend to be sure that they involve no breach of charity; and it is very hard for either to discover, when orthodoxy is disputed and authority necessarily silent, the true exponent of the Catholic idea. As the rise of heresies furnished the text which defined Catholicism to be the most perfect expression of Christianity, so the growth of internal controversy requires some further test to ascertain the purest form of thought on open questions within the Church. For the control of religion extends further than its dogmas; and a view which contradicts no prescribed doctrine may be a more serious symptom of estrangement from the spirit of the Church than some unconscious doctrinal errors. There are certain questions to which the test of orthodoxy does not apply, which yet are more significant than some of those which it decides. The liberty which prevails on doubtful points does not justify a resignation that acquiesces in doubt, and deprecates the efforts by which it may be dispelled. In the absence of the degrees of authority, such points may be settled by scientific inquiry, and an opinion which can never be enforced may claim to be received. Yet, though Catholics may be ready to adopt a criterion which excludes some of those who are in communion with them, they dread what may repel those who are not; and they naturally conceal in the presence of strangers a weapon which they use among themselves. It is impossible that varying parties which cannot agree in a common definition should accept a common term.

Protestant observers have adopted a designation to indicate the esoteric spirit of Catholicism, the real essence of the system they oppose. That designation is Ultramontanism. Unquestionably the significance attached to it has a certain reality and truth which ought to overcome the reluctance to admit the term. Ultramontanism stands in the same relation to Catholicism in matters of opinion as Catholicism to Christianity in matters of faith. It signifies a habit of intellect carrying forward the inquiries and supplementing the work of authority. It implies the legitimate union of religion with science, and the conscious intelligible harmony of Catholicism with the system of secular truth. Its basis is authority, but its domain is liberty, and it reconciles the one with the other. A Catholic may be utterly deficient in human learning, or he may possess it in such a measure as presents no difficulties to his faith, or he may find a ready and universal solution for all such difficulties in an un-hesitating sacrifice either of faith or of reason. In no one of these cases, whether he be a good or a bad Catholic, has he any pre-tensions to the name of Ultramontane. His religion derives no strength or resources from his knowledge, nor does his knowl-edge find a principle of unity or a guide in his religion. If neither of them has lost anything of its integrity and truth, neither has gained anything from the other. If there is no strug-gle in his mind, there has also been no combination—no genera-tion of something previously non-existent which neither science alone nor religion alone could have produced. His conscience has obtained no security against the necessity of sacrificing faith to truth or truth to faith, and no impulse to that reflection which recognises the ultimate unity.

It is plain that Ultramontanism, in this acceptation of the word, can only be a fruit of mature civilisation and of a very advanced stage of scientific investigation. Natural science be-fore it was purified by the methods of observation, and histori-cal science before it was regenerated by criticism, consorted better with superstition and error than with religion. But a change took place in their nature at the beginning of this century. There is an interval, as it were, of centuries which divides Cuvier from Buffon, Niebuhr from Gibbon, with a dis-tinctness almost as great as that which separates chemistry from alchemy, astronomy from astrology, history from legend. A simi-lar change ensued in the political system, and established in almost every country the theory and the desire of freedom. In one of the contests arising from this altered condition of society, about a quarter of a century ago, the term Ultramontane began to be applied to those who advocated the rights and principles of the Catholic Church. In one sense the designation was just: in another it was a strange inversion of the meaning which had been hitherto attached to the word.

During the period between the Reformation and the Revolu-tion, Ultramontanism, like Gallicanism, was used as a party term. It designated the strict Roman system as developed by the antagonism of the Gallican theories of the fifteenth century.

In comparison with the practice of the Middle Ages, it was a jealousy of liberties, stimulated by an equal jealousy of authority. Such a controversy, raising a false issue on the law and constitution of the Church, could only engage the masters of ecclesiastical learning during an age when history, the touchstone and solvent of extreme systems, was very imperfectly known. At a time when it raged, little had yet been done to illustrate the mediaeval Church, and men were still without the means of solving such historical problems as that of the Donation of Constantine, the spurious Decretals, the story of Pope Joan, and all the various fables which furnished the bases of the rival claims for an almost absolute national independence, and for an arbitrary and universal power. In those days Gallicans and Ultramontanes contended for narrow, extreme, subordinate, we might almost say, uneducated views. The conflict between them was an abatement of the true Catholic spirit, and was lamented by the saints as a disaster for the Church. "Je hais," says St Francis of Sales, "par inclination naturelle, et, je pense, par inspiration céleste, toutes les contentions et disputes qui se font entre Catholiques, et dont la fin est inutile; encore plus celles dont les effets ne peuvent être que dissensions et différends, surtout en ce temps plein d'esprits disposés aux controverses, aux médisances, aux censures et à la ruine de la charité. Je n'ai pas même trouvé à mon goût certains écrits d'un saint et très-excellent prélat, dans lequels il a touché du pouvoir indirect du Pape sur les princes; non que j'ai jugé s'il a tort ou raison, mais parce qu'en cet age où nous avons tant d'ennemis en dehors, nous ne devons rien émouvoir au dedans du corps de l'Église." St Francis also says: "Il est malaisé de dire choses qui n'offensent ceux qui, faisant les bons valets, soit du Pape, soit des princes, ne veulent pas que jamais on s'arrête hors des extremités."[1]

Intellectual indolence conspired with the ignorance of the age to promote these theories. Men were glad to find a formula which saved them the trouble of thinking, and a view which

---

[1] *Œuvres,* xi, 406, 401.

enabled them to shut their eyes. For the defence of a thesis is far easier than the discovery of truth. There is something alarming in the labour of distinguishing and comparing times and places, and of making due allowance for qualifying circumstances and conditions. The followers of a system dreaded lest the knowledge of facts should interfere with the certainty of their opinions, and lest the resistless stream of history should be let in upon their settled and compact conclusions.

The political condition of those times is an important element in the history of the controversy. Gallicanism and Ultramontanism both professed to represent liberty; but they both belonged to an age of absolute power. One system was the instrument by which absolute monarchs extended their power over the Church, whilst by the other the same principle of absolutism was introduced into the Church herself. Both were expedients by which ecclesiastical liberty was curtailed, and authority made superior to law. The source of their vitality and the reason of their existence disappeared when the Revolution put an end to the old society which tolerated, and even approved, the system of arbitrary government. At a later period, under the Restoration, the reverence for law, and the religious aversion for absolute power, which resisted the encroachment of civil government on the liberties of the Church, caused her to maintain, in her own internal system, the authority of law and tradition over the temporary will of her rulers. Instead of Church and State being rivals in absolutism, it came to be understood that both ought to obey their own legislation; while the horror of the lawless epochs they had lately traversed, in the Revolution and the Empire, came to be the predominant influence in the minds of men.

Early in the present century, while Chateaubriand was explaining the charm of religious emotions, and when in Germany the distinction of creeds was all but obliterated by the powerful current of Romanticism, it cannot be said that there were any distinguishable groups of Catholic opinions. Ecclesiastical literature was at a low ebb, and controversy was almost extinct. There was neither learning, nor leisure, nor definiteness enough to awaken the old discussions. They appeared again when peace and freedom were restored to religion, and literary activity revived, after 1814. In those days the memory of the revolutionary period and its unbelief was very vivid, and the ideas of the Holy Alliance found much favour with thinking Catholics. They dreamed of a league between Church and State, of a renovated loyalty identified with a revived religion, and of a combination between men of goodwill for the restoration of the great interests which had fallen before the common foe. It was hoped that religion might enable the State to protect society against the recurrence of such a catastrophe. There were many who relied for the realization of this scheme (half religious and half political) as much on the Czar as on the Pope. The strong practical purpose by which it was animated is one leading characteristic of the literary movement which followed. Another is, that its writers were chiefly laymen; for the problems of the day were rather social than ecclesiastical, and even theology was treated with a view to the State. Long before the French Revolution the schools of theology had generally declined, and then, for five and twenty years, ecclesiastical studies were almost everywhere suspended. No successors had sprung up to the great scholars who had lived far into the pontificate of Pius VI; and many of the most cultivated priests on the Continent were deeply marked with Rationalism. At the Restoration the clergy, as a body, were not in a condition to take an active part in literature. Their place in the van was supplied by laymen—often recent converts, seldom trained scholars, and all rather inspired by the lessons of recent history than versed in the older details of theological discussion.

The foremost of these men was the Comte de Maistre. During the evil days he had made himself a name by two political pamphlets, written with the power, the eloquence and depth of Burke, with more metaphysical ability than Burke possessed, but without his instinct for political truth, or his anxious attention to the voice of history. In these pamphlets he had laid down some of the most important principles of civil government, and had explained with special success the necessity of aristocracy for the establishment of freedom. His writings had displayed extensive knowledge, earnest faith, a pointed wit, and an almost unexampled union of common sense with love of paradox and passion for extremes. After his return from St Petersburg, in the first years of the Restoration, he published several works in rapid succession, which have earned for him perhaps the highest place next to Pascal among laymen who have defended religion without the advantage of a theological education.

Society, said M. de Maistre, has been ruined by the want of faith, or by its equivalent in the civil order, the weakness of authority. It is necessary that mankind should be taught the duty of unconditional obedience, the merit of suffering, the sinfulness of self-assertion, the peril of liberty, and the evil of securities against the abuse of power.[2] Tyranny, poverty and slavery are not the faults of society, but the penalties of sin. Monarchy is the only legitimate form of government, because monarchy alone gives the nations a master, and places the sovereign under the restraint of conscience. It is his duty to promote as well as to preserve religion, to suppress error and sinlike crime, and to defend the faith by prescribing knowledge [3] and encouraging superstition.[4]

---

[2] "Il est vrai au fond que les peuples ont des droits, mais non celui de les faire valoir ou d'en punir la violation par la force" (*Correspondance Diplomatique*, ii, 36). "Le dogme catholique, comme tout le monde sait, proscrit tout espèce de révolte sans distinction; et pour défendre ce dogme nos docteurs disent d'assez bonne raisons, philosophiques même, et politiques" (*Du Pape*, p. 161).

[3] "Les inconvénients inévitables de la science, dans tous les pays et dans tous les lieux, sont de rendre l'homme inhabile à la vie active, qui est la vraie vocation de l'homme; de le rendre souverainement orgueilleux, enivré de lui-même, et de ses propres idées, ennemi de toute subordination, frondeur de toute loi et de toute institution, et partisan-né de toute innovation. Elle tend donc nécessairement à tuer l'esprit public et à nuire à la société" (*Quatre Chapitres inédits sur la Russie*, 1859, p. 38). "Restreindre de même la science, de plusieurs manières, savoir . . . en supprimant tout enseignement public des connaissances qui peuvent être livrée au goût et au moyens de chaque particulier; comme l'histoire, la géographie, la métaphysique, la morale, la politique, le commerce" (*ibid.*, p. 147). "Il y a dans la science, si elle n'est pas entièrement subordonnée

In these writings de Maistre unquestionably relinquished or modified some of his earlier opinions. There was no longer that love of freedom which he had opposed to the violence of the Revolution, or that admiration for England with which he had been inspired by her long resistance to Napoleon.[5] His ideal state had become more centralized, his sovereign more absolute, his nobility less independent, his people less free. The dread of revolutionary despotism had given place to a horror of constitutionalism. This was the current of the hour. But it inspired de Maistre with the theory which is the chief cause of his celebrity, a theory new to the Catholic thinkers of his time. Catholicism, he maintained, inculcates the absolute authority of the sovereign, and forbids resistance even to the gravest wrong.[6] This

---

aux dogmes nationaux, quelque chose de caché qui tend à ravaler l'homme, et à le rendre surtout inutile ou mauvais citoyen. . . . Il faut subordonner toutes nos connaissances à la religion, croire fermement qu'on étudie en priant; et surtout lorsque nous nous occupons de philosophie rationnelle, ne jamais oublier que toute proposition de métaphysique, qui ne sort pas comme d'elle-même d'un dogme chrétien, n'est et ne peut pas être qu'un coupable extravagance" (*Soirées de St Petersburg*, ii, 221, 223).

[4] "Je crois que la superstition est un ouvrage avancé de la religion qu'il ne faut pas détruire, car il n'est pas bon qu'on puisse venir sans obstacle jusqu'au pied du mur, en mesurer la hauteur et planter les échelles. . . . Croyez-vous que les abus d'une chose divine n'aient pas dans la chose même certaines limites naturelles, et que les inconvénients de ces abus puissent jamais égaler le danger d'ébranler la croyance?" (*Soirées de St Petersburg*, ii, 234).

[5] "On a bien dit: 'Il faut des lois fondamentales, il faut une constitution'. Mais qui les établira, ces lois fondamentales, et qui les fera exécuter? Le corps ou l'individu qui en aurait la force serait souverain. . . . L'Angleterre seule a pu faire quelque chose dans ce genre; mais sa constitution n'a point encore subi l'épreuve du temps. . . . Qu'arrivera-t-il? Je l'ignore; mais quand les choses tourneraient comme je le désire, un exemple isolé de l'histoire prouverait peu en faveur des monarchies constitutionelles, d'autant que l'expérience universelle est contraire à cet example unique" (*Du Pape*, pp. 159, 160). Ten years earlier he had said: "La constitution est l'ouvrage des circonstances . . . l'unité la plus compliquée et le plus bel équilibre des forces politiques qu'on ait jamais vu dans le monde" (*Essai sur le Principe Générateur des Constitutions Politiques*, p. 16).

[6] "Si l'on veut s'exprimer exactement, il n'y a point de souveraineté limitée; toutes sont absolues et infaillibles, puisque nulle part il n'est permis de dire qu'elles se sont trompées. . . . Elle est toujours et partout

unity and absolutism of authority spring from the very nature of religion, and are not only necessary for the State, but essential to the Church. Civil society cannot subsist without the maxim that the king can do no wrong. The Church requires the same privilege for the Pope. Absolute infallibility in the one is a corollary of despotism in the other.[7] It is also its remedy. Denying to the people any part in the vindication of right, de Maistre transferred to the Pope alone the whole duty of moderating kings. Thus the argument for the Papal power flowed into two streams from one source—the theory of civil absolutism. Reasoning by analogy, the Pope ought to be an arbitrary ruler within the Church; while, by contrast, his power was extended over States, and the security of civil rights was to be sought in the completeness of hierarchical despotism.

Whoever studies the writings of de Maistre will find far more than the memorable theory by which he became the founder of a new school of Ultramontanism. He will find some of the best and wisest things ever written on religion and society—a generous one, an admirable style of discussion, and the Catholic system presented often in the noblest manner. These qualities have exercised a powerful and salutary influence on all the succeeding schools of Catholic thought; and some who differ most widely from de Maistre on the questions which he made more particularly his own owe much to his writings. But it was only in the course of years, as the publication of eight posthu-

---

absolue, sans que personne ait le droit de lui dire qu'elle est injuste ou trompée" (*Du Pape*, p. 165). "Il faudroit que les souverains protestants eussent perdu le sens pour ne pas apercevoir l'insigne folie qu'ils font, de soutenir une religion qui pose en maxime le jugement particulier et la souveraineté du peuple, contre une autre religion qui soutient que contre notre légitime souverain, fût-il même un Neron, nous n'avons d'autre droit que celui de nous laisser couper la tête en lui disant respectueusement la vérité" (*Correspondance Diplomatique*, ii, 132).

[7] "Il ne peut y avoir de société humaine sans gouvernement, ni de gouvernement sans souveraineté, sans infallibilité; et ce dernier privilège est si absolument nécessaire, qu'on est forcé de supposer l'infallibilité, même dans les souverainetés temporelles (où elle n'est pas), sous peine de voir l'association se dissoudre. L'église ne demande rien de plus que les autres souverainetés" (*Du Pape*, p. 147).

mous volumes defined more clearly and more amply the character of his mind, that men learned to separate the man from his
peculiar theory. At first, all the merits of his system and his style
served but to give attractiveness and splendour to the theory of
the Papal power, which became the symbol of a party, and gave
the impulse to an important movement. No distinct view had
yet been put forward so positively or so brilliantly; and its
influence on contemporaries was extraordinary. It appeared to a
large class of persons as the only perfect form of Catholicism.
Everything that fell short of it seemed to them treason or
surrender. To limit the Holy See in Church or State was to
attack religion, and open the door to Jansenism, Protestantism,
and infidelity. Inasmuch as authority was especially odious to
irreligious Catholics, it became the part of good Catholics to
vindicate it with at least a corresponding zeal. All qualification
was taken to be opposition, and was deemed to imply a secret
aversion.

Since the question raised by de Maistre was one of fact, and
not of speculation, its solution was to be found not in theory but
in history. For, as the standing object of his school was to
establish a prejudice favourable to the supreme authority of the
Church in every period, their labour would be in vain if it could
be shown that the pontifical power had manifested itself in
various degrees in various times, or that there had been serious
vicissitudes in its spirit. Here an entrance was found for a
personal element new to ecclesiastical literature, which caused
the discussion of character to become more prominent than the
discussion of principle. Those who defended a particular view
of canon law, history, or politics with orthodoxy obliged themselves to treat all objections to this view as blasphemies against
religious truth; whatever was inconsistent with the theory was
regarded as really equivalent to a denial of the continuity of
tradition.[8] Large tracts of history which had formally involved

---

[8] On February 5, 1820, Lamennais wrote to de Maistre on the publication of his book, *Du Pape:* "En défendant l'autorité du saint-siège, vous
défendez celle de l'église, et l'autorité même des souverains, et toute
vérité et tout ordre. Vous devez donc compter sur de nombreuses con-

no theological interest became the arena of controversy; and their adverse and telling facts were only in the brief to be explained away and amplified respectively. De Maistre had given the example of discussing these questions with the arts of advocacy. His rhetorical dexterity enabled him to put wit in the place of argument, to disconcert adversaries by spirited retaliation, or baffle them by ingenuously dissembling or boldly denying whatever might serve their purpose. Many followed him in good faith, fully persuaded that nothing opposed to the theory could be true; but he had other followers who were not in good faith.

The long opposition of science and philosophy to religion had brought their methods into a discredit which the practice of the writers of that time by no means tended to dissipate. Men doubted whether scientific method could be really reconciled to religious truth; and it was felt that so ambiguous a weapon was least unsafe when least used. Men suspected that it was altogether inadequate to give certain demonstration of the truths with which it is conversant,[9] and without the aid of external authority. On this idea a theory was founded which seemed at first to support de Maistre's argument for the Papal authority, though it ended in decided contradiction of it. Lamennais, the author of this new philosophy, taught that no evidence amounts to certain demonstration unless confirmed by the universal consent of the general testimony; and that the organ of this universal reason is the Holy See. This principle, laid down in the second volume of the *Essai sur l'Indifférence,* led necessarily to the rejection of that theory of the absolute authority of the civil power which had furnished de Maistre

---

tradictions; mais il est beau de les supporter pour une telle cause. L'opposition des méchants console le coeur de l'homme de bien, il se sent plus séparé d'eux, et des lors plus près de celui à qui le jugement appartient et à qui restera la victoire."

[9] "Je n'irai point tenter follement d'escaler l'enceinte salutaire dont la sagesse divine nous a environnés; je suis sûr d'être de cet côté sur les terres de la vérité: qui m'assure qu'au delà (pour ne point faire de supposition plus triste) je ne me trouverai pas sur les domaines de la superstition?" (*Soirées de St Petersburg,* ii, 227).

with the analogy he used with such effect. If the infallibility of universal opinion is the origin of certainty, it is the source of authority; and the Holy See is therefore exalted over princes as much as over philosophers and thinkers. When, therefore, the French monarchy became odious to the people, and, at the same time, hostile to the Church, Lamennais denied its right, and appealed against it to the people as the source of power, and to the Pope as their organ. This was the spirit of the *Avenir*,[10] and it still largely tinges the political Catholicism of France. The doctrine of the impotence of reason was wrought into a system by Father Ventura, and was adopted by the Traditionalists, who, on the plea of Rationalism, anathematized all the writers who did most honour to the clergy of France. During many years Traditionalism preserved an organ in the journal of the indefatigable M. Bonnetty, until it was condemned, and the claims of reason vindicated both by Pope and Council.[11]

This theory of the vanity of science applied to history made it as uninteresting as an old almanac, and at the same time as arbitrary, unreal and unreliable as the annual prophecy of a

---

[10] The Abbé Gerbet wrote in the number of February 21, 1831: "L'ordre légal peut cesser de la même manière qu'il a été établi, c'est-à-dire par voie de consentement."

[11] The decree of the Council of Amiens, quoted by Father Gratry, explains better than any description the extremes to which the school had come: "Dum rationalismum impugnant, caveant etiam, ne rationis humanae infirmitatem quasi ad impotentiam reducant. Hominem, rationis exercitio fruentem, hujus facultatis applicatione posse percipere aut etiam demonstrare plures veritates metaphysicas et morales . . . constanti scholarum catholicarum doctrina compertum est. Falsum est, rationem solvendis istis quaestionibus esse omnino impotentem, argumenta quae proponit nihil certe exhibere et argumentis oppositis ejusdem valoris destrui. Falsum est, hominem has veritates naturaliter admittere non posse, quin prius per actum fidei supernaturalis revelationi divinae credat." The *Congregatio Indici* defined the doctrine of the Church against the Traditionalists in four sentences, of which this is the second: "Ratiocinatio Dei existentiam, animae spiritualitatem, hominis libertatem cum certitudine probare potest. Fides posterior est revelatione, proindeque ad probandam Dei existentiam contra atheum, ad probandam animae rationalis spiritualitatem ac libertatem contra naturalismi ac fatalismi sectatorem allegari convenienter nequit."

new one. It made the teaching of the Church the sole foundation and test of certain knowledge, a criterion alike of the records of history and of the arguments of unbelief. It recognized no means of ascertaining the truth of facts, or the authenticity of documents, sufficiently trustworthy to interfere with theological opinions. It supposed the part of malice and ignorance to be so large, and the powers of unaided reason so minute, that ecclesiastical authority could be the only guide, even in matters foreign to its immediate domain—the next place given to the presumptive authority of the more probable opinion. Otherwise, it was thought, the constant fluctuations of profane science would oblige theology to obey all its movements, and religion would ape the mobility which passion, ignorance, and error impart to literature. Hence it was held impossible to verify the facts of religious history, or to argue from the monuments of tradition. Catholics had no basis of criticism in common with others. Every Protestant was *principia negans*. In all likelihood quite as strong a case might be made out against the Catholic view of the past as in its favour, and no appeal to history was expected to confound adversaries or to confirm belief. The immediate consequence was to set aside historical study as useless or dangerous; and that courageous logician, M. Veuillot, affirmed ignorance to be quite as serviceable as knowledge for the vindication of truth, and urged that no time should be wasted in exchanging the one for the other.

A particular suspicion rested on history, because, as the study of facts, it was less amenable to authority and less controllable by interest than philosophical speculation. In consequence partly of the denial of historical certainty, and partly of the fear of it, the historical study of Dogma in its original sources was abandoned, and the dialectical systematic treatment preferred. Theology became almost entirely scholastic. It was regarded as complete, not susceptible of development, looking backwards and not forwards, more interested in the vindication of authoritative names than in the cultivation of those original studies which are needed for its advance. This movement, which for a time had its centre at Rome, found its most brilliant expression in Father Kleutgen's work on the theology of the old times.

The principle of de Maistre's philosophy which is common to works so discordant in spirit and so dissimilar in execution as the *Essai sur l'Indifférence,* Ventura's *Traditionalism,* and the *Theologie der Vorzeit* of the accomplished Roman Jesuit, has displayed itself in politics as vividly as in theology. The same dread of an outward independent criterion, which causes divines to reject the facts of history, leads canonists, in disputes involving civil questions, to turn from the State to the sole and supreme authority of the Church. Building upon the weakness of human reason and the malice of the outer world, the men of this school arrived at the opinion that, as civil interests are subservient to those of religion, the civil law is necessarily subject to that of the Church. At the same time they could not admit that the interests of the Church might be sacrificed to the letter of her own law. They concluded that no merely political institution, no legislation which is so indirectly connected with the moral law that it can assume various forms in various Christian states, could be permitted to stand in the way of considerations of religious advantage. In canon law, they said, the Holy See can dispense from any obligation which is not of divine right. Why should civil law be more sacred? If the Pope can permit a brother and sister to marry for the sake of expediency, how can any opinion of political right and wrong be allowed to supersede that highest argument? They held, therefore, that no spiritual advantage could be surrendered in obedience to the variable legislation of any local power. Hence arose a system very remote from the servile loyalty of the Gallican Church, a system which assumed on many occasions a liberal and sometimes a revolutionary appearance. But if no civil authority was sacred beyond the limit of religious expediency, no civil rights could enjoy a higher immunity. The Church could make no distinction between political freedom and wrong, but must unite with that cause whose alliance promised most profit. The standard of political duty was held to exist for those only who recognized no higher law; those who did so felt no difficulty in bestowing an equal and consistent admiration for Gregory XVI, rebuking the Archbishop of Paris for his legitimist sympathies, and for Pius IX, supporting the Neapolitan Bourbons. Thus it was made to appear that Catholics are not guided in public life by sentiments which constitute the honour of other men, and that they absolutely repudiate political principle. A feeling of distrust and of contempt was thereby engendered in the minds of governments and nations. The religion which suffered by this conduct was appealed to by one party, and condemned by the other, as countenancing it. Catholic parties did duty for the Church, and eagerly transferred to her the obloquy which they themselves had incurred.

This theory, which has so much affected both theology and politics, has exercised a still deeper influence on the treatment of history; and in this field it has passed more gradually through the successive steps which have led to its complete display. First, it was held, the interests of religion, which are opposed to the study of history, require that precautions should be taken to make it innocuous where it cannot be quite suppressed. If it is lawful to conceal facts or statements, it is equally right to take out their sting when they must be brought forward. It is not truth, but error, which is suppressed by this process, the object of which is to prevent a false impression being made on the minds of men. For the effects of these facts or statements is to prejudice men against the Church, and to lead them to false conclusions concerning her nature. Whatever tends to weaken this adverse impression contributes really to baffle a falsehood and sustain the cause of truth. The statement, however true in its own subordinate place, will only serve to mislead in a higher order of truth, where the consequences may be fatal to the conscience and happiness of those who hear it without any qualification. Words, moreover, often convey to the uninstructed mind ideas contrary to their real significance, and the interpretation of facts is yet more delusive. Put the case of a Protestant sincerely seeking to be instructed, and earnestly inquiring into the spirit and practices of the Church, who perhaps on the very threshold of conversion, when the dogmatic difficulties are over and the longing for the sacraments is awakened, asks if it be true that the spiritual rulers of the Church have been sometimes men of scandalous lives, or whether Catholicism has encouraged or ordained persecution. If he finds the inquiry answered affirmatively in Catholic books, it is probable that he may be disappointed, or even disgusted, and that a few idle sentences of an indiscreet and superficial writer may undo the work of his conversion, and bring ruin to his soul. What end could that writer have in view that would bear comparison with the evil of such a consummation? Nothing obliged him to write at all, still less to write on so delicate a topic, and to handle it without reserve. If his words were true, they still deceived the reader who found in them the evidence of great defects in the Catholic system. The real duty of Catholics is not to gratify an idle curiosity or mere literary vanity, but to bring souls to Christ. The next step is to annul the effect of what has been said and what cannot be unsaid. This may be done in several ways. Reprisals are often successful; for in choosing between rival systems it is natural to compare them. But there are cases in which this argument does not apply, and minds on which it is without effect. Here there may be room for the simple contradiction—a favourite weapon with de Maistre. There have been many forgeries in the world, and it is natural to suspect that they proceed from enemies of truth. If documents on which the Church long relied are proved to be the works of fraud, it may reasonably be assumed that some of those on which her adversaries depend will ultimately meet with the same fate. And if the document is genuine, the writer may have been inspired with bad motives, or his text interpolated, or his information unauthentic. A great deal may be done in this way; and where there is really no room for doubt, it is still unnecessary to say so. For the object is not the discovery of objective truth, but the production of a right belief in a mind. When all is in vain—when the argument by reprisals, and the argument by denial, and the argument by insinuation of motives, or imputation of fraud, and last of all the argument by diversion, have failed, there is the last resource of admitting the fact and defending its righteousness. This may be done in two ways. The most common is to say that the only blame falls on those who shrink from heroic deeds, and judge them by the paltry cowardly standard of a selfish morality.[12] The other is to attribute acts which are hard to justify to the superior insight of those who committed them in the higher interests of religion, and their superiority to the conventional regulations which guide ordinary men. The examples of the Old Testament, the wisdom of the saints, the special illumination which God vouchsafes to those who rule His Church, may be appealed to in support of this argument. It is the duty of the son to cover the shame of his father; and the Catholic owes it to the Church to defend her against every adverse fact as he would defend the honour of his mother. He will not coldly examine the value of testimony, or concede any point because it is hard to meet, or assist with unbiased mind in the discovery of truth before he knows what its bearing may be. Assured that nothing injurious to the Church can be true, he will combat whatever bears an unfavourable semblance with every attainable artifice and weapon. Mindful of the guilt of those who scandalize the weak, or interpose between the waverer and the Church, and fully conscious that a lie may in some cases be the nearest approach to truth, he will allow no adverse statement to pass without contradiction, or without at least an antidote which may remove its danger. For there is but one thing needful; and all facts and all opinions are worthless except to minister to the salvation of men and the promotion of religion.

Those who traversed unconsciously the course which marks the genesis of these views, and arrived at the extreme we have

---

[12] M. de Falloux has shown, in his essay "Le Parti Catholique" (*Le Correspondant*, N.S. ii, 192), how this temper carried a party among the Catholics of France to defend the massacre of St Bartholomew and the revocation of the Edict of Nantes. He quotes the following characteristic passage from the *Univers*: "Aujourd'hui, avec les ridicules idées de liberté et de respect des opinions, avec l'opprobre public jeté sur l'inquisition et la crainte de la revivre, avec l'absence enfin de foi et de règle dans les consciences, peut-on supposer que les maires soupçonneront qu'ils ont en ce point quelque devoir à remplir."

indicated, were generally sincere at least in the belief that they were defending the cause of religion, and not merely their own interests or opinions; and they succeeded in communicating their belief to Protestants. The enemies of the Church supposed from their example that she could only be defended on the principle that the means are justified by the end; and this identification of her methods with those of a party within her led them to think that in exposing the latter they were tearing down a real outwork of Catholicism. They showed themselves expert in this, without discovering that they were really serving the Church which her own defenders were betraying. But those defenders were not conscious traitors, and honestly thought their own cause that of the Church. Hence they shrank from exposure and danger of scandal, and insisted that Catholics should not show them up, or renounce complicity with their arms, lest the world should lose all confidence in Catholic controversy, and come to believe that a cause so defended cannot be good. And when indignant men vindicated the Church from the suspicion which this conduct had brought upon her, they were accused of introducing discord into the sanctuary, of firing on their own troops, of exhibiting to adversaries the repulsive spectacle of internal discord in a Church whose mark is unity, of bringing sacred things before the incompetent judgement of the outer world. This consideration, and the fear of injuring influences that might be powerful for good, have restrained many from repudiating practices from which their hearts revolted.

The extracts which we are about to give in illustration of this spirit are taken chiefly from books of a popular kind, which have very little authority to lose. We might begin with Damberger's voluminous *History of the Middle Ages*. It would be hard to find in the whole range of Protestant literature since the Centuriators a more monstrous production. But the character of the work is so notorious that, in spite of the real erudition of the author, it has fallen into an obscurity which it is better not to disturb. A far cleverer writer, Wilhelm von Schütz, whose works were much read and admired twenty years ago, will supply us with an example of German aberrations in this direction. In the year 1845 he wrote a tract on the massacre of St Bartholomew, with a view to vindicate the Catholic cause from that long-standing imputation. He explains the case as follows: the massacre was planned for the purpose of ruining the Catholics, not the Huguenots; and its author was not the Catholic royal family, but the Protestant leader, Henry of Navarre, whose marriage to Margaret of Valois was part of a scheme to betray the Catholic Church and introduce a reactionary policy in favour of the Protestants. His accomplices were pseudo-Catholics acting in the Huguenot interest. The mistake is to suppose that the massacre was a blow aimed at the Huguenots, a conspiracy against them; it was a conspiracy in their favour . . . The court had sold Catholicism to Protestantism . . . Attention was to be diverted from the mixed marriage. Therefore the spectacle of a pretended Protestant massacre was instituted in order to deceive the Catholics.[13]

In short, it was a got-up thing, perfectly understood by the so-called victims, and a shameful deception on the unfortunate Catholics.

Whilst Schütz in Germany attributes the massacre to the Protestant interest, Rohrbacher in France shows that it proceeded from Protestant principles. His way of defending the Catholics is to lay the blame on Protestant doctrines. Judged by the

---

[13] "Darin beruht das Missverstehen der Geschichte, dass man sich einbildet die sogenannte Bluthochzeit sei ein Schlag gegen die Hugenotten, eine Verschwörung gegen sie gewesen: es war eine Verschwörung für die Hugenotten. Der Hof hatte den Katholizismus an den Protestantismus verkauft und gab dafür den betrogenen Katholiken ein Feuerwerk, das scheinen sollte einen Schlag gegen die Hugenotten, statt mit Raketen, mit Blut zu feiern. Das Wesentliche lag in dem Katholisch-Protestantischen Beilager. Dies sollte niemand sehen: von ihm wollte man die Blicke abwenden. Deshalb ward das Feuerwerk eines Protestantische sein sollenden Blutbades abgebrannt, dessen Prasseln die Katholiken zu täuschen die Bestimmung hatte. Die sogenannte Bluthochzeit war eine Anstiftung von Pseudo-Katholiken zu Gunsten einer Katholisch-Hugenottischen Reaktion. Dies geschah nur um die Katholiken zu täuschen und sie glauben zu machen, das, was in hugenottischem Interesse geschahen war, sei zugunsten der Katholiken verübt worden" (*Die aufgehellte Bartholomäusnacht,* pp. 11, 25, 31, 34).

Reformers' standard, "the massacre was a divine act, which deserves our respect and admiration"; and "Charles IX had a right to do what he did, not only as king but as private individual; and any one may go and do likewise, whenever he has the power and inclination." [14]

The sixteenth century offers many tempting opportunities for manipulations of this kind. Rohrbacher's tone and manner may be gathered from what he says of Queen Elizabeth. Speaking of her refusal to marry, he says: "L'histoire remarque en effet qu'elle n'a pas eu un mari, mais plus d'un: Lingard en nomme jusqu'à huit." [15] The heading of the paragraph where this occurs, in which the author follows a notorious calumny of Cobbett, runs thus: "La papesse Elizabeth, avec ses maris et ses bâtards, ses emportements et sa tyrannie." Rohrbacher is still more unscrupulous in dealing with the death of Henry III. He was stabbed by a Dominican, and fell crying that he had been murdered by "ce méchant moine." For fear of scandal the historian says not a word of all this. Jacques Clément had only been "educated in a Dominican monastery"; he was carried away by Protestant principles, which justify his act, and Rohrbacher insinuates that he defied the authority of the Pope, and was at heart a Huguenot. So that the reader would never learn that the regicide was a Dominican, but might be led to suppose that he was in fact a crypto-Calvinist. [16]

---

[14] "D'après la croyance des huguenots et de leurs patriarches Luther et Calvin, que Dieu opère en nous le mal comme le bien, c'est une opération divine qui mérite nos respects et notre admiration. D'après le principe fondamental du protestantisme, que chacun n'a d'autre règle ni d'autre juge que soi-même, Charles IX avait droit de faire ce qu'il a fait, non seulement comme roi, mais encore comme particulier; et à chacun il est permis d'en faire autant, dès qu'il en a l'envie et la puissance" (*Histoire Universelle de L'Église*, xxiv, 640).

[15] *Histoire Universelle de L'Église*, xxiv, 583.

[16] "Il fut tué la veille par Jacques Clément, né au village de Sorbonne, près de Sense, élevé au couvent des Dominicains de cette ville, et âgé alors de vingt-deux ans. Les assistants le mirent en pièces sur l'heure même. Il s'était porté à ce crime par de prétendue révélations. D'après le principe fondamental du Protestantisme, que chacun n'a de règle et de juge pour sa conscience que soi-même, Clément avait droit de faire ce qu'il a fait. D'après cet autre principe de Calvin et de Luther, que Dieu

In comparison with the systematic deceitfulness of Rohrbacher, the arts of Audin appear innocent. He is partial, unjust, and very often ill-informed or misguided, but he is rarely guilty of wilful mendacity. No man is honest who refuses to censure vice in persons of exalted station; but there is after all only a qualified dishonesty in such passages as that on the election of Alexander VI: "In these difficult times a man of the character of Alexander might well be regarded as an instrument of Providence. There is nothing, therefore, but what is quite natural in his election." Audin's irresolute wavering between straightforwardness and falsehood is fairly illustrated by his critical remark on the authority of Burchard: "Nous voudrions bien savoir comment on doit s'en rapporter aveuglément au Protestant, qui s'est chargé de déchiffrer ce journal." [17] He knew perfectly well that MSS. of the Journal abound—there are at least half a dozen at Paris alone—and they have often been consulted by historians; but he preferred to take advantage of the badness of the published text to excuse his refusal to avail himself of the authority of the journalist.

M. Nicolas, one of the most popular Catholic writers in France, in a volume written for the purpose of repudiating the co-operation proposed by M. Guizot for the defence of society against the principles of the Revolution, has been obliged to speak of the moral and social influence of the Protestant religion. Wishing to show that Luther encouraged polygamy, he quotes the Reformer's well-known answer to Brück, which, though sufficiently discreditable, is not enough so for M. Nicolas: "Luther lui répondit par cet oracle vraiment delphien: 'Il m'est impossible, en vertu de l'Écriture Sainte, de défendre à qui ce soit de prendre plusieurs femmes en même temps; mais je ne voudrais pas être le premier à introduire cette louable

opère en nous le mal comme le bien, le régicide de Jacques Clément était une action divine. Il est criminel comme Catholique d'avoir agi en Huguenot, pour mettre la main, lui particulier, sur un roi, sur le chef d'une nation, sans le jugement ni l'ordre d'aucun tribunal supérieur à ce roi et à cette nation" (*ibid.*, xxiv, 655).

[17] *Leon X*, i, 157, 304.

coutume chez les chrétiens,'" [18] Here every word is omitted by which Luther expresses his real sentiment on the matter; another is coolly introduced which converts an expression of dislike and disapproval into a positive recommendation, and the words "nollem primo introduci" are insidiously misinterpreted. Although the passage is well known, we must quote it for the purpose of comparison: "Ego sane fateor, me non posse prohibere, si quis plures vult uxores ducere, nec repugnat Sacris literis; verum tamen apud Christianos id exempli nollem primo introduci, apud quos decet etiam ea intermittere, quae licita sunt, pro vitando scandalo, et pro honestate vitae." [19]

It is recorded that when Papabroch, at the beginning of his long career as a Bollandist, visited Rome, and explained to the Pope the scheme of that great undertaking, Alexander VII expressed delight at hearing that there were methods by which the authentic Lives of the Saints might be distinguished from spurious fabrications. The art of criticism was then just beginning; it soon made progress in the hands of Mabillon, Ruinart, and Tillemont; and, in the perfection it has now attained, it is one of the surest defences of the Catholic system. But to writers of the school we have described its control is naturally unwelcome; for it prevents the arbitrary selection of facts and authorities, interferes with the perfect freedom of speech, and establishes something different from convenience as a test of truth. They therefore reject its laws, not only on principle, but in detail and in practice, and deliberately return to the traditions of a period when the means of distinguishing truth from falsehood in ecclesiastical literature did not exist. Dom Guéranger, the learned Abbot of Solesmes, is the most outspoken of these systematic adversaries of modern knowledge. The critical spirit of the close of the seventeenth century, in which the members of the orders took the lead, and in which they were followed by the most learned men among the Jesuits as well as the Jansenists, sprang, he says from a spirit of party, and be-

---

[18] *Du Protestantisme et de toutes les Hérésies dans leur Rapport avec la Socialisme*, p. 560.

[19] *Luther's Briefe*, ed. de Wette, ii, 459.

longs legitimately to the infidel Germans. If we would avoid scepticism, we must revise the canons of critical science, and we shall recover much contested literature.[20] On these principles, Dom Guéranger proceeds to rehabilitate many rejected documents and to revive exploded legends, such as the baptism of Constantine by Pope Sylvester. Before long we shall probably hear of writers who defend the authenticity of the Donation of Constantine, and the works of the Areopagite, and who will compensate for their credulity by an equally wilful rejection of authentic works; for the opposite exaggeration of literary scepticism and literary credulity are manifestations of the same reckless spirit.

Dom Guéranger's denial of the principles of science has necessarily conducted him to a position of hostility to all those who understand the manner in which learning serves religion. In particular, he has attacked the most accomplished layman among the French Catholics and the most eminent divine of the French clergy; and he has elicited replies from both. We will quote a passage from that of the Prince de Broglie, because it describes so accurately the method of the school of which Dom Guéranger is perhaps the most learned representative. He had assailed the *History of the Fourth Century* in three articles in the *Univers*, which were the beginning of those *Essays on Naturalism* from which we have already quoted. M. de Broglie says: "In the first and second articles I am a timorous Christian, who, to please the philosophers, attenuates dogmas, dissembles and tones down miracles, loves to give to the facts of the Gospel and Church history a natural character and a rational interpre-

---

[20] "On commence à se douter déjà que l'entrainement et l'esprit de parti ont été pour quelque chose dans la rénovation pour ainsi dire complète qui s'opéra, vers la fin du XVIIe siècle, dans la science de l'antiquité ecclésiastique. Les principes critique qui prévalurent alors, et que les écoles incroyantes de l'Allemagne appliquent de si bon coeur aux évangiles même, ont l'inconvénient de conduire logiquement au pyrrhonisme historique; les esprits sensés se trouvent donc réduits à les soumettre à l'examen; et l'on ne peut nier qu'il n'y ait là un profit tout clair pour la science, en même temps qu'un secours pour la religion et la société, qui ne sauraient s'accommoder du scepticisme" (*Essai sur le Naturalisme Contemporain*, i, 227).

tation. In the third, on the contrary, I am transformed into a blind enemy of reason, who denies it even the power of demonstrating the existence of God, and thus falls under the liberal decisions of the Church, so clearly confirmed by a recent document. By turns, I have passed so severe a judgement on the ancient nations as to cast doubts on the goodness of God, and on the other hand, have carried indulgence so far as completely to excuse idolatry. Either I am guilty of the most contrary things, or everything will serve to accuse me." [21]

While the Prince de Broglie treats his assailant with great consideration, the reply of Monseigneur Maret to the attack on his work on the Dignity of Human Reason and the Necessity of Divine Revelation strikes more vigorously home. Dom Guéranger had accused him of asserting the absolute necessity of revelation, and the impotence of the human reason. He was reminded that M. Maret teaches only the moral necessity of revelation, and that these words are in the heading of the chapter which he criticized. To this he replied that he had, indeed, seen the words in the summary, but that he had not paid regard to them, because they were contradicted—not by the text, but—by the title of the book.[22] Monseigneur Maret adds some touches to the description of the methods given by the Prince de Broglie: "I have shown that, in order to avenge some imaginary conces-

---

[21] "Réponse aux Attaques du R. P. Guéranger," *Questions de Religion et d'Histoire*, ii, 221.

[22] "Quand mon honorable ami M. l'Abbé Hugonin, s'étonnant d'une accusation que rien ne justifie, rappelle à D. Guéranger que je soutiens uniquement la nécessité morale de la révelation, et qu'il a pu lire ces mots dans le sommaire même du chapitre qu'il critique, que répond M. l'Abbé de Solesme? Il a vu en effet, dit-il, ces mots dans le sommaire; mais il n'en a pas tenu compte, parce qu'ils sont contredits par le titre du livre, qui porte, sans correctif, *Nécessité de la Révélation*. Est-il permis à un homme grave, à un religieux, à un prêtre, lorsqu'il s'agit de l'honneur d'un autre prêtre, de recourir à de pareilles échappatoires? Dans presque tous les traités de la religion, ne trouvons-nous pas un chapitre intitulé 'De necessitate revelationis', sans autre explication?" (Lettre de M. l'Abbé Maret, Doyen de la Faculté de Théologie de Paris à Nos Seigneurs les Evêques de France sur les attaques dirigées contre son livre: *Dignité de la Raison Humaine et Necessité de la Révélation Divine*, par le R. P. D. Guéranger, 1858, p. 15).

sions to a separatist philosophy, and perhaps also unconsciously gratifying the jealousies of party spirit, Dom Guéranger consents to misrepresent, mutilate, and suppress my texts. He makes me say exactly the contrary of what I say; and if his quotation had been entirely faithful, he could not have made himself the accuser of my book. Carried away by controversy, he goes so far as to affirm absolute propositions which, if so stated, would deserve severe censure, and would be reached by pontifical condemnations." [23]

Nothing is more characteristic of the spirit of Dom Guéranger's writing than his repudiation of the liberty of conscience, and his denial of the inclination of the Church to freedom. M. de Broglie had written: "C'est donc avec la liberté et non avec le pouvoir qu'est l'alliance fructueuse et naturelle de l'Église. Elle a été autrefois le plus éclairé des pouvoirs, elle doit être aujourd'hui la plus pure et la plus regulière des libertés." Perhaps this may not be a very philosophical or exact statement; but to Dom Guéranger it appears as an insult to the Church: "De quel droit osez-vous ainsi dégrader celle qui n'a été élevée à la dignité d'Épouse d'un Dieu que pour régner avec lui?" [24] And in asserting the rights of the Church he is careful to assert his enmity to freedom: "Est-ce que par hasard l'Église serait exclue de la liberté, par la raison que l'erreur n'y a pas droit?" [25]

In this matter of the freedom of conscience Father Perrone, the last writer whom we shall cite among the representatives of the unscrupulous school, speaks with much greater judgement. But as a historical question he treats it with as little reverence for the moral obligations of literature as an Orangeman could have shown. Whilst the State punishes open non-conformity, but is compelled to respect concealed dissent, the peculiarity of the penalties imposed by the Church consists in their being directed against the sin of the individual, not against the danger to society; hence they may be incurred by thought as well as by word or deed. The object of the Church is always the conver-

[23] *Ibid.*, p. 23.
[24] *Essais*, Preface, p. xxxv.
[25] *Ibid.*, p. xvii.

sion of the sinner, whilst that of the State is simply his exclusion or suppression. Therefore it has always been deemed unnatural that capital punishment for heresy should be inflicted by the priesthood; and those who, like de Maistre [26] or Balmez, have defended the Inquisition as a political tribunal in Spain, have denied that persecution ever raged in Rome. Father Perrone boldly denies that the Church proceeded against private opinions, and says that executions for heresy were rare or unknown in Rome.[27]

In his catechism of the Protestant religions he used arguments of the most calumnious kind in order to turn the mind of the people away from it—that the Reformers were men whose private lives were infamous; that Calvin died of a shameful disease, blaspheming and invoking the devil; and that the reform of morals and discipline commonly attributed to the Council of Trent, was proceeding prosperously, and the Church improving daily, when the Reformation interrupted the reform.[28] Such language, if it was not intended to mislead uneducated persons, would read like a satire on the Council of the Lateran.

[26] "Jamais le prêtre n'éleva d'échafaud; il y monte seulement comme martyr ou consolateur: il ne prêche que miséricorde et clémence; et sur tous les points du globe, il n'a versé d'autre sang que le sien. Voulez-vous de plus connaître, par l'expérience, le véritable esprit sacerdotal sur ce point essentiel? Étudiez-le dans le pays où le prêtre a tenue le sceptre ou le tient encore. . . . Assurément, c'est dans le gouvernement des pontifes que le véritable esprit du sacerdoce doit se montrer de la manière le moins équivoque" (*Lettres sur l'Inquisition Espagnole*, pp. 18, 21, 22).

[27] "La chiesa non ha mai proceduto contro le opinione finche questa rimaneano nella conscienza or nel cervello balzano di chi le aveva. In Roma poi o non v'e o appena v'e qualche rarissimo esempio di alcuno messo a molte per sola eresia" (*Catechismo intorno alla Chiesa Cattolica ad uso del Popolo*, pp. 93, 94).

[28] "Gia parecchi di essi ai tempi di Lutero reano tolti, ed altri scemati, e la riforma dei costumi e della disciplina si perfezionava oggidi, allorche risorsero quegli uomini ribelli contro la chiesa.—Tali sono i corifei del protestantismo, uomini cioe, che a detta di un protestante, erano tutti per la loro malvagita degni del capestro.—Calvino per ultimo mori disperato bestemmiando e invocando il diavolo, di una malattia la piu vergognosa, roso dai vermi" (*Catechismo intorno al Protestantismo ad uso del Popolo*, pp. 11, 23).

It would have been easy to quote from the writings of Monseigneur Gaume against the classics passages more striking than these; but his writings belong to a different movement, and the object of his attack is not knowledge in itself, but profane learning. "It is the devil," says Gregory the Great, "who takes away from certain persons the desire of mastering secular sciences, because he knows how much they serve us in religious questions." The *Vex Rongeur* was the prelude to a general attack on the pursuit of all learning that is not purely religious; but writers like Father Ventura and others whom we have quoted went beyond this, and thought that even the things of the Church cannot be the objects of scientific knowledge. There is but one step from the denial of certainty to the denial of truth; and the theory of the applicability of falsehood followed immediately on the theory of the utility of ignorance. By a similar process calumny was grafted on mendacity.

There are two things which it specially behooves every Catholic engaged in controversy to observe in his treatment of adversaries: that the discussion ought to be a means of converting them from error, instead of repelling them from truth by the fault of its defenders; and that no bitterness or personality should scandalize them by occasions of sin. The course enjoined by the Church is to win over opponents by considerate, gentle, generous, and affectionate treatment, joined to the most uncompromising and relentless exposure of their errors. If gentleness is a duty in the case of those errors against faith which are sinful in themselves, it is even more imperative where the error is a defect of knowledge, which, though indeed it may be a consequence of sin, can hardly be traced to its origin in the will. All Christians must in some measure feel and acknowledge this duty: but Catholics especially can judge of its importance by the horror with which the Church regards the giving of scandal, combined with her doctrine of exclusive salvation. It has been often disregarded in former disputes; but in our time a regular theory has been devised which inverts the law and renounces the Catholic spirit. Two paths appear to have led to this transition. One is the transfer of ecclesiastical language to another sphere. Those who have the sacramental power to bind and to loose, and who administer the ecclesiastical discipline, speak, by virtue of their office, in language of severity and commination even to individuals. It may fall within their province to utter the most solemn maledictions, and they may judge it probable that vehement denunciations will move to repentance those who are not utterly deaf to a voice that unites all the kinds of authority that belong to the father, the judge, and the king. Naturally, and almost imperceptibly, in an age when laymen exerted through the press an influence not less deep, and an authority often more extended, than the bishops themselves, they usurped the same weapons, spoke in the same tone, and affected to deal blows of equal weight. When the most illustrious prelates themselves, like the Bishops of Orléans and Mentz, mingled in the fray and placed themselves on equal terms with adversaries, it very easily happened that some of their privileges were forgotten by those who fought beside as well as against them, and that the thunder was sometimes imitated by those who could not wield the lightning.

Another course was more consciously followed with the same result. Catholics continually see things stated against the Church by educated and even learned men which, they are persuaded, cannot be sincerely believed. They are aware of the malignity of some, and are unable to credit the ignorance in which others persist with regard to Catholic matters. When, therefore, the inventions of men whose trade is lying are repeated by men whose profession is controversy, it is almost impossible to understand that ignorance can assume so closely the guise of wilful calumny. The plea of ignorance may be allowed in the case of Dr Cumming or Mr Whalley, but how can it be urged for Baron Bunsen, or M. Michelet, or Mr Buckle? It is scarcely possible for Catholics to avoid feeling aversion and contempt for men whom they conceive to be wilfully distorting truth; and therefore, instead of confining themselves to the refutation of falsehood, which they are persuaded their opponent does not desire, they endeavour to expose his iniquity. This temper of mind was gradually transferred from controversy with aliens to discussions among Catholics, where there was the new element of insubordination, to which the origins of errors might be attributed. A Catholic might reasonably be supposed to know the religion he had been taught from childhood, and in which he ought to have been more and more confirmed by the practices of piety. If he erred, there was at once a suspicion that he had neglected those practices; or that he was moved by the dislike of obedience to hold what was not held by his teachers; or that he had culpably turned away from the proper guides to hearken to the flattering seductions of hostile parties. In every such dispute a question of morality was directly at issue. Both antagonists could not be equally in harmony with the sentiment of authorities which both acknowledged. In casting off this blame from himself, each necessarily fixed it on the other as a prejudice against his virtue. But where a writer is persuaded that his adversary is persisting in his error insincerely, or from wrong motives, the triumph he seeks is not to convince but to convict him. He desires to produce an effect, not upon him, but upon the audience, which may be impressed by the exposure of the man, while he will be insensible to the confutation of his views. Therefore he strives less for truth than for effect, and abandons the argument in order to pursue the man. He tries to gain every advantage over him; and the best chance he has is to disturb his presence of mind by making him lose his temper. That which will irritate him most is most likely to make him expose himself and give an opening to reply. It would be too long to inquire how many things contributed to promote this habit: in some places, the want of that forbearance which public assemblies often engender between men subject in common to a local special disciplinary system; in others, the terror which anticipated or the temper which followed great social convulsions; in others, the extreme fierceness or perfidy of an infidel press. It was soon justified by theory; and in practice it seems becoming more general and more vehement.

To these combined causes it is due that a strong and vituperative opposition has been uniformly offered to the progress of Catholic thought. With scarcely one exception, all those who were most eminent in religious science have been denounced, by men not less zealous and devout than themselves, as the corrupters of doctrine and enemies of the Church; and the distance between the two parties was such as to justify a doubt as to their agreement in the same faith or in the same morality. This persecution of those who really advanced religious knowledge is, on the one hand, a natural and direct consequence of that common spirit which manifests itself in different ways in the philosophy of Ventura, the scholasticism of Kleutgen and Clemens, the politics of Donoso Cortés, the polemics of Veuillot, the educational theories of Gaume, and the historical method of Rohrbacher and Guéranger, and, on the other, the most characteristic symptom of the present condition of the Catholic Church. It assailed alike the two greatest thinkers among the Italian clergy, Rosmini and Gioberti, and in a less degree the best of their ecclesiastical historians, whom their knowledge of the Middle Ages prevents from becoming the supporters of things as they are—the Benedictine Tosti, the Oratorian Capecelatro, and the Dominican Marchese. In France it fell on the theoretical defenders of profane learning, like the Bishop of Orléans, and on the first Catholic authorities on theology and metaphysics, Monseigneur Maret and Father Gratry. The two foremost living divines in Germany, Döllinger and Kuhn, were accused in like manner—the one for his treatment of Church history, the other for a dogmatic method which seems heretical to the advocates of the scholastic theology; both alike for their theory of development. The few laymen out of Germany who occupy a rank in Catholic literature approaching that of the ecclesiastical leaders fared scarcely better. The Baron d'Eckstein was held a dreamer and an innovator, indifferent to the Dogma of the Church, for reasons such as in earlier times procured Gerbert and Bacon the reputation of wizards. The Prince de Broglie, while he was attacked by Donoso Cortés with the courteous arms of chivalry for preferring liberty to feudalism, incurred the ruder censures of Dom Guéranger because he recognized in history, besides the action of Providence, the operation of natural and secondary causes. Beyond the Atlantic the spirit is the same. When Dr Brownson, urged forward by his powerful and independent mind, emancipated himself from the narrow and intolerant school which in the first moments of his conversion he had been taught to consider the legitimate form of Catholic thought, his great services did not protect him from denunciations as violent as those which, in the immaturity of his Catholic ideas, he had heaped on Dr Newman. These, however, are difficulties in the way of improvement, which eminent men are able to overcome; and it is well that they should confront the obstacles which they alone can ultimately remove.

That which one class of Catholics sought by a sacrifice of truth on behalf of religion, others aimed at by making some scientific opinion the arbiter of doctrine. If there was a deliberate denial of the moral law, there was on the other hand an unconscious surrender of dogmatic truths. The philosophies of Hermes and Günther, Frohschammer's theory of the independence of speculation, and the extreme proposals of ecclesiastical reform made by Hirscher, before he became the adviser and defender of the Archbishop of Freiburg, are instances of such a failure resulting rather from confidence in human reason than from timid solicitude for the safety of God's Church. But the errors of these men proceed from no common principle, and in no wise agree together. The real antithesis to the spurious Ultramontanism that ramified from de Maistre into so many branches is to be found, not in the opposite errors, but in the true course which deflects on neither side.

The rise of the school we have considered depended, first, on the low ebb of scientific knowledge, and on its open hostility to religion, and, secondly, on the absence of any literary co-operation of Catholics with Protestants. Among its leaders there were men of great virtues and talents, and at least one man of genius; but there is not one to whom secular learning is really indebted. As they renounced more and more the results and spirit of modern science, they repelled Protestants, and ended by presenting religion in an aspect which did not entirely attract converts. The want of contact with men who believed in other religions left them in ignorance of real difficulties and of their true solution. To the opposite circumstance of familiarity with non-Catholic science we trace the formation of that Ultramontanism which we have described as the highest intellectual development of the Catholic system.

The prostration of religion on the Continent at the close of the last century was shared by the Protestants in an equal measure. But it was followed by a revived literary activity among them to which there is no parallel in modern history except the Revival of the fifteenth century, to which it bears a real resemblance. For, first, the intellectual movement which proceeded from Weimar to Jena, and Halle, and Heidelberg, and then to other German universities, like that of the Medicean age, obeyed no religious impulse, but was indifferent to doctrine. The Churches were not then either feared for their power or envied for their wealth; and Rationalism ignored, as it had no inducement to assail, them. Secondly, the mental exertion of the period of Goethe, like that of Erasmus, had no definite practical end to attain, no reward to earn but that of literary enjoyment, no mission to fulfil but that of satisfying the thirst for knowledge. Thirdly, the Revival of the nineteenth century, like that of the fifteenth, was distinguished principally by the recovery from oblivion of a forgotten age. But here the analogy is exhausted; for the effect of reviving antiquity was exactly contrary to that of the mediaeval restoration. The learning of the Renaissance was antiquarian. It overleapt a vast interval which it consigned to a complete neglect, in order to resuscitate an extinct society. It set up a remote ideal in all the arts of life, and bent its own civilization to fit the model it had disinterred. Therefore it predominated more in art than in science, because of its luxurious and idle temper, and it was also artificial, unnatural, imitative, and, like all imitators, arbitrary, and in theories of government absolute, and often revolutionary.

The character of the mediaeval Revival which is the distinctive achievement of the age in which we live was not antiquarian but historical. Its study was not of death, but of life—not of a world of ruins, but of that which is our own. Therefore its lesson was a lesson of continuity, not of sudden restoration of servile copying. It taught respect for the past, encouraged patriotic sentiments, and awakened the memory of hereditary rights. The study of national history, literature, and art was one of its more important results. This impulse was strongest in the north of Germany. There the feelings of men towards the Catholic Church were free from bitterness. She had been their companion in misfortune, had suffered under the same tyranny, and had been delivered by the same victories, and nowhere seemed to them formidable or oppressive. As the patriotic feeling carried back these thoughts to the preponderance of their country, the Reformation ceased to be the supreme glory of their nation, and the boundary of their retrospect. They recognized in its system one of the chief elements in their history, one of the most powerful influences over their ideas; but they also recalled a happier period of national greatness, when the princes of the Church were the best and the most beloved rulers of Germany. It was remembered that among the emperors who continued the long struggle with Rome there were many who could not be remembered by Germans with unmixed pride— that Henry IV and Henry VI were men of evil lives, Frederick I a tyrant, and Frederick II an alien; whilst the most devoted protectors of the Church—Charlemagne, St Henry, Otto the Great, Henry III, and Rudolph of Habsburg—were the greatest of the rulers of the Empire.

Men approached these studies with minds that had been trained in pursuits free from the temptations of party spirit, and from the influence of religious opinions. They came from the study of antiquity, which from the time of Heyne had its home in the schools of Germany; and they applied to the investigation of the mediaeval records the tone and method of classical philology. Other causes contributed to this indifferent rather than impartial temper. The union of the Prussian Protestants had expressed the ruling disregard of dogmatic definitions; and the vague theology which it established could not so heartily oppose Catholicism as a more consistent system. Something must also be attributed to the influence of the Hegelian philosophy on the Rationalists. The pantheism of that school, regarding all things alike as manifestations of the same universal nature, substituted the test of success, and even the order of succession, for the distinction of right and wrong. It was held that all religion is a form of truth, good of its kind; but that the law of life is progress, and the earlier is less perfect than the later. Therefore the advance constituted by Catholicism over the religions of antiquity was explained with the same curious interest as the progress, effected by the Reformation upon the mediaeval Church, or by the Philosophy of the Absolute on dogmatic Protestantism. The question of truth resolved itself into one of fact. Events were studied in their nature rather than in their character; and mankind was allowed to exhibit properties rather than qualities. The action of divine or human will was alike excluded; and accident was denied as well as morality. The Hegelians asserted the unbroken continuity of cause and effect, and held that all the phenomena of history are reasonable and intelligible. There ensued a kind of optimism very conducive to a dispassionate treatment of the past. Then out of the Hegelian philosophy arose the school of infidel and almost atheistic criticism, which ignored the dogmatic differences, and reserved its hardest blows for the foundations of Protestantism.

These causes did not indeed dissipate ignorance and prejudice, but they promoted a critical study of details, and prevented the interference of passion, or interest, or zeal. A school of historians arose who made it their business to write on the Middle Ages as they wrote on the Persian War; who spoke of the Church as they spoke of the Areopagus, and applied to the most obscure moments of her history those tests of credibility and authenticity which had been lavished on Herodotus and Livy. They had nothing of the spirit of panegyrists or accusers; but with all their learning, acuteness, and equity, most of these men were destitute of that faculty or experience which would have enabled them to understand the significance of religion. They understood, better than any Catholic writers before them, the outward action of the ecclesiastical organism, the moral, intellectual, and social influence of the Church; but they knew nothing of her religious character. They betrayed the same incapacity in the study of paganism; and their interpretation of the Hellenic theology was often as superficial as their explanation of Catholic doctrine. The most universal of all modern scholars believed that sacrifice originated in the idea that the gods required food; and the most learned of all writers on mythology explained its rise and power by the artifices of the priesthood.

Catholics were astonished to find that men who wrote with fairness, and often with admiration, of the Church, who made themselves the champions of her maligned or forgotten heroes, who threw a new splendour over the lives of saints, and gave meaning and reality to much that had seemed simply marvellous, cared nothing for the doctrines of the institution they laboriously defended, and repudiated with indignation the proposal to submit to its authority. Subsequently, under the influence of the rising Catholic literature, there were many conversions among the historians, such as Philipps, and Hurter, and Gfrörer; but the great schools of historians who wrote, like Luden and Menzel, under the influence of the War of Independence, the disciples of Eichhorn, who sought after legal antiquities, the pantheistic followers of Hegel, and the disciples of Ranke, who were the critics and commentators of the mediaeval texts, were generally as far as possible from the faith of the Church. But the method they pursued in the investigation of truth prevailed against all hostile inclinations; and the scientific spirit which arose out of the decomposition of Protestantism became in the hands of Catholics the safeguard of religious truth, and the most efficient weapon of controversy.

It is little more than thirty years since a class of writers arose so completely masters of the science of the age that they required to apply no other tests but its methods in order to judge of its results. The name of Ultramontane was given in consequence of their advocacy of the freedom of the Church against the civil power; but the characteristic of their advocacy was, that they spoke not specially for the interests of religion, but on behalf of a general principle which, while it asserted freedom for the Church, extended it likewise to other communities and institutions. Convinced of the efficacy and right of the fundamental precepts of politics, they knew that the Church desires nothing incompatible with them, and can no more require the suspension of political law than of the moral order from which it springs. Pursuing the strict analogy between science and polity, they carried out the same principle in the investigation of philosophy and history. In history, they sought to obtain for the ecclesiastical authority no immunity but that which it would enjoy from the promotion of political rights; and in philosophy, they provided no protection for religious doctrines but in the advancement of scientific truth.

The causes which in Germany gave rise to this school of Catholic apologists did not exist in Italy, and were but partially present in France. The overwhelming authority of de Maistre, and the subtle influence of the theories of Lamennais, were serious obstacles. The want of a severe scientific training was felt by many very accomplished men whose natural place would have been among the defenders of those higher principles. Yet if we compare the tone of the writings of Eckstein and Lenormant, Ozanam, Maret, and de Broglie, with the histories of the Counts Montalembert and Falloux, or with the works of Father Lacordaire, and Monseigneur Dupanloup, the difference between the more scientific and the more brilliant portion of the liberal party among French Catholics is very apparent. But it is due to the general spirit of this school of writers, rather than to the special character of its deeper scholars, that so large a portion of the higher intellects of France, formerly more or less separated from the Church, have during the last few years gradually approached her.[29] The strength of this school was necessarily confined to Germany, where its most eminent representatives were the divines Mohler, Döllinger, and Kuhn, the metaphysicians Baader and Molitor, the political writers Görres and Radowitz, and historians such as Movers and Gfrörer. On all the questions on the authority of science and its agreement

---

[29] Cousin, Villemain, Augustin Thierry, Barrante, and even Guizot.

with religion; of the influence of the Church on the state of intellectual and political liberty; of the propriety of concealment for fear of scandal; the example and the precepts of this Ultramontane school are diametrically opposite to those of the Catholics whose language we have quoted.

The first Catholic theologian who commenced the protest on behalf of Christian science against obscurantism was Gügler of Lucerne, a man not surpassed in knowledge of Scripture and originality of mind by any of those whom we shall have to name. The intensity of the antagonism reveals itself very clearly in the energy of his language, which the present state of literature would not justify. In a lecture against the opponents of a scientific and critical study of Holy Writ, he expresses himself in the following terms:

Timidity is a child of darkness. . . . Wherefore do you complain of us that we investigate the sacred writings? Because, indeed, we are in danger of falling away from the truth; as if truth resided only in unreason, as if the sun's light shone only for the blind! You may be led to unbelieving thoughts quite as easily by merely reading the Scriptures as by a deeper study of them; much more easily, indeed, for error floats upon the surface, while truth lies deep below. If you would be faithful to your cause, you must close these books, and conscientiously abstain from reading them; and this in fact, is what you really do, and so are secure not only from evil thoughts but from all ideas whatever. At least the lofty freedom of the Christian spirit is far from you, and you labour zealously to reach an opposite extreme. We are to believe the voice of the Church, you say, without seeking to understand; but where do we hear that voice? Not in your mouths certainly, or with the ears of the body; it must be sought for in history and in the written records of the Church. . . . We must examine each document historically, in order to know whether it is the authentic expression of the mind of the Church, without interpolation; only then does faith begin. . . . You endeavour to lull to sleep the spirit of inquiry, to suppress it when it is wakened, to check it in its growth; and by what means? Is it by a great intellectual preponderance and authority which enable you to assume the guardianship of the rest of the world? Far from it; but by ignorance, and by blindly casting suspicion on that which you do not understand. These are your arts, these are your only weapons; and thus you resemble madmen who would extinguish a conflagration, not by work, but by outcry. . . . The universal scorn under which you have fallen is of your own making; for as you will not listen to anything, and understand nothing, men deem that your cause is at an end, and you will seldom find any like ourselves who will honour you with a single word. . . . By your resistance you cast a hideous shadow on Christianity. When the ignorant, who are carried along by the current of the hour, look on you who profess to be true Christians, must they not believe that Christianity is taking darkness under its protection, and making it essential to its own existence? Will they not suppose that Christianity must dread all inquiry, and dare not approach the light? You have betrayed the sanctuary; you are the cause of the decline of faith, because its purity was long ago dimmed in yourselves. . . . Faith is not your motive, for it has no object but truth. . . . Embrace reason and science, become what you ought to be, and your kingdom will rise again from the dead. Give us a protection not only against unbelief, but one equally potent against superstition. It can only be truth, which lies hidden in the depths. To depart but a hair-breadth from it is as bad as to be a hundred miles away. . . . Your disposition is very remote from that love of truth which always asks, True or not true? Your question is, Shall we have it so or not? He that loves the truth has divested himself of all particular inclinations and preferences. He views everything with love or aversion as he finds it true or false. You, on the contrary, care only for externals, and, if the thing were not true, you still would not abandon it. This is the disposition that nailed Christ upon the cross, and made the Jews blind to the dazzling light.[30]

In 1826 the Baron d'Eckstein founded a review, *Le Catholique,* for the purpose of promoting these ideas in France. He pointed out the backwardness of the clergy in learning, and the necessity of a great improvement. The freedom of the press was requisite in order to restore to Catholicism its proper influence. Left without official protection, it would be obliged to look for support in all the sciences, and to furnish itself with new armour. But if the Church of France should make no effort to

---

[30] Gügler, *Rede gegen die Feinde wissenschaftlicher, besonders historisch-kritischer Untersuchung der heiligen Schrift, Nachgelassene Schriften,* i, 75–86.

recover the supremacy of learning, and to master religion intellectually as she practised it in life, she could not resist science and impiety.[31]

About the same time, Baader was expounding at Munich, in an obscure, unsystematic, and aphoristic style, the most profound philosophy yet attained by Catholic speculation. The understanding requires to be satisfied just as much as the religious feelings of men; we cannot therefore rest contented with faith alone. Faith is the basis of true knowledge, and knowledge the complement of faith; for uninstructed faith is liable to be shaken, but he who has proceeded from faith to knowledge is sure of his belief. Therefore he insisted on the necessary progress of science as the safeguard of religion against unbelief, the only conciliation of authority and liberty, and the only means of protecting the faithful from the burden of a merely external authority which, when it imposes itself on the processes of the understanding instead of confining itself to its own sphere in the will and the reason, becomes as arbitrary as the system of unbelievers.[32] Molitor, the only rival of Baader among the Catholic philosophers of his day, dwells more particularly on the union of faith and knowledge. Science, which seeks to clear up what our consciousness dimly and uncertainly perceives, is the

---

[31] *Le Catholique,* i, 100; iii, 202; vi, 536; vii, 326. "Nous insistons fortement sur ces points, parce que l'Église est plus que jamais appelée au combat, et que si elle néglige le soin d'unir le savoir aux croyances, toutes les connaissances, toutes les découvertes des hommes tourneraient au profit du mauvais esprit et non celui de la vérité. A l'avenir rien de ce qui constitue la science ne doit rester étranger à ses principaux défenseurs. Avec la simplicité de la foi on opère la conversion des barbares, et des sauvages; mais c'est avec la science unie a cette divine simplicité, que l'on peut conquérir les peuples vieillis au sein d'une longue civilisation. Il ne faut pas craindre les véritables lumières, et redouter de s'en servir, si l'on veut anéantir les fausses" (iii, 204).

[32] Hofmann, *Vorhalle zur spekulativen Lehre F. Baader's,* pp. 20, 31. "Es muss erkann werden, dass jede neugewonnene Wahrheit keine frühere aufhebt, sodern vielmehr bestätigt, indem sie dieselbe bestimmter entfaltet, und in der Aufzeichnung neue Beziehungen bereichert. . . . Sie müssen zur Erkenntnis kommen, dass eine neue Wahrheit möglich ist, wenn sie nicht in der schon gewonnenen ihre Wurzel hat, dass somit jede neue Wahrheit die alte voraussetzt, und derselben ihr offenbar gewordenes sein zu verdanken hat" (p. 35).

guide through the labyrinth of the feelings, and therefore harmonizes necessarily with faith. Human nature strives after unity with itself; and the union of faith and reason, things equally necessary and important, must be practically attainable at least to a certain extent.[33] "Knowledge," says Dr Döllinger, "is one of the forms, and a necessary portion of morality; and as without an enlightened understanding there can be no real and perfect morality, so also a true and comprehensive knowledge can subsist only in a mind disciplined by morality. . . . It is true that this love of wisdom, often as it is paraded and proclaimed, is as rare as it is precious; for he alone can claim to possess it who is willing and able to dedicate himself to Truth with an absolute and unreserved devotion, and to make even the most painful sacrifice in its behalf. This resolute determination ever to seek the truth, the whole truth, and nothing but the truth, is a most difficult and unusual thing; and a man of whom this may be fairly said is not more easy to find than a man who is really determined to fulfil God's will alone." He says more particularly in another passage: "The understanding of ethical matters, or of matters approaching the domain of ethics, cannot be acquired by the operation of the reason alone. Otherwise the clever and the educated would be infinitely superior to the poor and uninstructed even in the knowledge of good and evil. But it is not so, and by an equally wise and equitable law man cannot master with his head what he does not at the same time receive into his heart; and if he hardens his will, he hardens at the same time his understanding against the truth." [34]

Nothing is more striking in the contrasts which the opposite schools present in their treatment of religious opponents than the manner in which they speak of the Reformation. The difference cannot be explained by the national prejudices; for there

---

[33] *Über die Tradition,* ii, 215, 216.

[34] *Irrthum, Zweifel und Wahrheit,* pp. 25, 33, 37. "The real seat of certainty is in the conscience alone. . . . Do not expect that in return, as it were, for your supposed good intentions, a mere superficial acquaintance and dilettante occupation with science and its results will really lead you to truth and supply you with firm convictions."

are many Germans whose language is as sweeping as that of Audin or Perrone. The tone of the greater German writers is very different. Görres speaks as follows: "In truth, it was a great and noble movement in the German people that brought about the Reformation. The Latin nations may condemn it altogether, but we cannot, for it sprang from the inmost spirit of our race, and extended nearly to the same limits. It was the spirit of a lofty moral disgust at every outrage on what is holy, wherever it may appear; of that indignation that is roused by every abuse; of that indestructible love of freedom which is sure always to cast off every yoke that perfidious violence would impose; in a word, the whole mass of salutary qualities which God bestowed on this nation, in order, when need should be, to ward off the corruption to which the warm South so easily inclines." [35]

Möhler says in his *Symbolik:* "Protestantism arose from the opposition to much that was undeniably evil and defective in the Church, and this is its merit—a merit not indeed peculiarly its own, since those evils were incessantly attacked, both before and after, on Catholic principles. It sprang partly from hostility to certain scientific representations of dogma, and certain forms of ecclesiastical life, which we may designate by the common term mediaeval, although these, again, had been the object of transforming endeavours, on behalf of the true system of the Church, from the end of the fourteenth century. . . . The Lutheran system will appear more excusable, as it will be shown to have proceeded really from a true Christian zeal, which indeed was, as in most other cases, injudiciously directed." [36]
"At the beginning of the sixteenth century," says Döllinger, "a profound disgust at the Papacy of those days, and a not undeserved indignation at the abuses in the Church and the moral depravity of a too wealthy and too numerous clergy, had spread widely over Germany." [37]

It belongs to the nature of this school of divines that their theology is not scholastic. The systematic discussion of doc-

---

[35] *Der Katholik,* xv, 279.
[36] *Symbolik,* pp. 11, 113.
[37] *Kirche und Kirchen,* p. 10.

trines occupies a subordinate place in their method, as it is but one of several modes of ascertaining the teaching of the Church. The historic method, which considers less the convenience of imparting than the means of advancing the knowledge of religious truth, and which proceeds directly to the study of its sources and original records, alone suited their scientific spirit and the necessities of their position; whilst they renounced and condemned the other as barren and obsolete. In his letter to Bautain, Möhler thus describes it: "You have repeatedly and vehemently assailed the scholastic method, which still prevails in the schools of France, as incapable of embracing the boundless substance of the Christian religion, and bringing it to its full development. . . . You attack a form of theological science whose special characteristic I would describe as a love for external demonstration, with a theology that supplies a quantity of proofs, but does not help us to know the thing itself which is to be proved; a theology that never gets through the mass of arguments to the truth itself, and understands better how to hang Christianity round about a man than how to convert him into a Christian. . . . This appears to me your most signal merit." [38] Professor Kuhn expresses himself still more strongly in reference to Kleutgen: "If we believe the modern restorers of Scholasticism, the older divines taught with one voice exactly the same doctrine on all the chief points of science which they now proclaim as perfect wisdom and genuine Catholic science. . . . From this wholly unhistorical view of the theology of former days they draw conclusions for the pursuit of theology in our day, which must inevitably injure it; besides which the partisans of this view, by investing their own knowl-

---

[38] *Sendschreiben an Bautain, Gesammelte Schriften* ii, 142. Not long before, Eckstein had sketched the state of scholastic theology in France: "Mère céléste des sciences, la théologie n'est enseignée comme une scholastique stérile dans l'école cartésienne. Dans celle de M. Lamennais, elle dégénère en une vaine ostentation de polémique sur l'autorité. Nos aïeux, que nous appelons grossiers, étaient plus avancés que nous dans la science catholique: aujourd'hui un certain parti semble croire que tout a été dit, qu'il n'est plus besoin de penser, d'aimer de méditer, mais de croire et de s'endormir" (*Le Catholique*, viii, 650).

edge and opinions with the authority of the Catholic schools, make their own intellectual work much too easy, and that of others unnecessarily difficult." [39]

The principles of civil and intellectual freedom are maintained by the Ultramontane writers as the necessary condition of that harmony between religion and political as well as moral science which it is their object to obtain. Eckstein deplores, in the first number of his review, that the fear of revolution should have given to the writings of apologists a reactionary taint which was neither requisite nor useful for the maintenance of sound doctrine.[40] He thundered against that monstrous combination of politics and religion which was sought by the intervention of a religious police; and he warned the Royalists that a terrible explosion might be the fruit of such mean and secret efforts, and of an impotent oppression exercised by men who, unable to obtain a triumph by open combat, sought it by artifices.[41] A quarter of a century later, Döllinger appealed to the French clergy with a similar warning in favour of liberty: "The Church of France cannot expect that she will be allowed to constitute permanently an exceptional domain of freedom in a state which is not free. . . . She will obtain her just share of the general freedom and will find it more satisfactory and more secure than if she only forms an exception to the general rule." [42] The Bishop of Mentz speaks with the same frankness of the political claims of the Church: "It is perfectly untrue that the Church now claims for her external position all that in former times may have been laid down by a Pontiff when all Christendom revered him as a father. . . . The altered circumstances necessarily require a completely new arrangement of the rela-

---

[39] *Katholische Dogmatik,* i, 916.

[40] *Le Catholique,* i, 9.

[41] *Avant-propos,* pp. 85, 99: "La liberté eût conservé à la religion tout le terrain que les inquisitions lui on fait perdre."

[42] *Betrachtungen über die Kaiserkrönung,* 1853, p. 40. "It is the first principle of the constitutional system that the sovereignty resides, not in the person of the monarch alone, but in the monarch and the people in inseparable unity" (*Debates of the Bavarian Chamber of Deputies,* 1849, i, 432).

tions between Church and State. This is what our age is struggling to effect. From the Reformation to the present day it has
never been possible to realize it. The recollection of the old
Catholic unity survived in men's minds, and they attempted to
settle matters in accordance with these recollections in all the
lesser states, without reflecting that the old conditions had
departed. Thence arose a truly absurd imitation of mediaeval
institutions; and that which had been great and legitimate,
considered from the point of view of Catholic unity, became, in
different circumstances, unnatural and intolerable. Let the
world manage its relations with the Church after the manner of
the Middle Ages, when by God's mercy it has returned to the
unity of religious belief; till then another basis is needed, which
I can discover nowhere but in an honest recognition of the
freedom of all Christian communities admitted by the State." [43]

The defence of intellectual freedom is founded not on the
rights of reason so much as on the duty and on the interests of
the Church. The danger to the priest, wrote Eckstein, is less in a
momentary oppression than in exaggerated triumph. By every
act that does violence to intellect he deludes himself, and the
motive is either passionate anger or pure idleness. [44] Neither
academies nor universities, but the Church alone can reconcile
the unrestricted progress of science with human welfare; the
Church, not by acting as she did in the Middle Ages, or by
striving, as she strove through the Jesuits, to control the education of European society—for we are neither in the Middle
Ages, nor in the sixteenth century—but by employing all the
knowledge and reflection of mankind, without putting any
impediment in its way. [45] With Görres this was also a favourite
theme: "Where will this freedom of speech and writing end?
Will not the eternal pillars of religion, law, virtue, and society at

---

[43] Ketteler: *Soll die Kirche allein rechtlos sein?* p. 30. In the National
Parliament of 1848 he spoke in the same way for the freedom of instruction: "I desire that the unbeliever shall be allowed to bring up his children
in unbelief; but it must be lawful for the strictest Catholic to give his
children a Catholic education" (*Frankfort Debates,* p. 2183).

[44] *Historisch-politische Blätter,* xi, 578.

[45] *Ibid.,* p. 581.

last be undermined and washed away? Fools! to believe that God has made the enduring order of the universe to depend on your vigilance, and has planted the foundations of the moral world in the blind wit of man! . . . The mind tolerates no tyrants. You can measure off the fields, they bear your limits patiently; but draw your boundary round the flood, divide the air into compartments and districts, contain the fire—how shall you, with your rude instruments shut up ideas and arrest the beams of thought? All that you will gain is, that, by the indignation with which men will be animated at the sight of your violence, the spark that goes forth still and harmless will be transformed into a thunderbolt, and that which would have passed away in a mild electric glow will gather into a destroying tempest." [46]

In an address to King Lewis of Bavaria on his accession which he places in the mouth of the greatest prince of his line, Görres takes care to exhort him faithfully to protect the freedom of thought against the interference of the clergy: "Pride has ever been the rock on which the priesthood has most easily been wrecked. As they are always busy with exalted things . . . and are instituted by God Himself, it may but too easily happen that they will confound His spirit with their own, identify themselves with the sanctity of their vocation, and, instead of obeying the command to govern only by voluntary self-abasement, and to seek their pride in humility, will glory in their office, and extend its functions over a sphere from which by nature it is excluded." [47] The peculiar autonomy of science is accurately

---

[46] *Politische Schriften*, v, 166, 135. "Resist the advance of learning, and behold, the genius strikes with his staff, the waters are parted asunder, and the waves stand up like walls on either side; pursue with your hosts, with your warriors and chariots and horses, and the waters shall close over you, and Pharaoh shall be drowned with all his army. . . . Go rather and cultivate the new land in the sweat of your brow, and learn to adapt yourself to the altered times. Learn that, in order to govern, wisdom, understanding, ability, and virtue are henceforth required, and make your peace with the coming generation."

[47] *Maximilian der Erste an den König Ludwig von Baiern, Politische Schriften*, v, 256, 241. "While faith, which is internally free and inevitably tends to freedom, is externally bound within the Church . . .

defined by Möhler. Science, he says, resting on a law of internal necessity which is identical with truth, can arrive at a conscious knowledge of it only by freedom. External bonds produce in literature miserable, superficial, sophistical results. He that has penetrated, by means of original research, to the inmost sanctuary of science, knows how solemn is the reception she gives to her followers—what self-denial, what sacrifice of their own will, and what renunciation of all personal interest she demands—and how she exacts that they shall give themselves up to her own laws.[48]

These extracts must suffice towards the solution of the doubt whether the Church desires the establishment of freedom as the highest phase of civil society, independently of her own interest in it, and of the question of her attitude towards the promotion of learning. But it is necessary to notice briefly an opinion held by some who are either ignorant of the Catholic system or especially hostile to it, that an arbitrary authority exists in the Church which may deny what has been hitherto believed, and may suddenly impose upon the faithful, against their will, doctrines which, while there is no warrant for them in the past, may be in contradiction with the existing and received conclusions of ecclesiastical, or even profane, science. The Ultramontane

---

knowledge, on the contrary, inasmuch as it acts through conviction, and compels minds by internal force, must be outwardly free, and the interchange of ideas in its special sphere must be arrested and controlled by no unnatural restriction. . . . Be ye, therefore, a Christian prince, at once a pillar of faith and protector of the freedom of the intellect; and let your example put to silence the zealots of both kinds who hold the two things to be incompatible. . . . As deep as thought can penetrate into the nature of things, as high as it can breathe on the summits of the intellectual world, everywhere let its course be kept free by you; and be not frightened if in the ardour of its progress it quits the established paths."

[48] *Gesammelte Schriften,* i, 280. "The union of reason and faith must be produced by no external coalition; for nothing is more contrary to reason than the introduction of a foreign authority into its sphere, which is the case where faith is assumed as a postulate; namely, when speculation, unable to proceed farther in its one-sided course, despairing in the power of reason, throws itself violently into the arms of faith" (Molitor, *Über die Tradition,* ii, 215).

divines, having regard to this impression, have stated with special care the limited nature of the limits of the Papal authority. Möhler affirms that it was at one time greater than it has since come to be in consequence of the general progress of civilization and knowledge, which rendered its leading-strings insupportable. Rude times, he says, required a strong concentration of power to reform them; and the violence of internal forces called into existence a strong external control. In this way a dictatorship was given to the Pope. But it had no sooner done the work for which it was created than the absolute power was again restricted by the influence of such men as St Bernard. It is a proof of the efficiency with which the Popes used their power that men grew tired of it so soon. In proportion as intellectual and moral culture improved under it, the temporary form of the Roman supremacy necessarily became intolerable.[49]

Such as it now canonically exists, this authority is described by Döllinger in several places. "You must allow me," he said in the Frankfort Parliament, "to put aside once for all, as entirely groundless, the assertion that the Pope is an absolute ruler in the Catholic Church. . . . No authority is more hampered than his by divers established limitations, and by a legislation descending to the most minute details, which the Pope cannot set aside, and which binds him as much as every other Catholic. If you imagine that there is any room in the Catholic Church for a purely arbitrary power of Pope or bishop, you are greatly mistaken."[50] "There is no society in the world whose constitution is more carefully organized, or more exactly regulated, than the Catholic Church. In that Church it is provided that the means of oppression, the tyrannical abuse of entrusted power, shall enjoy the smallest possible scope that is possible among men. Like a vast encompassing net, our ecclesiastical law extends over the whole Church; and none can break through it without abandoning her communion. . . . Blind obedience is neither exacted of the Christian nor conceded by him; and he must reject it as soon as he discerns, or believes that he discerns,

---

[49] *Gesammelte Schriften*, ii, 27.
[50] *Debates*, p. 1674.

something sinful in it. At the same time, he knows that nothing can be proposed to him that is not founded on the immutable order and the laws of the Church."[51]

It is sufficient to appeal to the example of Möhler,[52] Döllinger,[53] and the other principal authors of the school, as a token of their opinion on the propriety of concealing truth for fear of scandal. "Everything must be told," says Gügler, "openly, clearly and without reserve, lest the deceit and suspicion that already surround all the relations of life should penetrate into the temple of science. Here no accommodation, no inherited custom, can be tolerated; whatever checks the free and genuine exhibition of character must be laid aside."[54] Some friends remonstrated with Görres on the manner in which he had spoken of the Popes in his Introduction to Cardinal Diepenbrook's *Suso*. In one of his letters he replies: "They are wrong in wishing truth to be disguised; that is always the worst possible policy, and now most of all. It is dangerous because it is dishonest, and quite unavailing besides. I vote everywhere fearlessly for the pure freshness of truth."[55] This was the maxim

---

[51] *Die Freiheit der Kirche,* pp. 18, 19.

[52] *Symbolik,* p. 353; *Neue Untersuchungen,* p. 382.

[53] *Lehrbuch der Kirchengeschichte,* ii, 229, 231, 234.

[54] *Nachgelassene Schriften,* i, 88. "La vérité est dans l'Église; elle possède donc les lumières; elle ne cessera jamais de dominer par la religion et la science; . . . on répétera ce vieux mot de Fontenelle, que toutes les vérités ne sont pas bonnes à dire. C'est une erreur. Il faut les proclamer toutes, si l'on ne veut que l'imposture se serve de la vérité partielle contre la vérité générale, et de la vérité générale contre elle-même" (Eckstein, *Le Catholique,* vii, 326).

[55] *Gesammelte Briefe,* i, 314. The following are the passages alluded to: "The Popes had become enslaved to their passions; . . . and that very French policy which they had invoked in the House of Anjou, to protect them against the violence of the Germans, was the appointed instrument to heap shame upon their heads, and to forge the fetters, to escape from which they, distrusting God and his divine order, and their own right, had played a senseless game, and had connected themselves with degraded things. The thirst for treasure was soon accompanied by the thirst for power, and the internal government of the Church sank more and more into the principles of the absolute dominion of the spiritual head: . . . a scandal on the side of the spiritual authority that raged irreconcilably, without measure, without dignity, without charity" (*Einleitung,* pp. xxvii, xxix).

with which Möhler inaugurated his lectures on ecclesiastical history: "It is obvious that the student of history must not pervert facts; and one may suppose that Christianity expressly prohibits falsehood. From the Christian point of view most of all, therefore, we are forbidden to be partial, to alter facts, to omit one thing, to be silent on another, or to add any thing which we have not found." [56]

The Catholic is subject to the correction of the Church when he is in contradiction with her truth, not when he stands in the way of her interests. For there is nothing arbitrary or extemporaneous in the authority which she wields; the laws of her government are of general application, ancient, public, and distinctly defined. There is a certain number of ideas which the Christian irrefragably believes, with such a faith as no scientific man thinks of reposing in any of the progressive realizations of inductive science. And he feels that such ideas as the existence of God, the immortality of the soul, and the punishment of sin, can neither by destroyed by knowledge nor impede its acquisition. Not that he thinks these great religious ideas ought to remain in sterile isolation. Like other general principles, each of them is capable of being made the basis of a vast superstructure of doctrine, proceeding from it with logical necessity. The work of this development has been performed by the organic action of the Church, which in the course of centuries has worked out a consistent system of doctrine, altogether free from accidental or arbitrary elements, the inevitable result of the principles of faith reacting upon the strict laws of thought and historical growth. Every part of this system is equally certain, and, if not equally necessary to be known, yet equally incapable of being denied. No part of it can be destroyed by the progress of knowledge, the last defined dogma no more than the first, no more than the existence of God, or the immortality of the thinking being.

But there is an outward shell of variable opinions constantly forming round this inward core of irreversible dogma, by its

---

[56] *Gesammelte Schriften*, ii, 284.

contact with human science or philosophy, as a coating of oxide forms round a mass of metal where it comes in contact with the shifting atmosphere. The Church must always put herself in harmony with existing ideas, and speak to each age and nation in its own language. A kind of amalgam between the eternal faith and temporal opinion is thus in constant process of generation, and by it Christians explain to themselves the bearings of their religion, so far as their knowledge allows. No wonder if, morally, this amalgam should be valued by its eternal rather than by its temporary element, and that its ideas should come to be regarded as almost equally sacred with the dogmas on which they are partly built. For they have the prestige of possession in their favour; they have come to be mixed up with social institutions and with philosophical speculation; and they form the outside line of defence in the controversial stronghold of Christendom.

But as opinion changes, as principles become developed, and as habits alter, one element of the amalgam is constantly losing its vitality, and the true dogma is left in an unnatural union with exploded opinion. From time to time a very extensive revision is required, hateful to conservative habits and feelings; a crisis occurs, and a new alliance has to be formed between religion and knowledge, between the Church and society. Every victory thus gained, though in its personal aspect it is a victory of innovators over those who seem to stand in the old paths, and to defend the interests of the unchangeable, is in reality a victory of truth over error, of science over opinion. It is a change not to be deplored but to be accepted with joy. It is a process which, though it has its crises, must be always progressing. There is always some mass or other in the temporary element of the amalgam which is becoming rusty and worn out, and fit only to be thrown aside. And as this purging process is one that involves opinions and feelings nearly conjoined with faith, there will always be an apparent danger, which, however, will at once disappear before the vigour of Catholics who will break the bonds of human tradition, and associate themselves with the progress of their times. The danger is only for those who fail to distinguish the essential from the accidental, and who cling to their religion, not for its substance, but for its appendages. Such men fall away altogether if their own way of explaining dogmas to themselves, and reconciling them with opinions, is cut from them. And even those who see clearly the difference between substance and accident must feel how important it is that their love and allegiance to the Church should be exhibited in those outer spheres where attachment takes the place of faith.

The fear of giving scandal, and the unwillingness to question too closely the limits of authority, are therefore the two motives which make the best-informed Catholics very circumspect in destroying opinions which have become amalgamated with faith. But these motives are misplaced in an age when Catholics can no longer shut themselves out from contact with the world, nor shelter themselves in ignorance. When all opinions are perpetually canvassed in a literature over which no authority and no consideration for others has any control, Catholics cannot help attempting to solve the problems which all the world is discussing. The point is, that while they solve them religiously, they should likewise solve them scientifically; that they should so comprehend them as to satisfy both conscience and reason—conscience, by a solution consistent with the infallible criterion of faith, and reason, by one defensible on grounds quite external to religion.

When a man has really performed this double task—when he has worked out the problem of science or politics, on purely scientific and political principles, and then controlled this process by the doctrine of the Church, and found its results to coincide with that doctrine, then he is an Ultramontane in the real meaning of the term—a Catholic in the highest sense of Catholicism. The Ultramontane is therefore one who makes no parade of his religion; who meets his adversaries on grounds which they understand and acknowledge; who appeals to no extrinsic considerations—benevolence, or force, or interest, or artifice—in order to establish his point; who discusses each topic on its intrinsic merits—answering the critic by a severer criticism, the metaphysician by closer reasoning, the historian by deeper learning, the politician by sounder politics, and indifference itself by a purer impartiality. In all these subjects the Ultramontane discovers a point pre-eminently Catholic, but also pre-eminently intellectual and true. He finds that there is a system of metaphysics, and of ethics, singularly agreeable to Catholicism, but entirely independent of it. Not that his labour is an easy one, or one capable of being brought to a close. Each generation has to carry it forward. None can complete it; for there will always be some progress to be made, some new discoveries to adopt and assimilate, some discord to harmonize, some half-truth which has become an error to lop away. It is a process never to be terminated, till God has finished the work of educating the human race to know Him and to love Him.

But it is a work which no Catholic can deem either impracticable or unnecessary. It is not an idle enterprise: if we seek, we shall find. Religion can be made intelligible if we take the pains to make it so; its proofs may be found, its laws ascertained, and the conscience and reason constrained to acknowledge them. And Catholics are the only persons who can enter on this field of labour with perfect freedom; for they alone have a religion perfectly defined, clearly marked off from all other spheres of thought; they alone therefore can enter these spheres free from all suspicion of doubt, and from all fear of discord between faith and knowledge. If this clear distinction has ever been forgotten by Catholics, defeat was sure to follow, and that defeat was the victory of truth. Authority may put itself in opposition to its own code; but the code is vindicated by the defeat of authority. Thus it was in politics during the drama of the Sicilian Vespers, and in physical science during the opposition to Galileo. Those experiments have taught authority its own bounds, and subjects the limits of obedience; and they have destroyed the last conceivable obstacle to the freedom with which a Catholic can move in the sphere of inductive truth.

VII

The Rise and Fall of the Mexican Empire

THE scene of the tragedy which I will attempt to describe is a country on which Nature's fairest gifts have been lavished with an unsparing hand, but where man has done his utmost to thwart the designs of Providence. Its social condition is so far removed from our experience that I must ask you to forget this evening the maxims and even the political terms we use nearer home.

Mexico possesses a territory more than thrice as large as France, with the fertility of the tropics, and the climate of the temperate zone, seated between two oceans, in the future centre of the commerce of the world. Its wealth in precious metals is so enormous that the time will come when the market will be flooded with silver, and its price will not allow the mines to be worked with profit. The only drawbacks on its prosperity are the badness of the harbours, the excessive dryness of the plains, and the disappearance of the forest timber, a curse which almost always follows the footstep of the Spaniard.

When England recognised the independence of the Spanish colonies, Mr. Canning declared that he had called a new world into existence to redress the balance of the old. But it was long before the new States justified the boast, and it is still generally believed that in point of political and material success they contrast much to their disadvantage with the North American Republic. In the greater part of South America this is no longer

A lecture delivered at the Bridgnorth Literary and Scientific Institution on March 10, 1868. Reprinted from Acton, *Historical Essays and Studies* (London: Macmillan, 1907).

true, for in several of those vast communities population and trade are growing at a rate that exceeds that of the Union.

Mexico is the saddest and most conspicuous exception in the midst of the general improvement. It is the pride of the colonial system of Spain, and the one merit in which it was superior to our own, that it succeeded in preserving and partially civilising the native race. The English settled in a region where the natives were hunters and wanderers, unskilled in the cultivation of the soil, who roamed into the West to elude the grasp of civilisation, or perished by its contact. The colonists retained their own congenial laws, the purity of European blood was maintained, and the portentous problem of race was happily averted. But in Mexico Cortez found a numerous and settled population, dwelling in cities, tilling the land, and brilliantly though superficially civilised. It was part of the Spanish system to protect, to preserve, and to convert the conquered heathens, whose number vastly exceeded that of their masters; a people of mixed blood sprang up between them, and thus there were three races separated by a very broad line, and isolated by the pride and the jealousy of colour. The Indian nobles were mostly exterminated, and the land was distributed among the families of a small group of conquerors. This arrangement of property remains unchanged. The natives are still without any interest in the land, and the immense estates have not been subdivided. In one of the richest districts on the Atlantic, the coast, for one hundred and fifty miles, is owned by one proprietor.

A society so constituted could not make a nation. There was no middle class, no impulse to industry, no common civilisation, no public spirit, no sense of patriotism. The Indians were not suffered to acquire wealth or knowledge, and every class was kept in ignorance and in rigorous seclusion; when, therefore, the Mexicans made themselves independent, the difficulty was to throw off, not the bondage, but the nonage in which they had been held, and to overcome the mental incapacity, the want of enterprise, the want of combination among themselves, and the want of the enlightenment which comes from intercourse with other nations. They formed a republic after the model of their more fortunate neighbours, and accepted those principles which are so inflexible in their consequences, and so unrelenting in their consistency. It soon appeared that there was not propelling power in the State equal to the heavy burden of a half-barbarous population. The intelligent minority was too undisciplined and too demoralised to elevate and to sway the degraded millions of the Indian race. The habits of authority and subordination departed with the Spaniards, and the faculty of organisation could not exist in a people that had never learned to help themselves. No man of very superior character and understanding arose. The leading men in the various provinces sought to maintain their own power by the continuance of anarchy; they combined against the central authority as fast as it changed hands, and overthrew thirty Presidents in thirty years. The requisite conditions of a Republican government did not exist. There was the greatest social inequality that can be conceived between the wealthy landowners and the Indian masses, who possessed neither the mental independence conferred by education nor the material independence which belongs to property. There was Democracy in the State, while society was intensely aristocratic.

The largest landowner in Mexico was the Church; and as there was no religious toleration, it was the Church of the whole nation, the only teacher of the moral law to the natives, the sole channel through which the majority of the people had access to the civilisation of Christendom. Therefore the clergy enjoyed an influence of which there has been no example in Europe for the last five hundred years, and formed a strong basis of aristocracy and the most serious barrier to the realisation of the Democratic principle that nominally prevailed. To establish a real Democracy the first thing to be done was to reduce this immense and artificial influence. For the last twelve years this has been the one constant object of the Democratic party. It was a war of principles, a struggle for existence, on either side, in which conciliation was impossible, and which could only terminate by the ruin of one of the contending forces.

Now, as long as the conflict was confined to America, the

Republicans could not be utterly defeated, for they could fall back on the unfailing sympathy and resources of the United States. Sooner or later the end would be the confiscation of the lands in mortmain, and the downfall of the Conservatives. Their only hope was in the assistance of Europe, and the establishment of a monarchy under foreign protection. Long before the antagonism became so definite and so extreme, the idea had begun to gain ground that a monarchy was the only form of government adapted to the character of Mexican society, and capable of arresting its decay; and the monarch, if he was not to be a party chief, must be a European prince. Negotiations for this object were opened as early as 1846; Mexican emissaries, acting in concert with the then President, addressed themselves to Prince Metternich, who received them coldly, to Bavaria, and then to France, where the plan was favourably entertained, when it was interrupted by the revolution of 1848. It was revived twelve years later by the progress of events in Mexico. In 1857 the Democratic party carried a new Constitution, abridging the privileges of the clergy, and including a law of mortmain which obliged them to convert their estates into money.

This was the signal for civil war. The Conservatives, led by a young man who, at the age of twenty-seven, had shown a remarkable capacity for war, Miguel Miramon, gained possession of the capital, and their President was recognised by Europe. The Constitutional President held the important seaport of Vera Cruz, and was recognised by the United States. His name, destined like that of his rival to a wide and melancholy celebrity, was Benito Juarez. He was an Indian of pure blood, nearly sixty years old. He had ascended to power by means of his eminence as a lawyer, and because, in the midst of almost universal corruption, he was deemed incorruptible. Unlike the intriguers and the soldiers of fortune who were his rivals, he had risen slowly, without perfidy and without violence,—a patient, steadfast man, and, as we should say, a man of extreme opinions. It would seem that in this educated, ambitious, successful Indian, the pent-up hatred of the oppressed race for the oppressor had broken forth, and formed his strongest political motive; and that he was striving for the social and political emancipation of his people when he tore down the privileges and annihilated the power of the class that lorded over them. He professed the principles of 1789, principles which had triumphed in France by a civil war, a reign of terror, ten years of military despotism, and sixty years of intermittent revolution. There was no reason to think they would succeed more easily in a country so backward as Mexico, but Juarez was ready to abide the issue. As there was no system of regular taxation, and all manufactured articles were imported by sea, the customs were the chief source of revenue. It was an advantage to Juarez to possess the chief seaport of the country, and as he dwelt under the cannon of European men-of-war, he was careful not to make enemies by plundering the foreigners.

Miramon, up in the interior, had neither the same resources nor the same restraint. There was no money to be had but that of foreign residents, or of the Church. He could not rob his own party, so he determined to turn to the other source of supply. He had so used his power, and his lieutenant, Marquez, had acted so ferociously, that the English Minister had left Mexico, when Miramon seized a sum of £130,000 belonging to British landholders, which was deposited at the Legation. He also contracted a loan with the Swiss banker, Jecker, on terms so exorbitant that it seems to have been a stratagem to embarrass those who were to come after him. These two measures were eventually fatal to Miramon, for they were the cause of the European intervention.

Juarez immediately obtained his recognition by England by promising to restore the stolen money, and to satisfy other British claims. He made the same promise to France. With this moral support, and by undertaking to grant away to his partisans the property of the Church, he obtained the means of expelling Miramon from Mexico, and in 1861 he was elected President for a term of four years. He at once dismissed the Spanish and the Papal envoys, decreed the absolute confiscation of the Church lands, and carried out with ruthless energy the triumph of his opinions. But he proved incapable as a ruler, and utterly unequal to the desperate task of restoring order in a country distracted by passion and ruined by anarchy.

The condition of affairs in the summer of 1861 is described by the English Minister in the following passages, which are important because they determined the policy of England:

As long as the present dishonest and incapable administration remains in power, things will go from bad to worse; but with a government formed of respectable men, could such be found, the resources of the country are so great that it might easily fulfil its engagements, and increase threefold the amount of its exportations, not only of the precious metals, but of those productions for which they receive British manufactured goods in exchange. Mexico furnishes two-thirds of the silver now in circulation, and might be made one of the richest and most prosperous countries of the world; so that it becomes the interest of Great Britain to put a stop by force, if necessary, to its present state of anarchy, and insist on its government paying what it owes to British subjects. All the respectable classes look forward with hope to a foreign intervention as the sole means of saving them from ruin, and preventing a dissolution of the Confederation, as well as a general rising of the Indians against the white population. Every day's experience duly tends to prove the utter absurdity of attempting to govern the country with the limited powers granted to the Executive by the present ultra-liberal Constitution, and I see no hope of improvement unless it comes from a foreign intervention, or the formation of a rational government, composed of the leading men of the moderate party, who, at present, are void of moral courage and afraid to move, unless with some material support from abroad. If the question was, what form of government would most conduce to the welfare of Mexico, by the establishment of order and a permanent state of things, there can be no doubt that a Constitutional monarchy is the one most likely to have central power sufficient to enable it to consolidate the nation, perhaps the only form of government that would give much hope of such a result; but as the question is not what is best for Mexico, but what are the wishes of the Mexican people, I fear that the answer must be that the great mass of the intelligent population are in favour of Republican institutions. Many well-educated and intelligent individuals who stand well in society form a well-grounded desire for a strong government, but these people are unfortunately timid, and passive in action, ready to accept what is done for them, but incapable of doing anything to bring about what they desire.

As it turned out, these were prophetic words. The sale of the Church property was carried on in a very disorderly way, and the money was squandered. A scheme to satisfy the urgent European claims with money lent by the United States, though entertained by the American Government, was rejected by the Senate, and in July 1861 the Mexican Congress resolved that all payments on European agreements should be suspended for two years.

The Powers most concerned in this act of repudiation—France, Spain, and Great Britain—now determined to intervene jointly, and to obtain by force of arms some real security for the property of their subjects, and for the establishment, if necessary, of a more trustworthy government. The conjuncture was favourable, for the Civil War had just broken out in the United States, and from that quarter there was no immediate danger of interruption. Spain took the lead, her military establishment at Cuba enabling her to act promptly, with some suspicion of a desire to recover her ancient dominion. England followed warily, with an eye only to mercantile interests. France did not yet reveal her intentions, and probably had not yet matured them.

The allied forces, amounting to about 6000 men, without means of transport or materials for a campaign in the interior, were placed under the command of the Spanish general Prim, a clever, showy, and ambitious officer, but a capricious and unstable politician. On their arrival, the town and fort of Vera Cruz were evacuated by the Mexican troops. In this extremity Juarez strengthened himself by putting at the head of the Ministry General Doblado, the leader of the moderate party, a man whose reputation for caution and ability stood high, and whose acts in office prove that it was well-deserved. In January 1862, he issued a decree directing all those who should be taken in arms against the Republic to be tried by court-martial and put to death as traitors. This is the law by which the Emperor was to die, and which gave a legal character to his execution.

Doblado had an interview with Prim, expatiated on the deplorable condition of the country, and undertook that the legitimate demands of the allies should be faithfully complied with, provided only they would recognise the existing government. These terms seemed acceptable to the allies, who were not equipped for a campaign, and they took Doblado at his word. But the agreement had to be sent to Europe for approval, and in the meantime it was arranged that the allies should move up from the pestilential swamp of Vera Cruz to healthier quarters on the first range of hills. This placed them within the outer line of the Mexican defences, and it was stipulated that if the preliminaries were not ratified, before commencing hostilities they should first withdraw to the plain below.

The claims of the three Powers had now to be specified. Those of Spain and England were clear, and easily ascertained. The French commissioners demanded, in addition to other large sums, three millions sterling for the banker Jecker. Their colleagues protested against this excessive demand. They affirmed that the sum advanced by the banker to Miramon was only £160,000, and they pointed out that he was not a Frenchman but a Swiss, and that the guardianship of Swiss interests in Mexico pertained to the American Legation. Jecker was immediately naturalised a Frenchman, and the French Government bought up his bonds. Agents were sent for this purpose with sealed instructions to America, two of whom, when they discovered the errand upon which they were employed, indignantly threw up the commission. Whilst this transaction was sowing discord in the allied camp, several Mexican exiles of the Conservative party made their appearance at Vera Cruz. One of these was Miramon. He was arrested and sent away by the British Commodore, on the ground that the expedition could not connect itself with one party while acknowledging the government of the other.

Miramon was speedily followed by General Almonte, for many years the chief agent of the Conservative party in Europe, and the secret councillor of the French Government, a man of high character and great influence. He stated that he came with a mission from France to establish a provisional government, to introduce a monarchy, and to procure the election of the Archduke Maximilian. The English and Spanish Commissioners demanded his expulsion, when General Lorencez arrived with French reinforcements, and announced that Napoleon had rejected the convention with Doblado, that he had sent Almonte to Mexico, and meant war. The alliance of the three Powers was at once dissolved; the Spaniards sailed for Cuba in English ships, and France was left alone, to accomplish the avowed design of erecting a throne beyond the Atlantic.

In the intention of the Emperor Napoleon, the Mexican expedition was the first step towards the execution of a bold and magnificent scheme, to which he gave the name of the regeneration of the Latin world. The ancient rivalry between France and England was expanded into the rivalry of the Latin with the Anglo-Saxon race. If we carry back our thoughts for a century, it will not be difficult to find in the history of the two nations the motives which suggested the idea. Scarcely one hundred years ago vast territories in Canada, on the Mississippi, and in the West Indies belonged to the Crown of France, and French adventurers of great daring and ability were laying the foundation of an Empire in Hindostan. One by one these possessions have gone, and France, watched by jealous neighbours, has nearly lost the power of expansion in Europe.

What has been, in the meantime, the progress of England? The colonies which France has lost have almost all been won by her. England, not France, wields the sceptre of the Great Mogul. Her people have encircled the globe with a girdle of British settlements. New continents, I may almost say, have arisen out of the Southern ocean to receive the incessant overflow of her population. Her colonial empire is a nursery of mighty nations, that carries to the distant places of the earth the language and the laws of home. George III. inherited dominions peopled perhaps by ten million human beings. His grand-daughter reigns over two hundred millions. In America the children of our race are waiting the time when the whole continent shall be theirs.

But on that continent there are thirty millions of men, not of French descent, but of a stock allied with the French, who derive their literary culture and intellectual impulse from Paris, whose traffic is carried on with French ports, who look up to France as their head, and turn to her to protect them from being absorbed by an alien race. The trade of France with South America is nearly equal to her trade with the United States, and is more profitable because it is carried in French ships. In the ten years before the expedition, it had grown from £6,000,000 to £20,000,000 a year. South America is the largest and safest opening that remains for the development of French commerce, the most increasing market for French industry. It was manifestly the interest of France to prevent it from falling under the control of the narrow mercantile policy of the United States, and to secure her own influence over nations with such a future. In the words of the Emperor: "It is not our interest that the United States should grasp the whole Gulf of Mexico, the Antilles, and South America, and become the sole dispensers of the produce of the New World. We have seen by sad experience how precarious is the fate of an industry which is forced to seek its raw material in a single market, under all the vicissitudes to which that market is liable." The establishment of a French dependency in Mexico would have checked the southward progress of the Union, and have cut the continent in two.

When Juarez repudiated his engagements with European creditors the Confederates had won their first victories, and the North was not able to repel the intervention upon its frontier. Shortly after, the Southern Commissioners were seized on board the *Trent*, and England began to arm. The French Emperor calculated that he would be able to do his work without interruption, and that England, in case of need, would help him to support the South. Therefore, from the end of 1861 he lent a willing ear to the Mexican exiles, who displayed the sufferings and the capabilities of their country, and allured him with the splendid vision of a nation to be regenerated by France. They persuaded him that the presence of his troops would be welcomed, that there would be no serious resistance, and that a powerful party would rally to his standard. In this belief, and with Almonte in their camp, the French advanced against Mexico, 6000 strong. On the 5th of May 1862, they appeared before Puebla, the second city in the land, on the road from Vera Cruz to the capital. They were received with so vigorous a cannonade that they were forced to retire to a position where they could await reinforcements without danger of being dislodged. After this military repulse, public opinion in France supported the Emperor in despatching an army of 30,000 men, provided with all the appliances of war. They landed in the autumn, and the winter was spent in preparations.

A whole year had been lost before Puebla fell, after an obstinate defence, and in June 1863 the French entered the city of Mexico. The early reverses and the long delays of the French greatly strengthened the position of Juarez. The invasion exalted the Indian leader of an extreme party into a champion of the dignity and the independence of the country, and his tenacity in upholding the cause did not allow this halo to depart from him even in the worst times. The capital was not fortified, and when the French appeared, Juarez carried the seat of his government to one of the Northern towns.

A new provisional government was instituted, in which Almonte was associated with the Archbishop of Mexico, and an assembly of notables, selected and convened by the French, met to decide on the future of the country. Many of the principal men in the capital who had been invited, refused to attend, and the assembly was composed of Conservatives who took their orders from Almonte and the French. The orders were to proclaim a monarchy, and to offer the Crown to the Archduke. They were obeyed on the 8th July 1863. The long-deferred hopes of the Mexican royalists seemed to be fulfilled, when a deputation proceeded to Europe to invite the Archduke to ascend the throne of Montezuma. Ferdinand Maximilian, the next brother of the Emperor of Austria, had long occupied a peculiar and exceptional position in his native country. There were circumstances which made him appear a possible rival to his brother, and the many errors of Francis Joseph, the waning confidence in his fortune and his judgment, kept alive the habit of looking to the Archduke, who was altogether excluded from the conduct of affairs, as a refuge in extremity. He possessed some of the best qualities of a ruler, honesty and firmness of purpose, a kind and true heart, and a mind fixed on high designs. In spite of much and various experience of mankind, he retained an unpractical imaginativeness, which is often connected with extreme cultivation, and a certain impetuous generosity frequently marred the effect of his sagacity. Though undoubtedly very intelligent, he was so often deceived that he must have lacked the faculty of judging men and choosing friends, without which there is no success in government. His ardent, lofty spirit, perpetually curbed and chafed by the prevailing dulness, selfishness, and incapacity in Austria, imparted something that was cold and sarcastic to his manner. His outspoken censure of his brother's unstable policy caused an estrangement between them, which was increased by his marriage with the daughter of the wise Leopold, a clever and accomplished woman, whose family has grown great by renouncing those principles of strict legitimacy which Austria specially represents. The Archduke was the last Austrian Governor of Lombardy. In that thankless office it was impossible to conciliate the Italians, and he could not permanently serve the interests of his country. But he made many friends, and men believed that he would willingly have been the Minister of a less unpopular system. It was even whispered that he had wished to set up a throne for himself in Lombardy and Venice, separate from the Austrian monarchy. At least he had so far deserted the ancient ways of his family as to fall under the ban of distrust and suspicion at Vienna. About the time of the marriage of the Princess Royal he visited the British Court, and made so favourable an impression that there were some who regretted that he could not have been a candidate for her hand. For who could then have dreamed that the reserved and unpretending Prussian was to be the spoilt darling of victory, while the genial, frank, and brilliant Austrian was destined to a traitor's death?

He devoted his care to the navy, a department always neglected in Austria, and the virtue of his administration became apparent when the fleet which he had created won the greatest sea-fight of our time. The war of 1859 deprived him of his high position, and reproaches and recriminations followed, which separated him yet more from the Emperor. He dwelt in his castle of Miramar at the head of the Adriatic, mourning over wasted talents, a ruined career, and an unsatisfied ambition.

Very soon the prospect of a new adventure opened before him. By a strange fatality his wife, the daughter of a Princess of the House of Orléans, was an enthusiastic Bonapartist, and not only admired, but trusted the Emperor Napoleon. When, therefore, he proposed to hand over his conquest to the Archduke, hoping thereby to conciliate Austria, the Archduchess Charlotte urged her husband to accept it. Their unsettled position must have become very irksome to her, for when they left their home Maximilian wept bitterly, and she showed no emotions but hope and joy. His brother's government employed strong measures to dissuade him from accepting, and it was decided that he must renounce his place in the succession, and be counted last after all the princes of the line.

When the vote of the Assembly of Notables was made known to him, he replied that he could not accept the crown unless he was assured of the support of the great Powers, or until it was offered to him by the free choice of the whole Mexican people. The French are skilled in managing the machinery of a spontaneous election; and in April 1864, a second deputation carried to Miramar a sceptre of Mexican gold, with the assurance that the whole nation had elected Maximilian Emperor. In reality the French were masters of a very small portion of the country, and the vast majority were not polled at all. Where the French were present there was no serious difficulty, though in some places the chief inhabitants were thrown into prison before they gave in their adhesion. Maximilian was fully informed that the pretended election was nothing but a ceremonious farce. A Mexican Republican made his way to Miramar, and warned him that the real feeling of the country was adverse to the invaders, and that the expedition would end in disaster.

But the promises of France were excessively enticing. The French army was to complete the pacification of the country, and a powerful corps was to be left for several years in the service of Maximilian. France negotiated a loan in his behalf, and seventeen chests filled with gold pieces found their way to Miramar. The Archduke was not in a position to disregard such inducements, for his private fortune was in disorder, and the first £300,000 of the Mexican loan went to clear his debts. Other points were raised which have been kept secret, and the friends of Maximilian still look for important revelations.

At his trial he instructed his counsel to say that Napoleon had required the cession of a portion of Mexican territory as large as Great Britain, and that he had indignantly refused to dismember the country which had given him a crown. He accepted it at a time when the tide of success had turned in the American War, and the prospects of the Confederacy were no longer hopeful. The Archduke demanded a pledge that he should be supported by a French alliance in case of war with the United States; and it is positively asserted that Napoleon gave the required pledge. He gave it believing that England would join him in recognising the South, if it was found that its resistance would be crushed without aid from Europe, and the time came when he made the proposal of a joint recognition to Lord Palmerston. It happened that the two foremost statesmen in the Ministry had made speeches in the provinces which appeared to show a disposition favourable to the Confederates; and the Emperor believed that they would carry their colleagues with them. This was the gravest miscalculation he made in the whole Mexican affair. The Cabinet, taking one of the most momentous resolutions ever adopted by a Ministry, rejected the proposal, and the Emperor shrank from a war single-handed with the United States.

Maximilian, on his part, undertook to pay a million a year while the French remained, and to liquidate all those accumulated claims which Juarez had rejected. In fact, he submitted to conditions impossible to meet, and commenced an undertaking predestined to financial ruin. He reached Mexico in June 1864, and was favourably if not warmly received. The French had ruled the country through the provisional government for a whole year, with almost uninterrupted military success. But they had encountered a difficulty of a formidable and unexpected kind. Juarez had had more than two years to accomplish the overthrow of the clergy, and their property had passed into the hands of speculators, chiefly foreigners, who, it was thought, would not easily be compelled to restore it. The Church party had called for intervention in the hope of recovering these losses, and when the French placed the leaders of the party at the head of the State, they preferred their claims with a sure expectation of success.

The Church in France is supported by the State, and owns no independent property. The French supposed that the practice of their own country could not be unsuitable to Mexico, where a revolution would be required to restore the ancient order, and where the clergy would not bear a comparison with the salaried priesthood of France. The demand was summarily refused. The Episcopate united to denounce the sacrilegious invaders, and the Archbishop ceased to be a member of the provisional government. The breach, for the moment, was complete; and the only hope of the clergy was in Maximilian. He knew that, for a Sovereign to be strong, he must be identified with no party. It was his mission to conciliate and blend together interests severed by years of antagonism. In declining the crown for the first time, he had signified that he would consent to receive it only as the gift of the entire nation. In accepting it afterwards, he made known that he looked upon himself as the elect of the nation, not as the nominee of a powerful interest. From the moment of his arrival he held out the olive branch to the Republicans, and sought their confidence by offering them place and power. Many accepted his offers, and he was surrounded by men who were hateful to those who had seated him on the throne. In adopting this policy it was impossible to draw a line, to examine antecedents, or to reject utterly any candidate for favour. The Emperor was often deceived, and lost on one side without gaining on the other.

After a long delay, which exasperated the trembling holders of Church property, as well as those whom they had despoiled, he decided that all legal purchases should be confirmed, and those which were fraudulent revised, but that nothing should be restored to the clergy, who were to be paid by the State. The Nuncio quarrelled with him upon this, and left the country. Maximilian, irritated by the hostile attitude of the clergy, went further, and restored what was called the *Exequatur*, a law forbidding any document to be published in ecclesiastical affairs without the consent of the civil power. This right has been abandoned by his brother, in Austria; by the Italian Government, last year; and even in Mexico, by Juarez, who adopted the voluntary principle. It could not be defended as a liberal law, and its revival seemed to be simply a blow at the independence of religion. The clergy protested that they had not borne the burden of civil war and brought foreign armies into the country, in order that a prince of their choosing should confirm decrees which had made their property the spoil of their enemies.

They declared that their position was worse under their friend than it had been under their persecutor Juarez. Thenceforth they withdrew their support, and observed a hostile neutrality, watching the time when the Emperor, driven to extremities, would be ready to purchase their assistance at any sacrifice they might demand. In some instances they even fomented the Republican opposition.

This was the first great and visible disaster that the Empire incurred. Another was soon known to be imminent. Financial capacity, rare in every country, was not to be found in Mexico; and Napoleon, who wished his creation to succeed, sent out a Chancellor of the Exchequer from France, with a staff of clerks. But the imported Minister died, and could not be replaced. The finances broke down so completely that Maximilian was obliged to ask for money from the military chest of the French army, and thus fell into the power of its commander. As he could not fulfil his engagements with the Emperor Napoleon, he was guilty of a breach of the treaty signed between them, and gave France an excuse, when her turn came, to justify her own breach of faith.

The year 1865 passed prosperously, on the whole. Maximilian visited many of the towns, saw what he could with his own eyes, and devoted his time to the fabrication of decrees by which he hoped to regenerate the country. These decrees are generally sensible and just; they incline in a good direction, but not always by the right road, and ornamental superfluities sometimes usurp the place of more difficult but more essential things. Maximilian was an anxious and determined educator, and his zeal was praiseworthy, for ninety per cent of the people could neither read or write. But it shows a want of practical capacity when in a community wanting the first necessaries of popular instruction the Sovereign founds an Academy of Sciences, and gravely inculcates on his Ministers the importance of encouraging the study of metaphysics. He found himself in the rare position of a lawgiver called to legislate in a country for which everything remained to be done, and he enjoyed the luxury of carrying out, at least on paper, systems nurtured in days of visionary retirement. He had not time or vigour to execute much of what he had projected.

There was one question that called for an act of high and generous statesmanship. The Indians had been reduced by their poverty and want of energy to the position of serfs. They were in debt to their landlords, and the whole hopeless labour of their lives, without the chance of profit or release, was due to their creditors. They had greeted the coming of Maximilian as the dawn of their deliverance, and he might have made them the willing prop of the imperial throne. In the 800,000 square miles of Mexico, peopled by 8,000,000 of men, but capable of sustaining 100,000,000, it would have been easy, without any spoliation, to distribute land among the countrymen of its ancient owners. Maximilian adopted a half measure. He abolished the debts of the Indians, and thus made them free; but he did no more, and left them to relapse, under pressure of the old causes, into the old degradation. The Indians were not satisfied, and the landowners were alienated.

Something, but not enough, was done for the creation of a native army to defend the crown and country when the French should depart. An Austrian and a Belgian corps were formed, but did not answer expectation. Next to the French, the most efficient body was the division of the Indian general Mejia, a man of a very pure fame. But the French were successful in all they undertook during the whole of 1865. The Republican bands were scattered, many of their generals made their submission, and Juarez, driven from place to place, disappeared at last at a point in the extreme north of Mexico, on the American frontier, more than a thousand miles from the capital. It was reported that he had escaped into the United States. At this time also the four years for which he had been elected expired, and it was impossible to convene a Congress for a new election. Many of his followers now held that he had ceased to govern, and the Vice-President Ortega, the defender of Puebla, claimed the vacant post. The strict legality which had been the strength of the position of Juarez was seriously impaired, and his authority was unquestionably shaken. The country was in a wretched state of insecurity and misery. Plunderers and assassins plied their trade under pretence of being real combatants. Mexican warfare is often scarcely distinguishable from armed robbery, and, as it was the plan of the Republicans to fight in small guerrilla bands, the line separating the soldier from the brigand was often indistinct. The Government thought the time had come to exterminate these bands, and to protect the inhabitants against their incursions. The victory over the regular army was complete, and it seemed that men who infested the roads, when organised resistance was over, did not deserve the treatment of prisoners of war.

On the 2nd of October Maximilian drew up a decree ordering all who should be taken with arms in their hands to be shot, and when he signed it he signed his own death-warrant. Immediately after its publication a Republican force, commanded by

Arteaga, was defeated, and the leaders were captured. In obedience to the new order the Imperial General Mendez put them to death. But the Republicans, though dispersed and dispirited, were not destroyed. A report made to the Emperor in November 1865 estimates their force at 24,000 men, and Juarez had not abandoned the struggle. He remained on Mexican territory, in a town on the Rio del Norte, from which a boat could take him in a few minutes to the American bank, and he remained in communication with the generals of his party. There he waited for the deliverance which he knew was coming. For at that moment, near the close of 1865, his cause was taken up by an ally so powerful and so much feared as to be able, without firing a shot or wasting a single life, to expel the French from Mexico, and to lay the Empire in the dust.

The United States had watched the intervention and the erection of the Empire with anger and alarm. They knew that it had sprung from a desire to cripple their influence, and they could not be indifferent to the presence of an European army on their frontier while they were embarrassed by a civil war. They denied that the Empire was the free choice of the Mexicans, and they highly disapproved of an Emperor that was absolute, for he retained in his own hands all the powers of the State. They refused to recognise him, but they remained neutral, determined not to act until they could act decisively. They rejected various schemes for assisting Juarez with money in return for land, and they declined not only the overtures of Napoleon and of Juarez, but one which was still more tempting. During the siege of Richmond the Confederates proposed that they should unite their armies for the conquest of Mexico and of Canada, but the North refused.

When the war of Secession was over, the Government of Washington had to apply a little diplomatic pressure to the Emperor Napoleon to hasten the recall of his troops. The pressure quickly took the form of threats, and Napoleon very speedily gave way. Events were passing in Europe which made him impatient that Maximilian should restore his legions. In June 1866 war broke out in Italy and in Germany, and in the first week of July Prussia had struck a blow that made half Europe tremble, and menaced the military supremacy and the pride of France. In these circumstances it was certain that the offensive language of America could not be resented, and Mr. Seward used his advantage with cruel complacency. Napoleon informed Maximilian that he must provide for himself, and he informed the American Government that he would retire from Mexico in March 1867.

Rumours of this strange correspondence, and of its probable result, reached Mexico and gave new spirit to the Republicans. Maximilian had refused permission to 25,000 confederates to settle in his dominions; but stragglers found their way to the armies of Juarez, and in June 1866 the important town of Matamoros was surrendered to Escobedo by Mejia. From the moment of that reverse fortune began rapidly to change; and as the French retired from more distant posts, swarms of Republicans appeared in every direction.

When Maximilian learnt the altered intention of Napoleon, he foresaw the end, and spoke of abdication. The Empress persuaded him to remain, while she undertook a journey to Europe. She would compel the French Emperor to fulfil his promises. She would induce the Pope to reconcile the clergy with the Empire. She failed utterly in both endeavours, and in her last interview with Pius IX., perceiving that all hope was ended, she went out of her mind. Early in October the news reached her husband, and then his courage gave way. He had lately exchanged what was called a Liberal for a Conservative Ministry, and had offered the principal departments to two French generals. But they were forbidden by Napoleon to accept, and still no substantial help came from the clergy. Worn out with illness and sorrow, deserted on all sides, and knowing that his Empire was crumbling, Maximilian started for the coast with an undefined intention of sailing for Europe. His most trusted adviser, a Belgian, who had accompanied the Empress, attempted at this conjuncture to draw him away by an appeal to his ambition. He described the discontent of the humbled Austrians and assured him that they wished his brother to abdicate, while sympathy for himself was increasing throughout the country.

Francis Joseph was aware of this intrigue, but he made a last effort to save his brother by restoring to him, if he would return, his position at the head of the princes of the blood. An aide-de-camp of Napoleon arrived in Mexico to hasten the departure of the troops, and was instructed to use everything but force to induce Maximilian to abdicate. The French did not like the dishonour of leaving him to his fate, and they hoped, if he ceased to reign, to make their own terms with the Mexicans, and to leave behind them a government not utterly hostile to themselves. That the expedition was a gigantic failure, injurious to the reputation of the army and the stability of the throne, could not be disguised. But the blow would be more keenly felt if the man on whom they had made war for four years, and with whom they had refused to treat, remained unshaken in his office, victorious over the arms and arts of Napoleon III. So great was their urgency that Maximilian felt insulted, and at last believed himself betrayed.

Whilst he was wavering and lingering near the coast, an American frigate appeared at Vera Cruz, conveying General Sherman and Mr. Campbell, accredited as envoys to Juarez. They had sailed from New York on the 11th of November, when it was supposed that Maximilian had abdicated, leaving the French in the country. The Government at Washington were determined that in that case their candidate, and not that of Napoleon, should prevail. Mr. Campbell was charged to offer support and aid to the Republic, and the presence of the ablest soldier of the Union indicated ostentatiously of what nature that aid was to be. When these envoys found that Maximilian had not departed, they understood that their mission was a blunder and withdrew. The Emperor did not believe that an American Minister, escorted by such a personage as Sherman, had come all the way to Vera Cruz and had gone away without doing anything. He persuaded himself that France and America had come to an understanding, and had made a bargain of which his crown was to be the price. The pressing invitations to depart with the French appeared to him perfidious, and he thought it would be disgraceful that his life should be rescued by those who had bartered his throne.

Meantime the Church party, which had so long coldly stood aloof, thought that the moment had arrived when it could impose its own conditions. It was represented to the Emperor that the disappearance of the invaders would remove the cause of his unpopularity, and that good patriots would support him now, who had refused to acknowledge the nominee of a foreign Power. Miramon arrived from Europe at the critical moment and offered his sword to Maximilian. The Prussian Minister also advised him to remain. The clergy promised their powerful aid, and he yielded. There was nothing for him to look forward to in Europe. No public career was open to the man who had failed so signally in an enterprise of his own seeking. His position in Austria, which was distressing before, would be intolerable now. He had quarrelled with his family, with his church, with the protector to whose temptations he had hearkened. And for him there was to be no more the happiness of the domestic hearth.

In Mexico there were no hopes to live for, but there was still a cause in which it would be glorious to die. There were friends whom he could not leave to perish in expiation of measures which had been his work. He knew what the vengeance of the victors would be. He knew that those who had been most faithful to him would be most surely slaughtered; and he deemed that he, who had never yet been seen on a field of battle, had no right to fly without fighting. Probably he felt that when a monarch cannot preserve his throne, nothing becomes him better than to make his grave beneath its ruins. He yielded, and returned, sullenly and slowly, to the capital. What concessions had been wrung from the party in whose hands he was, I do not know. But he addressed a letter to the Pope, expressing regret for the policy which had failed, and at Rome, where he was once regarded as a persecutor and almost an apostate, the letter was hailed as a solemn and complete retraction.

From that moment Maximilian was no longer the chief of a

national government, but a partisan leader, who had not even the control of his party. He laid aside the pomp of Majesty, and lived in private houses, especially as the guest of the clergy. He declared that he was only provisionally the chief of the State, and held office only until a national assembly had decided what should be the future of Mexico. He invited Juarez to submit his claim to the same peaceful arbitration, and proposed that there should be a general amnesty, to stop the shedding of blood. The Republicans saw nothing in all this but the signs of weakness, and of their own approaching triumph. They opposed no obstacles in the way of the departing French, but they closed in overwhelming numbers upon the feeble army of the Empire.

The defeat of Miramon on the great North road in February compelled Maximilian to take the field. He put himself for the first time at the head of his troops, and joined Miramon at Queretaro. On this day last year he was surrounded and besieged by Escobedo with an army which rose speedily to more than 40,000 men. Marquez was sent to Mexico for reinforcements, but he never returned, and spent the short time that remained in wringing money from the inhabitants. The siege proceeded slowly, and on the 24th of April Miramon made a successful sally, and opened for a moment the road to the capital. But the men were worn out with fighting, and the Emperor refused to leave them. He declared he had not come to Queretaro to fly from danger. To those who saw him during those anxious days, haggard and aged, with a long beard flowing over his breast, and the fever of despair in his eyes, conducting the defence and constantly under fire, it seemed that he was longing for the glory of a soldier's death. At length the supplies were nearly exhausted, the certainty of the treason of Marquez removed all hope of relief, and it was resolved that the garrison should make an attempt to cut its way through the enemy on the 15th of May. It was too late. For four days Lopez, the second in command, had been in communication with Escobedo, and had accepted a bribe of £1400. Late in the night of the 14th he saw the Emperor; and then, at two in the morning, he introduced a Republican general into the fort. This general was disguised, and carried concealed arms. He remained two hours, and examined the interior of the works. Then Lopez withdrew the Imperial sentries, and their posts were silently occupied by the soldiers of Riva Palacio, the only officer who had been excepted, by name, from the decree of October.

At daybreak the bells of the churches of Queretaro announced to the Republican camp that the place was won. The traitor went up to the Emperor's room, and told him that the enemy was in the town. Maximilian rushed forth, and was stopped by Republican soldiers, who did not recognise him. Lopez whispered to the officer who it was. Then the generous Mexican allowed the Emperor to pass, pretending to take him for a civilian; and he escaped to a fortified position at some distance. Here he was joined by the faithful Mejia, and as many officers and men as could hew their way through the columns of Republicans that were now pouring into the town. Miramon alone attempted a forlorn resistance. A shot struck him in the face, and he fell, blinded with blood, into the hands of his enemies.

The position occupied by the Imperialists was swept by artillery and could not be defended, and at eight o'clock they surrendered. Among the prisoners was Mendez, who had caused the decree of October to be executed on Arteaga and his companions. He was shot the same day. The Emperor was shut up, with Miramon and Mejia, in a cell of the Capuchin convent, and it was announced to them that they would be tried by court-martial, under the decree of January. From that moment Maximilian retained no hope of life. He presented his war-horse to Riva Palacio, the most chivalrous of his enemies, and telegraphed to Mexico for the Prussian Minister, and for legal advice in preparing his defence.

Mexico was already besieged by a Republican army, and hollow shells were thrown into the town, stuffed with telegrams proclaiming the fall of Queretaro. But Marquez, the most detested of the Imperial generals, wished to gain time, and he suppressed the news. Maximilian had deposited his abdication in the hands of the President of Council, to be produced if he died or fell a prisoner; but Marquez compelled him to keep it secret, and prevented for several days the departure of the defenders who had been summoned. The most eminent of these was the advocate Riva Palacio, the father of the general, a leading Republican, who had refused all solicitations to serve the Emperor in the days of his power. The others seem to have been less distinguished, but they were all chosen among the Republicans. The Prussian Minister, Baron Magnus, had lived on intimate terms with the Emperor, and had been one of the advisers of the expedition which had ended so fatally. No European Power was less compromised in Mexican affairs, or less obnoxious to the dominant party than Prussia, and it was thought that Baron Magnus would be the best mediator.

The seat of Government was at San Luis, 200 miles beyond Queretaro, but connected with it by telegraph. Two lawyers remained with the Emperor, while Riva Palacio and the Prussian Minister repaired to San Luis to intercede with Juarez. The court-martial which was to try the prisoners met on the stage of the theatre of Queretaro on the morning of Friday, the 14th of June. The house was lighted up and full of spectators. Maximilian had been ill in bed for several days, and self-respect forbade him to appear on such a scene. The two generals were present. Their case was manifestly desperate; yet the defender of Mejia caused a deep impression when he claimed for his client the same mercy which, in spite of stern decrees, he had always shown to his captives, and appealed to Escobedo to say how he had fared when he was Mejia's prisoner. The defence of Miramon was less dignified and less loyal. He pleaded that he had had no command while the French were in the country, that he had been hostile to the Empire which had sent him on an idle mission to Europe, and that he had offered his services to the chief of the Republic. These facts were true; and at Paris Miramon had said openly that the end of the intervention would be to make him President again. Maximilian knew all this, and he knew the manner of his defence. This must not be forgotten when we come to the last scene of all, and see how the Emperor bore himself towards the brave but ambitious soldier, who had been ready to desert the cause in which he was to die.

The strongest points of the indictment against Maximilian were, that he had known the decree of January, which had been published long before he came; that the necessity of foreign support must have proved to him that he was not the legitimate, national Sovereign, and that he could not therefore justify the October decree, by which it was pretended, with great exaggeration, that 40,000 Mexicans had suffered death; that he was responsible for the continuance of civil war after the departure of the French, and for the introduction of Belgian and Austrian soldiers, whose Governments were not at war with the Republic, and who came therefore in the character of filibusters and assassins. The reply to these charges was narrow and technical, and not worthy of the occasion. It amounted in substance to that which the Emperor had said himself: "You may dispute the original probability of my success, but not the sincerity of my motives." As to the decree of October, his advocates defied the prosecution to name a single instance in which he had refused a pardon.

A little before midnight on the 15th the prisoners were found guilty, and their sentence having been confirmed by Escobedo on the Sunday morning, they were informed that they would be shot at three o'clock on the same day. Meanwhile the issue of the trial had been foreseen, and the friends of the Emperor were pleading with Juarez for his pardon. On the ground of political expediency their position was undoubtedly more favourable than that of men restricted to legal arguments. During the war in Mexico a yet deadlier struggle had raged beyond the American border. The author of Secession was not a foreigner, like Maximilian, but a citizen of the country in which he had conspired. He too had been defeated and captured, and then, while European monarchies suppressed revolution with atrocious cruelty, Jefferson Davis had been released by the great Republic. Therefore, they said, the honour of Republican institutions was in the keeping of Juarez, and required that Mexico should follow that example of triumphant clemency, and should betray neither hatred for the past nor alarm for the future.

The President and his minister, Lerdo, listened patiently but coldly. They said that Europe could give no guarantee that it would not renew the same attempt, that Maximilian would continue, even in spite of himself, to be a pretext and a rallying cry for faction, and an instrument by which foreign Powers, when complications arose, might gain a party in the country. The decree of October cried for expiation, and the death of its author would enable them to spare the rest. Many Mexicans had been put to death under the decree of January, and the punishment of inferiors could not be justified if that of the leader was remitted. They seem to have believed that if the doorposts of the Republic were marked with the blood of a prince, the angel of destruction would pass them by. They showed no inclination to cast on others the responsibility of their act, but it is difficult to believe that it was determined by reason of state dispassionately weighed.

Juarez possessed but a precarious authority over the army; and the army was infuriated by strife, and thirsted to avenge the comrades who had been executed like murderers. We can imagine what their feelings would be towards the foreigner whose title was a vote extracted by the bayonets of invaders, who had ordered their countrymen and themselves to be slaughtered, and who was now convicted of having been a pretender and a usurper, as he was the champion of the weaker party. It is probable that the real author of the Emperor's execution is Escobedo, and that Juarez was powerless to save him. When the news that he was to die in three hours reached San Luis at noon on the Sunday, the Prussian Minister prayed for a short delay. He knew that Maximilian had matters to settle before death, and there was some hope that foreign intercession would be in time to save his life. But the American Government, at the request of the Emperor of Austria, had already interceded for his brother, and had interceded in vain. A delay of three days was granted, but the order did not reach Queretaro till the last moment, when the prisoners had made themselves ready for immediate death. For himself, indeed, Maximilian had no hope, and was perfectly resigned. A report that his wife was dead made him meet his fate with joy. On the eve of his execution he telegraphed to Juarez requesting that he might be the only victim.

At six in the morning of Wednesday, the 19th of last June, he was led forth to the doom he had not deserved. His last act before going to the place of execution had been to write the following letter to his implacable conqueror: "I give up my life willingly, if the sacrifice can promote the welfare of my new country. But nothing healthy can grow upon a soil saturated with blood, and therefore, I entreat you, let mine be the last you shed. The fortitude with which you upheld the cause that triumphs now won my admiration in happier days, and I pray that it may not fail you in the peaceful work of conciliation that is to come." When they came to the appointed place, he gave money to the soldiers by whose hands he was to fall, asking them to aim at his heart, for he wished that his mother might look upon his face again. The officer who was to give the word assured him that he detested the duty, and implored him not to die with a feeling of resentment against him. Maximilian thanked him, and said that he must obey orders. Mejia was in great trouble and dejection. His wife had just borne him a son, and as he left his prison he had seen her rushing through the streets, raving mad, with the child in her arms. The Emperor bade him farewell affectionately, saying: "There is a reward in the next world for that which is not requited here." He was standing between the Mexicans, but out of humility, or magnanimity, or because a solemn and sacred memory was present to his mind at that last awful moment, he turned to Miramon and said that out of esteem for his courage he would yield to him the place of honour. His last words were: "I die for a just cause—the independence and the liberty of Mexico. May my death close the era of the misfortunes of my adopted country: God save Mexico!" Then he crossed his hands upon his breast and fell, pierced by nine balls.

He fell, and carried with him in his fall the independence of the people he had come to save. Nothing henceforth remains that can permanently arrest the United States in the annexation of Spanish America. If they have prudence to avoid European war, and wisdom to compose their own dissensions, they may grasp the most glorious inheritance the earth affords. The conquest of Spanish America would be easy and certain, but beset with dangers. A confederacy loses its true character when it rules over dependencies; and a Democracy lives a threatened life that admits millions of a strange and inferior race which it can neither assimilate nor absorb. It is more likely that the Americans will bind their neighbours by treaties, which will throw open the whole continent to their own influence and enterprise, without destroying their separate existence.

The memory of the fair-haired stranger, who devoted his life to the good of Mexico, and died for guilt which was not his own, will live in sorrow rather than in anger among the people for whom he strove in vain. Already we may pronounce the verdict of history upon his sad career—his worst crime was in accepting the treacherous gift of Empire, but his misfortune was greater than his fault. I think he was well-nigh the noblest of his race, and fulfilled the promise of his words: "The fame of my ancestors will not degenerate in me."

VIII

The History of Freedom in Antiquity

LIBERTY, next to religion, has been the motive of good deeds
and the common pretext of crime, from the sowing of the seed
at Athens, two thousand four hundred and sixty years ago, until
the ripened harvest was gathered by men of our race. It is the
delicate fruit of a mature civilisation; and scarcely a century has
passed since nations, that knew the meaning of the term, resolved to be free. In every age its progress has been beset by its
natural enemies, but ignorance and superstition, by lust of
conquest and by love of ease, by the strong man's craving for
power, and the poor man's craving for food. During long intervals it has been utterly arrested, when nations were being
rescued from barbarism and from the grasp of strangers, and
when the perpetual struggle for existence, depriving men of all
interest and understanding in politics, has made them eager to
sell their birthright for a pottage, and ignorant of the treasure
they resigned. At all times sincere friends of freedom have been
rare, and its triumphs have been due to minorities, that have
prevailed by associating themselves with auxiliaries whose objects often differed from their own; and this association, which
is always dangerous, has been sometimes disastrous, by giving
to opponents just grounds of opposition, and by kindling dispute over the spoils in the hour of success. No obstacle has been
so constant, or so difficult to overcome, as uncertainty and
confusion touching the nature of true liberty. If hostile interests

An address delivered to the members of the Bridgnorth Institution at the
Agricultural Hall, February 26, 1877. Reprinted from Acton, *History of
Freedom and Other Essays* (London: Macmillan, 1907).

have wrought much injury, false ideas have wrought still more; and its advance is recorded in the increase of knowledge, as much as in the improvement of laws. The history of institutions is often a history of deception and illusions; for their virtue depends on the ideas that produce and on the spirit that preserves them, and the form may remain unaltered when the substance has passed away.

A few familiar examples from modern politics will explain why it is that the burden of my argument will lie outside the domain of legislation. It is often said that our Constitution attained its formal perfection in 1679, when the Habeas Corpus Act was passed. Yet Charles II. succeeded, only two years later, in making himself independent of Parliament. In 1789, while the States-General assembled at Versailles, the Spanish Cortes, older than Magna Charta and more venerable than our House of Commons, were summoned after an interval of generations, but they immediately prayed the King to abstain from consulting them, and to make his reforms of his own wisdom and authority. According to the common opinion, indirect elections are a safeguard of conservatism. But all the Assemblies of the French Revolution issued from indirect elections. A restricted suffrage is another reputed security for monarchy. But the Parliament of Charles X., which was returned by 90,000 electors, resisted and overthrew the throne; while the Parliament of Louis Philippe, chosen by a Constitution of 250,000, obsequiously promoted the reactionary policy of his Ministers, and in the fatal division which, by rejecting reform, laid the monarchy in the dust, Guizot's majority was obtained by the votes of 129 public functionaries. An unpaid legislature is, for obvious reasons, more independent than most of the Continental legislatures which receive pay. But it would be unreasonable in America to send a member as far as from here to Constantinople to live for twelve months at his own expense in the dearest of capital cities. Legally and to outward seeming the American President is the successor of Washington, and still enjoys powers devised and limited by the Convention of Philadelphia. In reality the new President differs from the Magistrate imagined by the Fathers of the Republic as widely as Monarchy from Democracy, for he is expected to make 70,000 changes in the public service; fifty years ago John Quincy Adams dismissed only two men. The purchase of judicial appointments is manifestly indefensible; yet in the old French monarchy that monstrous practice created the only corporation able to resist the king. Official corruption, which would ruin a commonwealth, serves in Russia as a salutary relief from the pressure of absolutism. There are conditions in which it is scarcely a hyperbole to say that slavery itself is a stage on the road to freedom. Therefore we are not so much concerned this evening with the dead letter of edicts and of statutes as with the living thoughts of men. A century ago it was perfectly well known that whoever had one audience of a Master in Chancery was made to pay for three, but no man heeded the enormity until it suggested to a young lawyer that it might be well to question and examine with rigorous suspicion every part of a system in which such things were done. The day on which that gleam lighted up the clear hard mind of Jeremy Bentham is memorable in the political calendar beyond the entire administration of many statesmen. It would be easy to point out a paragraph in St. Augustine, or a sentence of Grotius that outweighs in influence the Acts of fifty Parliaments, and our cause owes more to Cicero and Seneca, to Vinet and Tocqueville, than to the laws of Lycurgus or the Five Codes of France.

By liberty I mean the assurance that every man shall be protected in doing what he believes his duty against the influence of authority and majorities, custom and opinion. The State is competent to assign duties and draw the line between good and evil only in its immediate sphere. Beyond the limits of things necessary for its well-being, it can only give indirect help to fight the battle of life by promoting the influences which prevail against temptation,—religion, education, and the distribution of wealth. In ancient times the State absorbed authorities not its own, and intruded on the domain of personal freedom. In the Middle Ages it possessed too little authority, and suffered others to intrude. Modern States fall habitually into both excesses. The most certain test by which we judge whether a country is really free is the amount of security enjoyed by minorities. Liberty, by this definition, is the essential condition and guardian of religion; and it is in the history of the Chosen People, accordingly, that the first illustrations of my subject are obtained. The government of the Israelites was a Federation, held together by no political authority, but by the unity of race and faith, and founded, not on physical force, but on a voluntary covenant. The principle of self-government was carried out not only in each tribe, but in every group of at least 120 families; and there was neither privilege of rank nor inequality before the law. Monarchy was so alien to the primitive spirit of the community that it was resisted by Samuel in that momentous protestation and warning which all the kingdoms of Asia and many of the kingdoms of Europe have unceasingly confirmed. The throne was erected on a compact; and the king was deprived of the right of legislation among a people that recognised no lawgiver but God, whose highest aim in politics was to restore the original purity of the constitution, and to make its government conform to the ideal type that was hallowed by the sanctions of heaven. The inspired men who rose in unfailing succession to prophesy against the usurper and the tyrant, constantly proclaimed that the laws, which were divine, were paramount over sinful rulers, and appealed from the established authorities, from the king, the priests, and the princes of the people, to the healing forces that slept in the uncorrupted consciences of the masses. Thus the example of the Hebrew nation laid down the parallel lines on which all freedom has been won—the doctrine of national tradition and the doctrine of the higher law; the principle that a constitution grows from a root, by process of development, and not of essential change; and the principle that all political authorities must be tested and reformed according to a code which was not made by man. The operation of these principles, in unison, or in antagonism, occupies the whole of the space we are going over together.

The conflict between liberty under divine authority and the absolutism of human authorities ended disastrously. In the year

622 a supreme effort was made at Jerusalem to reform and preserve the State. The High Priest produced from the temple of Jehovah the book of the deserted and forgotten Law, and both king and people bound themselves by solemn oaths to observe it. But that early example of limited monarchy and of the supremacy of law neither lasted nor spread; and the forces by which freedom has conquered must be sought elsewhere. In the very year 586, in which the flood of Asiatic despotism closed over the city which had been, and was destined again to be, the sanctuary of freedom in the East, a new home was prepared for it in the West, where, guarded by the sea and the mountains, and by valiant hearts, that stately plant was reared under whose shade we dwell, and which is extending its invincible arms so slowly and yet so surely over the civilised world.

According to a famous saying of the most famous authoress of the Continent, liberty is ancient, and it is despotism that is new. It has been the pride of recent historians to vindicate the truth of that maxim. The heroic age of Greece confirms it, and it is still more conspicuously true of Teutonic Europe. Wherever we can trace the earlier life of the Aryan nations we discover germs which favouring circumstances and assiduous culture might have developed into free societies. They exhibit some sense of common interest in common concerns, little reverence for external authority, and an imperfect sense of the function and supremacy of the State. Where the division of property and labour is incomplete there is little division of classes and of power. Until societies are tried by the complex problems of civilisation they may escape despotism, as societies that are undisturbed by religious diversity avoid persecution. In general, the forms of the patriarchal age failed to resist the growth of absolute States when the difficulties and temptations of advancing life began to tell; and with one sovereign exception, which is not within my scope to-day, it is scarcely possible to trace their survival in the institutions of later times. Six hundred years before the birth of Christ absolutism held unbounded sway. Throughout the East it was propped by the unchanging influence of priests and armies. In the West, where there were no

sacred books requiring trained interpreters, the priesthood acquired no preponderance, and when the kings were overthrown
their powers passed to aristocracies of birth. What followed,
during many generations, was the cruel domination of class over
class, the oppression of the poor by the rich, and of the ignorant
by the wise. The spirit of that domination found passionate
utterance in the verses of the aristocratic poet Theognis, a man
of genius and refinement, who avows that he longed to drink
the blood of his political adversaries. From these oppressors the
people of many cities sought deliverance in the less intolerable
tyranny of revolutionary usurpers. The remedy gave new shape
and energy to the evil. The tyrants were often men of surprising
capacity and merit, like some of those who, in the fourteenth
century, made themselves lords of Italian cities; but rights
secured by equal laws and by sharing power existed nowhere.

From this universal degradation the world was rescued by
the most gifted of the nations. Athens, which like other cities
was distracted and oppressed by a privileged class, avoided
violence and appointed Solon to revise its laws. It was the
happiest choice that history records. Solon was not only the
wisest man to be found in Athens, but the most profound
political genius of antiquity; and the easy, bloodless, and pacific
revolution by which he accomplished the deliverance of his
country was the first step in a career which our age glories in
pursuing, and instituted a power which has done more than
anything, except revealed religion, for the regeneration of society. The upper class had possessed the right of making and
administering the laws, and he left them in possession, only
transferring to wealth what had been the privilege of birth. To
the rich, who alone had the means of sustaining the burden of
public service in taxation and war, Solon gave a share of power
proportioned to the demands made on their resources. The
poorest classes were exempt from direct taxes, but were excluded
from office. Solon gave them a voice in electing magistrates
from the classes above them, and the right of calling them to
account. This concession, apparently so slender, was the beginning of a mighty change. It introduced the idea that a man

ought to have a voice in selecting those to whose rectitude and wisdom he is compelled to trust his fortune, his family, and his life. And this idea completely inverted the notion of human authority, for it inaugurated the reign of moral influence where all political power had depended on moral force. Government by consent superseded government by compulsion, and the pyramid which had stood on a point was made to stand upon its base. By making every citizen the guardian of his own interest Solon admitted the element of Democracy into the State. The greatest glory of a ruler, he said, is to create a popular government. Believing that no man can be entirely trusted, he subjected all who exercised power to the vigilant control of those for whom they acted.

The only resource against political disorders that had been known till then was the concentration of power. Solon undertook to effect the same object by the distribution of power. He gave to the common people as much influence as he thought them able to employ, that the State might be exempt from arbitrary government. It is the essence of Democracy, he said, to obey no master but the law. Solon recognised the principle that political forms are not final or inviolable, and must adapt themselves to facts; and he provided so well for the revision of his constitution, without breach of continuity or loss of stability, that for centuries after his death the Attic orators attributed to him, and quoted by his name, the whole structure of Athenian law. The direction of its growth was determined by the fundamental doctrine of Solon, that political power ought to be commensurate with public service. In the Persian war the services of the Democracy eclipsed those of the Patrician orders, for the fleet that swept the Asiatics from the Aegean Sea was manned by the poorer Athenians. That class, whose valour had saved the State and had preserved European civilisation, had gained a title to increase of influence and privilege. The offices of State, which had been a monopoly of the rich, were thrown open to the poor, and in order to make sure that they should obtain their share, all but the highest commands were distributed by lot.

Whilst the ancient authorities were decaying, there was no accepted standard of moral and political right to make the framework of society fast in the midst of change. The instability that had seized on the forms threatened the very principles of government. The national beliefs were yielding to doubt, and doubt was not yet making way for knowledge. There had been a time when the obligations of public as well as private life were identified with the will of the gods. But that time had passed. Pallas, the ethereal goddess of the Athenians, and the Sun god whose oracles, delivered from the temple between the twin summits of Parnassus, did so much for the Greek nationality, aided in keeping up a lofty ideal of religion; but when the enlightened men of Greece learnt to apply their keen faculty of reasoning to the system of their inherited belief, they became quickly conscious that the conceptions of the gods corrupted the life and degraded the minds of the public. Popular morality could not be sustained by the popular religion. The moral instruction which was no longer supplied by the gods could not yet be found in books. There was no venerable code expounded by experts, no doctrine proclaimed by men of reputed sanctity like those teachers of the far East whose words still rule the fate of nearly half mankind. The effort to account for things by close observation and exact reasoning began by destroying. There came a time when the philosophers of the Porch and the Academy wrought the dictates of wisdom and virtue into a system so consistent and profound that it has vastly shortened the task of the Christian divines. But that time had not yet come.

The epoch of doubt and transition during which the Greeks passed from the dim fancies of mythology to the fierce light of science was the age of Pericles, and the endeavour to substitute certain truth for the prescriptions of impaired authorities, which was then beginning to absorb the energies of the Greek intellect, is the grandest movement in the profane annals of mankind, for to it we owe, even after the immeasurable progress accomplished by Christianity, much of our philosophy and far the better part of the political knowledge we possess. Pericles, who was at the head of the Athenian Government, was the first statesman who encountered the problem which the rapid weakening of traditions forced on the political world. No authority in morals or in politics remained unshaken by the motion that was in the air. No guide could be confidently trusted; there was no available criterion to appeal to, for the means of controlling or denying convictions that prevailed among the people. The popular sentiment as to what was right might be mistaken, but it was subject to no test. The people were, for practical purposes, the seat of the knowledge of good and evil. The people, therefore, were the seat of power.

The political philosophy of Pericles consisted of this conclusion. He resolutely struck away all the props that still sustained the artificial preponderance of wealth. For the ancient doctrine that power goes with land, he introduced the idea that power ought to be so equitably diffused as to afford equal security to all. That one part of the community should govern the whole, or that one class should make laws for another, he declared to be tyrannical. The abolition of privilege would have served only to transfer the supremacy from the rich to the poor, if Pericles had not redressed the balance by restricting the right of citizenship to Athenians of pure descent. By this measure the class which formed what we should call the third estate was brought down to 14,000 citizens, and became about equal in numbers with the higher ranks. Pericles held that every Athenian who neglected to take his part in the public business inflicted an injury on the commonwealth. That none might be excluded by poverty, he caused the poor to be paid for their attendance out of the funds of the State; for his administration of the federal tribute had brought together a treasure of more than two million sterling. The instrument of his sway was the art of speaking. He governed by persuasion. Everything was decided by argument in open deliberation, and every influence bowed before the ascendancy of mind. The idea that the object of constitutions is not to confirm the predominance of any interest, but to prevent it; to preserve with equal care the independence of labour and the security of property; to make the rich safe against envy, and the poor against oppression, marks the highest level attained by the statesmanship of Greece. It hardly survived the great patriot who conceived it; and all history has been occupied with the endeavour to upset the balance of power by giving the advantage to money, land, or numbers. A generation followed that has never been equalled in talent—a generation of men whose works, in poetry and eloquence, are still the envy of the world, and in history, philosophy, and politics remain unsurpassed. But it produced no successor to Pericles, and no man was able to wield the sceptre that fell from his hand.

It was a momentous step in the progress of nations when the principle that every interest should have the right and the means of asserting itself was adopted by the Athenian Constitution. But for those who were beaten in the vote there was no redress. The law did not check the triumph of majorities or rescue the minority from the dire penalty of having been outnumbered. When the overwhelming influence of Pericles was removed, the conflict between classes raged without restraint, and the slaughter that befell the higher ranks in the Peloponnesian war gave an irresistible preponderance to the lower. The restless and inquiring spirit of the Athenians was prompt to unfold the reason of every institution and the consequences of every principle, and their Constitution ran its course from infancy to decrepitude with unexampled speed.

Two men's lives span the interval from the first admission of popular influence, under Solon, to the downfall of the State. Their history furnishes the classic example of the peril of Democracy under conditions singularly favourable. For the Athenians were not only brave and patriotic and capable of generous sacrifice, but they were the most religious of the Greeks. They venerated the Constitution which had given them prosperity, and equality, and freedom, and never questioned the fundamental laws which regulated the enormous power of the Assembly. They tolerated considerable variety of opinion and great license of speech; and their humanity towards their slaves roused the indignation even of the most intelligent partisan of aristocracy. Thus they became the only people of antiquity that grew great by democratic institutions. But the possession of unlimited power, which corrodes the conscience, hardens the heart, and confounds the understanding of monarchs, exercised its demoralising influence on the illustrious democracy of Athens. It is bad to be oppressed by a minority, but it is worse to be oppressed by a majority. For there is a reserve of latent power in the masses which, if it is called into play, the minority can seldom resist. But from the absolute will of an entire people there is no appeal, no redemption, no refuge but treason. The humblest and most numerous class of the Athenians united the legislative, the judicial, and, in part, the executive power. The philosophy that was then in the ascendant taught them that there is no law superior to that of the State—the lawgiver is above the law.

It followed that the sovereign people had a right to do whatever was within its power, and was bound by no rule of right or wrong but its own judgment of expediency. On a memorable occasion the assembled Athenians declared it monstrous that they should be prevented from doing whatever they chose. No force that existed could restrain them; and they resolved that no duty should restrain them, and that they would be bound by no laws that were not of their own making. In this way the emancipated people of Athens became a tyrant; and their Government, the pioneer of European freedom, stands condemned with a terrible unanimity by all the wisest of the ancients. They ruined their city by attempting to conduct war by debate in the marketplace. Like the French Republic, they put their unsuccessful commanders to death. They treated their dependencies with such injustice that they lost their maritime Empire. They plundered the rich until the rich conspired with the public enemy, and they crowned their guilt by the martyrdom of Socrates.

When the absolute sway of numbers had endured for near a quarter of a century, nothing but bare existence was left for the State to lose; and the Athenians, wearied and despondent, confessed the true cause of their ruin. They understood that for liberty, justice, and equal laws, it is as necessary that Democracy should restrain itself as it had been that it should restrain the

Oligarchy. They resolved to take their stand once more upon the ancient ways, and to restore the order of things which had subsisted when the monopoly of power had been taken from the rich and had not been acquired by the poor. After a first restoration had failed, which is only memorable because Thucydides, whose judgment in politics is never at fault, pronounced it the best Government Athens had enjoyed, the attempt was renewed with more experience and greater singleness of purpose. The hostile parties were reconciled, and proclaimed an amnesty, the first in history. They resolved to govern by concurrence. The laws, which had the sanction of tradition, were reduced to a code; and no act of the sovereign assembly was valid with which they might be found to disagree. Between the sacred lines of the Constitution which were to remain inviolate, and the decrees which met from time to time the needs and notions of the day, a broad distinction was drawn; and the fabric of a law which had been the work of generations was made independent of momentary variations in the popular will. The repentance of the Athenians came too late to save the Republic. But the lesson of their experience endures for all times, for it teaches that government by the whole people, being the government of the most numerous and most powerful class, is an evil of the same nature as unmixed monarchy, and requires, for nearly the same reasons, institutions that shall protect it against itself, and shall uphold the permanent reign of law against arbitrary revolutions of opinion.

Parallel with the rise and fall of Athenian freedom, Rome was employed in working out the same problems, with greater constructive sense, and greater temporary success, but ending at last in a far more terrible catastrophe. That which among the ingenious Athenians had been a development carried forward by the spell of plausible argument, was in Rome a conflict between rival forces. Speculative politics had no attraction for the grim and practical genius of the Romans. They did not consider what would be the cleverest way of getting over a difficulty, but what way was indicated by analogous cases; and

they assigned less influence to the impulse and spirit of the
moment, than to precedent and example. Their peculiar character prompted them to ascribe the origin of their laws to early
times, and in their desire to justify the continuity of their
institutions, and to get rid of the reproach of innovation, they
imagined the legendary history of the kings of Rome. The
energy of their adherence to traditions made their progress
slow, they advanced only under compulsion of almost unavoidable necessity, and the same questions recurred often, before
they were settled. The constitutional history of the Republic
turns on the endeavours of the aristocracy, who claimed to be
the only true Romans, to retain in their hands the power they
had wrested from the kings, and of the plebeians to get an
equal share in it. And this controversy, which the eager and
restless Athenians went through in one generation, lasted for
more than two centuries, from a time when the *plebs* were
excluded from the government of the city, and were taxed, and
made to serve without pay, until, in the year 285, they were
admitted to political equality. Then followed one hundred and
fifty years of unexampled prosperity and glory; and then, out of
the original conflict which had been compromised, if not theo-
retically settled, a new struggle arose which was without an
issue.

The mass of poorer families, impoverished by incessant service in war, were reduced to dependence on an aristocracy of
about two thousand wealthy men, who divided among themselves the immense domain of the State. When the need became
intense the Gracchi tried to relieve it by inducing the richer
classes to allot some share in the public lands to the common
people. The old and famous aristocracy of birth and rank had
made a stubborn resistance, but it knew the art of yielding. The
later and more selfish aristocracy was unable to learn it. The
character of the people was changed by the sterner motives of
dispute. The fight for political power had been carried on with
the moderation which is so honourable a quality of party contests in England. But the struggle for the objects of material
existence grew to be as ferocious as civil controversies in

France. Repulsed by the rich, after a struggle of twenty-two years, the people, three hundred and twenty thousand of whom depended on public rations for food, were ready to follow any man who promised to obtain for them by revolution what they could not obtain by law.

For a time the Senate, representing the ancient and threatened order of things, was strong enough to overcome every popular leader that arose, until Julius Caesar, supported by an army which he had led in an unparalleled career of conquest, and by the famished masses which he won by his lavish liberality, and skilled beyond all other men in the art of governing, converted the Republic into a Monarchy by a series of measures that were neither violent nor injurious.

The Empire preserved the Republican forms until the reign of Diocletian; but the will of the Emperors was as uncontrolled as that of the people had been after the victory of the Tribunes. Their power was arbitrary even when it was most wisely employed, and yet the Roman Empire rendered greater services to the cause of liberty than the Roman Republic. I do not mean by reason of the temporary accident that there were emperors who made good use of their immense opportunities, such as Nerva, of whom Tacitus says that he combined monarchy and liberty, things otherwise incompatible; or that the Empire was what its panegyrists declared it, the perfection of Democracy. In truth it was at best an ill-disguised and odious despotism. But Frederic the Great was a despot; yet he was a friend to toleration and free discussion. The Bonapartes were despotic; yet no liberal ruler was ever more acceptable to the masses of the people than the First Napoleon, after he had destroyed the Republic, in 1805, and the Third Napoleon at the height of his power in 1859. In the same way, the Roman Empire possessed merits which, at a distance, and especially at a great distance of time, concern men more deeply than the tragic tyranny which was felt in the neighbourhood of the Palace. The poor had what they had demanded in vain of the Republic. The rich fared better than during the Triumvirate. The rights of Roman citizens were extended to the people of the provinces. To the imperial epoch belong the better part of Roman literature and nearly the entire Civil Law; and it was the Empire that mitigated slavery, instituted religious toleration, made a beginning of the law of nations, and created a perfect system of the law of property. The Republic which Caesar overthrew had been anything but a free State. It provided admirable securities for the rights of citizens; it treated with savage disregard the rights of men; and allowed the free Roman to inflict atrocious wrongs on his children, on debtors and dependents, on prisoners and slaves. Those deeper ideas of right and duty, which are not found on the tables of municipal law, but with which the generous minds of Greece were conversant, were held of little account, and the philosophy which dealt with such speculations was repeatedly proscribed, as a teacher of sedition and impiety.

At length, in the year 155, the Athenian philosopher Carneades appeared at Rome, on a political mission. During an interval of official business he delivered two public orations, to give the unlettered conquerors of his country a taste of the disputations that flourished in the Attic schools. On the first day he discoursed of natural justice. On the next he denied its existence, arguing that all our notions of good and evil are derived from positive enactment. From the time of that memorable display, the genius of the vanquished held its conquerors in thrall. The most eminent of the public men of Rome, such as Scipio and Cicero, formed their minds on Grecian models, and her jurists underwent the rigorous discipline of Zeno and Chrysippus.

If, drawing the limit in the second century, when the influence of Christianity becomes perceptible, we should form our judgment of the politics of antiquity by its actual legislation, our estimate would be low. The prevailing notions of freedom were imperfect, and the endeavours to realise them were wide of the mark. The ancients understood the regulation of power better than the regulation of liberty. They concentrated so many prerogatives in the State as to leave no footing from which a man could deny its jurisdiction or assign bounds to its activity. If I may employ an expressive anachronism, the vice of the classic State was that it was both Church and State in one. Morality was undistinguished from religion and politics from morals; and in religion, morality, and politics there was only one legislator and one authority. The State, while it did deplorably little for education, for practical science, for the indigent and helpless, or for the spiritual needs of man, nevertheless claimed the use of all his faculties and the determination of all his duties. Individuals and families, associations and dependencies were so much material that the sovereign power consumed for its own purposes. What the slave was in the hands of his master, the citizen was in the hands of the community. The most sacred obligations vanished before the public advantage. The passengers existed for the sake of the ship. By their disregard for private interests, and for the moral welfare and improvement of the people, both Greece and Rome destroyed the vital elements on which the prosperity of nations rests, and perished by the decay of families and the depopulation of the country. They survive not in their institutions, but in their ideas, and by their ideas, especially on the art of government, they are—

> The dead, but sceptred sovereigns who still rule
> Our spirits from their urns.

To them, indeed, may be tracked nearly all the errors that are undermining political society—Communism, Utilitarianism, the confusion between tyranny and authority, and between lawlessness and freedom.

The notion that men lived originally in a state of nature, by violence and without laws, is due to Critias. Communism in its grossest form was recommended by Diogenes of Sinope. According to the Sophists, there is no duty above expediency and no virtue apart from pleasure. Laws are an invention of weak men to rob their betters of the reasonable enjoyment of their superiority. It is better to inflict than to suffer wrong; and as there is no greater good than to do evil without fear of retribution, so there is no worse evil than to suffer without the consolation of revenge. Justice is the mask of a craven spirit; injustice is

worldly wisdom; and duty, obedience, self-denial are the im-
postures of hypocrisy. Government is absolute, and may ordain
what it pleases, and no subject can complain that it does him
wrong, but as long as he can escape compulsion and punishment, he is always free to disobey. Happiness consists in obtaining power and in eluding the necessity of obedience; and he
that gains a throne by perfidy and murder, deserves to be truly
envied.

Epicurus differed but little from the propounders of the code
of revolutionary despotism. All societies, he said, are founded
on contracts for mutual protection. Good and evil are conventional terms, for the thunderbolts of heaven fall alike on the just
and the unjust. The objection to wrongdoing is not the act, but
in its consequences to the wrongdoer. Wise men contrive laws,
not to bind, but to protect themselves; and when they prove to
be unprofitable they cease to be valid. The illiberal sentiments
of even the most illustrious metaphysicians are disclosed in the
saying of Aristotle, that the mark of the worst governments is
that they leave men free to live as they please.

If you will bear in mind that Socrates, the best of the pagans,
knew of no higher criterion for men, of no better guide of
conduct, than the laws of each country; that Plato, whose sublime doctrine was so near an anticipation of Christianity that
celebrated theologians wished his works to be forbidden, lest
men should be content with them, and indifferent to any higher
dogma—to whom was granted that prophetic vision of the Just
Man, accused, condemned and scourged, and dying on a
Cross—nevertheless employed the most splendid intellect ever
bestowed on man to advocate the abolition of the family and
the exposure of infants; that Aristotle, the ablest moralist of
antiquity, saw no harm in making raids upon a neighbouring
people, for the sake of reducing them to slavery—still more, if
you will consider that, among the moderns, men of genius equal
to these have held political doctrines not less criminal or absurd—it will be apparent to you how stubborn a phalanx of
error blocks the paths of truth; that pure reason is as powerless
as custom to solve the problem of free government; that it can

only be the fruit of long, manifold, and painful experience; and that the tracing of the methods by which divine wisdom has educated the nations to appreciate and to assume the duties of freedom, is not the least part of that true philosophy that studies to

> Assert eternal Providence,
> And justify the ways of God to men.

But, having sounded the depth of their errors, I should give you a very inadequate idea of the wisdom of the ancients if I allowed it to appear that their precepts were no better than their practice. While statesmen and senates and popular assemblies supplied examples of every description of blunder, a noble literature arose, in which a priceless treasure of political knowledge was stored, and in which the defects of the existing institutions were exposed with unsparing sagacity. The point on which the ancients were most nearly unanimous is the right of the people to govern, and their inability to govern alone. To meet this difficulty, to give to the popular element a full share without a monopoly of power, they adopted very generally the theory of a mixed Constitution. They differed from our notion of the same thing, because modern Constitutions have been a device for limiting monarchy; with them they were invented to curb democracy. The idea arose in the time of Plato—though he repelled it—when the early monarchies and oligarchies had vanished, and it continued to be cherished long after all democracies had been absorbed in the Roman Empire. But whereas a sovereign prince who surrenders part of his authority yields to the argument of superior force, a sovereign people relinquishing its own prerogative succumbs to the influence of reason. And it has in all times proved more easy to create limitations by the use of force than by persuasion.

The ancient writers saw very clearly that each principle of government standing alone is carried to excess and provokes a reaction. Monarchy hardens into despotism. Aristocracy contracts into oligarchy. Democracy expands into the supremacy of numbers. They therefore imagined that to restrain each element by combining it with the others would avert the natural process of self-destruction, and endow the State with perpetual youth. But this harmony of monarchy, aristocracy, and democracy blended together, which was the ideal of many writers, and which they supposed to be exhibited by Sparta, by Carthage, and by Rome, was a chimera of philosophers never realised by antiquity. At last Tacitus, wiser than the rest, confessed that the mixed Constitution, however admirable in theory, was difficult to establish and impossible to maintain. His disheartening avowal is not disowned by later experience.

The experiment has been tried more often than I can tell, with a combination of resources that were unknown to the ancients—with Christianity, parliamentary government, and a free press. Yet there is no example of such a balanced Constitution having lasted a century. If it has succeeded anywhere it has been in our favoured country and in our time; and we know not yet how long the wisdom of the nation will preserve the equipoise. The Federal check was as familiar to the ancients as the Constitutional. For the type of all their Republics was the government of a city by its own inhabitants meeting in the public place. An administration embracing many cities was known to them only in the form of the oppression which Sparta exercised over the Messenians, Athens over her Confederates, and Rome over Italy. The resources which, in modern times, enabled a great people to govern itself through a single centre did not exist. Equality could be preserved only by Federalism; and it occurs more often amongst them than in the modern world. If the distribution of power among the several parts of the State is the most efficient restraint on monarchy, the distribution of power among several States is the best check on democracy. By multiplying centres of government and discussion it promotes the diffusion of political knowledge and the maintenance of healthy and independent opinion. It is the protectorate of minorities, and the consecration of self-government. But although it must be enumerated among the better achievements of practical genius in antiquity, it arose from necessity, and its properties were imperfectly investigated in theory.

When the Greeks began to reflect on the problems of society, they first of all accepted things as they were, and did their best to explain and defend them. Inquiry, which with us is stimulated by doubt, began with them in wonder. The most illustrious of the early philosophers, Pythagoras, promulgated a theory for the preservation of political power in the educated class, and ennobled a form of government which was generally founded on popular ignorance and on strong class interests. He preached authority and subordination, and dwelt more on duties than on rights, on religion than on policy; and his system perished in the revolution by which oligarchies were swept away. The revolution afterwards developed its own philosophy, whose excesses I have described.

But between the two eras, between the rigid didactics of the early Pythagoreans and the dissolving theories of Protagoras, a philosopher arose who stood aloof from both extremes, and whose difficult sayings were never really understood or valued until our time. Heraclitus, of Ephesus, deposited his book in the temple of Diana. The book has perished, like the temple and the worship, but its fragments have been collected and interpreted with incredible ardour, by the scholars, the divines, the philosophers, and politicians who have been engaged the most intensely in the toil and stress of this century. The most renowned logician of the last century adopted every one of his propositions; and the most brilliant agitator among Continental Socialists composed a work of eight hundred and forty pages to celebrate his memory.

Heraclitus complained that the masses were deaf to truth, and knew not that one good man counts for more than thousands; but he held the existing order in no superstitious reverence. Strife, he says, is the source and the master of all things. Life is perpetual motion, and repose is death. No man can plunge twice into the same current, for it is always flowing and passing, and is never the same. The only thing fixed and certain in the midst of change is the universal and sovereign reason, which all men may not perceive, but which is common to all. Laws are sustained by no human authority, but by virtue of their derivation from the one law that is divine. These sayings, which recall the grand outlines of political truth which we have found in the Sacred Books, and carry us forward to the latest teaching of our most enlightened contemporaries, would bear a good deal of elucidation and comment. Heraclitus is, unfortunately, so obscure that Socrates could not understand him, and I won't pretend to have succeeded better.

If the topic of my address was the history of political science, the highest and the largest place would belong to Plato and Aristotle. The *Laws* of the one, the *Politics* of the other, are, if I may trust my own experience, the books from which we may learn the most about the principles of politics. The penetration with which those great masters of thought analysed the institutions of Greece, and exposed their vices, is not surpassed by anything in later literature; by Burke or Hamilton, the best political writers of the last century; by Tocqueville or Roscher, the most eminent of our own. But Plato and Aristotle were philosophers, studious not of unguided freedom, but of intelligent government. They saw the disastrous effects of ill-directed striving for liberty; and they resolved that it was better not to strive for it, but to be content with a strong administration, prudently adapted to make men prosperous and happy.

Now liberty and good government do not exclude each other; and there are excellent reasons why they should go together. Liberty is not a means to a higher political end. It is itself the highest political end. It is not for the sake of a good public administration that it is required, but for security in the pursuit of the highest objects of civil society, and of private life. Increase of freedom in the State may sometimes promote mediocrity, and give vitality to prejudice; it may even retard useful legislation, diminish the capacity for war, and restrict the boundaries of Empire. It might be plausibly argued that, if many things would be worse in England or Ireland under an intelligent despotism, some things would be managed better;

that the Roman Government was more enlightened under Augustus and Antoninus than under the Senate, in the days of Marius or of Pompey. A generous spirit prefers that his country should be poor, and weak, and of no account, but free, rather than powerful, prosperous, and enslaved. It is better to be the citizen of a humble commonwealth in the Alps, without a prospect of influence beyond the narrow frontier, than a subject of the superb autocracy that overshadows half of Asia and of Europe. But it may be urged, on the other side, that liberty is not the sum or the substitute of all the things men ought to live for; that to be real it must be circumscribed, and that the limits of circumscription vary; that advancing civilisation invests the State with increased rights and duties, and imposes increased burdens and constraint on the subject; that a highly instructed and intelligent community may perceive the benefit of compulsory obligations which, at a lower stage, would be thought unbearable; that liberal progress is not vague or indefinite, but aims at a point where the public is subject to no restrictions but those of which it feels the advantage; that a free country may be less capable of doing much for the advancement of religion, the prevention of vice, or the relief of suffering, than one that does not shrink from confronting great emergencies by some sacrifice of individual rights, and some concentration of power; and that the supreme political object ought to be sometimes postponed to still higher moral objects. My argument involves no collision with these qualifying reflections. We are dealing, not with the effects of freedom, but with its causes. We are seeking out the influences which brought arbitrary government under control, either by the diffusion of power, or by the appeal to an authority which transcends all government, and among those influences the greatest philosophers of Greece have no claim to be reckoned.

It is the Stoics who emancipated mankind from its subjugation to despotic rule, and whose enlightened and elevated views of life bridged the chasm that separates the ancient from the Christian state, and led the way to freedom. Seeing how little security there is that the laws of any land shall be wise or just, and that the unanimous will of a people and the assent of nations are liable to err, the Stoics looked beyond those narrow barriers, and above those inferior sanctions, for the principles that ought to regulate the lives of men and the existence of society. They made it known that there is a will superior to the collective will of man, and a law that overrules those of Solon and Lycurgus. Their test of good government is its conformity to principles that can be traced to a higher legislator. That which we must obey, that to which we are bound to reduce all civil authorities, and to sacrifice every earthly interest, is that immutable law which is perfect and eternal as God Himself, which proceeds from His nature, and reigns over heaven and earth and over all the nations.

The great question is to discover, not what governments prescribe, but what they ought to prescribe; for no prescription is valid against the conscience of mankind. Before God, there is neither Greek nor barbarian, neither rich nor poor, and the slave is as good as his master, for by birth all men are free; they are citizens of that universal commonwealth which embraces all the world, brethren of one family, and children of God. The true guide of our conduct is no outward authority, but the voice of God, who comes down to dwell in our souls, who knows all our thoughts, to whom are owing all the truth we know, and all the good we do; for vice is voluntary, and virtue comes from the grace of the heavenly spirit within.

What the teaching of that divine voice is, the philosophers who had imbibed the sublime ethics of the Porch went on to expound: It is not enough to act up to the written law, or to give all men their due; we ought to give them more than their due, to be generous and beneficent, to devote ourselves for the good of others, seeking our reward in self-denial and sacrifice, acting from the motive of sympathy and not of personal advantage. Therefore we must treat others as we wish to be treated by them, and must persist until death in doing good to our enemies, regardless of unworthiness and ingratitude. For we must be at war with evil, but at peace with men, and it is better to suffer than to commit injustice. True freedom, says the most eloquent of the Stoics, consists in obeying God. A State governed by such principles as these would have been free far beyond the measure of Greek or Roman freedom; for they open a door to religious toleration, and close it against slavery. Neither conquest nor purchase, said Zeno, can make one man the property of another.

These doctrines were adopted and applied by the great jurists of the Empire. The law of nature, they said, is superior to the written law, and slavery contradicts the law of nature. Men have no right to do what they please with their own, or to make profit out of another's loss. Such is the political wisdom of the ancients, touching the foundations of liberty, as we find it in its highest development, in Cicero, and Seneca, and Philo, a Jew of Alexandria. Their writings impress upon us the greatness of the work of preparation for the Gospel which had been accomplished among men on the eve of the mission of the Apostles. St. Augustine, after quoting Seneca, exclaims: "What more could a Christian say than this Pagan has said?" The enlightened pagans had reached nearly the last point attainable without a new dispensation, when the fulness of time was come. We have seen the breadth and the splendour of the domain of Hellenic thought, and it has brought us to the threshold of a greater kingdom. The best of the later classics speak almost the language of Christianity, and they border on its spirit.

But in all that I have been able to cite from classical literature, three things are wanting,—representative government, the emancipation of the slaves, and liberty of conscience. There were, it is true, deliberative assemblies, chosen by the people; and confederate cities, of which, both in Asia and Africa, there were so many leagues, sent their delegates to sit in Federal Councils. But government by an elected Parliament was even in theory a thing unknown. It is congruous with the nature of Polytheism to admit some measure of toleration. And Socrates, when he avowed that he must obey God rather than the Athenians, and the Stoics, when they set the wise man above the law, were very near giving utterance to the principle. But it was first proclaimed and established by enactment, not in polytheis-

tic and philosophical Greece, but in India, by Asoka, the earliest
of the Buddhist kings, two hundred and fifty years before the
birth of Christ.

Slavery has been, far more than intolerance, the perpetual
curse and reproach of ancient civilisation, and although its
rightfulness was disputed as early as the days of Aristotle, and
was implicitly, if not definitely, denied by several Stoics, the
moral philosophy of the Greeks and Romans, as well as their
practice, pronounced decidedly in its favour. But there was one
extraordinary people who, in this as in other things, anticipated
the purer precept that was to come. Philo of Alexandria is one
of the writers whose views on society were most advanced. He
applauds not only liberty but equality in the enjoyment of
wealth. He believes that a limited democracy, purged of its
grosser elements, is the most perfect government, and will extend itself gradually over all the world. By freedom he understood the following of God. Philo, though he required that the
condition of the slave should be made compatible with the
wants and claims of his higher nature, did not absolutely condemn slavery. But he has put on record the customs of the
Essenes of Palestine, a people who, uniting the wisdom of the
Gentiles with the faith of the Jews, led lives which were uncon-
taminated by the surrounding civilisation, and were the first to
reject slavery both in principle and practice. They formed a
religious community rather than a State, and their numbers did
not exceed 4000. But their example testifies to how great a
height religious men were able to raise their conception of
society even without the succour of the New Testament, and
affords the strongest condemnation of their contemporaries.

This, then, is the conclusion to which our survey brings us:
There is hardly a truth in politics or in the system of the rights
of man that was not grasped by the wisest of the Gentiles and
the Jews, or that they did not declare with a refinement of
thought and a nobleness of expression that later writers could
never surpass. I might go on for hours, reciting to you passages
on the law of nature and the duties of man, so solemn and
religious that though they come from the profane theatre on the

Acropolis, and from the Roman Forum, you would deem that you were listening to the hymns of Christian Churches and the discourse of ordained divines. But although the maxims of the great classic teachers, of Sophocles, and Plato, and Seneca, and the glorious examples of public virtue were in the mouths of all men, there was no power in them to avert the doom of that civilisation for which the blood of so many patriots and the genius of such incomparable writers had been wasted in vain. The liberties of the ancient nations were crushed beneath a hopeless and inevitable despotism, and their vitality was spent, when the new power came forth from Galilee, giving what was wanting to the efficacy of human knowledge to redeem societies as well as men.

It would be presumptuous if I attempted to indicate the numberless channels by which Christian influence gradually penetrated the State. The first striking phenomenon is the slowness with which an action destined to be so prodigious became manifest. Going forth to all nations, in many stages of civilisation and under almost every form of government, Christianity had none of the character of a political apostolate, and in its absorbing mission to individuals did not challenge public authority. The early Christians avoided contact with the State, abstained from the responsibilities of office, and were even reluctant to serve in the army. Cherishing their citizenship of a kingdom not of this world, they despaired of an empire which seemed too powerful to be resisted and too corrupt to be converted, whose institutions, the work and the pride of untold centuries of paganism, drew their sanctions from the gods whom the Christians accounted devils, which plunged its hands from age to age in the blood of martyrs, and was beyond the hope of regeneration and foredoomed to perish. They were so much overawed as to imagine that the fall of the State would be the end of the Church and of the world, and no man dreamed of the boundless future of spiritual and social influence that awaited their religion among the race of destroyers that were bringing the empire of Augustus and of Constantine to humiliation and ruin. The duties of government were less in their thoughts than the private virtues and duties of subjects; and it was long before they became aware of the burden of power in their faith. Down almost to the time of Chrysostom, they shrank from contemplating the obligation to emancipate the slaves.

Although the doctrine of self-reliance and self-denial, which is the foundation of political economy, was written as legibly in the New Testament as in the *Wealth of Nations,* it was not recognised until our age. Tertullian boasts of the passive obedience of the Christians. Melito writes to a pagan Emperor as if he were incapable of giving an unjust command; and in Christian times Optatus thought that whoever presumed to find fault with his sovereign exalted himself almost to the level of a god. But this political quietism was not universal. Origen, the ablest writer of early times, spoke with approval of conspiring for the destruction of tyranny.

After the fourth century the declarations against slavery are earnest and continual. And in a theological but yet pregnant sense, divines of the second century insist on liberty, and divines of the fourth century on equality. There was one essential and inevitable transformation in politics. Popular governments had existed, and also mixed and federal governments, but there had been no limited government, no State the circumference of whose authority had been defined by a force external to its own. That was the great problem which philosophy had raised, and which no statesmanship had been able to solve. Those who proclaimed the assistance of a higher authority had indeed drawn a metaphysical barrier before the governments, but they had not known how to make it real. All that Socrates could effect by way of protest against the tyranny of the reformed democracy was to die for his convictions. The Stoics could only advise the wise man to hold aloof from politics, keeping the unwritten law in his heart. But when Christ said: "Render unto Caesar the things that are Caesar's, and unto God the things that are God's," those words, spoken on His last visit to the Temple, three days before His death, gave to the civil power, under the protection of conscience, a sacredness it had never enjoyed, and bounds it had never acknowledged; and they were the repudiation of absolutism and the inauguration of freedom. For our Lord not only delivered the precept, but created the force to execute it. To maintain the necessary immunity in one supreme sphere, to reduce all political authority within defined limits, ceased to be an aspiration of patient reasoners, and was made the perpetual charge and care of the most energetic institution and the most universal association in the world. The new law, the new spirit, the new authority, gave to liberty a meaning and a value it had not possessed in the philosophy or in the constitution of Greece or Rome before the knowledge of the truth that makes us free.

IX

The History of Freedom in Christianity

WHEN Constantine the Great carried the seat of empire from Rome to Constantinople he set up in the market-place of the new capital a porphyry pillar which had come from Egypt, and of which a strange tale is told. In a vault beneath he secretly buried the seven sacred emblems of the Roman State, which were guarded by the virgins in the temple of Vesta, with the fire that might never be quenched. On the summit he raised a statue of Apollo, representing himself, and enclosing a fragment of the Cross; and he crowned it with a diadem of rays consisting of the nails employed at the Crucifixion, which his mother was believed to have found at Jerusalem.

The pillar still stands, the most significant monument that exists of the converted empire; for the notion that the nails which had pierced the body of Christ became a fit ornament for a heathen idol as soon as it was called by the name of a living emperor indicates the position designed for Christianity in the imperial structure of Constantine. Diocletian's attempt to transform the Roman Government into a despotism of the Eastern type had brought on the last and most serious persecution of the Christians; and Constantine, in adopting their faith, intended neither to abandon his predecessor's scheme of policy nor to renounce the fascinations of arbitrary authority, but to strengthen his throne with the support of a religion which had astonished the world by its power of resistance, and to ob-

An address delivered to the members of the Bridgnorth Institution at the Agricultural Hall, May 28, 1877. Reprinted from Acton, *History of Freedom and Other Essays* (London: Macmillan, 1907).

tain that support absolutely and without a drawback he fixed the seat of his government in the East, with a patriarch of his own creation.

Nobody warned him that by promoting the Christian religion he was tying one of his hands, and surrendering the prerogative of the Caesars. As the acknowledged author of the liberty and superiority of the Church, he was appealed to as the guardian of her unity. He admitted the obligation; he accepted the trust; and the divisions that prevailed among the Christians supplied his successors with many opportunities of extending that protectorate, and preventing any reduction of the claims or of the resources of imperialism.

Constantine declared his own will equivalent to a canon of the Church. According to Justinian, the Roman people had formally transferred to the emperors the entire plenitude of its authority, and, therefore, the Emperor's pleasure, expressed by edict or by letter, had force of law. Even in the fervent age of its conversion the Empire employed its refined civilisation, the accumulated wisdom of ancient sages, the reasonableness and sublety of Roman law, and the entire inheritance of the Jewish, the Pagan, and the Christian world, to make the Church serve as a gilded crutch of absolutism. Neither an enlightened philosophy, nor all the political wisdom of Rome, nor even the faith and virtue of the Christians availed against the incorrigible tradition of antiquity. Something was wanted beyond all the gifts of reflection and experience—a faculty of self-government and self-control, developed like its language in the fibre of a nation, and growing with its growth. This vital element, which many centuries of warfare, of anarchy, of oppression had extinguished in the countries that were still draped in the pomp of ancient civilisation, was deposited on the soil of Christendom by the fertilising stream of migration that overthrew the empire of the West.

In the height of their power the Romans became aware of a race of men that had not abdicated freedom in the hands of a monarch; and the ablest writer of the empire pointed to them with a vague and bitter feeling that, to the institutions of these barbarians, not yet crushed by despotism, the future of the world belonged. Their kings, when they had kings, did not preside at their councils; they were sometimes elective; they were sometimes deposed; and they were bound by oath to act in obedience with the general wish. They enjoyed real authority only in war. This primitive Republicanism, which admits monarchy as an occasional incident, but holds fast to the collective supremacy of all free men, of the constituent authority over all constituted authorities, is the remote germ of Parliamentary government. The action of the State was confined to narrow limits; but, besides his position as head of the State, the king was surrounded by a body of followers attached to him by personal or political ties. In these, his immediate dependents, disobedience or resistance to orders was no more tolerated than in a wife, a child, or a soldier; and a man was expected to murder his own father if his chieftain required it. Thus these Teutonic communities admitted an independence of government that threatened to dissolve society; and a dependence on persons that was dangerous to freedom. It was a system very favourable to corporations, but offering no security to individuals. The State was not likely to oppress its subjects; and was not able to protect them.

The first effect of the great Teutonic migration into the regions civilised by Rome was to throw back Europe many centuries to a condition scarcely more advanced than that from which the institutions of Solon had rescued Athens. Whilst the Greeks preserved the literature, the arts, and the science of antiquity and all the sacred monuments of early Christianity with a completeness of which the rended fragments that have come down to us give no commensurate idea, and even the peasants of Bulgaria knew the New Testament by heart, Western Europe lay under the grasp of masters the ablest of whom could not write their names. The faculty of exact reasoning, of accurate observation, became extinct for five hundred years, and even the sciences most needful to society, medicine and geometry, fell into decay, until the teachers of the West went to school at the feet of Arabian masters. To bring order out of chaotic ruin, to rear a new civilisation and blend hostile and unequal races into a nation, the thing wanted was not liberty but force. And for centuries all progress is attached to the action of men like Clovis, Charlemagne, and William the Norman, who were resolute and peremptory, and prompt to be obeyed.

The spirit of immemorial paganism which had saturated ancient society could not be exorcised except by the combined influence of Church and State; and the universal sense that their union was necessary created the Byzantine despotism. The divines of the Empire who could not fancy Christianity flourishing beyond its borders, insisted that the State is not in the Church, but the Church in the State. This doctrine had scarcely been uttered when the rapid collapse of the Western Empire opened a wider horizon; and Salvianus, a priest at Marseilles, proclaimed that the social virtues, which were decaying amid the civilised Romans, existed in greater purity and promise among the Pagan invaders. They were converted with ease and rapidity; and their conversion was generally brought about by their kings.

Christianity, which in earlier times had addressed itself to the masses, and relied on the principle of liberty, now made its appeal to the rulers, and threw its mighty influence into the scale of authority. The barbarians, who possessed no books, no secular knowledge, no education, except in the schools of the clergy, and who had scarcely acquired the rudiments of religious instruction, turned with childlike attachment to men whose minds were stored with the knowledge of Scripture, of Cicero, of St. Augustine; and in the scanty world of their ideas, the Church was felt to be something infinitely vaster, stronger, holier than their newly founded States. The clergy supplied the means of conducting the new governments, and were made exempt from taxation, from the jurisdiction of the civil magistrate, and of the political administrator. They taught that power ought to be conferred by election; and the Councils of Toledo furnished the framework of the Parliamentary system of Spain, which is, by a long interval, the oldest in the world. But the monarchy of the Goths in Spain, as well as that of the Saxons in England, in both of which the nobles and the prelates surrounded the throne with the semblance of free institutions, passed away; and the people that prospered and overshadowed the rest were the Franks, who had no native nobility, whose law of succession to the Crown became for one thousand years the fixed object of an unchanging superstition, and under whom the feudal system was developed to excess.

Feudalism made land the measure and the master of all things. Having no other source of wealth than the produce of the soil, men depended on the landlord for the means of escaping starvation; and thus his power became paramount over the liberty of the subject and the authority of the State. Every baron, said the French maxim, is sovereign in his own domain. The nations of the West lay between the competing tyrannies of local magnates and of absolute monarchs, when a force was brought upon the scene which proved for a time superior alike to the vassal and his lord.

In the days of the Conquest, when the Normans destroyed the liberties of England, the rude institutions which had come with the Saxons, the Goths, and the Franks from the forests of Germany were suffering decay, and the new element of popular government afterwards supplied by the rise of towns and the formation of a middle class was not yet active. The only influence capable of resisting the feudal hierarchy was the ecclesiastical hierarchy; and they came into collision, when the process of feudalism threatened the independence of the Church by subjecting the prelates severally to that form of personal dependence on the kings which was peculiar to the Teutonic state.

To that conflict of four hundred years we owe the rise of civil liberty. If the Church had continued to buttress the thrones of the king whom it anointed, or if the struggle had terminated speedily in an undivided victory, all Europe would have sunk down under a Byzantine or Muscovite despotism. For the aim of both contending parties was absolute authority. But although liberty was not the end for which they strove, it was the means by which the temporal and the spiritual power called the nations to their aid. The towns of Italy and Germany won their franchises, France got her States-General, and England her Parliament out of the alternate phases of the contest; and as long as it lasted it prevented the rise of divine right. A disposition existed to regard the crown as an estate descending under the law of real property in the family that possessed it. But the authority of religion, and especially of the papacy, was thrown on the side that denied the indefeasible title of kings. In France what was afterwards called the Gallican theory maintained that the reigning house was above the law, and that the sceptre was not to pass away from it as long as there should be princes of the royal blood of St. Louis. But in other countries the oath of fidelity itself attested that it was conditional, and should be kept only during good behaviour; and it was in conformity with the public law to which all monarchs were held subject, that King John was declared a rebel against the barons, and that the men who raised Edward III. to the throne from which they had deposed his father invoked the maxim *Vox populi Vox Dei.*

And this doctrine of the divine right of the people to raise up and pull down princes, after obtaining the sanctions of religion, was made to stand on broader grounds, and was strong enough to resist both Church and king. In the struggle between the House of Bruce and the House of Plantagenet for the possession of Scotland and Ireland, the English claim was backed by the censures of Rome. But the Irish and the Scots refused it, and the address in which the Scottish Parliament informed the Pope of their resolution shows how firmly the popular doctrine had taken root. Speaking of Robert Bruce, they say: "Divine Providence, the laws and customs of the country, which we will defend till death, and the choice of the people, have made him our king. If he should ever betray his principles, and consent that we should be subjects of the English king, then we shall treat him as an enemy, as the subverter of our rights and his own, and shall elect another in his place. We care not for glory or for wealth, but for that liberty which no true man will give up but with his life." This estimate of royalty was natural among men accustomed to see those whom they most respected in constant strife with their rulers. Gregory VII. had begun the disparagement of civil authorities by saying that they are the work of the devil; and already in his time both parties were driven to acknowledge the sovereignty of the people, and appealed to it as the immediate source of power.

Two centuries later this political theory had gained both in definiteness and in force among the Guelphs, who were the Church party, and among the Ghibellines, or Imperialists. Here are the sentiments of the most celebrated of all the Guelphic writers: "A king who is unfaithful to his duty forfeits his claim to obedience. It is not rebellion to depose him, for he is himself a rebel whom the nation has a right to put down. But it is better to abridge his power, that he may be unable to abuse it. For this purpose, the whole nation ought to have a share in governing itself; the Constitution ought to combine a limited and elective monarchy, with an aristocracy of merit, and such an admixture of democracy as shall admit all classes to office, by popular election. No government has a right to levy taxes beyond the limit determined by the people. All political authority is derived from popular suffrage, and all laws must be made by the people or their representatives. There is no security for us as long as we depend on the will of another man." This language, which contains the earliest exposition of the Whig theory of the revolution, is taken from the works of St. Thomas Aquinas, of whom Lord Bacon says that he had the largest heart of the school divines. And it is worth while to observe that he wrote at the very moment when Simon de Montfort summoned the Commons; and that the politics of the Neapolitan friar are centuries in advance of the English statesman's.

The ablest writer of the Ghibelline party was Marsilius of Padua. "Laws," he said, "derive their authority from the nation, and are invalid without its assent. As the whole is greater than any part, it is wrong that any part should legislate for the whole; and as men are equal, it is wrong that one should be bound by laws made by another. But in obeying laws to which all men have agreed, all men, in reality, govern themselves. The monarch, who is instituted by the legislature to execute its will, ought to be armed with a force sufficient to coerce individuals, but not sufficient to control the majority of the people. He is responsible to the nation, and subject to the law; and the nation that appoints him, and assigns him his duties, has to see that he obeys the Constitution, and has to dismiss him if he breaks it. The rights of citizens are independent of the faith they profess; and no man may be punished for his religion." This writer, who saw in some respects farther than Locke or Montesquieu, who, in regard to the sovereignty of the nation, representative government, the superiority of the legislature over the executive, and the liberty of conscience, had so firm a grasp of the principles that were to sway the modern world, lived in the reign of Edward II., five hundred and fifty years ago.

It is significant that these two writers should agree on so many of the fundamental points which have been, ever since, the topic of controversy; for they belonged to hostile schools, and one of them would have thought the other worthy of death. St. Thomas would have made the papacy control all Christian governments. Marsilius would have had the clergy submit to the law of the land; and would have put them under restrictions both as to property and numbers. As the great debate went on, many things gradually made themselves clear, and grew into settled convictions. For these were not only the thoughts of prophetic minds that surpassed the level of contemporaries; there was some prospect that they would master the practical world. The ancient reign of the barons was seriously threatened. The opening of the East by the Crusades had imparted a great stimulus to industry. A stream set in from the country to the towns, and there was no room for the government of towns in the feudal machinery. When men found a way of earning a livelihood without depending for it on the good will of the class that owned the land, the landowner lost much of his importance, and it began to pass to the possessors of moveable wealth. The townspeople not only made themselves free from the control of prelates and barons, but endeavoured to obtain for their own class and interest the command of the State.

The fourteenth century was filled with the tumult of this

struggle between democracy and chivalry. The Italian towns, foremost in intelligence and civilisation, led the way with democratic constitutions of an ideal and generally an impracticable type. The Swiss cast off the yoke of Austria. Two long chains of free cities arose, along the valley of the Rhine, and across the heart of Germany. The citizens of Paris got possession of the king, reformed the State, and began their tremendous career of experiments to govern France. But the most healthy and vigorous growth of municipal liberties was in Belgium, of all countries on the Continent, that which has been from immemorial ages the most stubborn in its fidelity to the principle of self-government. So vast were the resources concentrated in the Flemish towns, so widespread was the movement of democracy, that it was long doubtful whether the new interest would not prevail, and whether the ascendency of the military aristocracy would not pass over to the wealth and intelligence of the men that lived by trade. But Rienzi, Marcel, Artevelde, and the other champions of the unripe democracy of those days, lived and died in vain. The upheaval of the middle class had disclosed the need, the passions, the aspirations of the suffering poor below; ferocious insurrections in France and England caused a reaction that retarded for centuries the readjustment of power, and the red spectre of social revolution arose in the track of democracy. The armed citizens of Ghent were crushed by the French chivalry; and monarchy alone reaped the fruit of the change that was going on in the position of classes, and stirred the minds of men.

Looking back over the space of a thousand years, which we call the Middle Ages, to get an estimate of the work they had done, if not towards perfection in their institutions, at least towards attaining the knowledge of political truth, this is what we find: Representative government, which was unknown to the ancients, was almost universal. The methods of election were crude; but the principle that no tax was lawful that was not granted by the class that paid it—that is, that taxation was inseparable from representation—was recognised, not as the privilege of certain countries, but as the right of all. Not a prince in the world, said Philip de Commines, can levy a penny without the consent of the people. Slavery was almost everywhere extinct; and absolute power was deemed more intolerable and more criminal than slavery. The right of insurrection was not only admitted but defined, as a duty sanctioned by religion. Even the principles of the Habeas Corpus Act, and the method of the Income Tax, were already known. The issue of ancient politics was an absolute state planted on slavery. The political produce of the Middle Ages was a system of states in which authority was restricted by the representation of powerful classes, by privileged associations, and by the acknowledgment of duties superior to those which are imposed by man.

As regards the realisation in practice of what was seen to be good, there was almost everything to do. But the great problems of principle had been solved, and we come to the question, How did the sixteenth century husband the treasure which the Middle Ages had stored up? The most visible sign of the times was the decline of the religious influence that had reigned so long. Sixty years passed after the invention of printing, and thirty thousand books had issued from European presses, before anybody undertook to print the Greek Testament. In the days when every State made the unity of faith its first care, it came to be thought that the rights of men, and the duties of neighbours and of rulers towards them, varied according to their religion; and society did not acknowledge the same obligations to a Turk or a Jew, a pagan or a heretic, or a devil worshipper, as to an orthodox Christian. As the ascendency of religion grew weaker, this privilege of treating its enemies on exceptional principles was claimed by the State for its own benefit; and the idea that the ends of government justify the means employed was worked into system by Machiavelli. He was an acute politician, sincerely anxious that the obstacles to the intelligent government of Italy should be swept away. It appeared to him that the most vexatious obstacle to intellect is conscience, and that the vigorous use of statecraft necessary for the success of difficult schemes would never be made if governments allowed themselves to be hampered by the precepts of the copy-book.

His audacious doctrine was avowed in the succeeding age by men whose personal character stood high. They saw that in critical times good men have seldom strength for their goodness, and yield to those who have grasped the meaning of the maxim that you cannot make an omelette if you are afraid to break the eggs. They saw that public morality differs from private, because no Government can turn the other cheek, or can admit that mercy is better than justice. And they could not define the difference or draw the limits of exception; or tell what other standard for a nation's acts there is than the judgment which Heaven pronounces in this world by success.

Machiavelli's teaching would hardly have stood the test of Parliamentary government, for public discussion demands at least the profession of good faith. But it gave an immense impulse to absolutism by silencing the consciences of very religious kings, and made the good and the bad very much alike. Charles V. offered 5000 crowns for the murder of an enemy. Ferdinand I. and Ferdinand II., Henry III. and Louis XIII., each caused his most powerful subject to be treacherously dispatched. Elizabeth and Mary Stuart tried to do the same to each other. The way was paved for absolute monarchy to triumph over the spirit and institutions of a better age, not by isolated acts of wickedness, but by a studied philosophy of crime and so thorough a perversion of the moral sense that the like of it had not been since the Stoics reformed the morality of paganism.

The clergy, who had in so many ways served the cause of freedom during the prolonged strife against feudalism and slavery, were associated now with the interest of royalty. Attempts had been made to reform the Church on the Constitutional model; they had failed, but they had united the hierarchy and the crown against the system of divided power as against a common enemy. Strong kings were able to bring the spirituality under subjection in France and Spain, in Sicily and in England. The absolute monarchy of France was built up in the two following centuries by twelve political cardinals. The kings of Spain obtained the same effect almost at a single stroke by reviving and appropriating to their own use the tribunal of the Inquisition, which had been growing obsolete, but now served to arm them with terrors which effectually made them despotic. One generation beheld the change all over Europe, from the anarchy of the days of the Roses to the passionate submission, the gratified acquiescence in tyranny that marks the reign of Henry VIII. and the kings of his time.

The tide was running fast when the Reformation began at Wittenberg, and it was to be expected that Luther's influence would stem the flood of absolutism. For he was confronted everywhere by the compact alliance of the Church with the state; and a great part of his country was governed by hostile potentates who were prelates of the Court of Rome. He had, indeed, more to fear from temporal than from spiritual foes. The leading German bishops wished that the Protestant demands should be conceded; and the Pope himself vainly urged on the Emperor a conciliatory policy. But Charles V. had outlawed Luther, and attempted to waylay him; and the Dukes of Bavaria were active in beheading and burning his disciples, whilst the democracy of the towns generally took his side. But the dread of revolution was the deepest of his political sentiments; and the gloss by which the Guelphic divines had got over the passive obedience of the apostolic age was characteristic of that mediaeval method of interpretation which he rejected. He swerved for a moment in his later years; but the substance of his political teaching was eminently conservative, the Lutheran States became the stronghold of rigid immobility, and Lutheran writers constantly condemned the democratic literature that arose in the second age of the Reformation. For the Swiss reformers were bolder than the Germans in mixing up their cause with politics. Zürich and Geneva were Republics, and the spirit of their governments influenced both Zwingli and Calvin.

Zwingli indeed did not shrink from the mediaeval doctrine that evil magistrates must be cashiered; but he was killed too early to act either deeply or permanently on the political character of Protestantism. Calvin, although a Republican, judged that the people are unfit to govern themselves, and declared the popular assembly an abuse that ought to be abolished. He desired an aristocracy of the elect, armed with the means of punishing not only crime but vice and error. For he thought that the severity of the mediaeval laws was insufficient for the need of the times; and he favoured the most irresistible weapon which the inquisitorial procedure put into the hand of the Government, the right of subjecting prisoners to intolerable torture, not because they were guilty, but because their guilt could not be proved. His teaching, though not calculated to promote popular institutions, was so adverse to the authority of the surrounding monarchs, that he softened down the expression of his political views in the French edition of his *Institutes*.

The direct political influence of the Reformation effected less than has been supposed. Most States were strong enough to control it. Some, by intense exertion, shut out the pouring flood. Others, with consummate skill, diverted it to their own uses. The Polish Government alone at that time left it to its course. Scotland was the only kingdom in which the Reformation triumphed over the resistance of the State; and Ireland was the only instance where it failed, in spite of Government support. But in almost every other case, both the princes that spread their canvas to the gale and those that faced it, employed the zeal, the alarm, the passions it aroused as instruments for the increase of power. Nations eagerly invested their rulers with every prerogative needed to preserve their faith, and all the care to keep Church and State asunder, and to prevent the confusion of their powers, which had been the work of ages, was renounced in the intensity of the crisis. Atrocious deeds were done, in which religious passion was often the instrument, but policy was the motive.

Fanaticism displays itself in the masses, but the masses were rarely fanaticised, and the crimes ascribed to it were commonly due to the calculations of dispassionate politicians. When the King of France undertook to kill all the Protestants, he was obliged to do it by his own agents. It was nowhere the spontaneous act of the population, and in many towns and in entire provinces the magistrates refused to obey. The motive of the

Court was so far from mere fanaticism that the Queen immediately challenged Elizabeth to do the like to the English Catholics. Francis I. and Henry II. sent nearly a hundred Huguenots to the stake, but they were cordial and assiduous promoters of the Protestant religion in Germany. Sir Nicholas Bacon was one of the ministers who suppressed the mass in England. Yet when the Huguenot refugees came over he liked them so little that he reminded Parliament of the summary way in which Henry V. at Agincourt dealt with the Frenchmen who fell into his hands. John Knox thought that every Catholic in Scotland ought to be put to death, and no man ever had disciples of a sterner or more relentless temper. But his counsel was not followed.

All through the religious conflict policy kept the upper hand. When the last of the Reformers died, religion, instead of emancipating the nations, had become an excuse for the criminal art of despots. Calvin preached and Bellarmine lectured, but Machiavelli reigned. Before the close of the century three events occurred which mark the beginning of a momentous change. The massacre of St. Bartholomew convinced the bulk of Calvinists of the lawfulness of rebellion against tyrants, and they became advocates of that doctrine in which the Bishop of Winchester had led the way,[1] and which Knox and Buchanan had received, through their master at Paris, straight from the mediaeval schools. Adopted out of aversion to the King of France, it was soon put in practice against the King of Spain. The revolted Netherlands, by a solemn Act, deposed Philip II., and made themselves independent under the Prince of Orange, who had been, and continued to be, styled his Lieutenant. Their example was important, not only because subjects of one religion deposed a monarch of another, for that had been seen in Scotland, but because, moreover, it put a republic in the place of a monarchy, and forced the public law of Europe to recognise the accomplished revolution. At the same time, the French Catholics, rising against Henry III., who was the most contemptible of tyrants, and against his heir, Henry of Navarre,

---

[1] Poynet, in his *Treatise on Political Power*.

who, as a Protestant, repelled the majority of the nation, fought for the same principles with sword and pen.

Many shelves might be filled with the books which came out in their defence during half a century, and they include the most comprehensive treatises on laws ever written. Nearly all are vitiated by the defect which disfigured political literature in the Middle Ages. That literature, as I have tried to show, is extremely remarkable, and its services in aiding human progress are very great. But from the death of St. Bernard until the appearance of Sir Thomas More's *Utopia,* there was hardly a writer who did not make his politics subservient to the interest of either Pope or King. And those who came after the Reformation were always thinking of laws as they might affect Catholics or Protestants. Knox thundered against what he called *the Monstrous Regiment of Women,* because the Queen went to mass, and Mariana praised the assassin of Henry III. because the King was in league with Huguenots. For the belief that it is right to murder tyrants, first taught among Christians, I believe, by John of Salisbury, the most distinguished English writer of the twelfth century, and confirmed by Roger Bacon, the most celebrated Englishman of the thirteenth, had acquired about this time a fatal significance. Nobody sincerely thought of politics as a law for the just and the unjust, or tried to find out a set of principles that should hold good alike under all changes of religion. Hooker's *Ecclesiastical Polity* stands almost alone among the works I am speaking of, and is still read with admiration by every thoughtful man as the earliest and one of the finest prose classics in our language. But though few of the others have survived, they contributed to hand down masculine notions of limited authority and conditional obedience from the epoch of theory to generations of free men. Even the coarse violence of Buchanan and Boucher was a link in the chain of tradition that connects the Hildebrandine controversy with the Long Parliament, and St. Thomas with Edmund Burke.

That men should understand that governments do not exist by divine right, and that arbitrary government is the violation of divine right, was no doubt the medicine suited to the malady under which Europe languished. But although the knowledge of this truth might become an element of salutary destruction, it could give little aid to progress and reform. Resistance to tyranny implied no faculty of constructing a legal government in its place. Tyburn tree may be a useful thing, but it is better still that the offender should live for repentance and reformation. The principles which discriminate in politics between good and evil, and make States worthy to last, were not yet found.

The French philosopher Charron was one of the men least demoralised by party spirit, and least blinded by zeal for a cause. In a passage almost literally taken from St. Thomas, he describes our subordination under a law of nature, to which all legislation must conform; and he ascertains it not by the light of revealed religion, but by the voice of universal reason, through which God enlightens the consciences of men. Upon this foundation Grotius drew the lines of real political science. In gathering the materials of international law, he had to go beyond national treaties and denominational interests for a principle embracing all mankind. The principles of law must stand, he said, even if we suppose that there is no God. By these inaccurate terms he meant that they must be found independently of revelation. From that time it became possible to make politics a matter of principle and of conscience, so that men and nations differing in all other things could live in peace together, under the sanctions of a common law. Grotius himself used his discovery to little purpose, as he deprived it of immediate effect by admitting that the right to reign may be enjoyed as a freehold, subject to no conditions.

When Cumberland and Pufendorf unfolded the true significance of his doctrine, every settled authority, every triumphant interest recoiled aghast. None were willing to surrender advantages won by force or skill, because they might be in contradiction, not with the Ten Commandments, but with an unknown code, which Grotius himself had not attempted to draw up, and touching which no two philosophers agreed. It was manifest that all persons who had learned that political science is an affair of conscience rather than of might or expediency, must regard their adversaries as men without principle, that the controversy between them would perpetually involve morality, and could not be governed by the plea of good intentions, which softens down the asperities of religious strife. Nearly all the greatest men of the seventeenth century repudiated the innovation. In the eighteenth, the two ideas of Grotius, that there are certain political truths by which every State and every interest must stand or fall, and that society is knit together by a series of real and hypothetical contracts, became, in other hands, the lever that displaced the world. When, by what seemed the operation of an irresistible and constant law, royalty had prevailed over all enemies and all competitors, it became a religion. Its ancient rivals, the baron and the prelate, figured as supporters by its side. Year after year, the assemblies that represented the self-government of provinces and of privileged classes, all over the Continent, met for the last time and passed away, to the satisfaction of the people, who had learned to venerate the throne as the constructor of their unity, the promoter of prosperity and power, the defender of orthodoxy, and the employer of talent.

The Bourbons, who had snatched the crown from a rebellious democracy, the Stuarts, who had come in as usurpers, set up the doctrine that States are formed by the valour, the policy, and the appropriate marriages of the royal family; that the king is consequently anterior to the people, that he is its maker rather than its handiwork, and reigns independently of consent. Theology followed up divine right with passive obedience. In the golden age of religious science, Archbishop Ussher, the most learned of Anglican prelates, and Bossuet, the ablest of the French, declared that resistance to kings is a crime, and that they may lawfully employ compulsion against the faith of their subjects. The philosophers heartily supported the divines. Bacon fixed his hope of all human progress on the strong hand of kings. Descartes advised them to crush all those who might be able to resist their power. Hobbes taught that authority is always in the right. Pascal considered it absurd to reform laws, or to set up an ideal justice against actual force. Even Spinoza, who was a Republican and a Jew, assigned to the State the absolute control of religion.

Monarchy exerted a charm over the imagination, so unlike the unceremonious spirit of the Middle Ages, that, on learning of the execution of Charles I., men died of the shock; and the same thing occurred at the death of Louis XVI. and of the Duke of Enghien. The classic land of absolute monarchy was France. Richelieu held that it would be impossible to keep the people down if they were suffered to be well off. The Chancellor affirmed that France could not be governed without the right of arbitrary arrest and exile; and that in case of danger to the State it may be well that a hundred innocent men should perish. The Minister of Finance called it sedition to demand that the Crown should keep faith. One who lived on intimate terms with Louis XIV. says that even the slightest disobedience to the royal will is a crime to be punished with death. Louis employed these precepts to their fullest extent. He candidly avows that kings are no more bound by the terms of a treaty than by the words of a compliment; and that there is nothing in the possession of their subjects which they may not lawfully take from them. In obedience to this principle, when Marshal Vauban, appalled by the misery of the people, proposed that all existing imposts should be repealed for a single tax that would be less onerous, the King took his advice, but retained all the old taxes whilst he imposed the new. With half the present population, he maintained an army of 450,000 men; nearly twice as large as that which the late Emperor Napoleon assembled to attack Germany. Meanwhile the people starved on grass. France, said Fénelon, is one enormous hospital. French historians believe that in a single generation six millions of people died of want. It would be easy to find tyrants more violent, more malignant, more odious than Louis XIV., but there was not one who ever used his power to inflict greater suffering or greater wrong; and the admiration with which he inspired the most illustrious men of his time denotes the lowest depth to which the turpitude of absolutism has ever degraded the conscience of Europe.

The Republics of that day were, for the most part, so governed as to reconcile men with the less opprobrious vices of monarchy. Poland was a State made up of centrifugal forces. What the nobles called liberty was the right of each of them to veto the acts of the Diet, and to persecute the peasants on his estates—rights which they refused to surrender up to the time of the partition, and thus verified the warning of a preacher spoken long ago: "You will perish, not by invasion or war, but by your infernal liberties." Venice suffered from the opposite evil of excessive concentration. It was the most sagacious of Governments, and would rarely have made mistakes if it had not imputed to others motives as wise as its own, and had taken account of passions and follies of which it had little cognisance. But the supreme power of the nobility had passed to a committee, from the committee to a Council of Ten, from the Ten to three Inquisitors of State; and in this intensely centralised form it became, about the year 1600, a frightful despotism. I have shown you how Machiavelli supplied the immoral theory needful for the consummation of royal absolutism; the absolute oligarchy of Venice required the same assurance against the revolt of conscience. It was provided by a writer as able as Machiavelli, who analysed the wants and resources of aristocracy, and made known that its best security is poison. As late as a century ago, Venetian senators of honourable and even religious lives employed assassins for the public good with no more compunction than Philip II. or Charles IX.

The Swiss Cantons, especially Geneva, profoundly influenced opinion in the days preceding the French Revolution, but they had had no part in the earlier movement to inaugurate the reign of law. That honour belongs to the Netherlands alone among the Commonwealths. They earned it, not by their form of government, which was defective and precarious, for the Orange party perpetually plotted against it, and slew the two most eminent of the Republican statesmen, and William III. himself intrigued for English aid to set the crown upon his head; but by the freedom of the press, which made Holland the vantage-ground from which, in the darkest hour of oppression, the victims of the oppressors obtained the ear of Europe.

The ordinance of Louis XIV., that every French Protestant should immediately renounce his religion, went out in the year in which James II. became king. The Protestant refugees did what their ancestors had done a century before. They asserted the deposing power of subjects over rulers who had broken the original contract between them, and all the Powers, excepting France, countenanced their argument, and sent forth William of Orange on that expedition which was the faint dawn of a brighter day.

It is to this unexampled combination of things on the Continent, more than to her own energy, that England owes her deliverance. The efforts made by the Scots, by the Irish, and at last by the Long Parliament to get rid of the misrule of the Stuarts had been foiled, not by the resistance of Monarchy, but by the helplessness of the Republic. State and Church were swept away; new institutions were raised up under the ablest ruler that had ever sprung from a revolution; and England, seething with the toil of political thought, had produced at least two writers who in many directions saw as far and as clearly as we do now. But Cromwell's Constitution was rolled up like a scroll; Harrington and Lilburne were laughed at for a time and forgotten, the country confessed the failure of its striving, disavowed its aims, and flung itself with enthusiasm, and without any effective stipulations, at the feet of a worthless king.

If the people of England had accomplished no more than this to relieve mankind from the pervading pressure of unlimited monarchy, they would have done more harm than good. By the fanatical treachery with which, violating the Parliament and the law, they contrived the death of King Charles, by the ribaldry of the Latin pamphlet with which Milton justified the act before the world, by persuading the world that the Republicans were hostile alike to liberty and to authority, and did not believe in themselves, they gave strength and reason to the current of Royalism, which, at the Restoration, overwhelmed their work. If there had been nothing to make up for this defect of certainty and of constancy in politics England would have gone the way of other nations.

At that time there was some truth in the old joke which describes the English dislike of speculation by saying that all our philosophy consists of a short catechism in two questions: "What is mind? No matter. What is matter? Never mind." The only accepted appeal was to tradition. Patriots were in the habit of saying that they took their stand upon the ancient ways, and would not have the laws of England changed. To enforce their argument they invented a story that the constitution had come from Troy, and that the Romans had allowed it to subsist untouched. Such fables did not avail against Strafford; and the oracle of precedent sometimes gave responses adverse to the popular cause. In the sovereign question of religion, this was decisive, for the practice of the sixteenth century, as well as of the fifteenth, testified in favour of intolerance. By royal command, the nation had passed four times in one generation from one faith to another, with a facility that made a fatal impression on Laud. In a country that had proscribed every religion in turn, and had submitted to such a variety of penal measures against Lollard and Arian, against Augsburg and Rome, it seemed there could be no danger in cropping the ears of a Puritan.

But an age of stronger conviction had arrived; and men resolved to abandon the ancient ways that led to the scaffold and the rack, and to make the wisdom of their ancestors and the statutes of the land bow before an unwritten law. Religious liberty had been the dream of great Christian writers in the age of Constantine and Valentinian, a dream never wholly realised in the Empire, and rudely dispelled when the barbarians found that it exceeded the resources of their art to govern civilised populations of another religion, and unity of worship was imposed by laws of blood and by theories more cruel than the laws. But from St. Athanasius and St. Ambrose down to Erasmus and More, each age heard the protest of earnest men in behalf of the liberty of conscience, and the peaceful days before the Reformation were full of promise that it would prevail.

In the commotion that followed, men were glad to get tolerated themselves by way of privilege and compromise, and willingly renounced the wider application of the principle. Socinus was the first who, on the ground that Church and State ought to be separated, required universal toleration. But Socinus disarmed his own theory, for he was a strict advocate of passive obedience.

The idea that religious liberty is the generating principle of civil, and that civil liberty is the necessary condition of religious, was a discovery reserved for the seventeenth century. Many years before the names of Milton and Taylor, of Baxter and Locke were made illustrious by their partial condemnation of intolerance, there were men among the Independent congregations who grasped with vigour and sincerity the principle that it is only by abridging the authority of States that the liberty of Churches can be assured. That great political idea, sanctifying freedom and consecrating it to God, teaching men to treasure the liberties of others as their own, and to defend them for the love of justice and charity more than as a claim of right, has been the soul of what is great and good in the progress of the last two hundred years. The cause of religion, even under the unregenerate influence of worldly passion, had as much to do as any clear notions of policy in making this country the foremost of the free. It had been the deepest current in the movement of 1641, and it remained the strongest motive that survived the reaction of 1660.

The greatest writers of the Whig party, Burke and Macaulay, constantly represented the statesmen of the Revolution as the legitimate ancestors of modern liberty. It is humiliating to trace a political lineage to Algernon Sidney, who was the paid agent of the French king; to Lord Russell, who opposed religious toleration at least as much as absolute monarchy; to Shaftesbury, who dipped his hands in the innocent blood shed by the perjury of Titus Oates; to Halifax, who insisted that the plot must be supported even if untrue; to Marlborough, who sent his comrades to perish on an expedition which he had betrayed to the French; to Locke, whose notion of liberty involves nothing more spiritual than the security of property, and is consistent with slavery and persecution; or even to Addison, who conceived that the right of voting taxes belonged to no country but his own. Defoe affirms that from the time of Charles II. to that of George I. he never knew a politician who truly held the faith of either party; and the perversity of the statesmen who led the assault against the later Stuarts threw back the cause of progress for a century.

When the purport of the secret treaty became suspected by which Louis XIV. pledged himself to support Charles II. with an army for the destruction of Parliament, if Charles would overthrow the Anglican Church, it was found necessary to make concession to the popular alarm. It was proposed that whenever James should succeed, great part of the royal prerogative and patronage should be transferred to Parliament. At the same time, the disabilities of Nonconformists and Catholics would have been removed. If the Limitation Bill, which Halifax supported with signal ability, had passed, the Monarchical constitution would have advanced, in the seventeenth century, farther than it was destined to do until the second quarter of the nineteenth. But the enemies of James, guided by the Prince of Orange, preferred a Protestant king who should be nearly absolute, to a constitutional king who should be a Catholic. The scheme failed. James succeeded to a power which, in more cautious hands, would have been practically uncontrolled, and the storm that cast him down gathered beyond the sea.

By arresting the preponderance of France, the Revolution of 1688 struck the first real blow at Continental despotism. At home it relieved Dissent, purified justice, developed the national energies and resources, and ultimately, by the Act of Settlement, placed the crown in the gift of the people. But it neither introduced nor determined any important principle, and, that both parties might be able to work together, it left untouched the fundamental question between Whig and Tory. For the divine right of kings it established, in the words of Defoe, the divine right of freeholders; and their domination extended for seventy years, under the authority of John Locke, the philosopher of government by the gentry. Even Hume did not enlarge the bounds of his ideas; and his narrow materialistic belief in the connection between liberty and property captivated even the bolder mind of Fox.

By his idea that the powers of government ought to be divided according to their nature, and not according to the division of classes, which Montesquieu took up and developed with consummate talent, Locke is the originator of the long reign of English institutions in foreign lands. And his doctrine of resistance, or, as he finally termed it, the appeal to Heaven, ruled the judgment of Chatham at a moment of solemn transition in the history of the world. Our Parliamentary system, managed by the great revolution families, was a contrivance by which electors were compelled, and legislators were induced to vote against their convictions; and the intimidation of the constituencies was rewarded by the corruption of their representatives. About the year 1770 things had been brought back, by indirect ways, nearly to the condition which the Revolution had been designed to remedy for ever. Europe seemed incapable of becoming the home of free States. It was from America that the plain ideas that men ought to mind their own business, and that the nation is responsible to Heaven for the acts of the State,—ideas long locked in the breast of solitary thinkers, and hidden among Latin folios,—burst forth like a conqueror upon the world they were destined to transform, under the title of the Rights of Man. Whether the British legislature had a constitutional right to tax a subject colony was hard to say, by the letter of the law. The general presumption was immense on the side of authority; and the world believed that the will of the constituted ruler ought to be supreme, and not the will of the subject people. Very few bold writers went so far as to say that lawful power may be resisted in cases of extreme necessity. But the colonisers of America, who had gone forth not in search of gain, but to escape from laws under which other Englishmen were content to live, were so sensitive even to appearances that the Blue Laws of Connecticut forbade men to walk to church within ten feet of their wives. And the proposed tax, of only £12,000 a year, might have been easily borne. But the reasons why Edward I. and his Council were not allowed to tax England were reasons why George III. and his Parliament should not tax America. The dispute involved a principle, namely, the right of controlling government. Furthermore, it involved the conclusion that the Parliament brought together by a decisive election had no just right over the unrepresented nation, and it called on the people of England to take back its power. Our best statesmen saw that whatever might be the law, the rights of the nation were at stake. Chatham, in speeches better remembered than any that have been delivered in Parliament, exhorted America to be firm. Lord Camden, the late Chancellor, said: "Taxation and representation are inseparably united. God hath joined them. No British Parliament can separate them."

From the elements of that crisis Burke built up the noblest political philosophy in the world. "I do not know the method," said he, "of drawing up an indictment against a whole people. The natural rights of mankind are indeed sacred things, and if any public measure is proved mischievously to affect them, the objection ought to be fatal to that measure, even if no charter at all could be set up against it. Only a sovereign reason, paramount to all forms of legislation and administration, should dictate." In this way, just a hundred years ago, the opportune reticence, the politic hesitancy of European statesmanship, was at last broken down; and the principle gained ground, that a nation can never abandon its fate to an authority it cannot control. The Americans placed it at the foundation of their new government. They did more; for having subjected all civil authorities to the popular will, they surrounded the popular will with restrictions that the British legislature would not endure.

During the revolution in France the example of England, which had been held up so long, could not for a moment compete with the influence of a country whose institutions were so wisely framed to protect freedom even against the perils of democracy. When Louis Philippe became king, he assured the old Republican, Lafayette, that what he had seen in the United States had convinced him that no government can be so good as a Republic. There was a time in the Presidency of Monroe, about fifty-five years ago, which men still speak of as "the era of good feeling," when most of the incongruities that had come down from the Stuarts had been reformed, and the motives of later divisions were yet inactive. The causes of old-world trouble,—popular ignorance, pauperism, the glaring contrast between rich and poor, religious strife, public debts, standing armies and war,—were almost unknown. No other age or country had solved so successfully the problems that attend the growth of free societies, and time was to bring no further progress.

But I have reached the end of my time, and have hardly come to the beginning of my task. In the ages of which I have spoken, the history of freedom was the history of the thing that was not. But since the Declaration of Independence, or, to speak more justly, since the Spaniards, deprived of their king, made a new government for themselves, the only known forms of liberty, Republics and Constitutional Monarchy, have made their way over the world. It would have been interesting to trace the reaction of America on the Monarchies that achieved its independence; to see how the sudden rise of political economy suggested the idea of applying the methods of science to the art of government; how Louis XVI., after confessing that despotism was useless, even to make men happy by compulsion, appealed to the nation to do what was beyond his skill, and thereby resigned his sceptre to the middle class, and the intelligent men of France, shuddering at the awful recollections of their own experience, struggled to shut out the past, that they might deliver their children from the prince of the world and rescue the living from the clutch of the dead, until the finest opportunity ever given to the world was thrown away, because the passion for equality made vain the hope of freedom.

And I should have wished to show you that the same deliberate rejection of the moral code which smoothed the paths of absolute monarchy and of oligarchy, signalised the advent of the democratic claim to unlimited power,—that one of its leading champions avowed the design of corrupting the moral sense of men, in order to destroy the influence of religion, and a famous apostle of enlightenment and toleration wished that the last king might be strangled with the entrails of the last priest. I would have tried to explain the connection between the doctrine of Adam Smith, that labour is the original source of all wealth, and the conclusion that the producers of wealth virtually compose the nation, by which Sieyès subverted historic France; and to show that Rousseau's definition of the social compact as a voluntary association of equal partners conducted Marat, by short and unavoidable stages, to declare that the poorer classes were absolved, by the law of self-preservation, from the conditions of a contract which awarded to them misery and death; that they were at war with society, and had a right to all they could get by exterminating the rich, and that their inflexible theory of equality, the chief legacy of the Revolution, together with the avowed inadequacy of economic science to grapple with problems of the poor, revived the idea of renovating society on the principle of self-sacrifice, which had been the generous aspiration of the Essenes and the early Christians, of Fathers and Canonists and Friars; of Erasmus, the most celebrated precursor of the Reformation; of Sir Thomas More, its most illustrious victim; and of Fénelon, the most popular of bishops, but which, during the forty years of its revival, has been associated with envy and hatred and bloodshed, and is now the most dangerous enemy lurking in our path.

Last, and most of all, having told so much of the unwisdom of our ancestors, having exposed the sterility of the convulsion that burned what they adored, and made the sins of the Republic mount up as high as those of the monarchy, having shown that Legitimacy, which repudiated the Revolution, and Imperialism, which crowned it, were but disguises of the same element of violence and wrong, I should have wished, in order that my address might not break off without a meaning or a moral, to relate by whom, and in what connection, the true law of the formation of free States was recognised, and how that discovery, closely akin to those which, under the names of development, evolution, and continuity, have given a new and deeper method to other sciences, solved the ancient problem between stability and change, and determined the authority of tradition on the progress of thought; how that theory, which Sir James Mackintosh expressed by saying that Constitutions are not made, but grow; the theory that custom and the national qualities of the governed, and not the will of the government, are the makers of the law; and therefore that the nation, which is the source of its own organic institutions, should be charged with the perpetual custody of their integrity, and with the duty of bringing the form into harmony with the spirit, was made, by the singular co-operation of the purest Conservative intellect with red-handed revolution, of Niebuhr with Mazzini, to yield the idea of nationality, which, far more than the idea of liberty, has governed the movement of the present age.

I do not like to conclude without inviting attention to the impressive fact that so much of the hard fighting, the thinking, the enduring that has contributed to the deliverance of man from the power of man, has been the work of our countrymen and of their descendants in other lands. We have had to contend, as much as any people, against monarchs of strong will and of resources secured by their foreign possession, against men of rare capacity, against whole dynasties of born tyrants. And yet that proud prerogative stands out on the background of our history. Within a generation of the Conquest, the Normans were compelled to recognise, in some grudging measure, the claims of the English people. When the struggle between Church and State extended to England, our Churchmen learned to associate themselves with the popular cause; and, with few exceptions, neither the hierarchical spirit of the foreign divines, nor the monarchical bias peculiar to the French, characterised the writers of the English school. The Civil Law, transmitted from the degenerate Empire to be the common prop of absolute power, was excluded from England. The Canon Law was restrained, and this country never admitted the Inquisition, nor fully accepted the use of torture which invested Continental royalty with so many terrors. At the end of the Middle Ages foreign writers acknowledged our superiority, and pointed to these causes. After that, our gentry maintained the means of local self-government such as no other country possessed. Divisions in religion forced toleration. The confusion of the common law taught the people that their best safeguard was the independence and the integrity of the judges.

All these explanations lie on the surface, and are as visible as the protecting ocean; but they can only be successive effects of a constant cause which must lie in the same native qualities of perseverance, moderation, individuality, and manly sense of duty, which give to the English race its supremacy in the stern art of labour, which has enabled it to thrive as no other can on inhospitable shores, and which (although no great people has less of the bloodthirsty craving for glory and an army of 50,000 English soldiers has never been seen in battle) caused Napoleon to exclaim, as he rode away from Waterloo, "It has always been the same since Crécy."

Therefore, if there is reason for pride in the past, there is more for hope in the time to come. Our advantages increase, while other nations fear their neighbours or covet their neighbours' goods. Anomalies and defects there are, fewer and less intolerable, if not less flagrant than of old.

But I have fixed my eyes on the spaces that Heaven's light illuminates, that I may not lay too heavy a strain on the indulgence with which you have accompanied me over the dreary and heart-breaking course by which men have passed to freedom; and because the light that has guided us is still unquenched, and the causes that have carried us so far in the van of free nations have not spent their power; because the story of the future is written in the past, and that which hath been is the same thing that shall be.

X

Inaugural Lecture on the Study of History

FELLOW STUDENTS—I look back to-day to a time before the middle of the century, when I was reading at Edinburgh and fervently wishing to come to this University. At three colleges I applied for admission, and, as things then were, I was refused by all. Here, from the first, I vainly fixed my hopes, and here, in a happier hour, after five-and-forty years, they are at last fulfilled.

I desire, first, to speak to you of that which I may reasonably call the Unity of Modern History, as an easy approach to questions necessary to be met on the threshold by any one occupying this place, which my predecessor has made so formidable to me by the reflected lustre of his name.

You have often heard it said that Modern History is a subject to which neither beginning nor end can be assigned. No beginning, because the dense web of the fortunes of man is woven without a void; because, in society as in nature, the structure is continuous, and we can trace things back uninterruptedly, until we dimly descry the Declaration of Independence in the forests of Germany. No end, because, on the same principle, history made and history making are scientifically inseparable and separately unmeaning.

"Politics," said Sir John Seeley, "are vulgar when they are not liberalised by history, and history fades into mere literature when it loses sight of its relation to practical politics." Everybody perceives the sense in which this is true. For the science of

Delivered at Cambridge, June, 1895. Reprinted from *Lectures on Modern History* (London: Macmillan, 1906).

politics is the one science that is deposited by the stream of history, like grains of gold in the sand of a river; and the knowledge of the past, the record of truths revealed by experience, is eminently practical, as an instrument of action and a power that goes to the making of the future.[1] In France, such is the weight attached to the study of our own time, that there is an appointed course of contemporary history, with appropriate text-books.[2] That is a chair which, in the progressive division of labour by which both science and government prosper,[3] may some day be founded in this country. Meantime, we do well to acknowledge the points at which the two epochs diverge. For the contemporary differs from the modern in this, that many of its facts cannot by us be definitely ascertained. The living do not give up their secrets with the candour of the dead; one key is always excepted, and a generation passes before we can ensure accuracy. Common report and outward seeming are bad copies of the reality, as the initiated know it. Even of a thing so memorable as the war of 1870, the true cause is still obscure; much that we believed has been scattered to the winds in the last six months, and further revelations by important witnesses are about to appear. The use of history turns far more on certainty than on abundance of acquired information.

Beyond the question of certainty is the question of detachment. The process by which principles are discovered and

---

[1] No political conclusions of any value for practice can be arrived at by direct experience. All true political science is, in one sense of the phrase, *a priori*, being deduced from the tendencies of things, tendencies known either through our general experience of human nature, or as the result of an analysis of the course of history, considered as a progressive evolution. —Mill, *Inaugural Address*, 51.

[2] Contemporary history is, in Dr. Arnold's opinion, more important than either ancient or modern; and in fact superior to it by all the superiority of the end to the means.—Seeley, *Lectures and Essays*, 306.

[3] The law of all progress is one and the same, the evolution of the simple into the complex by successive differentiations.—*Edinburgh Review*, clvii. 428. Die Entwickelung der Völker vollzieht sich nach zwei Gesetzen. Das erste Gesetz ist das der Differenzierung. Die primitiven Einrichtungen sind einfach und einheitlich, die der Civilisation zusammengesetzt und geteilt, und die Arbeitsteilung nimmt beständig zu.— Sickel, *Goettingen Gelehrte Anzeigen*, 1890, 563.

appropriated is other than that by which, in practice, they are applied; and our most sacred and disinterested convictions ought to take shape in the tranquil regions of the air, above the tumult and the tempest of active life.[4] For a man is justly despised who has one opinion in history and another in politics, one for abroad and another at home, one for opposition and another for office. History compels us to fasten on abiding issues, and rescues us from the temporary and transient. Politics and history are interwoven, but are not commensurate. Ours is a domain that reaches farther than affairs of state, and is not subject to the jurisdiction of governments. It is our function to keep in view and to command the movement of ideas, which are not the effect but the cause of public events;[5] and even to allow some priority to ecclesiastical history over civil, since, by reason of the graver issues concerned, and the vital consequences of error, it opened the way in research, and was the first to be treated by close reasoners and scholars of the higher rank.[6]

In the same manner, there is wisdom and depth in the philosophy which always considers the origin and the germ, and glories in history as one consistent epic.[7] Yet every student

---

[4] Nous risquons toujours d'être influencés par les préjugés de notre époque; mais nous sommes libres des préjugés particuliers aux époques antérieures.—E. Naville, *Christianisme de Fénelon,* 9.

[5] La nature n'est qu'un écho de l'esprit. L'idée est la mère du fait, elle façonne graduellement le monde à son image.—Feuchtersleben, in Caro, *Nouvelles Études Morales,* 132. Il n'est pas d'étude morale qui vaille l'histoire d'une idée.—Laboulaye, *Liberté Religieuse,* 25.

[6] Il y a des savants qui raillent le sentiment religieux. Ils ne savent pas que c'est à ce sentiment, et par son moyen, que la science historique doit d'avoir pu sortir de l'enfance. . . . Depuis des siècles les âmes indépendantes discutaient les textes et les traditions de l'église, quand les lettrés n'avaient pas encore eu l'idée de porter un regard critique sur les textes de l'antiquité mondaine.—*La France Protestante,* ii. 17.

[7] In our own history, above all, every step in advance has been at the same time a step backwards. It has often been shown how our latest constitution is, amidst all external differences, essentially the same as our earliest, how every struggle for right and freedom, from the thirteenth century onwards, has simply been a struggle for recovering something old. —Freeman, *Historical Essays,* iv. 253. Nothing but a thorough knowledge

ought to know that mastery is acquired by resolved limitation. And confusion ensues from the theory of Montesquieu and of his school, who, adapting the same term to things unlike, insist that freedom is the primitive condition of the race from which we are sprung.[8] If we are to account mind not matter, ideas not force, the spiritual property that gives dignity and grace and intellectual value to history, and its action on the ascending life of man, then we shall not be prone to explain the universal by the national, and civilisation by custom.[9] A speech of Antigone, a single sentence of Socrates, a few lines that were inscribed on an Indian rock before the Second Punic War, the footsteps of a silent yet prophetic people who dwelt by the Dead Sea, and perished in the fall of Jerusalem, come nearer to our lives than the ancestral wisdom of barbarians who fed their swine on the Hercynian acorns.

For our present purpose, then, I describe as Modern History that which begins four hundred years ago, which is marked off

---

of the social system, based upon a regular study of its growth, can give us the power we require to affect it.—Harrison, *Meaning of History,* 19. Eine Sache wird nur völlig auf dem Wege verstanden, wie sie selbst entsteht. —In dem genetischen Verfahren sind die Gründe der Sache, auch die Gründe des Erkennens.—Trendelenburg, *Logische Untersuchungen,* ii. 395, 388.

[8] Une telle liberté . . . n'a rien de commun avec le savant système de garanties qui fait libres les peuples modernes.—Boutmy, *Annales des Sciences Politiques,* i. 157. Les trois grandes réformes qui ont renouvelé l'Angleterre, la liberté religieuse, la réforme parlementaire, et la liberté économique, ont été obtenues sous la pression des organisations extra-constitutionnelles.—Ostrogorski, *Revue Historique,* lii. 272.

[9] The question which is at the bottom of all constitutional struggles, the question between the national will and the national law.—Gardiner, *Documents,* xviii. Religion, considered simply as the principle which balances the power of human opinion, which takes man out of the grasp of custom and fashion, and teaches him to refer himself to a higher tribunal, is an infinite aid to moral strength and elevation.—Channing, *Works,* iv. 83. Je tiens que le passé ne suffit jamais au présent. Personne n'est plus disposé que moi à profiter de ses leçons; mais en même temps, je le demande, le présent ne fournit-il pas toujours les indications qui lui sont propres?—Molé, in Falloux, *Études et Souvenirs,* 130. Admirons la sagesse de nos pères, et tachons de l'imiter, en faisant ce qui convient à notre siècle.—Galiani, *Dialogues,* 40.

by an evident and intelligible line from the time immediately preceding, and displays in its course specific and distinctive characteristics of its own.[10] The modern age did not proceed from the medieval by normal succession, with outward tokens of legitimate descent. Unheralded, it founded a new order of things, under a law of innovation, sapping the ancient reign of continuity. In those days Columbus subverted the notions of the world, and reversed the conditions of production, wealth, and power; in those days Machiavelli released government from the restraint of law; Erasmus diverted the current of ancient learning from profane into Christian channels; Luther broke the chain of authority and tradition at the strongest link; and Copernicus erected an invincible power that set for ever the mark of progress upon the time that was to come. There is the same unbound originality and disregard for inherited sanctions in the rare philosophers as in the discovery of Divine Right, and the intruding Imperialism of Rome. The like effects are visible everywhere, and one generation beheld them all. It was an awakening of new life; the world revolved in a different orbit, determined by influences unknown before. After many ages persuaded of the headlong decline and impending dissolution of society,[11] and governed by usage and the will of masters who were in their graves, the sixteenth century went forth armed for untried experience, and ready to watch with hopefulness a prospect of incalculable change.

That forward movement divides it broadly from the older world; and the unity of the new is manifest in the universal spirit of investigation and discovery which did not cease to

---

[10] Ceterum in legendis Historiis malim te ductum animi, quam anxias leges sequi. Nullae sunt, quae non magnas habeant utilitates; et melius haerent, quae libenter legimus. In universum tamen, non incipere ab antiquissimis, sed ab his, quae nostris temporibus nostraeque notitiae propius cohaerent, ac paulatim deinde in remotiora eniti, magis è re arbitror. —Grotius, *Epistolae*, 18.

[11] The older idea of a law of degeneracy, of a "fatal drift towards the worse," is as obsolete as astrology or the belief in witchcraft. The human race has become hopeful, sanguine.—Seeley, *Rede Lecture*, 1887. *Fortnightly Review*, July 1887, 124.

operate, and withstood the recurring efforts of reaction, until, by the advent of the reign of general ideas which we call the Revolution, it at length prevailed.[12] This successive deliverance and gradual passage, for good and evil, from subordination to independence is a phenomenon of primary import to us, because historical science has been one of its instruments.[13] If the

---

[12] Formuler des idées générales, c'est changer le salpêtre en poudre.— A. de Musset, *Confessions d'un Enfant du Siècle*, 15. Les révolutions c'est l'avènement des idées libérales. C'est presque toujours par les révolutions qu'elles prévalent et se fondent, et quand les idées libérales en sont véritablement le principe et le but, quand elles leur ont donné naissance, et quand elles les couronnent à leur dernier jour, alors ces révolutions sont légitimes—Rémusat, 1839, in *Revue des Deux Mondes*, 1875, vi. 335. Il y a même des personnes de piété qui prouvent par raison qu'il faut renoncer à la raison; que ce n'est point la lumière, mais la foi seule qui doit nous conduire, et que l'obéissance aveugle est la principale vertu des chrétiens. La paresse des inférieurs et leur esprit flatteur s'accommode souvent de cette vertu prétendue, et l'orgueil de ceux qui commandent en est toujours très content. De sorte qu'il se trouvera peut-être des gens qui seront scandalisés que je fasse cet honneur à la raison, de l'élever au-dessus de toutes les puissances, et qui s'imagineront que je me révolte contre les autorités légitimes à cause que je prends son parti et que je soutiens que c'est à elle à décider et à regner.—Malebranche, *Morale*, i. 2, 13. That great statesman (Mr. Pitt) distinctly avowed that the application of philosophy to politics was at that time an innovation, and that it was an innovation worthy to be adopted. He was ready to make the same avowal in the present day which Mr. Pitt had made in 1792.—Canning, 1st June 1827. *Parliamentary Review*, 1828, 71. American history knows but one avenue of success in American legislation, freedom from ancient prejudice. The best lawgivers in our colonies first became as little children. —Bancroft, *History of the United States*, i. 494. Every American, from Jefferson and Gallatin down to the poorest squatter, seemed to nourish an idea that he was doing what he could to overthrow the tyranny which the past had fastened on the human mind.—Adams, *History of the United States*, i. 175.

[13] The greatest changes of which we have had experience as yet are due to our increasing knowledge of history and nature. They have been produced by a few minds appearing in three or four favoured nations, in comparatively a short period of time. May we be allowed to imagine the minds of men everywhere working together during many ages for the completion of our knowledge? May not the increase of knowledge transfigure the world?—Jowett, *Plato*, i. 414. Nothing, I believe, is so likely to beget in us a spirit of enlightened liberality, of Christian forbearance, of large-hearted moderation, as the careful study of the history of doctrine and the history of interpretation.—Perowne, *Psalms*, i. p. xxxi.

Past has been an obstacle and a burden, knowledge of the Past is the safest and the surest emancipation. And the earnest search for it is one of the signs that distinguish the four centuries of which I speak from those that went before. The Middle Ages, which possessed good writers of contemporary narrative, were careless and impatient of older fact. They became content to be deceived, to live in a twilight of fiction, under clouds of false witness, inventing according to convenience, and glad to welcome the forger and the cheat.[14] As time went on, the atmosphere of accredited mendacity thickened, until, in the Renaissance, the art of exposing falsehood dawned upon keen Italian minds. It was then that History as we understand it began to be understood, and the illustrious dynasty of scholars arose to whom we still look both for method and material. Unlike the dreaming prehistoric world, ours knows the need and the duty to make itself master of the earlier times, and to forfeit nothing of their wisdom or their warnings,[15] and has devoted its best energy and treasure to the sovereign purpose of detecting error and vindicating entrusted truth.[16]

In this epoch of full-grown history men have not acquiesced in the given conditions of their lives. Taking little for granted they have sought to know the ground they stand on, and the road they travel, and the reason why. Over them, therefore, the historian has obtained an increasing ascendency.[17] The law of

---

[14] Ce n'est guère avant la seconde moitié du XVIIᵉ siècle qu'il devint impossible de soutenir l'authenticité des fausses décrétales, des Constitutions apostoliques, des Récognitions Clémentines, du faux Ignace, du pseudo-Dionys, et de l'immense fatras d'œuvres anonymes ou pseudonymes qui grossissait souvent du tiers ou de la moitié l'héritage littéraire des auteurs les plus considérables.—Duchesne, *Témoins anténicéens de la Trinité,* 1883, 36.

[15] A man who does not know what has been thought by those who have gone before him is sure to set an undue value upon his own ideas.— M. Pattison, *Memoirs,* 78.

[16] Travailler à discerner, dans cette discipline, le solide d'avec le frivole, le vrai d'avec le vraisemblable, la science d'avec l'opinion, ce qui forme le jugement d'avec ce qui ne fait que charger la mémoire.—Lamy, *Connoissance de soi-même,* v. 459.

[17] All our hopes of the future depend on a sound understanding of the past.—Harrison, *The Meaning of History,* 6.

stability was overcome by the power of ideas, constantly varied and rapidly renewed; [18] ideas that give life and motion, that take wing and traverse seas and frontiers, making it futile to pursue the consecutive order of events in the seclusion of a separate nationality.[19] They compel us to share the existence of societies wider than our own, to be familiar with distant and exotic types, to hold our march upon the loftier summits, along the central range, to live in the company of heroes, and saints, and men of genius, that no single country could produce. We cannot afford wantonly to lose sight of great men and memorable lives, and are bound to store up objects for admiration as far as may be; [20] for the effect of implacable research is constantly

[18] The real history of mankind is that of the slow advance of resolved deed following laboriously just thought; and all the greatest men live in their purpose and effort more than it is possible for them to live in reality. —The things that actually happened were of small consequence—the thoughts that were developed are of infinite consequence.—Ruskin. Facts are the mere dross of history. It is from the abstract truth which interpenetrates them, and lies latent among them like gold in the ore, that the mass derives its value.—Macaulay, *Works*, v. 131.

[19] Die Gesetze der Geschichte sind eben die Gesetze der ganzen Menschheit, gehen nicht in die Geschicke eines Volkes, einer Generation oder gar eines Einzelnen auf. Individuen und Geschlechter, Staaten und Nationen, können zerstäuben, die Menschheit bleibt.—A. Schmidt, *Züricher Monatsschrift*, i. 45.

[20] Le grand péril des âges démocratiques, soyez-en sûr, c'est la destruction ou l'affaiblissement excessif des parties du corps social en présence du tout. Tout ce qui relève de nos jours l'idée de l'individu est sain.— Tocqueville, 3rd January 1840, *Oeuvres*, vii. 97. En France, il n'y a plus d'hommes. On a systématiquement tué l'homme au profit du peuple, des masses, comme disent nos législateurs écervelés. Puis un beau jour, on s'est aperçu que ce peuple n'avait jamais existé qu'en projet, que ces masses étaient un troupeau mi-partie de moutons et de tigres. C'est une triste histoire. Nous avons à relever l'âme humaine contre l'aveugle et brutale tyrannie des multitudes.—Lanfrey, 23rd March 1855. M. du Camp, *Souvenirs Littéraires*, ii. 273. C'est le propre de la vertu d'être invisible, même dans l'histoire, à tout autre œil que celui de la conscience. —Vacherot, *Comptes Rendus de l'Institut*, lxix. 319. Dans l'histoire où la bonté est la perle rare, qui a été bon passe presque avant qui a été grand. —V. Hugo, *Les Misérables*, vii. 46. Grosser Maenner Leben und Tod der Wahrheit gemaess mit Liebe zu schildern, ist zu allen Zeiten herzerhebend; am meisten aber dann, wenn im Kreislauf der irdischen Dinge die Sterne wieder aehnlich stehen wie damals als sie unter uns lebten.—

to reduce their number. No intellectual exercise, for instance, can be more invigorating than to watch the working of the mind of Napoleon, the most entirely known as well as the ablest of historic men. In another sphere, it is the vision of a higher world to be intimate with the character of Fénelon, the cherished model of politicians, ecclesiastics, and men of letters, the witness against one century and precursor of another, the advocate of the poor against oppression, of liberty in an age of arbitrary power, of tolerance in an age of persecution, of the humane virtues among men accustomed to sacrifice them to authority, the man of whom one enemy says that his cleverness was enough to strike terror, and another, that genius poured in torrents from his eyes. For the minds that are greatest and best alone furnish the instructive examples. A man of ordinary proportion or inferior metal knows not how to think out the rounded circle of his thought, how to divest his will of its surroundings and to rise above the pressure of time and race and circumstance,[21] to choose the star that guides his course, to correct, and test, and assay his convictions by the light within,[22] and, with a resolute conscience and ideal courage, to remodel and reconstitute the character which birth and education gave him.[23]

Lasaulx, *Sokrates*, 3. Instead of saying that the history of mankind is the history of the masses, it would be much more true to say that the history of mankind is the history of its great men.—Kingsley, *Lectures*, 329.

[21] Le génie n'est que la plus complète émancipation de toutes les influences de temps, de mœurs et de pays.—Nisard, *Souvenirs*, ii. 43.

[22] Meine kritische Richtung zieht mich in der Wissenschaft durchaus zur Kritik meiner eigenen Gedanken hin, nicht zu der der Gedanken Anderer.—Rothe, *Ethik*, i. p. xi.

[23] When you are in young years the whole mind is, as it were, fluid, and is capable of forming itself into any shape that the owner of the mind pleases to order it to form itself into.—Carlyle, *On the Choice of Books*, 131. Nach allem erscheint es somit unzweifelhaft als eine der psychologischen Voraussetzungen des Strafrechts, ohne welche der Zurechnungsbegriff nicht haltbar wäre, dass der Mensch für seinen Charakter verantwortlich ist und ihn muss abändern können.—Rümelin, *Reden und Aufsätze*, ii. 60. An der tiefen und verborgenen Quelle, woraus der Wille entspringt, an diesem Punkt, nur hier steht die Freiheit, und führt das Steuer und lenkt den Willen. Wer nicht bis zu dieser Tiefe in sich einkehren und seinen natürlichen Charakter von hier aus bemeistern kann,

For ourselves, if it were not the quest of the higher level and the extended horizon, international history would be imposed by the exclusive and insular reason that parliamentary reporting is younger than parliaments. The foreigner has no mystic fabric in his government, and no *arcanum imperii.* For him the foundations have been laid bare; every motive and function of the mechanism is accounted for as distinctly as the works of a watch. But with our indigenous constitution, not made with hands or written upon paper, but claiming to develop by a law of organic growth; with our disbelief in the virtue of definitions and general principles and our reliance on relative truths, we can have nothing equivalent to the vivid and prolonged debates in which other communities have displayed the inmost secrets of political science to every man who can read. And the discussions of constituent assemblies, at Philadelphia, Versailles and Paris, at Cadiz and Brussels, at Geneva, Frankfort and Berlin, above nearly all, those of the most enlightened States in the American Union, when they have recast their institutions, are paramount in the literature of politics, and proffer treasures which at home we have never enjoyed.

To historians the later part of their enormous subject is precious because it is inexhaustible. It is the best to know because it is the best known and the most explicit. Earlier scenes stand out from a background of obscurity. We soon reach the sphere of hopeless ignorance and unprofitable doubt. But hundreds and even thousands of the moderns have borne testimony against themselves, and may be studied in their private correspondence and sentenced on their own confession. Their deeds are done in the daylight. Every country opens its archives and invites us to penetrate the mysteries of State. When Hallam wrote his chapter on James II., France was the only Power whose reports were available. Rome followed, and the Hague;

---

der hat nicht den Gebrauch seiner Freiheit, der ist nicht frei, sondern unterworfen dem Triebwerk seiner Interessen, und dadurch in der Gewalt des Weltlaufs, worin jede Begebenheit und jede Handlung eine nothwendige Folge ist aller vorhergehenden.—Fischer, *Problem der Freiheit,* 27.

and then came the stores of the Italian States, and at last the Prussian and the Austrian papers, and partly those of Spain. Where Hallam and Lingard were dependent on Barillon, their successors consult the diplomacy of ten governments. The topics indeed are few on which the resources have been so employed that we can be content with the work done for us and never wish it to be done over again. Part of the lives of Luther and Frederic, a little of the Thirty Years' War, much of the American Revolution and the French Restoration, the early years of Richelieu and Mazarin, and a few volumes of Mr. Gardiner, show here and there like Pacific islands in the ocean. I should not even venture to claim for Ranke, the real originator of the heroic study of records, and the most prompt and fortunate of European pathfinders, that there is one of his seventy volumes that has not been overtaken and in part surpassed. It is through his accelerating influence mainly that our branch of study has become progressive, so that the best master is quickly distanced by the better pupil.[24] The Vatican archives alone, now made accessible to the world, filled 3239 cases when they were sent to France; and they are not the richest. We are still at the beginning of the documentary age, which will tend to make history independent of historians, to develop learning at the expense of writing, and to accomplish a revolution in other sciences as well.[25]

---

[24] I must regard the main duty of a Professor to consist, not simply in communicating information, but in doing this in such a manner, and with such an accompaniment of subsidiary means, that the information he conveys may be the occasion of awakening his pupils to a vigorous and varied exertion of their faculties.—Sir W. Hamilton, *Lectures,* i. 14. No great man really does his work by imposing his maxims on his disciples, he evokes their life. The pupil may become much wiser than his instructor, he may not accept his conclusions, but he will own, "You awakened me to be myself; for that I thank you."—Maurice, *The Conscience,* 7, 8.

[25] Ich sehe die Zeit kommen, wo wir die neuere Geschichte nicht mehr auf die Berichte selbst nicht der gleichzeitigen Historiker, ausser in so weit ihnen neue originale Kenntniss beiwohnte, geschweige denn auf die weiter abgeleiteten Bearbeitungen zu gründen haben, sondern aus den Relationen der Augenzeugen und der ächten und unmittelbarsten Urkunden aufbauen werden.—Ranke, *Reformation,* Preface, 1838. Ce qu'on

To men in general I would justify the stress I am laying on Modern History, neither by urging its varied wealth, nor the rupture with precedent, nor the perpetuity of change and increase of pace, nor the growing predominance of opinion over belief, and of knowledge over opinion, but by the argument that it is a narrative told of ourselves, the record of a life which is our own, of efforts not yet abandoned to repose, of problems that still entangle the feet and vex the hearts of men. Every part of it is weighty with inestimable lessons that we must learn by experience and at a great price, if we know not how to profit by the example and teaching of those who have gone before us, in a society largely resembling the one we live in.[26] Its study fulfils its purpose even if it only makes us wiser, without producing books, and gives us the gift of historical thinking, which is better than historical learning.[27] It is a most powerful ingredient

a trouvé et mis en œuvre est considérable en soi: c'est peu de chose au prix de ce qui reste à trouver et à mettre en œuvre.—Aulard, *Études sur la Révolution*, 21.

[26] N'attendez donc pas les leçons de l'expérience; elles coûtent trop cher aux nations.—O. Barrot, *Mémoires*, ii. 435. Il y a des leçons dans tous les temps, pour tous les temps; et celles qu'on emprunte à des ennemis ne sont pas les moins précieuses.—Lanfrey, *Napoléon*, v. p. ii. Old facts may always be fresh, and may give out a fresh meaning for each generation.—Maurice, *Lectures*, 62. The object is to lead the student to attend to them; to make him take interest in history not as a mere narrative, but as a chain of causes and effects still unwinding itself before our eyes, and full of momentous consequences to himself and his descendants—an unremitting conflict between good and evil powers, of which every act done by any one of us, insignificant as we are, forms one of the incidents; a conflict in which even the smallest of us cannot escape from taking part, in which whoever does not help the right side is helping the wrong.—Mill, *Inaugural Address*, 59.

[27] I hold that the degree in which Poets dwell in sympathy with the Past, marks exactly the degree of their poetical faculty.—Wordsworth, in C. Fox, *Memoirs*, June 1842. In all political, all social, all human questions whatever, history is the main resource of the inquirer.—Harrison, *Meaning of History*, 15. There are no truths which more readily gain the assent of mankind, or are more firmly retained by them, than those of an historical nature, depending upon the testimony of others.—Priestley, *Letters to French Philosophers*, 9. Improvement consists in bringing our opinions into nearer agreement with facts; and we shall not be likely to do this while we look at facts only through glasses coloured by those very opinions.—Mill, *Inaugural Address*, 25.

in the formation of character and the training of talent, and our historical judgments have as much to do with hopes of heaven as public or private conduct. Convictions that have been strained through the instances and the comparisons of modern times differ immeasurably in solidity and force from those which every new fact perturbs, and which are often little better than illusions or unsifted prejudice.[28]

The first of human concerns is religion, and it is the salient feature of the modern centuries. They are signalised as the scene of Protestant developments. Starting from a time of extreme indifference, ignorance, and decline, they were at once occupied with that conflict which was to rage so long, and of which no man could imagine the infinite consequences. Dogmatic conviction—for I shun to speak of faith in connection with many characters of those days—dogmatic conviction rose to be the centre of universal interest, and remained down to Cromwell the supreme influence and motive of public policy. A time came when the intensity of prolonged conflict, when even

---

[28] He who has learnt to understand the true character and tendency of many succeeding ages is not likely to go very far wrong in estimating his own.—Lecky, *Value of History*, 21. C'est à l'histoire qu'il faut se prendre, c'est le fait que nous devons interroger, quand l'idée vacille et fuit à nos yeux.—Michelet, *Disc. d'Ouverture*, 263. C'est la loi des faits telle qu'elle se manifeste dans leur succession. C'est la règle de conduite donnée par la nature humaine et indiquée par l'histoire. C'est la logique, mais cette logique qui ne fait qu'un avec l'enchaînement des choses. C'est l'enseignement de l'expérience.—Scherer, *Mélanges*, 558. Wer seine Vergangenheit nicht als seine Geschichte hat und weiss wird und ist characterlos Wem ein Ereigniss sein plötzlich abreisst von seinem Jetzt wird leicht wurzellos.—Kliefoth, *Rheinwalds Repertorium*, xliv. 20. La politique est une des meilleures écoles pour l'esprit. Elle force à chercher la raison de toutes choses, et ne permet pas cependant de la chercher hors des faits.—Rémusat, *Le Temps Passé*, i. 31. It is an unsafe partition that divides opinions without principle from unprincipled opinions.—Coleridge, *Lay Sermons*, 373.

Wer nicht von drei tausend Jahren sich weiss Rechenschaft zu geben,
Bleib 'im Dunkeln unerfahren, mag von Tag zu Tage leben!

GOETHE.

What can be rationally required of the student of philosophy is not a preliminary and absolute, but a gradual and progressive, abrogation of prejudices.—Sir W. Hamilton, *Lectures*, iv. 92.

the energy of antagonistic assurance abated somewhat, and the controversial spirit began to make room for the scientific; and as the storm subsided, and the area of settled questions emerged, much of the dispute was abandoned to the serene and soothing touch of historians, invested as they are with the prerogative of redeeming the cause of religion from many unjust reproaches, and from the graver evil of reproaches that are just. Ranke used to say that Church interests prevailed in politics until the Seven Years' War, and marked a phase of society that ended when the hosts of Brandenburg went into action at Leuthen, chaunting their Lutheran hymns.[29] That bold proposition would be disputed even if applied to the present age. After Sir Robert Peel had broken up his party, the leaders who followed him declared that no popery was the only basis on which it could be reconstructed.[30] On the other side may be urged that, in July 1870, at the outbreak of the French war, the only government that insisted on the abolition of the temporal power was Austria; and since then we have witnessed the fall of Castelar, because he attempted to reconcile Spain with Rome.

Soon after 1850 several of the most intelligent men in France, struck by the arrested increase of their own population and by the telling statistics from Further Britain, foretold the coming preponderance of the English race. They did not foretell, what none could then foresee, the still more sudden growth of Prussia, or that the three most important countries of the globe would, by the end of the century, be those that chiefly belonged to the conquests of the Reformation. So that in Religion, as in so many things, the product of these centuries has favoured the

---

[29] Die Schlacht bei Leuthen ist wohl die letzte, in welcher diese religiösen Gegensätze entscheidend eingewirkt haben.—Ranke, *Allgemeine Deutsche Biographie,* vii. 70.

[30] The only real cry in the country is the proper and just old No Popery cry.—*Major Beresford,* July 1847. Unfortunately the strongest bond of union amongst them is an apprehension of Popery.—*Stanley,* 12th September 1847. The great Protectionist party having degenerated into a No Popery, No Jew Party, I am still more unfit now than I was in 1846 to lead it.—*G. Bentinck,* 26th December 1847; *Croker's Memoirs,* iii. 116, 132, 157.

new elements; and the centre of gravity, moving from the Mediterranean nations to the Oceanic, from the Latin to the Teuton, has also passed from the Catholic to the Protestant.[31]

Out of these controversies proceeded political as well as historical science. It was in the Puritan phase, before the restoration of the Stuarts, that theology, blending with politics, effected a fundamental change. The essentially English reformation of the seventeenth century was less a struggle between churches than between sects, often subdivided by questions of discipline and self-regulation rather than by dogma. The sectaries cherished no purpose or prospect of prevailing over the nations; and they were concerned with the individual more than with the congregation, with conventicles, not with State churches. Their view was narrowed, but their sight was sharpened. It appeared to them that governments and institutions are made to pass away, like things of earth, whilst souls are immortal; that there is no more proportion between liberty and power than between eternity and time; that, therefore, the sphere of enforced command ought to be restricted within fixed limits, and that which had been done by authority, and outward discipline, and organised violence, should be attempted by division of power, and committed to the intellect and the conscience of free men.[32] Thus was exchanged the dominion of will

---

[31] In the case of Protestantism, this constitutional instability is now a simple matter of fact, which has become too plain to be denied. The system is not fixed, but in motion; and the motion is for the time in the direction of complete self-dissolution.—We take it for a transitory scheme, whose breaking up is to make room in due time for another and far more perfect state of the Church.—The new order in which Protestantism is to become thus complete cannot be reached without the co-operation and help of Romanism.—Nevin, *Mercersburg Review*, iv. 48.

[32] Diese Heiligen waren es, die aus dem unmittelbaren Glaubensleben und den Grundgedanken der christlichen Freiheit zuerst die Idee allgemeiner Menschenrechte abgeleitet und rein von Selbstsucht vertheidigt haben. —Weingarten, *Revolutionskirchen*, 447. Wie selbst die Idee allgemeiner Menschenrechte, die in dem gemeinsamen Character der Ebenbildlichkeit Gottes gegründet sind, erst durch das Christenthum zum Bewusstsein gebracht werden, während jeder andere Eifer für politische Freiheit als ein mehr oder weniger selbstsüchtiger und beschränkter sich erwiesen

over will for the dominion of reason over reason. The true apostles of toleration are not those who sought protection for their own beliefs, or who had none to protect; but men to whom, irrespective of their cause, it was a political, a moral, and a theological dogma, a question of conscience involving both religion and policy.[33] Such a man was Socinus; and others arose in the smaller sects,—the Independent founder of the colony of Rhode Island, and the Quaker patriarch of Pennsylvania. Much of the energy and zeal which had laboured for authority of doctrine was employed for liberty of prophesying. The air was filled with the enthusiasm of a new cry; but the cause was still the same. It became a boast that religion was the mother of freedom, that freedom was the lawful offspring of religion; and this transmutation, this subversion of established forms of political life by the development of religious thought, brings us to the heart of my subject, to the significant and central feature of the historic cycles before us. Beginning with the strongest religious movement and the most refined despotism ever known, it has led to the superiority of politics over divinity in the life of nations, and terminates in the equal claim of every man to be unhindered by man in the fulfilment of duty

hat.—Neander, *Pref. to Uhden's Wilberforce*, p. v. The rights of individuals and the justice due to them are as dear and precious as those of states; indeed the latter are founded on the former, and the great end and object of them must be to secure and support the rights of individuals, or else vain is government.—Cushing, in Conway, *Life of Paine*, i. 217. As it is owned the whole scheme of Scripture is not yet understood; so, if it ever comes to be understood, before the restitution of all things, and without miraculous interpositions, it must be in the same way as natural knowledge is come at—by the continuance and progress of learning and liberty.—Butler, *Analogy*, ii. 3.

[33] Comme les lois elles-mêmes sont faillibles, et qu'il peut y avoir une autre justice que la justice écrite, les sociétés modernes ont voulu garantir les droits de la conscience à la poursuite d'une justice meilleure que celle qui existe; et là est le fondement de ce qu'on appelle liberté de conscience, liberté d'écrire, liberté de pensée.—Janet, *Philosophie Contemporaine*, 308. Si la force matérielle a toujours fini par céder à l'opinion, combien plus ne sera-t-elle pas contrainte de céder à la conscience? Car la conscience, c'est l'opinion renforcée par le sentiment de l'obligation.—Vinet, *Liberté Religieuse*, 3.

to God [34]—a doctrine laden with storm and havoc, which is the secret essence of the Rights of Man, and the indestructible soul of Revolution.

When we consider what the adverse forces were, their sustained resistance, their frequent recovery, the critical moments when the struggle seemed for ever desperate, in 1685, in 1772, in 1808, it is no hyperbole to say that the progress of the world towards self-government would have been arrested but for the strength afforded by the religious motive in the seventeenth century. And this constancy of progress, of progress in the direction of organised and assured freedom, is the characteristic fact of Modern History, and its tribute to the theory of Providence.[35] Many persons, I am well assured, would detect that

---

[34] Après la volonté d'un homme, la raison d'état; après la raison d'état, religion; après la religion, la liberté. Voilà toute la philosophie de l'histoire.—Flottes, *La Souveraineté du Peuple,* 1851, 192. La répartition plus égale des biens et des droits dans ce monde est le plus grand objet que doivent se proposer ceux qui mènent les affaires humaines. Je veux seulement que l'égalité en politique consiste à également libre.—Tocqueville, 10th September 1856. $M^{me.}$ *Swetchine,* i. 455. On peut concevoir une législation très simple, lorsqu'on voudra en écarter tout ce qui est arbitraire, ne consulter que les deux premières lois de la liberté et de la propriété, et ne point admettre de lois positives qui ne tirent leur raison de ces deux lois souveraines de la justice essentielle et absolue.—Letrosne, *Vues sur la Justice Criminelle,* 16. Summa enim libertas est, ad optimum recta ratione cogi.—Nemo optat sibi hanc libertatem, volendi quae velit, sed potius volendi optima.—Leibniz, *De Fato.* Trendelenburg, *Beiträge zur Philosophie,* ii. 190.

[35] All the world is, by the very law of its creation, in eternal progress; and the cause of all the evils of the world may be traced to that natural, but most deadly error of human indolence and corruption, that our business is to preserve and not to improve—Arnold, *Life,* i. 259. In whatever state of knowledge we may conceive man to be placed, his progress towards a yet higher state need never fear a check, but must continue till the last existence of society.—Herschel, *Prel. Dis.* 360. It is in the development of thought as in every other development; the present suffers from the past, and the future struggles hard in escaping from the present.—Max Müller, *Science of Thought,* 617. Most of the great positive evils of the world are in themselves removable, and will, if human affairs continue to improve, be in the end reduced within narrow limits. Poverty in any sense implying suffering may be completely extinguished by the wisdom of society combined with the good sense and providence of individuals.—All the grand sources, in short, of human suffering are in a

great degree, many of them almost entirely, conquerable by human care and effort.—J. S. Mill, *Utilitarianism*, 21, 22. The ultimate standard of worth is personal worth, and the only progress that is worth striving after, the only acquisition that is truly good and enduring, is the growth of the soul.—Bixby, *Crisis of Morals*, 210. La science, et l'industrie qu'elle produit, ont, parmi tous les autres enfants du génie de l'homme, ce privilège particulier, que leur vol non-seulement ne peut pas s'interrompre, mais qu'il s'accélère sans cesse.—Cuvier, *Discours sur la Marche des Sciences*, 24 Avril 1816. Aucune idée parmi celles qui se réfèrent à l'ordre des faits naturels, ne tient de plus près à la famille des idées religieuses que l'idée du progrès, et n'est plus propre à devenir le principe d'une sorte de foi religieuse pour ceux qui n'en ont pas d'autres. Elle a, comme la foi religieuse, la vertu de relever les âmes et les caractères.—Cournot, *Marche des Idées*, ii. 425. Dans le spectacle de l'humanité errante, souffrante et travaillant toujours à mieux voir, à mieux penser, à mieux agir, à diminuer l'infirmité de l'être humain, à apaiser l'inquiétude de son cœur, la science découvre une direction et un progrès.—A. Sorel, *Discours de Réception*, 14. Le jeune homme qui commence son éducation quinze ans après son père, à une époque où celui-ci, engagé dans une profession spéciale et active, ne peut que suivre les anciens principes, acquiert une supériorité théorique dont on doit tenir compte dans la hiérarchie sociale. Le plus souvent le père n'est-il pas pénétré de l'esprit de routine, tandis que le fils représente et défend la science progressive? En diminuant l'écart qui existait entre l'influence des jeunes générations et celle de la vieillesse ou de l'âge mûr, les peuples modernes n'auraient donc fait que reproduire dans leur ordre social un changement de rapports qui s'était déjà accompli dans la nature intime des choses.—Boutmy, *Revue Nationale*, xxi. 393. Il y a dans l'homme individuel des principes de progrès viager; il y a, en toute société, des causes constantes qui transforment ce progrès viager en progrès héréditaire. Une société quelconque tend à progresser tant que les circonstances ne touchent pas aux causes de progrès que nous avons reconnues, l'imitation des dévanciers par les successeurs, des étrangers par les indigènes.—Lacombe, *L'Histoire comme Science*, 292. Veram creatae mentis beatitudinem consistere in non impedito progressu ad bona majora.—Leibniz to Wolf, 21st February 1705. In cumulum etiam pulchritudinis perfectionisque universalis operum divinorum progressus quidam perpetuus liberrimusque totius universi est agnoscendus, ita ut ad majorem semper cultum procedat.—Leibniz, ed. Erdmann, 150*a*. Der Creaturen und also auch unsere Vollkommenheit bestehen in einem ungehinderten starken Forttrieb zu neuen und neuen Vollkommenheiten.—Leibniz, *Deutsche Schriften*, ii. 36. Hegel, welcher annahm, der Fortschritt der Neuzeit gegen das Mittelalter sei dieser, dass die Principien der Tugend und des Christenthums, welche im Mittelalter sich allein im Privatleben und der Kirche zur Geltung gebracht hätten, nun auch anfingen, das politische Leben zu durchdringen.—Fortlage, *Allg. Monatsschrift*, 1853, 777. Wir Slawen wissen, dass die Geister einzelner Menschen und ganzer Völker sich nur durch die Stufe ihrer Entwicklung unterscheiden. —Mickiewicz, *Slawische Literatur*, ii. 436. Le progrès ne disparait jamais, mais il se déplace souvent. Il va des gouvernants aux gouvernés. La tendance des révolutions est de le ramener toujours parmi les gouvernants. Lorsqu'il est à la tête des sociétés, il marche hardiment, car il conduit. Lorsqu'il est dans la masse, il marche à pas lents, car il lutte.—Napoleon III., *Des Idées Napoléoniennes.* La loi du progrès avait jadis l'inexorable rigueur du destin; elle prend maintenant de jour en jour la douce puissance de la Providence. C'est l'erreur, c'est l'iniquité, c'est le vice, que la civilisation tend à emporter dans sa marche irrésistible; mais la vie des individus et des peuples est devenue pour elle une chose sacrée. Elle transforme plutôt qu'elle ne détruit les choses qui s'opposent à son développement; elle procède par absorption graduelle plutôt que par brusque exécution; elle aime à conquérir par l'influence des idées plutôt que par la force des armes, un peuple, une classe, une institution qui résiste au progrès.—Vacherot, *Essais de Philosophie Critique*, 443. Peu à peu l'homme intellectuel finit par effacer l'homme physique.—Quetelet, *De l'Homme*, ii. 285. In dem Fortschritt der ethischen Anschauungen liegt daher der Kern des geschichtlichen Fortschritts überhaupt.—Schäfer, *Arbeitsgebiet der Geschichte*, 24. Si l'homme a plus de devoirs à mesure qu'il avance en âge, ce qui est mélancolique, mais ce qui est vrai, de même aussi l'humanité est tenue d'avoir une morale plus sévère à mesure qu'elle prend plus de siècles.—Faguet, *Revue des Deux Mondes*, 1894, iii. 871. Si donc il y a une loi de progrès, elle se confond avec la loi morale, et la condition fondamentale du progrès, c'est la pratique de cette loi.—Carrau, *Ib.* 1875, v. 585. L'idée du progrès, du développement, me paraît être l'idée fondamentale contenue sous le mot de civilisation.—Guizot, *Cours d'Histoire*, 1828, 15. Le progrès n'est sous un autre nom, que la liberté en action.—Broglie, *Journal des Débats*, 28th January 1869. Le progrès social est continu. Il a ses périodes de fièvre ou d'atonie, de surexcitation ou de léthargie; il a ses soubresauts et ses haltes, mais il avance toujours.—De Decker, *La Providence*, 174. Ce n'est pas au bonheur seul, c'est au perfectionnement que notre destin nous appelle; et la liberté politique est le plus puissant, le plus énergique moyen de perfectionnement que le ciel nous ait donné.—B. Constant, *Cours de Politique*, ii. 559. To explode error, on whichever side it lies, is certainly to secure progress.—Martineau, *Essays*, i. 114. Die sämmtlichen Freiheitsrechte, welche der heutigen Menschheit so theuer sind, sind im Grunde nur Anwendungen des Rechts der Entwickelung.—Bluntschli, *Kleine Schriften*, i. 51. Geistiges Leben ist auf Freiheit beruhende Entwicklung, mit Freiheit vollzogene That und geschichtlicher Fortschritt.—*Münchner Gel. Anzeigen*, 1849, ii. 83. Wie das Denken erst nach und nach reift, so wird auch der freie Wille nicht fertig geboren, sondern in der Entwickelung erworben.—Trendelenburg, *Logische Untersuchungen*, ii. 94. Das Liberum Arbitrium im vollen Sinne (die vollständig aktuelle Macht der Selbstbestimmung) lässt sich seinem Begriff zufolge schlechterdings nicht unmittelbar geben; es kann nur erworben werden durch das Subjekt selbst, in sich moralisch hervorgebracht werden kraft seiner eigenen Entwickelung.—Rothe, *Ethik*, 1. 360. So gewaltig sei der Andrang der Erfindungen und Entdeckungen, dass "Entwicklungsperioden, die in früheren Zeiten erst in Jahrhunderten

this is a very old story, and a trivial commonplace, and would challenge proof that the world is making progress in aught but intellect, that it is gaining in freedom, or that increase in freedom is either a progress or a gain. Ranke, who was my own master, rejected the view that I have stated; [36] Comte, the master of better men, believed that we drag a lengthening chain under the gathered weight of the dead hand; [37] and many of our recent classics—Carlyle, Newman, Froude—were persuaded that there is no progress justifying the ways of God to man, and that the mere consolidation of liberty is like the motion of creatures whose advance is in the direction of their tails. They deem that anxious precaution against bad government is an obstruction to good, and degrades morality and mind by placing the capable at the mercy of the incapable, dethroning enlightened virtue for the benefit of the average man. They hold that great and salutary things are done for mankind by power concentrated, not by power balanced and cancelled and dispersed, and that the whig theory, sprung from decomposing sects, the theory that authority is legitimate only by virtue of its checks, and that the sovereign is dependent on the subject, is rebellion against the divine will manifested all down the stream of time.

---

durchlaufen wurden, die im Beginn unserer Zeitperiode noch der Jahrzehnte bedurften, sich heute in Jahren vollenden, häufig schon in voller Ausbildung ins Dasein treten."—Philippovich, *Fortschritt und Kulturentwicklung*, 1892, i., quoting Siemens, 1886. Wir erkennen dass dem Menschen die schwere körperliche Arbeit, von der er in seinem Kampfe um's Dasein stets schwer niedergedrückt war und grossenteils noch ist, mehr und mehr durch die wachsende Benutzung der Naturkräfte zur mechanischen Arbeitsleistung abgenommen wird, dass die ihm zufallende Arbeit immer mehr eine intellektuelle wird.—Siemens, 1886, *Ib.* 6.

[36] Once, however, he wrote:—Darin könnte man den idealen Kern der Geschichte des menschlichen Geschlechtes überhaupt sehen, dass in den Kämpfen, die sich in den gegenseitigen Interessen der Staaten und Völker vollziehen, doch immer höhere Potenzen emporkommen, die das Allgemeine demgemäss um gestalten und ihm wieder einen anderen Charakter verleihen.—Ranke, *Weltgeschichte*, iii. 1, 6.

[37] Toujours et partout, les hommes furent de plus en plus dominés par l'ensemble de leurs prédécesseurs, dont ils purent seulement modifier l'empire nécessaire.—Comte, *Politique Positive*, iii. 621.

I state the objection not that we may plunge into the crucial controversy of a science that is not identical with ours, but in order to make my drift clear by the defining aid of express contradiction. No political dogma is as serviceable to my purpose here as the historian's maxim to do the best he can for the other side, and to avoid pertinacity or emphasis on his own. Like the economic precept *laissez faire*,[38] which the eighteenth century derived from Colbert, it has been an important, if not a final step in the making of method. The strongest and most impressive personalities, it is true, like Macaulay, Thiers, and the two greatest of living writers, Mommsen and Treitschke, project their own broad shadow upon their pages. This is a practice proper to great men, and a great man may be worth several immaculate historians. Otherwise there is virtue in the saying that a historian is seen at his best when he does not appear.[39] Better for us is the example of the Bishop of Oxford, who never lets us know what he thinks of anything but the matter before him; and of his illustrious French rival, Fustel de Coulanges, who said to an excited audience: "Do not imagine you are listening to me; it is history itself that speaks."[40] We can found no philosophy on the observation of four hundred years, excluding three thousand. It would be an imperfect and a fallacious induction. But I hope that even this narrow and disedifying section of history will aid you to see that the action of Christ who is risen on mankind whom he redeemed fails not, but increases;[41] that the wisdom of divine rule appears not in

---

[38] La liberté est l'âme du commerce.—Il faut laisser faire les hommes qui s'appliquent sans peine à ce qui convient le mieux; c'est ce qui apporte le plus d'avantage.—Colbert, in *Comptes Rendus de l'Institut*, xxxix. 93.

[39] Il n'y a que les choses humaines exposées dans leur vérité, c'est-à-dire avec leur grandeur, leur variété, leur inépuisable fécondité, qui aient le droit de retenir le lecteur et qui le retiennent en effet. Si l'écrivain paraît une fois, il ennuie ou fait sourire de pitié les lecteurs sérieux.—Thiers to Ste. Beuve, *Lundis,* iii. 195. Comme l'a dit Taine, la disparition du style, c'est la perfection du style.—Faguet, *Revue Politique,* lii. 67.

[40] Ne m'applaudissez pas; ce n'est pas moi qui vous parle; c'est l'histoire qui parle par ma bouche.—*Revue Historique,* xli. 278.

[41] Das Evangelium trat als Geschichte in die Welt, nicht als Dogma— wurde als Geschichte in der christlichen Kirche deponiert.—Rothe, *Kir-*

the perfection but in the improvement of the world; [42] and that achieved liberty is the one ethical result that rests on the converging and combined conditions of advancing civilisation.[43]

chengeschichte, ii. p. x. Das Christenthum ist nicht der Herr Christus, sondern dieser macht es. Es ist sein Werk, und zwar ein Werk, das er stets unter der Arbeit hat.—Er selbst, Christus der Herr, bleibt, der er ist in alle Zukunft, dagegen liegt es ausdrücklich im Begriffe seines Werks, des Christenthums, dass es nicht so bleibt, wie es anhebt.—Rothe, *Allgemeine kirchliche Zeitschrift,* 1864, 299. Dieses Werk, weil es dem Wesen der Geschichte zufolge eine Entwickelung ist, muss über Stufen hinweggehen, die einander ablösen, und von denen jede folgende neue immer nur unter der Zertrümmerung der ihr vorangehenden Platz greifen kann.—Rothe, *ib.* 19th April 1865. Je grösser ein geschichtliches Princip ist, desto langsamer und über mehr Stufen hinweg entfaltet es seinen Gehalt; desto langlebiger ist es aber ebendeshalb auch in diesen seinen unaufhörlichen Abwandelungen.—Rothe, *Stille Stunden,* 301. Der christliche Glaube geht nicht von der Anerkennung abstracter Lehrwahrheiten aus, sondern von der Anerkennung einer Reihe von Thatsachen, die in der Erscheinung Jesu ihren Mittelpunkt haben.—Nitzsch, *Dogmengeschichte,* i. 17. Der Gedankengang der evangelischen Erzählung gibt darum auch eine vollständige Darstellung der christlichen Lehre in ihren wesentlichen Grundzügen; aber er gibt sie im allseitigen lebendigen Zusammenhange mit der Geschichte der christlichen Offenbarung, und nicht in einer theoretisch zusammenhängenden Folgenreihe von ethischen und dogmatischen Lehrsätzen.—Deutinger, *Reich Gottes,* i. p. v.

[42] L'Univers ne doit pas estre considéré seulement dans ce qu'il est; pour le bien connoître, il faut le voir aussi dans ce qu'il doit estre. C'est cet avenir surtout qui a été le grand objet de Dieu dans la création, et c'est pour cet avenir seul que le présent existe.—D'Houteville, *Essai sur la Providence,* 273. La Providence emploie les siècles à élever toujours un plus grand nombre de familles et d'individus à ces biens de la liberté et de l'égalité légitimes que, dans l'enfance des sociétés, la force avait rendus le privilège de quelques-uns.—Guizot, *Gouvernement de la France,* 1820, 9. La marche de la Providence n'est pas assujettie à d'étroites limites; elle ne s'inquiète pas de tirer aujourd'hui la conséquence du principe qu'elle a posé hier; elle la tirera dans des siècles, quand l'heure sera venue; et pour raisonner lentement selon nous, sa logique n'est pas moins sûr.—Guizot, *Histoire de la Civilisation,* 20. Der Keim fortschreitender Entwicklung ist, auch auf göttlichem Geheisse, der Menschheit eingepflanzt. Die Weltgeschichte ist der blosse Ausdruck einer vorbestimmten Entwicklung.—A. Humboldt, 2nd January 1842, *Im Neuen Reich,* 1872, i. 197. Das historisch grosse ist religiös gross; es ist die Gottheit selbst, die sich offenbart.—Raumer, April 1807, *Erinnerungen,* i. 85.

[43] Je suis arrivé à l'âge où je suis, à travers bien des évènements différents, mais avec une seule cause, celle de la liberté régulière.—Tocqueville, 1st May 1852, *Œuvres Inédites,* ii. 185. Me trouvant dans un pays où la religion et le libéralisme sont d'accord, j'avais respiré.—J'exprimais ce sentiment, il

y a plus de vingt ans, dans l'avant-propos de la *Démocratie*. Je l'éprouve aujourd'hui aussi vivement que si j'étais encore jeune, et je ne sais s'il y a une seule pensée qui ait été plus constamment présente à mon esprit.—5th August 1857, *Œuvres*, vi. 395. Il n'y a que la liberté (j'entends la modérée et la régulière) et la religion, qui, par un effort combiné, puissent soulever les hommes au-dessus du bourbier où l'égalité démocratique les plonge naturellement.—1st December 1852, *Œuvres*, vii. 295. L'un de mes rêves, le principal en entrant dans la vie politique, était de travailler à concilier l'esprit libéral et l'esprit de religion, la société nouvelle et l'église.—15th November 1843. *Œuvres Inédites*, ii. 121. La véritable grandeur de l'homme n'est que dans l'accord du sentiment libéral et du sentiment religieux.—17th September 1853, *Œuvres Inédites*, ii. 228. Qui cherche dans la liberté autre chose qu'elle-même est fait pour servir.—*Ancien Régime*, 248. Je regarde, ainsi que je l'ai toujours fait, la liberté comme le premier des biens; je vois toujours en elle l'une des sources les plus fécondes des vertus mâles et des actions grandes. Il n'y a pas de tranquillité ni de bien-être qui puisse me tenir lieu d'elle.—7th January 1856, *Mme· Swetchine*, i. 452. La liberté a un faux air d'aristocratie; en donnant pleine carrière aux facultés humaines, en encourageant le travail et l'economie, elle fait ressortir les supériorités naturelles ou acquises.—Laboulaye, *L'État et ses Limites*, 154. Dire que la liberté n'est point par elle-même, qu'elle dépend d'une situation, d'une opportunité, c'est lui assigner une valeur négative. La liberté n'est pas dès qu'on la subordonne. Elle n'est pas un principe purement négatif, un simple élément de contrôle et de critique. Elle est le principe actif, créateur organisateur par excellence. Elle est le moteur et la règle, la source de toute vie, et le principe de l'ordre. Elle est, en un mot, le nom que prend la conscience souveraine, lorsque, se posant en face du monde social et politique, elle émerge du moi pour modeler les sociétés sur les données de la raison.—Brisson, *Revue Nationale*, xxiii. 214. Le droit, dans l'histoire, est le développement progressif de la liberté, sous la loi de la raison.—Lerminier, *Philosophie du Droit*, i. 211. En prouvant par les leçons de l'histoire que la liberté fait vivre les peuples et que le despotisme les tue, en montrant que l'expiation suit la faute et que la fortune finit d'ordinaire par se ranger du côté de la vertu, Montesquieu n'est ni moins moral ni moins religieux que Bossuet.—Laboulaye, *Œuvres de Montesquieu*, ii. 109. Je ne comprendrais pas qu'une nation ne plaçât pas les libertés politiques au premier rang, parce que c'est des libertés politiques que doivent découler toutes les autres.—Thiers, *Discours*, x. 8, 28th March 1865. Nous sommes arrivés à une époque où la liberté est le but sérieux de tous, où le reste n'est plus qu'une question de moyens.—J. Lebeau, *Observations sur le Pouvoir Royal:* Liège, 1830, p. 10. Le libéralisme, ayant la prétention de se fonder uniquement sur les principes de la raison, croit d'ordinaire n'avoir pas besoin de tradition. Là est son erreur. L'erreur de l'école libérale est d'avoir trop cru qu'il est facile de créer la liberté par la réflexion, et de n'avoir pas vu qu'un établissement n'est solide que quand il a des racines historiques.—Renan, 1858, *Nouvelle Revue*, lxxix. 596. Le respect des individus et des droits existants est autant au-dessus du bonheur de tous, qu'un intérêt moral surpasse un intérêt purement

Then you will understand what a famous philosopher said, that History is the true demonstration of Religion.[44]

---

temporel.—Renan, 1858, *Ib.* lxxix. 597. Die Rechte gelten nichts, wo es sich handelt um das Recht, und das Recht der Freiheit kann nie verjähren, weil es die Quelle alles Rechtes selbst ist.—C. Frantz, *Ueber die Freiheit*, 110. Wir erfahren hienieden nie die ganze Wahrheit: wir geniessen nie die ganze Freiheit.—Reuss, *Reden*, 56. Le gouvernement Constitutionnel, comme tout gouvernement libre, présente et doit présenter un état de lutte permanent. La liberté est la perpétuité de la lutte.—De Serre. Broglie, *Nouvelles Études*, 243. The experiment of free government is not one which can be tried once for all. Every generation must try it for itself. As each new generation starts up to the responsibilities of manhood, there is, as it were, a new launch of Liberty, and its voyage of experiment begins afresh.—Winthrop, *Addresses*, 163. L'histoire perd son véritable caractère du moment que la liberté en a disparu; elle devient une sorte de physique sociale. C'est l'élément personnel de l'histoire qui en fait la réalité.—Vacherot, *Revue des Deux Mondes*, 1869, iv. 215. Demander la liberté pour soi et la refuser aux autres, c'est la définition du despotisme.—Laboulaye, 4th December 1874. Les causes justes profitent de tout, des bonnes intentions comme des mauvaises, des calculs personnels comme des dévouemens courageux, de la démence, enfin, comme de la raison.—B. Constant, *Les Cent Jours*, ii. 29. Sie ist die Kunst, das Gute der schon weit gediehenen Civilisation zu sichern.—Baltisch, *Politische Freiheit*, 9. In einem Volke, welches sich zur bürgerlichen Gesellschaft, überhaupt zum Bewusstseyn der Unendlichkeit des Freien—entwickelt hat, ist nur die constitutionelle Monarchie möglich.—Hegel's *Philosophie des Rechts*, § 137, *Hegel und Preussen*, 1841, 31. Freiheit ist das höchste Gut. Alles andere ist nur das Mittel dazu: gut falls es ein Mittel dazu ist, übel falls es dieselbe hemmt.—Fichte, *Werke*, iv. 403. You are not to inquire how your trade may be increased, nor how you are to become a great and powerful people, but how your liberties can be secured. For liberty ought to be the direct end of your government.—Patrick Henry, 1788; Wirt, *Life of Henry*, 272.

[44] Historiae ipsius praeter delectationem utilitas nulla est, quam ut religionis Christianae veritas demonstretur, quod aliter quam per historiam fieri non potest.—Leibniz, *Opera*, ed. Dutens, vi. 297. The study of Modern History is, next to Theology itself, and only next in so far as Theology rests on a divine revelation, the most thoroughly religious training that the mind can receive. It is no paradox to say that Modern History, including Medieval History in the term, is coextensive in its field of view, in its habits of criticism, in the persons of its most famous students, with Ecclesiastical History.—Stubbs, *Lectures*, 9. Je regarde donc l'étude de l'histoire comme l'étude de la providence.—L'histoire est vraiment une seconde philosophie.—Si Dieu ne parle pas toujours, il agit toujours en Dieu.—D'Aguesseau, *Œuvres*, xv. 34, 31, 35. Für diejenigen, welche das Wesen der menschlichen Freiheit erkannt haben, bildet die denkende Betrachtung der Weltgeschichte, besonders des christlichen

But what do people mean who proclaim that liberty is the palm, and the prize, and the crown, seeing that it is an idea of which there are two hundred definitions, and that this wealth of interpretation has caused more bloodshed than anything, except theology? Is it Democracy as in France, or Federalism as in America, or the national independence which bounds the Italian view, or the reign of the fittest, which is the ideal of Germans? [45] I know not whether it will ever fall within my sphere of duty to trace the slow progress of that idea through

Weltalters, die höchste, und umfassendste Theodicee.—Vatke, *Die Menschliche Freiheit,* 1841, 516. La théologie, que l'on regarde volontiers comme la plus étroite et la plus stérile des sciences, en est, au contraire, la plus étendue et la plus féconde. Elle confine à toutes les études et touche à toutes les questions. Elle renferme tous les éléments d'une instruction libérale.—Scherer, *Mélanges,* 522. The belief that the course of events and the agency of man are subject to the laws of a divine order, which it is alike impossible for any one either fully to comprehend or effectually to resist—this belief is the ground of all our hope for the future destinies of mankind.—Thirlwall, *Remains,* iii. 282. A true religion must consist of ideas and facts both; not of ideas alone without facts, for then it would be mere philosophy; nor of facts alone without ideas, of which those facts are the symbols, or out of which they are grounded; for then it would be mere history.—Coleridge, *Table Talk,* 144. It certainly appears strange that the men most conversant with the order of the visible universe should soonest suspect it empty of directing mind; and, on the other hand, that humanistic, moral and historical studies—which first open the terrible problems of suffering and grief, and contain all the reputed provocatives of denial and despair—should confirm, and enlarge rather than disturb, the prepossessions of natural piety.—Martineau, *Essays,* i. 122. Die Religion hat nur dann eine Bedeutung für den Menschen, wenn er in der Geschichte einen Punkt, findet, dem er sich völlig unbedingt hingeben kann.—Steffens, *Christliche Religionsphilosophie,* 440, 1839. Wir erkennen darin nur eine Thätigkeit des zu seinem ächten und wahren Leben, zu seinem verlornen, objectiven Selbstverständnisse such zurücksehnenden christlichen Geistes unserer Zeit, einen Ausdruck für das Bedürfniss desselben, sich aus den unwahren und unächten Verkleidungen, womit ihn der moderne, subjective Geschmack der letzten Entwicklungsphase des theologischen Bewusstseyns umhüllt hat, zu seiner historischen allein wahren und ursprünglichen Gestalt wiederzugebären, zu derjenigen Bedeutung zurückzukehren, die ihm in dem Bewusstseyn der Geschichte allein zukommt und deren Verständniss in dem wogenden luxuriösen Leben der modernen Theologie längst untergegangen ist.—Georgii, *Zeitschrift für Hist. Theologie,* ix. 5, 1839.

[45] Liberty, in fact, means just so far as it is realised, the right man in the right place.—Seeley, *Lectures and Essays,* 109.

the chequered scenes of our history, and to describe how subtle speculations touching the nature of conscience promoted a nobler and more spiritual conception of the liberty that protects it,[46] until the guardian of rights developed into the guardian of duties which are the cause of rights,[47] and that which had been prized as the material safeguard for treasures of earth became sacred as security for things that are divine. All that we require is a work-day key to history, and our present need can be supplied without pausing to satisfy philosophers. Without inquiring how far Sarasa or Butler, Kant or Vinet, is right as to the infallible voice of God in man, we may easily agree in this, that where absolutism reigned, by irresistible arms, concentrated possessions, auxiliary churches, and inhuman laws, it reigns no more; that commerce having risen against land, labour against wealth, the State against the forces dominant in society,[48] the division of power against the State, the thought of individuals against the practice of ages, neither authorities, nor minorities, nor majorities can command implicit obedience; and, where there has been long and arduous experience, a rampart of tried conviction and accumulated knowledge,[49] where there is a fair

---

[46] In diesem Sinne ist Freiheit und sich entwickelnde moralische Vernunft und Gewissen gleichbedeutend. In diesen Sinne ist der Mensch frei, sobald sich das Gewissen in ihm entwickelt.—Scheidler, *Ersch und Gruber*, xlix. 20. Aus der unendlichen und ewigen Geltung der menschlichen Persönlichkeit vor Gott, aus der Vorstellung von der in Gott freien Persönlichkeit, folgt auch der Anspruch auf das Recht derselben in der weltlichen Sphäre, auf bürgerliche und politische Freiheit, auf Gewissen und Religionsfreiheit, auf freie wissenschaftliche Forschung u.s.w., und namentlich die Forderung, dass niemand lediglich zum Mittel für andere diene.—Martensen, *Christliche Ethik*, i. 50.

[47] Es giebt angeborne Menschenrechte, weil es angeborne Menschenpflichten giebt.—Wolff, *Naturrecht;* Loeper, *Einleitung zu Faust*, lvii.

[48] La constitution de l'état reste jusqu'à un certain point à notre discrétion. La constitution de la société ne dépend pas de nous; elle est donnée par la force des choses, et si l'on veut élever le langage, elle est l'œuvre de la Providence.—Rémusat, *Revue des Deux Mondes*, 1861, v. 795.

[49] Die Freiheit ist bekanntlich kein Geschenk der Götter, sondern ein Gut das jedes Volk sich selbst verdankt und das nur bei dem erforderlichen Mass moralischer Kraft und Würdigkeit gedeiht.—Ihering, *Geist des Römischen Rechts*, ii. 290. Liberty, in the very nature of it, absolutely requires, and even supposes, that people be able to govern themselves in

level of general morality, education, courage, and self-restraint, there, if there only, a society may be found that exhibits the condition of life towards which, by elimination of failures, the world has been moving through the allotted space.[50] You will know it by outward signs: Representation, the extinction of slavery, the reign of opinion, and the like; better still by less apparent evidences: the security of the weaker groups [51] and the liberty of conscience, which, effectually secured, secures the rest.

Here we reach a point at which my argument threatens to abut on a contradiction. If the supreme conquests of society are won more often by violence than by lenient arts, if the trend and drift of things is towards convulsions and catastrophes,[52] if the world owes religious liberty to the Dutch Revolution, constitutional government to the English, federal republicanism to the American, political equality to the French and its succes-

those respects in which they are free; otherwise their wickedness will be in proportion to their liberty, and this greatest of blessings will become a curse.—Butler, *Sermons*, 331. In each degree and each variety of public development there are corresponding institutions, best answering the public needs; and what is meat to one is poison to another. Freedom is for those who are fit for it.—Parkman, *Canada*, 396. Die Freiheit ist die Wurzel einer neuen Schöpfung in der Schöpfung.—Sederholm, *Die ewigen That-sachen*, 86.

[50] La liberté politique, qui n'est qu'une complexité plus grande, de plus en plus grande, dans le gouvernement d'un peuple, à mesure que le peuple lui-même contient un plus grand nombre de forces diverses ayant droit et de vivre et de participer à la chose publique, est un fait de civilisation qui s'impose lentement à une société organisée, mais qui n'apparaît point comme un principe à une société qui s'organise.—Faguet, *Revue des Deux Mondes*, 1889, ii. 942.

[51] Il y a bien un droit du plus sage, mais non pas un droit du plus fort.—La justice est le droit du plus faible.—Joubert, *Pensées*, i. 355, 358.

[52] Nicht durch ein pflanzenähnliches Wachsthum, nicht aus den dunklen Gründen der Volksempfindung, sondern durch den männlichen Willen, durch die Ueberzeugung, durch die That, durch den Kampf entsteht, behauptet, entwickelt sich das Recht. Sein historisches Werden ist ein bewusstes, im hellen Mittagslicht der Erkenntniss und der Gesetzgebung. —*Rundschau*, November 1893, 13. Nicht das Normale, Zahme, sondern das Abnorme, Wilde, bildet überall die Grundlage und den Anfang einer neuen Ordnung.—Lasaulx, *Philosophie der Geschichte*, 143.

sors,[53] what is to become of us, docile and attentive students of
the absorbing Past? The triumph of the Revolutionist annuls the
historian.[54] By its authentic exponents, Jefferson and Sieyès, the
Revolution of the last century repudiates history. Their followers renounced acquaintance with it, and were ready to destroy
its records and to abolish its inoffensive professors. But the
unexpected truth, stranger than fiction, is that this was not the
ruin but the renovation of history. Directly and indirectly, by
process of development and by process of reaction, an impulse
was given which made it infinitely more effectual as a factor of
civilisation than ever before, and a movement began in the
world of minds which was deeper and more serious than the
revival of ancient learning.[55] The dispensation under which we

---

[53] Um den Sieg zu vervollständigen, erübrigte das zweite Stadium oder
die Aufgabe: die Berechtigung der Mehrheit nach allen Seiten hin zur
gleichen Berechtigung aller zu erweitern, d.h. bis zur Gleichstellung aller
Bekenntnisse im Kirchenrecht, aller Völker im Völkerrecht, aller Staats-
bürger im Staatsrecht und aller socialen Interessen im Gesellschaftsrecht
fortzuführen.—A. Schmidt, *Züricher Monatsschrift*, i. 68.

[54] Notre histoire ne nous enseignait nullement la liberté. Le jour où la
France voulut être libre, elle eut tout à créer, tout à inventer dans cet
ordre de faits.—Cependant il faut marcher, l'avenir appelle les peuples.
Quand on n'a point pour cela l'impulsion du passé, il faut bien se confier à
la raison.—Dupont White, *Revue des Deux Mondes*, 1861, vi. 191. Le
peuple français a peu de goût pour le développement graduel des institutions. Il ignore son histoire, il ne s'y reconnaît pas, elle n'a pas laissé de
trace dans sa conscience.—Scherer, *Études Critiques*, i. 100. Durch die
Revolution befreiten sich die Franzosen von ihrer Geschichte.—
Rosenkranz, *Aus einem Tagebuch*, 199.

[55] The discovery of the comparative method in philology, in mythology—let me add in politics and history and the whole range of human
thought—marks a stage in the progress of the human mind at least as
great and memorable as the revival of Greek and Latin learning.—
Freeman, *Historical Essays*, iv. 301. The diffusion of a critical spirit in
history and literature is affecting the criticism of the Bible in our own day
in a manner not unlike the burst of intellectual life in the fifteenth and
sixteenth centuries.—Jowett, *Essays and Reviews*, 346. As the revival of
literature in the sixteenth century produced the Reformation, so the
growth of the critical spirit, and the change that has come over mental
science, and the mere increase of knowledge of all kinds, threaten now a
revolution less external but not less profound.—Haddan, *Replies*, 348.

live and labour consists first in the recoil from the negative spirit that rejected the law of growth, and partly in the endeavour to classify and adjust the Revolution, and to account for it by the natural working of historic causes. The Conservative line of writers, under the name of the Romantic or Historical School, had its seat in Germany, looked upon the Revolution as an alien episode, the error of an age, a disease to be treated by the investigation of its origin, and strove to unite the broken threads and to restore the normal conditions of organic evolution. The Liberal School, whose home was France, explained and justified the Revolution as a true development, and the ripened fruit of all history.[56] These are the two main arguments of the genera-

---

[56] In his just contempt and detestation of the crimes and follies of the Revolutionists, he suffers himself to forget that the revolution itself is a process of the Divine Providence, and that as the folly of men is the wisdom of God, so are their iniquities instruments of His goodness.— Coleridge, *Biographia Literaria*, ii. 240. In other parts of the world, the idea of revolutions in government is, by a mournful and indissoluble association, connected with the idea of wars, and all the calamities attendant on wars. But happy experience teaches us to view such revolutions in a very different light—to consider them only as progressive steps in improving the knowledge of government, and increasing the happiness of society and mankind.—J. Wilson, 26th November 1787, *Works*, iii. 293. La Révolution, c'est-à-dire l'œuvre des siècles, ou, si vous voulez, le renouvellement progressif de la société, ou encore, sa nouvelle constitution.—Rémusat, *Correspondance*, 11th October 1818. A ses yeux loin d'avoir rompu le cours naturel des évènements, ni la Révolution d'Angleterre, ni la nôtre, n'ont rien dit, rien fait, qui n'eût été dit, souhaité, fait, ou tenté cent fois avant leur explosion. "Il faut en ceci," dit-il, "tout accorder à leurs adversaires, les surpasser même en sévérité, ne regarder à leurs accusations que pour y ajouter, s'ils en oublient; et puis les sommer de dresser, à leur tour, le compte des erreurs, des crimes, et des maux de ces temps et de ces pouvoirs qu'ils ont pris sous leur garde."—*Revue de Paris*, xvi. 303, on Guizot. Quant aux nouveautés mises en œuvre par la Révolution française on les retrouve une à une, en remontant d'âge en âge, chez les philosophes du XVIII⁰ siècle, chez les grands penseurs du XVI⁰, chez certains Pères d'Église et jusque dans la République de Platon. —En présence de cette belle continuité de l'histoire, qui ne fait pas plus de sauts que la nature, devant cette solidarité nécessaire des révolutions avec le passé qu'elles brisent.—Krantz, *Revue Politique*, xxxiii. 264. L'esprit du XIX⁰ siècle est de comprendre et de juger les choses du passé. Notre œuvre est d'expliquer ce que le VIII⁰ siècle avait mission de nier.— Vacherot, *De la Démocratie*, pref., 28.

tion to which we owe the notion and the scientific methods that make history so unlike what it was to the survivors of the last century. Severally, the innovators were not superior to the men of old. Muratori was as widely read, Tillemont as accurate, Leibniz as able, Fréret as acute, Gibbon as masterly in the craft of composite construction. Nevertheless, in the second quarter of this century, a new era began for historians.

I would point to three things in particular, out of many, which constitute the amended order. Of the incessant deluge of new and unsuspected matter I need say little. For some years, the secret archives of the papacy were accessible at Paris; but the time was not ripe, and almost the only man whom they availed was the archivist himself.[57] Towards 1830 the documentary studies began on a large scale, Austria leading the way. Michelet, who claims, towards 1836, to have been the pioneer,[58] was preceded by such rivals as Mackintosh, Bucholtz, and Mignet. A new and more productive period began thirty years later, when the war of 1859 laid open the spoils of Italy. Every country in succession has now allowed the exploration of its records, and there is more fear of drowning than of drought. The result has been that a lifetime spent in the largest collection of printed books would not suffice to train a real master of modern history. After he had turned from literature to sources, from Burnet to Pocock, from Macaulay to Madame Campana, from Thiers to the interminable correspondence of the Bonapartes, he would still feel instant need of inquiry at Venice or Naples, in the Ossuna library or at the Hermitage.[59]

---

[57] La commission recherchera, dans toutes les parties des archives pontificales, les pièces relatives à l'abus que les papes ont fait de leur ministère spirituel contre l'autorité des souveraines et la tranquillité des peuples.—Daunou, *Instructions*, 3rd January 1811. Laborde, *Inventaires*, p. cxii.

[58] Aucun des historiens remarquables de cette époque n'avait senti encore le besoin de chercher les faits hors des livres imprimés, aux sources primitives, la plupart inédites alors, aux manuscrits de nos bibliothèques, aux documents de nos archives.—Michelet, *Histoire de France*, 1869, i. 2.

[59] Doch besteht eine Grenze, wo die Geschichte aufhört und das Archiv anfängt, und die von der Geschichtschreibung nicht überschritten werden sollte. *Unsere Zeit*, 1866, ii. 635. Il faut avertir nos jeunes historiens à la

These matters do not now concern us. For our purpose, the main thing to learn is not the art of accumulating material, but the sublimer art of investigating it, of discerning truth from falsehood and certainty from doubt. It is by solidity of criticism more than by the plenitude of erudition, that the study of history strengthens, and straightens, and extends the mind.[60] And the accession of the critic in the place of the indefatigable compiler, of the artist in coloured narrative, the skilled limner of character, the persuasive advocate of good, or other, causes, amounts to a transfer of government, to a change of dynasty, in the historic realm. For the critic is one who, when he lights on an interesting statement, begins by suspecting it. He remains in suspense until he has subjected his authority to three operations. First, he asks whether he has read the passage as the author wrote it. For the transcriber, and the editor, and the

---

fois de la nécessité inéluctable du document et, d'autre part, du danger qu'il présente.—M. Hanotaux.

[60] This process consists in determining with documentary proofs, and by minute investigations duly set forth, the literal, precise, and positive inferences to be drawn at the present day from every authentic statement, without regard to commonly received notions, to sweeping generalities, or to possible consequences.—Harrisse, *Discovery of America*, 1892, p. vi. Perhaps the time has not yet come for synthetic labours in the sphere of History. It may be that the student of the Past must still content himself with critical inquiries.—*Ib.* p. v. Few scholars are critics, few critics are philosophers, and few philosophers look with equal care on both sides of a question.—W. S. Landor in Holyoake's *Agitator's Life*, ii. 15. Introduire dans l'histoire, et sans tenir compte des passions politiques et religieuses, le doute méthodique que Descartes, le premier, appliqua à l'étude de la philosophie, n'est-ce pas là une excellente méthode? n'est-ce pas même la meilleure?—Chantelauze, *Correspondant*, 1883, i. 129. La critique historique ne sera jamais populaire. Comme elle est de toutes les sciences la plus délicate, la plus déliée, elle n'a de crédit qu'auprès des esprits cultivés.—Cherbuliez, *Revue des Deux Mondes*, xcvii. 517. Nun liefert aber die Kritik, wenn sie rechter Art ist, immer nur einzelne Data, gleichsam die Atome des Thatbestandes, und jede Kombination, jede Zusammenfassung und Schlussfolgerung, ohne die es doch einmal nicht abgeht, ist ein subjektiver Akt des Forschers. Demnach blieb Waitz, bei des eigenen Arbeit wie bei jener des anderen, immer höchst mistrauisch gegen jedes Résumé, jede Definition, jedes abschliessende Wort.—Sybel, *Historische Zeitschrift*, lvi. 484. Mit blosser Kritik wird darin nichts ausgerichtet, denn die ist nur eine Vorarbeit, welche da aufhört, wo die echte historische Kunst anfängt.—Lasaulx, *Philosophie der Künste*, 212.

official or officious censor on the top of the editor, have played strange tricks, and have much to answer for. And if they are not to blame, it may turn out that the author wrote his book twice over, that you can discover the first jet, the progressive variations, things added, and things struck out. Next is the question where the writer got his information. If from a previous writer, it can be ascertained, and the inquiry has to be repeated. If from unpublished papers, they must be traced, and when the fountain-head is reached, or the track disappears, the question of veracity arises. The responsible writer's character, his position, antecedents, and probable motives have to be examined into; and this is what, in a different and adapted sense of the word, may be called the higher criticism, in comparison with the servile and often mechanical work of pursuing statements to their root. For a historian has to be treated as a witness, and not believed unless his sincerity is established.[61] The maxim that a man must be presumed to be innocent until his guilt is proved, was not made for him.

For us, then, the estimate of authorities, the weighing of testimony, is more meritorious than the potential discovery of new matter.[62] And modern history, which is the widest field of application, is not the best to learn our business in; for it is too wide, and the harvest has not been winnowed as in antiquity, and further on to the Crusades. It is better to examine what has been done for questions that are compact and circumscribed, such as the sources of Plutarch's *Pericles*, the two tracts on Athenian government, the origin of the epistle to Diognetus, the date of the life of St. Antony; and to learn from Schwegler how this analytical work began. More satisfying because more deci-

---

[61] The only case in which such extraneous matters can be fairly called in is when facts are stated resting on testimony; then it is not only just, but it is necessary for the sake of truth, to inquire into the habits of mind of him by whom they are adduced.—Babbage, *Bridgewater Treatise*, p. xiv.

[62] There is no part of our knowledge which it is more useful to obtain at first hand—to go to the fountain-head for—than our knowledge of History. —J. S. Mill, *Inaugural Address*, 34. The only sound intellects are those which, in the first instance, set their standard of proof high.—J. S. Mill, *Examination of Hamilton's Philosophy*, 525.

sive has been the critical treatment of the medieval writers, parallel with the new editions, on which incredible labour has been lavished, and of which we have no better examples than the prefaces of Bishop Stubbs. An important event in this series was the attack on Dino Compagni, which, for the sake of Dante, roused the best Italian scholars to a not unequal contest. When we are told that England is behind the Continent in critical faculty, we must admit that this is true as to quantity, not as to quality of work. As they are no longer living, I will say of two Cambridge professors, Lightfoot and Hort, that they were critical scholars whom neither Frenchman nor German has surpassed.

The third distinctive note of the generation of writers who dug so deep a trench between history as known to our grandfathers and as it appears to us, is their dogma of impartiality. To an ordinary man the word means no more than justice. He considers that he may proclaim the merits of his own religion, of his prosperous and enlightened country, of his political persuasion, whether democracy, or liberal monarchy, or historic conservatism, without transgression or offence, so long as he is fair to the relative, though inferior, merits of others, and never treats men as saints or as rogues for the side they take. There is no impartiality, he would say, like that of a hanging judge. The men who, with the compass of criticism in their hands, sailed the uncharted sea of original research proposed a different view. History, to be above evasion or dispute, must stand on documents, not on opinions. They had their own notion of truthfulness, based on the exceeding difficulty of finding truth, and the still greater difficulty of impressing it when found. They thought it possible to write, with so much scruple, and simplicity, and insight, as to carry along with them every man of good will, and, whatever his feelings, to compel his assent. Ideas which, in religion and in politics, are truths, in history are forces. They must be respected; they must not be affirmed. By dint of a supreme reserve, by much self-control, by a timely and discreet indifference, by secrecy in the matter of the black cap, history might be lifted above contention, and made an accepted tribunal, and the same for all.[63] If men were truly sincere, and delivered judgment by no canons but those of evident morality, then Julian would be described in the same terms by Christian and pagan, Luther by Catholic and Protestant, Washington by Whig and Tory, Napoleon by patriotic Frenchman and patriotic German.[64]

[63] There are so few men mentally capable of seeing both sides of a question; so few with consciences sensitively alive to the obligation of seeing both sides; so few placed under conditions either of circumstance or temper, which admit of their seeing both sides.—Greg, *Political Problems*, 1870, 173. Il n'y a que les Allemands qui sachent être aussi complètement objectifs. Ils se dédoublent, pour ainsi dire, en deux hommes, l'un qui a des principes très arrêtés et des passions très vives, l'autre qui sait voir et observer comme s'il n'en avait point.—Laveleye, *Revue des Deux Mondes*, 1868, i. 431. L'écrivain qui penche trop dans le sens où il incline, et qui ne se défie pas de ses qualités presque autant que ses défauts, cet écrivain tourne à la manière.—Scherer, *Mélanges*, 484. Il faut faire volteface, et vivement, franchement, tourner le dos au moyen âge, à ce passé morbide, qui, même quand il n'agit pas, influe terriblement par la contagion de la mort. Il ne faut ni combattre, ni critiquer, mais oublier. Oublions et marchons!—Michelet, *La Bible de l'Humanité*, 483. It has excited surprise that Thucydides should speak of Antiphon, the traitor to the democracy, and the employer of assassins, as "a man inferior in virtue to none of his contemporaries." But neither here nor elsewhere does Thucydides pass moral judgments.—Jowett, *Thucydides*, ii. 501.

[64] Non theologi provinciam suscepimus; scimus enim quantum hoc ingenii nostri tenuitatem superet: ideo sufficit nobis τὸ ὅτι fideliter ex antiquis auctoribus retulisse.—Morinus, *De Poenitentia*, ix. 10.—Il faut avouer que la religion chrétienne a quelque chose d'étonnant! C'est parce que vous y êtes né, dira-t-on. Tant s'en faut, je me roidis contre par cette raison-là même, de peur que cette prévention ne me suborne.—Pascal, *Pensées*, xvi. 7.—I was fond of Fleury for a reason which I express in the advertisement; because it presented a sort of photograph of ecclesiastical history without any comment upon it. In the event, that simple representation of the early centuries had a good deal to do with unsettling me.—Newman, *Apologia*, 152.—Nur was sich vor dem Richterstuhl einer ächten, unbefangenen, nicht durch die Brille einer philosophischen oder dogmatischen Schule stehenden Wissenschaft als wahr bewährt, kann zur Erbauung, Belehrung und Warnung tüchtig seyn.—Neander, *Kirchengeschichte*, i. p. vii. Wie weit bei katholischen Publicisten bei der Annahme der Ansicht von der Staatsanstalt apologetische Gesichtspunkte massgebend gewesen sind, mag dahingestellt bleiben. Der Historiker darf sich jedoch nie durch apologetische Zwecke leiten lassen; sein einziges Ziel soll die Ergründung der Wahrheit sein.—Pastor, *Geschichte der Päbste*, ii. 545. Church history falsely written is a school of vainglory, hatred and uncharitableness; truly

I speak of this school with reverence, for the good it has done, by the assertion of historic truth and of its legitimate authority over the minds of men. It provides a discipline which every one of us does well to undergo, and perhaps also well to relinquish. For it is not the whole truth. Lanfrey's essay on Carnot, Chuquet's wars of the Revolution, Ropes's military histories, Roget's Geneva in the time of Calvin, will supply you with examples of a more robust impartiality than I have described. Renan calls it the luxury of an opulent and aristocratic society, doomed to

---

written, it is a discipline of humility, of charity, of mutual love.—Sir W. Hamilton, *Discussions*, 506. The more trophies and crowns of honour the Church of former ages can be shown to have won in the service of her adorable head, the more tokens her history can be brought to furnish of his powerful presence in her midst, the more will we be pleased and rejoice, Protestant though we be.—Nevin, *Mercersburg Review*, 1851, 168. S'il est une chose à laquelle j'ai donné tous mes soins, c'est à ne pas laisser influencer mes jugements par les opinions politiques ou religieuses; que si j'ai quelquefois péché par quelque excès, c'est par la bienveillance pour les œuvres n'avons nul intérêt à faire parler l'histoire en faveur de nos propres opinions. C'est son droit imprescriptible que le narrateur reproduise tous les faits sans aucune réticence et range toutes les évolutions dans leur ordre naturel. Notre récit restera complètement en dehors des préoccupations de la dogmatique et des déclamations de la polémique. Plus les questions auxquelles nous aurons à toucher agitent et passionnent de nos jours les esprits, plus il est du devoir de l'historien de s'effacer devant les faits qu'il veut faire connaître.—Reuss, *Nouvelle Revue de Théologie*, vi. 193, 1860. To love truth for truth's sake is the principal part of human perfection in this world, and the seed-plot of all other virtues.—Locke, *Letter to Collins*. Il n'est plus possible aujourd'hui à l'historien d'être national dans le sens étroit du mot. Son patriotisme à lui c'est l'amour de la vérité. Il n'est pas l'homme d'une race ou d'un pays, il est l'homme de tous les pays, il parle au nom de la civilisation générale.—Lanfrey, *Hist. de Nap.* iii. 2, 1870. Juger avec les parties de soi-même qui sont le moins des formes du tempérament, et le plus des facultés pénétrées et modelées par l'expérience, par l'étude, par l'investigation, par le non-moi.—Faguet, *R. de Paris*, i. 151. Aucun critique n'est aussi impersonnel que lui, aussi libre de partis pris et d'opinions preconçues, aussi objectif.—Il ne mêle ou paraît mêler à ses appréciations ni inclinations personnelles de goût ou d'humeur, ou théories d'aucune sorte. G. Monod, of Faguet, *Revue Historique*, xlii. 417. On dirait qu'il a peur, et généralisant ses observations, en systématisant ses connaissances, de mêler de lui-même aux choses.—Je lis tout un volume de M. Faguet, sans penser une fois à M. Faguet: je ne vois que les originaux qu'il montre.—J'envisage toujours une réalité objective, jamais l'idée de M. Faguet, jamais la doctrine de M. Faguet.—Lanson, *Revue Politique*, 1894, i. 98.

vanish in an age of fierce and sordid striving. In our universities it has a magnificent and appointed refuge; and to serve its cause, which is sacred, because it is the cause of truth and honour, we may import a profitable lesson from the highly unscientific region of public life. There a man does not take long to find out that he is opposed by some who are abler and better than himself. And, in order to understand the cosmic force and the true connection of ideas, it is a source of power, and an excellent school of principle, not to rest until, by excluding the fallacies, the prejudices, the exaggerations which perpetual contention and the consequent precautions breed, we have made out for our opponents a stronger and more impressive case than they present themselves.[65] Excepting one to which we are coming before I release you, there is no precept less faithfully observed by historians.

Ranke is the representative of the age which instituted the modern study of History. He taught it to be critical, to be colourless, and to be new. We meet him at every step, and he has done more for us than any other man. There are stronger books than any one of his, and some may have surpassed him in political, religious, philosophic insight, in vividness of the

---

[65] It should teach us to disentangle principles first from parties, and again from one another; first of all as showing how imperfectly all parties represent their own principles, and then how the principles themselves are a mingled tissue.—Arnold, *Modern History*, 184. I find it a good rule, when I am contemplating a person from whom I want to learn, always to look out for his strength, being confident that the weakness will discover itself.—Maurice, *Essays*, 305. We may seek for agreement somewhere with our neighbours, using that as a point of departure for the sake of argument. It is this latter course that I wish here to explain and defend. The method is simple enough, though not yet very familiar.—It aims at conciliation; it proceeds by making the best of our opponent's case, instead of taking him at his worst.—The most interesting part of every disputed question only begins to appear when the rival ideals admit each other's right to exist.—A. Sidgwick, *Distinction and the Criticism of Beliefs*, 1892, 211. That cruel reticence in the breasts of wise men which makes them always hide their deeper thought.—Ruskin, *Sesame and Lilies*, i. 16. Je offener wir die einzelnen Wahrheiten des Sozialismus anerkennen, desto erfolgreicher können wir seine fundamentalen Unwahrheiten widerlegen.—Roscher, *Deutsche Vierteljahrschrift*, 1849, i. 177.

creative imagination, in originality, elevation, and depth of thought; but by the extent of important work well executed, by his influence on able men, and by the amount of knowledge which mankind receives and employs with the stamp of his mind upon it, he stands without a rival. I saw him last in 1877, when he was feeble, sunken, and almost blind, and scarcely able to read or write. He uttered his farewell with kindly emotion, and I feared that the next I should hear of him would be the news of his death. Two years later he began a Universal History, which is not without traces of weakness, but which, composed after the age of eighty-three, and carried, in seventeen volumes, far into the Middle Ages, brings to a close the most astonishing career in literature.

His course had been determined, in early life, by *Quentin Durward*. The shock of the discovery that Scott's Lewis the Eleventh was inconsistent with the original in Commynes made him resolve that his object thenceforth should be above all things to follow, without swerving, and in stern subordination and surrender, the lead of his authorities. He decided effectually to repress the poet, the patriot, the religious or political partisan, to sustain no cause, to banish himself from his books, and to write nothing that would gratify his own feelings or disclose his private convictions.[66] When a strenuous divine,

---

[66] Dann habe ihn die Wahrnehmung, dass manche Angaben in den historischen Romanen Walter Scott's, mit den gleichzeitigen Quellen im Widerspruch standen, "mit Erstaunen" erfüllt, und ihn zu dem Entschlusse gebracht, auf das Gewissenhafteste an der Ueberlieferung der Quellen festzuhalten.—Sybel, *Gedächtnissrede auf Ranke. Akad. der Wissenschaften*, 1887, p. 6. Sich frei zu halten von allem Widerschein der Gegenwart, sogar, soweit das menschenmöglich, von dem der eignen subjectiven Meinung in den Dingen des Staates, der Kirche und der Gesellschaft.—A. Dove, *Im Neuen Reich*, 1875, ii. 967. Wir sind durchaus nicht für die leblose und schemenartige Darstellungsweise der Ranke'schen Schule eingenommen; es wird uns immer kühl bis ans Herz heran, wenn wir derartige Schilderungen der Reformation und der Revolution lesen, welche so ganz im kühlen Element des Pragmatismus sich bewegen und dabei so ganz Undinenhaft sind und keine Seele haben.—Wir lassen es uns lieber gefallen, dass die Männer der Geschichte hier und dort gehofmeistert werden, als dass sie uns mit Glasaugen ansehen, so meisterhaft immer die Kunst sein mag, die sie ihnen eingesetzt hat.—Gottschall, *Unsere Zeit*,

who, like him, had written on the Reformation, hailed him as a comrade, Ranke repelled his advances. "You," he said, "are in the first place a Christian: I am in the first place a historian. There is a gulf between us." [67] He was the first eminent writer who exhibited what Michelet calls *le désintéressement des morts*. It was a moral triumph for him when he could refrain from judging, show that much might be said on both sides, and leave the rest to Providence.[68] He would have felt sympathy with the two famous London physicians of our day, of whom it is told that they could not make up their minds on a case and reported dubiously. The head of the family insisted on a positive opinion. They answered that they were unable to give one, but he might easily find fifty doctors who could.

Niebuhr had pointed out that chroniclers who wrote before the invention of printing generally copied one predecessor at a time, and knew little about sifting or combining authorities. The suggestion became luminous in Ranke's hands, and with his light and dexterous touch he scrutinised and dissected the principal historians, from Machiavelli to the *Mémoires d'un Homme d'État*, with a rigour never before applied to moderns. But whilst Niebuhr dismissed the traditional story, replacing it with a construction of his own, it was Ranke's mission to preserve, not to undermine, and to set up masters whom, in their proper sphere, he could obey. The many excellent dissertations

1866, ii. 636, 637. A vivre avec des diplomates, il leur a pris des qualités qui sont un défaut chez un historien. L'historien n'est pas un témoin, c'est un juge; c'est à lui d'accuser et de condamner au nom du passé opprimé et dans l'intérêt de l'avenir.—Laboulaye on Ranke; *Débats,* 12th January 1852.

[67] Un théologien qui a composé une éloquente histoire de la Réformation, rencontrant à Berlin un illustre historien qui, lui aussi, a raconté Luther et le XVIe siècle, l'embrassa avec effusion en le traitant de confrère. "Ah! permettez," lui répondit l'autre en se dégageant, "il y a une grande différence entre nous: vous êtes avant tout chrétien, et je suis avant tout historien."—Cherbuliez, *Revue des Deux Mondes,* 1872, i. 537.

[68] Nackte Wahrheit ohne allen Schmuck; gründliche Erforschung des Einzelnen; das Uebrige, Gott befohlen.—*Werke,* xxxiv. 24. Ce ne sont pas les théories qui doivent nous servir de base dans la recherche des faits, mais ce sont les faits qui doivent nous servir de base pour la composition des théories.—Vincent, *Nouvelle Revue de Théologie,* 1859, ii. 252.

in which he displayed this art, though his successors in the next generation matched his skill and did still more thorough work, are the best introduction from which we can learn the technical process by which within living memory the study of modern history has been renewed. Ranke's contemporaries, weary of his neutrality and suspense, and of the useful but subordinate work that was done by beginners who borrowed his wand, thought that too much was made of these obscure preliminaries which a man may accomplish for himself, in the silence of his chamber, with less demand on the attention of the public.[69] That may be reasonable in men who are practised in these fundamental technicalities. We who have to learn them, must immerse ourselves in the study of the great examples.

Apart from what is technical, method is only the reduplication of common sense, and is best acquired by observing its use by the ablest men in every variety of intellectual employment.[70]

---

[69] Die zwanglose Anordnungs—die leichte und leise Andeutungskunst des grossen Historikers voll zu würdigen, hinderte ihn in früherer Zeit sein Bedürfniss nach scharfer begrifflicher Ordnung und Ausführung, später, und in immer zunehmenden Grade, sein Sinn für strenge Sachlichkeit, und genaue Erforschung der ursächlichen Zusammenhänge, noch mehr aber regte sich seine geradherzige Offenheit seine männliche Ehrlichkeit, wenn er hinter den fein verstrichenen Farben der Rankeschen Erzählungsbilder die gedeckte Haltung des klugen Diplomaten zu entdecken glaubte.— Haym, *Duncker's Leben*, 437. The ground of criticism is indeed, in my opinion, nothing else but distinct attention, which every reader should endeavour to be master of.—Hare, December 1736; *Warburton's Works*, xiv. 98. Wenn die Quellenkritik so verstanden wird, als sei sie der Nachweis, wie ein Autor den andern benutzt hat, so ist das nur ein gelegentliches Mittel—eins unter anderen—ihre Aufgabe, den Nachweis der Richtigkeit zu lösen oder vorzubereiten.—Droysen, *Historik*, 18.

[70] L'esprit scientifique n'est autre en soi que l'instinct du travail et de la patience, le sentiment de l'ordre, de la réalité et de la mesure.—Papillon, *R. des Deux Mondes*, 1873, v. 704. Non seulement les sciences, mais toutes les institutions humaines s'organisent de même, et sous l'empire des mêmes idées régulatrices.—Cournot, *Idées Fondamentales*, i. 4. There is no branch of human work whose constant laws have not close analogy with those which govern every other mode of man's exertion. But more than this, exactly as we reduce to greater simplicity and surety any one group of these practical laws, we shall find them passing the mere condition of connection or analogy, and becoming the actual expression of some ultimate nerve or fibre of the mighty laws which govern the moral

Bentham acknowledged that he learned less from his own profession than from writers like Linnaeus and Cullen; and Brougham advised the student of Law to begin with Dante. Liebig described his *Organic Chemistry* as an application of ideas found in Mill's *Logic,* and a distinguished physician, not to be named lest he should overhear me, read three books to enlarge his medical mind; and they were Gibbon, Grote, and Mill. He goes on to say, "An educated man cannot become so on one study alone, but must be brought under the influence of natural, civil, and moral modes of thought." [71] I quote my col-

---

world.—Ruskin, *Seven Lamps,* 4. The sum total of all intellectual excellence is good sense and method. When these have passed into the instinctive readiness of habit, when the wheel revolves so rapidly that we cannot see it revolve at all, then we call the combination genius. But in all modes alike, and in all professions, the two sole component parts, even of genius, are good sense and method.—Coleridge, June 1814, *Mem. of Coleorton,* ii. 172. Si l'exercice d'un art nous empêche d'en apprendre un autre, il n'en est pas ainsi dans les sciences: la connoissance d'une vérité nous aide à en découvrir une autre.—Toutes les sciences sont tellement liées ensemble qu'il est bien plus facile de les apprendre toutes à la fois que d'en apprendre une seule en la détachant des autres.—Il ne doit songer qu'à augmenter les lumières naturelles de sa raison, non pour résoudre telle ou telle difficulté de l'école, mais pour que dans chaque circonstance de la vie son intelligence montre d'avance à sa volonté le parti qu'elle doit prendre.—Descartes, *Œuvres Choisies,* 300, 301. *Règles pour la Direction de l'Esprit.* La connaissance de la méthode qui a guidé l'homme de génie n'est pas moins utile au progrès de la science et même à sa propre gloire, que ses découvertes.—Laplace, *Système du Monde,* ii. 371. On ne fait rien sans idées préconçues, il faut avoir seulement la sagesse de ne croire à leurs déductions qu'autant que l'expérience les confirme. Les idées préconçues, soumises au contrôle sévère de l'expérimentation, sont la flamme vivante des sciences d'observation; les idées fixes en sont le danger. —Pasteur, in *Histoire d'un Savant,* 284. Douter des vérités humaines, c'est ouvrir la porte aux découvertes; en faire des articles de foi, c'est la fermer.—Dumas, *Discours,* i. 123.

[71] We should not only become familiar with the laws of phenomena within our own pursuit, but also with the modes of thought of men engaged in other discussions and researches, and even with the laws of knowledge itself, that highest philosophy.—Above all things, know that we call you not here to run your minds into our moulds. We call you here on an excursion, on an adventure, on a voyage of discovery into space as yet uncharted.—Allbutt, *Introductory Address at St. George's,* October 1889. Consistency in regard to opinions is the slow poison of intellectual life.— Davy, *Memoirs,* 68.

league's golden words in order to reciprocate them. If men of science owe anything to us, we may learn much from them that is essential.[72] For they can show how to test proof, how to secure fulness and soundness in induction, how to restrain and to employ with safety hypothesis and analogy. It is they who hold the secret of the mysterious property of the mind by which error ministers to truth, and truth slowly but irrevocably prevails.[73] Theirs is the logic of discovery,[74] the demonstration of

---

[72] Ce sont vous autres physiologistes des corps vivants, qui avez appris à nous autres physiologistes de la société (qui est aussi un corps vivant) la manière de l'observer et de tirer des conséquences de nos observations.— J. B. Say to De Candolle, 1st June 1827; De Candolle, *Mémoires*, 567.

[73] Success is certain to the pure and true: success to falsehood and corruption, tyranny and aggression, is only the prelude to a greater and an irremediable fall.—Stubbs, *Seventeen Lectures*, 20. The Carlylean faith, that the cause we fight for, so far as it is true, is sure of victory, is the necessary basis of all effective activity for good.—Caird, *Evolution of Religion*, ii. 43. It is the property of truth to be fearless, and to prove victorious over every adversary. Sound reasoning and truth, when adequately communicated, must always be victorious over error.—Godwin, *Political Justice* (Conclusion). Vice was obliged to retire and give place to virtue. This will always be the consequence when truth has fair play. Falsehood only dreads the attack, and cries out for auxiliaries. Truth never fears the encounter; she scorns the aid of the secular arm, and triumphs by her natural strength.—Franklin, *Works*, ii. 292. It is a condition of our race that we must ever wade through error in our advance towards truth: and it may even be said that in many cases we exhaust almost every variety of error before we attain the desired goal.—Babbage, *Bridgewater Treatise*, 27. Les hommes ne peuvent, en quelque genre que ce soit, arriver à quelque chose de raisonnable qu'après avoir, en ce même genre, épuisé toutes les sottises imaginables. Que de sottises ne dirions-nous pas maintenant, si les anciens ne les avaient pas déjà dites avant nous, et ne nous les avaient, pour ainsi dire, enlevées!—Fontenelle. Without premature generalisations the true generalisation would never be arrived at.—H. Spencer, *Essays*, ii. 57. The more important the subject of difference,—the greater, not the less, will be the indulgence of him who has learned to trace the sources of human error,—of error, that has its origin not in our weakness and imperfection merely, but often in the most virtuous affections of the heart.—Brown, *Philosophy of the Human Mind*, i. 48, 1824. Parmi les châtiments du crime qui ne lui manquent jamais, à côté de celui que lui inflige la conscience, l'histoire lui en inflige un autre encore, éclatant et manifeste, l'impuissance.—Cousin, *Phil. Mod.* ii. 24. L'avenir de la science est garanti; car dans le grand livre scientifique tout s'ajoute et rien ne se perd. L'erreur ne fonde pas; aucune erreur ne dure très longtemps.—Renan, *Feuilles Détachées*, xiii. Toutes les fois que deux

hommes sont d'un avis contraire sur la même chose, à coup sûr, l'un ou l'autre se trompe; bien plus, aucun ne semble posséder la vérité; car si les raisons de l'un étoient certaines et évidentes, it pourroit les exposer à l'autre de telle manière qu'il finiroit par le convaincre également.—Descartes, *Règles; Œuvres Choisies*, 302. Le premier principe de la critique est qu'une doctrine ne captive ses adhérents que par ce qu'elle a de légitime.—Renan, *Essais de Morale*, 184. Was dem Wahn solche Macht giebt ist wirklich nicht er selbst, sondern die ihm zu Grunde liegende und darin nur verzerrte Wahrheit.—Frantz, *Schelling's Philosophie*, i. 62. Quand les hommes ont vu une fois la vérité dans son éclat, ils ne peuvent plus l'oublier. Elle reste debout, et tôt ou tard elle triomphe, parce qu'elle est la pensée de Dieu et le besoin du monde.—Mignet, *Portraits*, ii. 295. C'est toujours le sens commun inapperçu qui fait la fortune des hypothèses auxquelles il se mêle.—Cousin, *Fragments Phil.* i, 51, Preface of 1826. Wer da sieht, wie der Irrthum selbst ein Träger mannigfaltigen und bleibenden Fortschritts wird, der wird auch nicht so leicht aus dem thatsächlichen Fortschritt der Gegenwart auf Unumstösslichkeit unserer Hypothesen schliessen.—Das richtigste Resultat der geschichtlichen Betrachtung ist die akademische Ruhe, mit welcher unsere Hypothesen und Theorieen ohne Feindschaft und ohne Glauben als das betrachtet werden, was sie sind; als Stufen in jener unendlichen Annäherung an die Wahrheit, welche die Bestimmung unserer intellectuellen Entwickelung zu sein scheint.—Lange, *Geschichte des Materialismus*, 502, 503. Hominum errores divina providentia reguntur, ita ut saepe male jacta bene cadant.—Leibniz, ed. Klopp, i. p. lii. Sainte-Beuve n'était même pas de la race des libéraux, c'est-à-dire de ceux qui croient que, tout compte fait, et dans un état de civilisation donné, le bien triomphe du mal à armes égales, et la vérité de l'erreur.—D'Haussonville, *Revue des Deux Mondes*, 1875, i. 567. In the progress of the human mind, a period of controversy amongst the cultivators of any branch of science must necessarily precede the period of unanimity.—Torrens, *Essay on the Production of Wealth*, 1821, p. xiii. Even the spread of an error is part of the wide-world process by which we stumble into mere approximations to truth.—L. Stephen, *Apology of an Agnostic*, 81. Errors, to be dangerous, must have a great deal of truth mingled with them; it is only from this alliance that they can ever obtain an extensive circulation.—S. Smith, *Moral Philosophy*, 7. The admission of the few errors of Newton himself is at least of as much importance to his followers in science as the history of the progress of his real discoveries.—Young, *Works*, iii. 621. Error is almost always partial truth, and so consists in the exaggeration or distortion of one verity by the suppression of another, which qualifies and modifies the former.—Mivart, *Genesis of Species*, 3. The attainment of scientific truth has been effected, to a great extent, by the help of scientific errors.—Huxley: Ward, *Reign of Victoria*, ii. 337. Jede neue tief eingreifende Wahrheit hat meiner Ansicht nach erst das Stadium der Einseitigkeit durchzumachen.—Ihering, *Geist des R. Rechts*, ii. 22. The more readily we admit the possibility of our own cherished convictions being mixed with error, the more vital and helpful whatever is right in them will become.—Ruskin, *Ethics of the Dust*, 225. They

the advance of knowledge and the development of ideas, which as the earthly wants and passions of men remain almost unchanged, are the charter of progress and the vital spark in history. And they often give us invaluable counsel when they attend to their own subjects and address their own people. Remember Darwin taking note only of those passages that raised difficulties in his way; the French philosopher complaining that his work stood still, because he found no more contradicting facts; Baer, who thinks error treated thoroughly nearly as remunerative as truth, by the discovery of new objections; for, as Sir Robert Ball warns us, it is by considering objections that we often learn.[75] Faraday declares that "in knowledge, that

hardly grasp the plain truth unless they examine the error which it cancels. —Cory, *Modern English History*, 1880, i. 109. Nur durch Irrthum kommen wir, der eine kürzeren und glücklicheren Schrittes, als der andere, zur Wahrheit; und die Geschichte darf nirgends diese Verirrungen übergehen, wenn sie Lehrerin und Warnerin für die nachfolgenden Geschlechter werden will.—*München Gel. Anzeigen*, 1840. i. 737.

[74] Wie die Weltgeschichte das Weltgericht ist, so kann in noch allgemeinerem Sinne gesagt werden, dass das gerechte Gericht, d.h. die wahre Kritik einer Sache, nur in ihrer Geschichte liegen kann. Insbesondere in der Hinsicht lehrt die Geschichte denjenigen, der ihr folgt, ihre eigene Methode, dass ihr Fortschritt niemals ein reines Vernichten, sondern nur ein Aufheben im philosophischen Sinne ist.—Strauss, *Hallische Jahrbücher*, 1839, 120.

[75] Dans tous les livres qu'il lit, et il en dévore des quantités, Darwin ne note que les passages qui contrarient ses idées systématiques.—Il collectionne les difficultés, les cas épineux, les critiques possibles.—Vernier, *Le Temps*, 6th Décembre 1887. Je demandais à un savant célèbre où il en était de ses recherches. "Cela ne marche plus," me dit-il, "je ne trouve plus de faits contradictoires." Ainsi le savant cherche à se contredire lui-même pour faire avancer sa pensée.—Janet, *Journal des Savants*, 1892, 20. Ein Umstand, der uns die Selbständigkeit des Ganges der Wissenschaft anschaulich machen kann, ist auch der: dass der Irrthum, wenn er nur gründlich behandelt wird, fast ebenso fördernd ist als das Finden der Wahrheit, denn er erzeugt fortgesetzten Widerspruch.—Baer, *Blicke auf die Entwicklung der Wissenschaft*, 120. It is only by virtue of the opposition which it has surmounted that any truth can stand in the human mind.—Archbishop Temple; Kinglake, *Crimea, Winter Troubles*, app. 104. I have for many years found it expedient to lay down a rule for my own practice, to confine my reading mainly to those journals the general line of opinons in which is adverse to my own.—Hare, *Means of Unity*, i. 19. Kant had a harder struggle with himself than he could possibly have had with any critic or opponent of his philosophy.—Caird, *Philosophy of Kant*, 1889, i. p. ix.

man only is to be condemned and despised who is not in a state of transition." And John Hunter spoke for all of us when he said: "Never ask me what I have said or what I have written; but if you will ask me what my present opinions are, I will tell you."

From the first years of the century we have been quickened and enriched by contributors from every quarter. The jurists brought us that law of continuous growth which has transformed history from a chronicle of casual occurrences into the likeness of something organic.[76] Towards 1820 divines began to recast their doctrines on the lines of development, of which Newman said, long after, that evolution had come to confirm it.[77] Even the Economists who were practical men, dissolved

---

[76] The social body is no more liable to arbitrary changes than the individual body.—A full perception of the truth that society is not a mere aggregate, but an organic growth, that it forms a whole, the laws of whose growth can be studied apart from those of the individual atom, supplies the most characteristic postulate of modern speculation.—L. Stephen, *Science of Ethics*, 31. Wie in dem Leben des einzelnen Menschen kein Augenblick eines vollkommenen Stillstandes wahrgenommen wird, sondern stete organische Entwicklung, so verhält es sich auch in dem Leben der Völker, und in jedem einzelnen Element, woraus dieses Gesammtleben besteht. So finden wir in der Sprache stete Fortbildung und Entwicklung, und auf gleiche Weise in dem Recht. Und auch diese Fortbildung steht unter demselben Gesetz der Erzeugung aus innerer Kraft und Nothwendigkeit, unabhängig von Zufall und individueller Willkür, wie die ursprüngliche Entstehung.—Savigny, *System*, i. 16, 17. Seine eigene Entdeckung, dass auch die geistige Produktion, bis in einem gewissen Punkte wenigstens, unter dem Gesetze der Kausalität steht, dass jedeiner nur geben kann, was er hat, nur hat, was er irgendwoher bekommen, muss auch für ihn selber gelten.—Bekker, *Das Recht des Besitzes bei den Römern*, 3, 1880. Die geschichtliche Wandlung des Rechts, in welcher vergangene Jahrhunderte halb ein Spiel des Zufalls und halb ein Werk vernünftelnder Willkür sahen, als gesetzmässige Entwickelung zu begreifen, war das unsterbliche Verdienst der von Männern wie Savigny, Eichhorn und Jacob Grimm geführten historischen Rechtsschule.—Gierke, *Rundschau*, xviii. 205.

[77] The only effective way of studying what is called the philosophy of religion, or the philosophical criticism of religion, is to study the history of religion. The true science of war is the history of war, the true science of religion is, I believe, the history of religion.—M. Müller, *Theosophy*, 3, 4. La théologie ne doit plus être que l'histoire des efforts spontanés tentés pour résoudre le problème divin. L'histoire, en effet, est la forme nécessaire de la science de tout ce qui est soumis aux lois de la vie changeante et successive. La science de l'esprit humain, c'est de même, l'histoire de l'esprit humain.—Renan, *Averroës*, Pref. vi.

their science into liquid history, affirming that it is not an auxiliary, but the actual subject-matter of their inquiry.[78] Philos-

[78] Political economy is not a science, in any strict sense, but a body of systematic knowledge gathered from the study of common processes, which have been practised all down the history of the human race in the production and distribution of wealth.—Bonamy Price, *Social Science Congress*, 1878. Such a study is in harmony with the best intellectual tendencies of our age, which is, more than anything else, characterised by the universal supremacy of the historical spirit. To such a degree has this spirit permeated all our modes of thinking, that with respect to every branch of knowledge, no less than with respect to every institution and every form of human activity, we almost instinctively ask, not merely what is its existing condition, but what were its earliest discoverable germs, and what has been the course of its development.—Ingram, *History of Political Economy*, 2. Wir dagegen stehen keinen Augenblick an, die Nationalökonomie für eine reine Erfahrungswissenschaft zu erklären, und die Geschichte ist uns daher nicht Hülfsmittel, sondern Gegenstand selber.— Roscher, *Deutsche Vierteljahrschrift*, 1849, i. 182. Der bei weitem grösste Theil menschlicher Irrthümer beruhet darauf, dass man zeitlich und örtlich Wahres oder Heilsames für absolut wahr oder heilsam ausgiebt. Für jede Stufe der Volksentwickelung passt eine besondere Staatsverfassung, die mit allen übrigen Verhältnissen des Volks als Ursache und Wirkung auf's Innigste verbunden ist; so passt auch für jede Entwickelungsstufe eine besondere Landwirthschaftsverfassung.—Roscher, *Archiv f. p. Oek.* viii. 2 Heft 1845. Seitdem vor allen Roscher, Hildebrand und Knies den Werth, die Berechtigung und die Nothwendigkeit derselben unwiderleglich dargethan, hat sich immer allgemeiner der Gedanke Bahn gebrochen, dass diese Wissenschaft, die bis dahin nur auf die Gegenwart, auf die Erkenntniss der bestehenden Verhältnisse und die in ihnen sichtbaren Gesetze den Blick gerichtet hatte, auch in die Vergangenheit, in die Erforschung der bereits hinter uns liegenden wirthschaftlichen Entwicklung der Völker sich vertiefen müsse.—Schonberg, *Jahrbücher f. Nationalökonomie und Statistik,* Neue Folge, 1867, i. 1. Schmoller, moins dogmatique et mettant comme une sorte de coquetterie à être incertain, démontre, par les faits, la fausseté ou l'arbitraire de tous ces postulats, et laisse l'économie politique se dissoudre dans l'histoire.—Breton, *R. de Paris*, ix. 67. Wer die politische Oekonomie Feuerlands unter dieselben Gesetze bringen wollte mit der des heutigen Englands, würde damit augenscheinlich nichts zu Tage fördern als den allerbanalsten Gemeinplatz. Die politische Oekonomie ist somit wesentlich eine historische Wissenschaft. Sie behandelt einen geschichtlichen, das heisst einen stets wechselnden Stoff. Sie untersucht zunächst die besondern Gesetze jeder einzelnen Entwicklungsstufe der Produktion und des Austausches, und wird erst am Schluss dieser Untersuchung die wenigen, für Produktion und Austausch überhaupt geltenden, ganz allgemeinen Gesetze aufstellen können.—Engels, *Dührings Umwälzung der Wissenschaft*, 1878, 121.

ophers claim that, as early as 1804, they began to bow the metaphysical neck beneath the historical yoke. They taught that philosophy is only the amended sum of all philosophies, that systems pass with the age whose impress they bear,[79] that the problem is to focus the rays of wandering but extant truth, and that history is the source of philosophy, if not quite a substitute for it.[80] Comte begins a volume with the words that the prepon-

---

[79] History preserves the student from being led astray by a too servile adherence to any system.—Wolowski. No system can be anything more than a history, not in the order of impression, but in the order of arrangement by analogy.—Davy, *Memoirs,* 68. Avec des matériaux si nombreux et si importants, il fallait bien du courage pour résister à la tentation de faire un système. De Saussure eut ce courage, et nous en ferons le dernier trait et le trait principal de son éloge.—Cuvier, *Éloge de Saussure,* 1810.

[80] C'était, en 1804, une idée heureuse et nouvelle, d'appeler l'histoire au secours de la science, d'interroger les deux grandes écoles rivales au profit de la vérité.—Cousin, *Fragments Littéraires,* 1843, 95, on Dégerando. No branch of philosophical doctrine, indeed, can be fairly investigated or apprehended apart from its history. All our systems of politics, morals, and metaphysics would be different if we knew exactly how they grew up, and what transformations they have undergone; if we knew, in short, the true history of human ideas.—Cliffe Leslie, *Essays in Political and Moral Philosophy,* 1879, 149. The history of philosophy must be rational and philosophic. It must be philosophy itself, with all its elements, in all their relations, and under all their laws represented in striking characters by the hands of time and of history, in the manifested progress of the human mind.—Sir William Hamilton, *Edin. Rev.* l. 200, 1829. Il n'est point d'étude plus instructive, plus utile que l'étude de l'histoire de la philosophie; car on y apprend à se désabuser des philosophes, et l'on y désapprend la fausse science de leurs systèmes.—Royer Collard, *Œuvres de Reid,* iv. 426. On ne peut guère échapper à la conviction que toutes les solutions des questions philosophiques n'aient été développées ou indiquées avant le commencement du dix-neuvième siècle, et que par conséquent il ne soit très difficile, pour ne pas dire impossible, de tomber, en pareille matière, sur une idée neuve de quelque importance. Or si cette conviction est fondée, il s'ensuit que la science est faite.—Jouffroy, in Damiron, *Philosophie du XIXᵉ Siècle,* 363. Le but dernier de tous mes efforts, l'âme de mes écrits et de tout mon enseignement, c'est l'identité de la philosophie et de son histoire.—Cousin, *Cours de 1829.* Ma route est historique, il est vrai, mais mon but est dogmatique; je tends à une théorie, et cette théorie je la demande à l'histoire.—Cousin, *Ph. du XVIIIᵉ Siècle,* 15. L'histoire de la philosophie est contrainte d'emprunter d'abord à la philosophie la lumière qu'elle doit lui rendre un jour avec usure.—Cousin, *Du Vrai,* 1855, 14. M. Cousin, durant tout son professorat de 1816 à 1829, a pensé que l'histoire

de la philosophie était la source de la philosophie même. Nous ne croyons pas exagérer en lui prêtant cette opinion.—B. St. Hilaire, *Victor Cousin*, i. 302. Il se hâta de convertir le fait en loi, et proclama que la philosophie, étant identique à son histoire, ne pouvait avoir une loi différente, et était vouée à jamais à l'évolution fatale des quatre systèmes, se contredisant toujours, mais se limitant, et se modérant, par cela même de manière à maintenir l'équilibre, sinon l'harmonie de la pensée humaine.—Vacherot, *Revue des Deux Mondes*, 1868, iii. 957. Er hat überhaupt das unvergängliche Verdienst, zuerst in Frankreich zu der Erkenntniss gelangt zu sein, dass die menschliche Vernunft nur durch das Studium des Gesetzes ihrer Entwickelungen begriffen werden kann.—Lauser, *Unsere Zeit*, 1868, i. 459. Le philosophe en quête du vrai en soi, n'est plus réduit à ses conceptions individuelles; il est riche du trésor amassé par l'humanité.—Boutroux, *Revue Politique*, xxxvii. 802. L'histoire, je veux dire l'histoire de l'esprit humain, est en ce sens la vraie philosophie de notre temps.—Renan, *Études de Morale*, 83. Die Philosophie wurde eine höchst bedeutende Hülfswissenschaft der Geschichte, sie hat ihre Richtung auf das Allgemeine gefördert, ihren Blick für dasselbe geschärft, und sie, wenigstens durch ihre Vermittlung, mit Gesichtspuncten, Ideen, bereichert, die sie aus ihrem eigenen Schoosse sobald noch nicht erzeugt haben würde. Weit die fruchtbarste darunter war die aus der Naturwissenschaft geschöpfte Idee des organischen Lebens, dieselbe auf der die neueste Philosophie selbst beruht. Die seit zwei bis drei Jahrzehnten in der Behandlung der Geschichte eingetretene durchgreifende Veränderung, wie die völlige Umgestaltung so mancher anderen Wissenschaft . . . ist der Hauptsache nach ihr Werk.—Haug, *Allgemeine Geschichte*, 1841, i. 22. eine Geschichte der Philosophie in eigentlichen Sinne wurde erst möglich, als man an die Stelle der Philosophen deren Systeme setzte, den inneren Zusammenhang zwischen diesen feststellte und—wie Dilthey sagt—mitten in Wechsel der Philosophien ein siegreiches Fortschreiten zur Wahrheit nachwies. Die Gesammtheit der Philosophie stellt sich also dar als eine geschichtliche Einheit.—Saul, *Rundschau*, February 1894, 307. Warum die Philosophie eine Geschichte habe und haben müsse, blieb unerörtert, ja ungeahnt, dass die Philosophie am meisten von allen Wissenschaften historisch sei, denn man hatte in der Geschichte den Begriff der Entwicklung nicht entdeckt.—Marbach, *Griechische Philosophie*, 15. Was bei oberflächlicher Betrachtung nur ein Gewirre einzelner Personen und Meinungen zu sein schien, zeigt sich bei genauerer und gründlicherer Untersuchung als eine geschichtliche Entwicklung, in der alles, bald näher, bald entfernter, mit allem anderen zusammenhängt.—Zeller, *Rundschau*, February 1894, 307. Nur die Philosophie, die an die geschichtliche Entwickelung anknüpft kann auf bleibenden Erfolg auch für die Zukunft rechnen und fortschreiten zu dem, was in der bisherigen philosophischen Entwickelung nur erst unvollkommen erreicht oder angestrebt worden ist. Kann sich doch die Philosophie überhaupt und insbesondere die Metaphysik ihrer eigenen geschichtlichen Entwickelung nicht entschlagen, sondern hat eine Geschichte der Philosophie als eigene und zwar zugleich historische und spekulative Disziplin, in deren geschichtlichen Entwickelungsphasen und

derance of history over philosophy was the characteristic of the
time he lived in.[81] Since Cuvier first recognised the conjunction
between the course of inductive discovery and the course of
civilisation,[82] science had its share in saturating the age with

geschichtlich aufeinanderfolgenden Systemen der Philosophen die neuere
Spekulation seit Schelling und Hegel zugleich die Philosophie selbst als ein
die verschiedenen geschichtlichen Systeme umfassendes ganzes in seiner
dialektischen Gliederung erkannt hat.—Gloatz, *Spekulative Theologie,* i.
23. Die heutige Philosophie führt uns auf einen Standpunkt von dem aus
die philosophische Idee als das innere Wesen der Geschichte selbst erscheint. So trat an die Stelle einer abstrakt philosophischen Richtung,
welche das Geschichtliche verneinte, eine abstrakt geschichtliche Richtung, welche das Philosophische verläugnete. Beide Richtungen sind als
überschrittene und besiegte zu betrachten.—Berner, *Strafrecht,* 75. Die
Geschichte der Philosophie hat uns fast schon die Wissenschaft der
Philosophie selbst ersetzt.—Hermann, *Phil. Monatshefte,* ii. 198, 1889.

[81] La siècle actuel sera principalement caractérisé par l'irrévocable pré-
pondérance de l'histoire, en philosophie, en politique, et même en
poésie.—Comte, *Politique Positive,* iii. 1.

[82] The historical or comparative method has revolutionised not only the
sciences of law, mythology, and language, of anthropology and sociology,
but it has forced its way even into the domain of philosophy and natural
science. For what is the theory of evolution itself, with all its far-reaching
consequences, but the achievement of the historical method?—Prothero,
Inaugural; National Review, December 1894, 461. To facilitate the advancement of all the branches of useful science, two things seem to be
principally requisite. The first is, an historical account of their rise,
progress, and present state. Without the former of these helps, a person
every way qualified for extending the bounds of science labours under
great disadvantages; wanting the lights which have been struck out by
others, and perpetually running the risk of losing his labour, and finding
himself anticipated.—Priestley, *History of Vision,* 1772, i., Pref. i. Cuvier
se proposait de montrer l'enchaînement scientifique des découvertes, leurs
relations avec les grands évènements historiques, et leur influence sur les
progrès et le développement de la civilisation.—Dareste, *Biographie Générale,* xii. 685. Dans ses éloquentes leçons, l'histoire des sciences est
devenue l'histoire même de l'esprit humain; car, remontant aux causes de
leurs progrès et de leurs erreurs, c'est toujours dans les bonnes ou mauvaises routes suivies par l'esprit humain, qu'il trouve ces causes.—
Flourens, *Éloge de Cuvier,* xxxi. Wie keine fortlaufende Entwickelungs-
reihe von nur einem Punkte aus vollkommen aufzufassen ist, so wird auch
keine lebendige Wissenschaft nur aus der Gegenwart begriffen werden
können.—Deswegen ist aber eine solche Darstellung doch noch nicht der
gesammten Wissenschaft adäquat, und sie birgt, wenn sie damit ver-
wechselt wird, starke Gefahren der Einseitigkeit, des Dogmatismus und
damit der Stagnation in sich. Diesen Gefahren kann wirksam nur begegnet

historic ways of thought, and subjecting all things to that influence for which the depressing names historicism and histori-
cal-mindedness have been divised.

There are certain faults which are corrigible mental defects
on which I ought to say a few denouncing words, because they
are common to us all. First: the want of an energetic understanding of the sequence and real significance of events, which
would be fatal to a practical politician, is ruin to a student of
history, who is the politician with his face turned backwards.[83]
It is playing at study, to see nothing but the unmeaning and
unsuggestive surface, as we generally do. Then we have a
curious proclivity to neglect, and by degrees to forget, what has
been certainly known. An instance or two will explain my idea.
The most popular English writer relates how it happened in his
presence that the title of Tory was conferred upon the Conservative party. For it was an opprobrious name at the time, applied
to men for whom the Irish Government offered head-money; so
that if I have made too sure of progress, I may at least compla-
cently point to this instance of our mended manners. One day,
Titus Oates lost his temper with the men who refused to believe
him, and, after looking about for a scorching imprecation, he
began to call them Tories.[84] The name remained; but its origin,

---

werden durch die verständige Betrachtung der Geschichte der Wissenschaften, welche diese selbst in stetem Flusse zeigt und die Tendenz ihres
Fortschreitens in offenbarer und sicherer Weise klarlegt.—Rosenberger,
Geschichte der Physik, iii. p. vi. Die Continuität in der Ausbildung aller
Auffassungen tritt um so deutlicher hervor, je vollständiger man sich damit
wie sie zu verschiedenen Zeiten waren, vertraut macht.—Klopp, *Entwickelung der Chemie*, 814.

[83] Die Geschichte und die Politik sind Ein und derselbe Janus mit dem
Doppelgesicht, das in der Geschichte in die Vergangenheit, in der Politik
in die Zukunft hinschaut.—Gügler's *Leben*, ii. 59.

[84] The papers inclosed, which give an account of the killing of two men
in the county of Londonderry; if they prove to be Tories, 'tis very well
they are gone.—I think it will not only be necessary to grant those a
pardon who killed them, but also that they have some reward for their
own and others' encouragement.—Essex, *Letters*, 10, 10th January 1675.
The author of this happened to be present. There was a meeting of some
honest people in the city, upon the occasion of the discovery of some
attempt to stifle the evidence of the witnesses.—Bedloe said he had letters

attested by Defoe, dropped out of common memory, as if one party were ashamed of their godfather, and the other did not care to be identified with his cause and character. You all know, I am sure, the story of the news of Trafalgar, and how, two days after it had arrived, Mr. Pitt, drawn by an enthusiastic crowd, went to dine in the city. When they drank the health of the minister who had saved his country, he declined the praise. "England," he said, "has saved herself by her own energy; and I hope that after having saved herself by her energy, she will save Europe by her example." In 1814, when this hope had been realised, the last speech of the great orator was remembered, and a medal was struck upon which the whole sentence was engraved, in four words of compressed Latin: *Seipsam virtute, Europam exemplo.* Now it was just at the time of his last appearance in public that Mr. Pitt heard of the overwhelming success of the French in Germany, and of the Austrian surrender at Ulm. His friends concluded that the contest on land was hopeless, and that it was time to abandon the Continent to the conqueror, and to fall back upon our new empire of the sea. Pitt did not agree with them. He said that Napoleon would meet with a check whenever he encountered a national resistance; and he declared that Spain was the place for it, and that then England would intervene.[85] General Wellesley, fresh from India, was present. Ten years later, when he had accomplished that which Pitt had seen in the lucid prescience of his last days, he

---

from Ireland, that there were some Tories to be brought over hither, who were privately to murder Dr. Oates and the said Bedloe. The doctor, whose zeal was very hot, could never after this hear any man talk against the plot, or against the witnesses, but he thought he was one of these Tories, and called almost every man a Tory that opposed him in discourse; till at last the word Tory became popular.—Defoe, *Edinburgh Review*, l. 403.

[85] La España serà el primer pueblo en donde se encenderà esta guerra patriotica que solo puede libertar á Europa.—Hemos oido esto en Inglaterra à varios de los que estaban alli presentes. Muchas veces ha oido lo mismo al duque de Wellington el general Don Miguel de Alava, y dicho duque refirió el suceso en una comida diplomatica que dió en Paris el duque de Richelieu en 1816.—Toreno, *Historia del Levantamiento de España*, 1838, i. 508.

related at Paris what I scarcely hesitate to call the most astounding and profound prediction in all political history, where such things have not been rare.

I shall never again enjoy the opportunity of speaking my thoughts to such an audience as this, and on so privileged an occasion a lecturer may well be tempted to bethink himself whether he knows of any neglected truth, any cardinal proposition, that might serve as his selected epigraph, as a last signal, perhaps even as a target. I am not thinking of those shining precepts which are the registered property of every school; that is to say—Learn as much by writing as by reading; be not content with the best book; seek sidelights from the others; have no favourites; keep men and things apart; guard against the prestige of great names; [86] see that your judgments are your own, and do not shrink from disagreement; no trusting without testing; be more severe to ideas than to actions; [87] do not overlook the strength of the bad cause or the weakness of the good; [88] never be surprised by the crumbling of an idol or the disclosure of a skeleton; judge talent at its best and character at its worst; suspect power more than vice,[89] and study problems in prefer-

---

[86] Nunquam propter auctoritatem illorum, quamvis magni sint nominis (supponimus scilicet semper nos cum eo agere qui scientiam historicam vult consequi), sententias quas secuti sunt ipse tamquam certas admittet, sed solummodo ob vim testimoniorum et argumentorum quibus eas confirmarunt.—De Smedt, *Introductio ad historian critice tractandam*, 1866, i. 5.

[87] Hundert schwere Verbrechen wiegen nicht so schwer in der Schale der Unsittlichkeit, als ein unsittliches Princip.—*Hallische Jahrbücher*, 1839, 308. Il faut flétrir les crimes; mais il faut aussi, et surtout, flétrir les doctrines et les systèmes qui tendent à les justifier.—Mortimer Ternaux, *Histoire de la Terreur.*

[88] We see how good and evil mingle in the best of men and in the best of causes; we learn to see with patience the men whom we like best often in the wrong, and the repulsive men often in the right; we learn to bear with patience the knowledge that the cause which we love best has suffered, from the awkwardness of its defenders, so great disparagement, as in strict equity to justify the men who were assaulting it.—Stubbs, *Seventeen Lectures*, 97.

[89] *Caeteris paribus*, on trouvera tousjours que ceux qui ont plus de puissance sont sujets à pécher davantage; et il n'y a point de théorème de

ence to periods; for instance: the derivation of Luther, the scientific influence of Bacon, the predecessors of Adam Smith, the medieval masters of Rousseau, the consistency of Burke, the identity of the first Whig. Most of this, I suppose, is undisputed, and calls for no enlargement. But the weight of opinion is against me when I exhort you never to debase the moral currency or to lower the standard of rectitude, but to try others by the final maxim that governs your own lives, and to suffer no man and no cause to escape the undying penalty which history has the power to inflict on wrong.[90] The plea in extenuation of guilt and mitigation of punishment is perpetual. At every step we are met by arguments which go to excuse, to palliate, to confound right and wrong, and reduce the just man to the level of the reprobate. The men who plot to baffle and resist us are, first of all, those who made history what it has become. They set up the principle that only a foolish Conservative judges the present time with the ideas of the past; that only a foolish Liberal judges the past with the ideas of the present.[91]

géométrie qui soit plus asseuré que cette proposition.—Leibniz, 1688, ed. Rommel, ii. 197. Il y a toujours eu de la malignité dans la grandeur, et de l'opposition à l'esprit de l'Évangile; mais maintenant il y en a plus que jamais, et il semble que comme le monde va á sa fin, celui qui est dans l'élévation fait tous ses efforts pour dominer avec plus de tyrannie, et pour étouffer les maximes du Christianisme et le règne de Jésus-Christ, voiant qu'il s'approche.—Godeau, *Lettres*, 423, 27th March 1667. There is, in fact, an unconquerable tendency in all power, save that of knowledge, acting by and through knowledge, to injure the mind of him by whom that power is exercised.—Wordsworth, 22nd June 1817; *Letters of Lake Poets*, 369.

[90] I cieli han messo sulla terra due giudici delle umane azioni, la coscienza e la storia.—Colletta. Wenn gerade die edelsten Männer um des Nachruhmes willen gearbeitet haben, so soll die Geschichte ihre Belohnung sein, sie auch die Strafe für die Schlechten.—Lasaulx, *Philosophie der Künste*, 211. Pour juger ce qui est bon et juste dans la vie actuelle ou passée, il faut posséder un criterium, qui ne soit pas tiré du passé ou du présent, mais de la nature humaine.—Ahrens, *Cours de Droit Naturel*, i. 67.

[91] L'homme de notre temps! La conscience moderne! Voilà encore de ces termes qui nous ramènent la prétendue philosophie de l'histoire et la doctrine du progrès, quand il s'agit de la justice, c'est-à-dire de la conscience pure et de l'homme rationnel, que d'autres siècles encore que le nôtre ont connu.—Renouvier, *Crit. Phil.* 1873, ii. 55.

The mission of that school was to make distant times, and
especially the Middle Ages, then most distant of all, intelligible
and acceptable to a society issuing from the eighteenth century.
There were difficulties in the way; and among others this, that,
in the first fervour of the Crusades, the men who took the Cross,
after receiving communion, heartily devoted the day to the
extermination of Jews. To judge them by a fixed standard, to
call them sacrilegious fanatics or furious hypocrites, was to
yield a gratuitous victory to Voltaire. It became a rule of policy
to praise the spirit when you could not defend the deed. So that
we have no common code; our moral notions are always fluid;
and you must consider the times, the class from which men
sprang, the surrounding influences, the masters in their schools,
the preachers in their pulpits, the movement they obscurely
obeyed, and so on, until responsibility is merged in numbers,
and not a culprit is left for execution.[92] A murderer was no

---

[92] Il faut pardonner aux grands hommes le marchepied de leur grandeur.—Cousin, in J. Simon, *Nos Hommes d'État*, 1887, 55. L'esprit du
XVIIIᵉ siècle n'a pas besoin d'apologie: l'apologie d'un siècle est dans son
existence.—Cousin, *Fragments*, iii. 1826. Suspendus aux lèvres éloquentes
de M. Cousin, nous l'entendîmes s'écrier que la meilleure cause l'emportait
toujours, que c'était la loi de l'histoire, le rhythme immuable du
progrès.—Gasparin, *La Liberté Morale*, ii. 63. Cousin verurtheilen heisst
darum nichts Anderes als jenen Geist historischer Betrachtung verdammen,
durch welchen das 19. Jahrhundert die revolutionäre Kritik des 18. Jahr-
hunderts ergänzt, durch welchen insbesondere Deutschland die geistigen
Wohlthaten vergolten hat, welche es im Zeitalter der Aufklärung von
seinen westlichen Nachbarn empfangen.—Idol, *Gesch. der Ethik*, ii. 295.
Der Gang der Weltgeschichte steht ausserhalb der Tugend, des Lasters,
und der Gerechtigkeit.—Hegel, *Werke*, viii. 425. Die Vermischung des
Zufälligen im Individuum mit dem an ihm Historischen führt zu
unzähligen falschen Ansichten und Urtheilen. Hierzu gehört namentlich
alles Absprechen über die moralische Tüchtigkeit der Individuen, und die
Verwunderung, welche bis zur Verzweiflung an göttlicher Gerechtigkeit
sich steigert, dass historisch grosse Individuen moralisch nichtswürdig
erscheinen können. Die moralische Tüchtigkeit besteht in der Unterord-
nung alles dessen, was zufällig am Einzelnen unter das an ihm dem
Allgemeinen Angehörige.—Marbach, *Geschichte der Griechischen Philosophie*, 7. Das Sittliche der Neuseeländer, der Mexikaner ist vielmehr ebenso
sittlich, wie das der Griechen, der Römer; und das Sittliche der Christen
des Mittelalters ist ebenso sittlich, wie das der Gegenwart.—Kirchmann,
Grundbegriffe des Richts, 194. Die Geschichtswissenschaft als solche kennt

criminal if he followed local custom, if neighbours approved, if he was encouraged by official advisers or prompted by just authority, if he acted for the reason of state or the pure love of religion, or if he sheltered himself behind the complicity of the Law. The depression of morality was flagrant; but the motives were those which have enabled us to contemplate with distressing complacency the secret of unhallowed lives. The code that is greatly modified by time and place, will vary according to the cause. The amnesty is an artifice that enables us to make exceptions, to tamper with weights and measures, to deal unequal justice to friends and enemies.

It is associated with that philosophy which Cato attributes to the gods. For we have a theory which justifies Providence by the event, and holds nothing so deserving as success, to which there can be no victory in a bad cause; prescription and duration legitimate; [93] and whatever exists is right and reasonable; and as God manifests His will by that which He tolerates, we must conform to the divine decree by living to shape the future after the ratified image of the past. [94] Another theory, less con-

---

nur ein zeitliches und mithin auch nur ein relatives Maass der Dinge. Alle Werthbeurtheilung der Geschichte kann daher nur relativ und aus zeitlichen Momenten fliessen, und wer sich nicht selbst täuschen und den Dingen nicht Gewalt anthun will, muss ein für allemal in dieser Wissenschaft auf absolute Werthe verzichten.—Lorenz, *Schlosser*, 80. Only according to his faith is each man judged. Committed as this deed has been by a pure-minded, pious youth, it is a beautiful sign of the time.—De Wette to Sand's Mother; Cheyne, *Founders of Criticism*, 44. The men of each age must be judged by the ideal of their own age and country, and not by the ideal of ours.—Lecky, *Value of History*, 50.

[93] La durée ici-bas, c'est le droit, c'est la sanction de Dieu.—Guiraud, *Philosophie Catholique de l'Histoire*.

[94] Ceux qui ne sont pas contens de l'ordre des choses ne sçauroient se vanter d'aimer Dieu comme il faut.—Il faut toujours estre content de l'ordre du passé, parce qu'il est conforme à la volonté de Dieu absolue, qu'on connoît par l'évènement. Il faut tâcher de rendre l'avenir, autant qu'il dépend de nous, conforme à la volonté de Dieu présomptive.—Leibniz, *Werke*, ed. Gerhardt, ii. 136. Ich habe damals bekannt und bekenne jetzt, dass die politische Wahrheit aus denselben Quellen zu schöpfen ist, wie alle anderen, aus dem göttliche Willen und dessen Kundgebung in der Geschichte des Menschengeschlechts.—Radowitz, *Neue Gespräche*, 65.

fidently urged, regards History as our guide, as much by showing errors to evade as examples to pursue. It is suspicious of
illusions in success, and, though there may be hope of ultimate
triumph for what is true, if not by its own attraction, by the
gradual exhaustion of error, it admits no corresponding promise
for what is ethically right. It deems the canonisation of the
historic past more perilous than ignorance or denial, because it
would perpetuate the reign of sin and acknowledge the sovereignty of wrong, and conceives it the part of real greatness to
know how to stand and fall alone, stemming, for a lifetime, the
contemporary flood.[95]

Ranke relates, without adornment, that William III. ordered
the extirpation of a Catholic clan, and scouts the faltering
excuse of his defenders. But when he comes to the death and
character of the international deliverer, Glencoe is forgotten,
the imputation of murder drops, like a thing unworthy of notice.[96] Johannes Mueller, a great Swiss celebrity, writes that the

---

[95] A man is great as he contends best with the circumstances of his
age.—Froude, *Short Studies*, i. 388. La persuasion que l'homme est avant
tout une personne morale et libre, et qu'ayant conçu seul, dans sa
conscience et devant Dieu, la règle de sa conduite, il doit s'employer tout
entier à l'appliquer en lui, hors de lui, absolument, obstinément, inflexible-
ment, par une résistance perpétuelle opposée aux autres; et par une
contrainte perpétuelle exercée sur soi, voilà la grande idée anglaise.—
Taine; Sorel, *Discours de Réception*, 24. In jeder Zeit des Christenthums
hat es einzelne Männer gegeben, die über ihrer Zeit standen und von ihren
Gegensätzen nicht berührt wurden.—Bachmann, *Hengstenberg*, i. 160.
Eorum enim qui de iisdem rebus mecum aliquid ediderunt, aut solus
insanio ego, aut solus non insanio; tertium enim non est, nisi (quod dicet
forte aliquis) insaniamus omnes.—Hobbes, quoted by De Morgan, 3rd
June 1858: *Life of Sir W. R. Hamilton*, iii. 552.

[96] I have now to exhibit a rare combination of good qualities, and a
steady perseverance in good conduct, which raised an individual to be an
object of admiration and love to all his contemporaries, and have made
him to be regarded by succeeding generations as a model of public and
private virtue.—The evidence shows that upon this occasion he was not
only under the influence of the most vulgar credulity, but that he violated
the plainest rules of justice, and that he really was the murderer of two
innocent women.—Hale's motives were most laudable.—Campbell's *Lives
of the Chief Justices*, i. 512, 561, 566. It was not to be expected of the
colonists of New England that they should be the first to see through a
delusion which befooled the whole civilised world, and the gravest and

British Constitution occurred to somebody, perhaps to Halifax. This artless statement might not be approved by rigid lawyers as a faithful and felicitous indication of the manner of that mysterious growth of ages, from occult beginnings, that was never profaned by the invading wit of man; [97] but it is less grotesque than it appears. Lord Halifax was the most original writer of political tracts in the pamphleteering crowd between Harrington and Bolingbroke; and in the Exclusion struggle he produced a scheme of limitations which, in substance, if not in form, foreshadowed the position of the monarchy in the later Hanoverian reigns. Although Halifax did not believe in the plot,[98] he insisted that innocent victims should be sacrificed to content the multitude. Sir William Temple writes: "We only disagreed in one point, which was the leaving some priests to the law upon the accusation of being priests only, as the House of Commons had desired; which I thought wholly unjust. Upon this point Lord Halifax and I had so sharp a debate at Lord Sunderland's lodgings, that he told me, if I would not concur in points which were so necessary for the people's satisfaction, he

---

most knowing persons in it.—The people of New England believed what the wisest men of the world believed at the end of the seventeenth century.—Palfrey, *New England*, iv. 127, 129 (also speaking of witch-craft). Il est donc bien étrange que sa sévérité tardive s'exerce aujourd'hui sur un homme auquel elle n'a d'autre reproche à faire que d'avoir trop bien servi l'état par des mesures politiques, injustes peut-être, violentes, mais qui, en aucune manière, n'avaient l'intérêt personnel du coupable pour objet.—M. Hastings peut sans doute paraître répréhensible aux yeux des étrangers, des particuliers même, mais il est assez extraordinaire qu'une nation usurpatrice d'une partie de l'Indostan veuille mêler les règles de la morale à celles d'une administration forcée, injuste et violente par essence, et à laquelle il faudrait renoncer à jamais pour être conséquent.—Mallet du Pan, *Mémoires*, ed. Sayous, i. 102.

[97] On parle volontiers de la stabilité de la constitution anglaise. La vérité est que cette constitution est toujours en mouvement et en oscillation et qu'elle se prête merveilleusement au jeu de ses différentes parties. Sa solidité vient de sa souplesse; elle plie et ne rompt pas.—Boutmy, *Nouvelle Revue*, 1878, 49.

[98] This is not an age for a man to follow the strict morality of better times, yet sure mankind is not yet so debased but that there will ever be found some few men who will scorn to join concert with the public voice when it is not well grounded.—*Savile Correspondence*, 173.

would tell everybody I was a Papist. And upon his affirming that the plot must be handled as if it were true, whether it were so or no, in those points that were so generally believed." In spite of this accusing passage, Macaulay, who prefers Halifax to all the statesmen of his age, praises him for his mercy: "His dislike of extremes, and a forgiving and compassionate temper which seems to have been natural to him, preserved him from all participation in the worst crimes of his time."

If, in our uncertainty, we must often err, it may be sometimes better to risk excess in rigour than in indulgence, for then at least we do no injury by loss of principle. As Bayle has said, it is more probable that the secret motives of an indifferent action are bad than good; [99] and this discouraging conclusion does not depend upon theology, for James Mozley supports the sceptic from the other flank, with all the artillery of Tractarian Oxford. "A Christian," he says, "is bound by his very creed to suspect evil, and cannot release himself. . . . He sees it where others do not; his instinct is divinely strengthened; his eye is supernaturally keen; he has a spiritual insight, and senses exercised to discern. . . . He owns the doctrine of original sin; that doctrine puts him necessarily on his guard against appearances, sustains his apprehension under perplexity, and prepares him for recognising anywhere what he knows to be everywhere." [100] There is

---

[99] Cette proposition: L'homme est incomparablement plus porté au mal qu'au bien, et il se fait dans le monde incomparablement plus de mauvaises actions que de bonnes—est aussi certaine qu'aucun principe de métaphysique. Il est donc incomparablement plus probable qu'une action faite par un homme, est mauvaise, qu'il n'est probable qu'elle soit bonne. Il est incomparablement plus probable que ces secrets ressorts qui l'ont produite sont corrompus, qu'il n'est probable qu'ils soient honnêtes. Je vous avertis que je parle d'une action qui n'est point mauvaise extérieurement.—Bayle, Œuvres, ii. 248.

[100] A Christian is bound by his very creed to suspect evil, and cannot release himself.—His religion has brought evil to light in a way in which it never was before; it has shown its depth, subtlety, ubiquity; and a revelation, full of mercy on the one hand, is terrible in its exposure of the world's real state on the other. The Gospel fastens the sense of evil upon the mind; a Christian is enlightened, hardened, sharpened, as to evil; he sees it where others do not.—Mozley, Essays, i. 308. All satirists, of course, work in the direction of Christian doctrine, by the support they give to the

a popular saying of Madame de Staël, that we forgive whatever we really understand. The paradox has been judiciously pruned by her descendant, the Duke de Broglie, in the words: "Beware of too much explaining, lest we end by too much excusing." [101] History, says Froude, does teach that right and wrong are real distinctions. Opinions alter, manners change, creeds rise and fall, but the moral law is written on the tablets of eternity.[102] And if there are moments when we may resist the teaching of Froude, we have seldom the chance of resisting when he is supported by Mr. Goldwin Smith: "A sound historical morality will sanction strong measures in evil times; selfish ambition, treachery, murder, perjury, it will never sanction in the worst of times, for these are the things that make times evil.—Justice has been justice, mercy has been mercy, honour has been honour, good faith has been good faith, truthfulness has been truthful-

---

doctrine of original sin, making a sort of meanness and badness a law of society.—Mozley, *Letters*, 333. Les critiques, même malveillants, sont plus près de la vérité dernière que les admirateurs.—Nisard, *Lit. fr.*, Conclusion. Les hommes supérieurs doivent nécessairement passer pour méchants. Où les autres ne voient ni un défaut, ni un ridicule, ni un vice, leur implacable œil l'aperçoit.—Barbey d'Aurevilly, *Figaro*, 31st March 1888.

[101] Prenons garde de ne pas trop expliquer, pour ne pas fournir des arguments à ceux qui veulent tout excuser.—Broglie, *Réception de Sorel*, 46.

[102] The eternal truths and rights of things exist, fortunately, independent of our thoughts or wishes, fixed as mathematics, inherent in the nature of man and the world. They are no more to be trifled with than gravitation.—Froude, *Inaugural Lecture at St. Andrews*, 1869, 41. What have men to do with interests? There is a right way and a wrong way. That is all we need think about.—Carlyle to Froude, *Longman's Magazine*, December 1892, 151. As to History, it is full of indirect but very effective moral teaching. It is not only, as Bolingbroke called it, "Philosophy teaching by examples," but it is morality teaching by examples.—It is essentially the study which best helps the student to conceive large thoughts.—It is impossible to overvalue the moral teaching of History.—Fitch, *Lectures on Teaching*, 432. Judging from the past history of our race, in ninety-nine cases out of a hundred, war is a folly and a crime.—Where it is so, it is the saddest and the wildest of all follies, and the most heinous of all crimes.—Greg, *Essays on Political and Social Science*, 1853, i. 562. La volonté de tout un peuple ne peut rendre juste ce qui est injuste: les représentants d'une nation n'ont pas le droit de faire ce que la nation n'a pas le droit de faire elle-même.—B. Constant, *Principes de Politique*, i. 15.

ness from the beginning." The doctrine that, as Sir Thomas Browne says, morality is not ambulatory,[103] is expressed as follows by Burke, who, when true to himself, is the most intelligent of our instructors: "My principles enable me to form my judgment upon men and actions in history, just as they do in common life; and are not formed out of events and characters, either present or past. History is a preceptor of prudence, not of principles. The principles of true politics are those of morality enlarged; and I neither now do, nor ever will admit of any other." [104]

Whatever a man's notions of these later centuries are, such, in the main, the man himself will be. Under the name of History, they cover the articles of his philosophic, his religious, and his political creed.[105] They give his measure; they denote his character: and, as praise is the shipwreck of historians, his preferences betray him more than his aversions. Modern History touches us so nearly, it is so deep a question of life and death, that we are bound to find our own way through it, and to owe our insight to ourselves. The historians of former ages, unapproachable for us in knowledge and in talent, cannot be our limit. We have the power to be more rigidly impersonal,

---

[103] Think not that morality is ambulatory; that vices in one age are not vices in another, or that virtues, which are under the everlasting seal of right reason, may be stamped by opinion.—Sir Thomas Browne, Works, iv. 64.

[104] Osons croire qu'il seroit plus à propos de mettre de côté ces traditions, ces usages, et ces coutumes souvent si imparfaites, si contradictoires, si incohérentes, ou de ne les consulter que pour saisir les inconvéniens et les éviter; et qu'il faudroit chercher non-seulement les éléments d'une nouvelle législation, mais même ses derniers détails dans une étude approfondie de la morale.—Letrosne, Réflexions sur la Législation Criminelle, 137. M. Renan appartient à cette famille d'esprits qui ne croient pas en réalité la raison, la conscience, le droit applicables à la direction des sociétés humaines, et qui demandent à l'histoire, à la tradition, non à la morale, les régles de la politique. Ces esprits sont atteints de la maladie du siècle, le scepticisme moral.—Pillon, Critique Philosophique, i. 49.

[105] The subject of modern History is of all others, to my mind, the most interesting, inasmuch as it includes all questions of the deepest interest relating not to human things only, but to divine.—Arnold, Modern History, 311.

disinterested and just than they; and to learn from undisguised and genuine records to look with remorse upon the past, and to the future with assured hope of better things; bearing this in mind, that if we lower our standard in History, we cannot uphold it in Church or State.

XI

The Heralds of the Revolution

THE revenue of France was near twenty millions when Lewis XVI., finding it inadequate, called upon the nation for supply. In a single lifetime it rose to far more than one hundred millions, while the national income grew still more rapidly; and this increase was wrought by a class to whom the ancient monarchy denied its best rewards, and whom it deprived of power in the country they enriched. As their industry effected change in the distribution of property, and wealth ceased to be the prerogative of a few, the excluded majority perceived that their disabilities rested on no foundation of right and justice, and were unsupported by reasons of State. They proposed that the prizes in the Government, the Army, and the Church should be given to merit among the active and necessary portion of the people, and that no privilege injurious to them should be reserved for the unprofitable minority. Being nearly an hundred to one, they deemed that they were virtually the substance of the nation, and they claimed to govern themselves with a power proportioned to their numbers. They demanded that the State should be reformed, that the ruler should be their agent, not their master.

That is the French Revolution. To see that it is not a meteor from the unknown, but the product of historic influences which, by their union were efficient to destroy, and by their division powerless to construct, we must follow for a moment the

Reprinted from Acton, *Lectures on the French Revolution* (London: Macmillan, 1925).

procession of ideas that went before, and bind it to the law of continuity and the operation of constant forces.

If France failed where other nations have succeeded, and if the passage from the feudal and aristocratic forms of society to the industrial and democratic was attended by convulsions, the cause was not in the men of that day, but in the ground on which they stood. As long as the despotic kings were victorious abroad, they were accepted at home. The first signals of revolutionary thinking lurk dimly among the oppressed minorities during intervals of disaster. The Jansenists were loyal and patient; but their famous jurist Domat was a philosopher, and is remembered as the writer who restored the supremacy of reason in the chaotic jurisprudence of the time. He had learnt from St. Thomas, a great name in the school he belonged to, that legislation ought to be for the people and by the people, that the cashiering of bad kings may be not only a right but a duty. He insisted that law shall proceed from common sense, not from custom, and shall draw its precepts from an eternal code. The principle of the higher law signifies Revolution. No government founded on positive enactments only can stand before it, and it points the way to that system of primitive, universal, and indefeasible rights which the lawyers of the Assembly, descending from Domat, prefixed to their constitution.

Under the edict of Nantes the Protestants were decided royalists; so that, even after the Revocation, Bayle, the apostle of Toleration, retained his loyalty in exile at Rotterdam. His enemy, Jurieu, though intolerant as a divine, was liberal in his politics, and contracted in the neighbourhood of William of Orange the temper of a continental Whig. He taught that sovereignty comes from the people and reverts to the people. The Crown forfeits powers it has made ill use of. The rights of the nation cannot be forfeited. The people alone possess an authority which is legitimate without conditions, and their acts are valid even when they are wrong. The most telling of Jurieu's seditious propositions, preserved in the transparent amber of Bossuet's reply, shared the immortality of a classic, and in time contributed to the doctrine that the democracy is irresponsible and must have its way.

Maultrot, the best ecclesiastical lawyer of the day, published three volumes in 1790 on the power of the people over kings, in which, with accurate research among sources very familiar to him and to nobody else, he explained how the Canon Law approves the principles of 1688 and rejects the modern invention of divine right. His book explains still better the attitude of the clergy in the Revolution, and their brief season of popularity.

The true originator of the opposition in literature was Fénelon. He was neither an innovating reformer nor a discoverer of new truth; but as a singularly independent and most intelligent witness, he was the first who saw through the majestic hypocrisy of the court, and knew that France was on the road to ruin. The revolt of conscience began with him before the glory of the monarchy was clouded over. His views grew from an extraordinary perspicacity and refinement in the estimate of men. He learnt to refer the problem of government, like the conduct of private life, to the mere standard of morals, and extended further than any one the plain but hazardous practice of deciding all things by the exclusive precepts of enlightened virtue. If he did not know all about policy and international science, he could always tell what would be expected of a hypothetically perfect man. Fénelon feels like a citizen of Christian Europe, but he pursues his thoughts apart from his country or his church, and his deepest utterances are in the mouth of pagans. He desired to be alike true to his own beliefs, and gracious towards those who dispute them. He approved neither the deposing power nor the punishment of error, and declared that the highest need of the Church was not victory but liberty. Through his friends, Fleury and Chevreuse, he favoured the recall of the Protestants, and he advised a general toleration. He would have the secular power kept aloof from ecclesiastical concerns, because protection leads to religious servitude and persecution to religious hypocrisy. There were moments when his steps seemed to approach the border of the undiscovered land where Church and State are parted.

He has written that a historian ought to be neutral between other countries and his own, and he expected the same discipline in politicians, as patriotism cannot absolve a man from his duty to mankind. Therefore no war can be just, unless a war to which we are compelled in the sole cause of freedom. Fénelon wished that France should surrender the ill-gotten conquests of which she was so proud, and especially that she should withdraw from Spain. He declared that the Spaniards were degenerate and imbecile, but that nothing could make that right which was contrary to the balance of power and the security of nations. Holland seemed to him the hope of Europe, and he thought the allies justified in excluding the French dynasty from Spain for the same reason that no claim of law could have made it right that Philip II. should occupy England. He hoped that his country would be thoroughly humbled, for he dreaded the effects of success on the temperament of the victorious French. He deemed it only fair that Lewis should be compelled to dethrone his grandson with his own guilty hand.

In the judgment of Fénelon, power is poison; and as kings are nearly always bad, they ought not to govern, but only to execute the law. For it is the mark of barbarians to obey precedent and custom. Civilised society must be regulated by a solid code. Nothing but a constitution can avert arbitrary power. The despotism of Lewis XIV. renders him odious and contemptible, and is the cause of all the evils which the country suffers. If the governing power which rightfully belonged to the nation was restored, it would save itself by its own exertion; but absolute authority irreparably saps its foundations, and is bringing on a revolution by which it will not be moderated, but utterly destroyed. Although Fénelon has no wish to sacrifice either the monarchy or the aristocracy, he betrays sympathy with several tendencies of the movement which he foresaw with so much alarm. He admits the state of nature, and thinks civil society not the primitive condition of man, but a result of the passage from savage life to husbandry. He would transfer the duties of government to local and central assemblies; and he demands entire freedom of trade, and education provided by law, because children belong to the State first and to the family afterwards. He does not resign the hope of making men good by act of parliament, and his belief in public institutions as a means of moulding individual character brings him nearly into touch with a distant future.

He is the Platonic founder of revolutionary thinking. Whilst his real views were little known, he became a popular memory; but some complained that his force was centrifugal, and that a church can no more be preserved by suavity and distinction than a state by liberty and justice. Lewis XVI., we are often told, perished in expiation of the sins of his forefathers. He perished, not because the power he inherited from them had been carried to excess, but because it had been discredited and undermined. One author of this discredit was Fénelon. Until he came, the ablest men, Bossuet and even Bayle, revered the monarchy. Fénelon struck it at the zenith, and treated Lewis XIV. in all his grandeur more severely than the disciples of Voltaire treated Lewis XV. in all his degradation. The season of scorn and shame begins with him. The best of his later contemporaries followed his example, and laid the basis of opposing criticism on motives of religion. They were the men whom Cardinal Dubois describes as dreamers of the same dreams as the chimerical archbishop of Cambray. Their influence fades away before the great change that came over France about the middle of the century.

From that time unbelief so far prevailed that even men who were not professed assailants, as Montesquieu, Condillac, Turgot, were estranged from Christianity. Politically, the consequence was this: men who did not attribute any deep significance to church questions never acquired definite notions on Church and State, never seriously examined under what conditions religion may be established or disestablished, endowed or disendowed, never even knew whether there exists any general solution, or any principle by which problems of that kind are decided. This defect of knowledge became a fact of importance at a turning-point in the Revolution. The theory of the relations between states and churches is bound up with the theory of

Toleration, and on that subject the eighteenth century scarcely rose above an intermittent, embarrassed, and unscientific view. For religious liberty is composed of the properties both of religion and of liberty, and one of its factors never became an object of disinterested observation among actual leaders of opinion. They preferred the argument of doubt to the argument of certitude, and sought to defeat intolerance by casting out revelation as they had defeated the persecution of witches by casting out the devil. There remained a flaw in their liberalism, for liberty apart from belief is liberty with a good deal of the substance taken out of it. The problem is less complicated and the solution less radical and less profound. Already, then, there were writers who held somewhat superficially the conviction, which Tocqueville made a corner-stone, that nations that have not the self-governing force of religion within them are unprepared for freedom.

The early notions of reform moved on French lines, striving to utilise the existing form of society, to employ the parliamentary aristocracy, to revive the States-General and the provincial assemblies. But the scheme of standing on the ancient ways, and raising a new France on the substructure of the old, brought out the fact that whatever growth of institutions there once had been had been stunted and stood still. If the medieval polity had been fitted to prosper, its fruit must be gathered from other countries, where the early notions had been pursued far ahead. The first thing to do was to cultivate the foreign example: and with that what we call the eighteenth century began. The English superiority, proclaimed first by Voltaire, was further demonstrated by Montesquieu. For England had recently created a government which was stronger than the institutions that had stood on antiquity. Founded upon fraud and treason, it had yet established the security of law more firmly than it had ever existed under the system of legitimacy, of prolonged inheritance, and of religious sanction. It flourished on the unaccustomed belief that theological dissensions need not detract from the power of the State, while political dissensions are the very secret of its prosperity. The men of questionable character who accomplished the change and had governed for the better part of sixty years, had successfully maintained public order, in spite of conspiracy and rebellion; they had built up an enormous system of national credit, and had been victorious in continental war. The Jacobite doctrine, which was the basis of European monarchy, had been backed by the arms of France, and had failed to shake the newly planted throne. A great experiment had been crowned by a great discovery. A novelty that defied the wisdom of centuries had made good its footing, and revolution had become a principle of stability more sure than tradition.

Montesquieu undertook to make the disturbing fact avail in political science. He valued it because it reconciled him with monarchy. He had started with the belief that kings are an evil, and not a necessary evil, and that their time was running short. His visit to Walpolean England taught him a plan by which they might be reprieved. He still confessed that a republic is the reign of virtue; and by virtue he meant love of equality and renunciation of self. But he had seen a monarchy that throve by corruption. He said that the distinctive principle of monarchy is not virtue but honour, which he once described as a contrivance to enable men of the world to commit almost every offense with impunity. The praise of England was made less injurious to French patriotism by the famous theory that explains institutions and character by the barometer and the latitude. Montesquieu looked about him, and abroad, but not far ahead. His admirable skill in supplying reason for every positive fact sometimes confounds the cause which produces with the argument that defends. He knows so many pleas for privilege that he almost overlooks the class that has none; and having no friendship for the clergy, he approves their immunities. He thinks that aristocracy alone can preserve monarchies, and makes England more free than any commonwealth. He lays down the great conservative maxim, that success generally depends on knowing the time it will take; and the most purely Whig maxim in his works, that the duty of a citizen is a crime when it obscures the duty of man, is Fénelon's. His liberty is of a Gothic type, and not insatiable. But the motto of his work, *Prolem sine matre creatam,* was intended to signify that the one thing wanting was liberty; and he had views on taxation, equality, and the division of powers that gave him a momentary influence in 1789. His warning that a legislature may be more dangerous than the executive remained unheard. The *Esprit des lois* had lost ground in 1767, during the ascendancy of Rousseau. The mind of the author moved within the conditions of society familiar to him, and he did not heed the coming democracy. He assured Hume that there would be no revolution, because the nobles were without civic courage.

There was more divination in d'Argenson, who was Minister of Foreign Affairs in 1745, and knew politics from the inside. Less acquiescent than his brilliant contemporary, he was perpetually contriving schemes of fundamental change, and is the earliest writer from whom we can extract the system of 1789. Others before him had perceived the impending revolution; but d'Argenson foretold that it would open with the slaughter of priests in the streets of Paris. Thirty-eight years later these words came true at the gate of St. Germain's Abbey. As the supporter of the Pretender he was quite uninfluenced by admiration for England, and imputed, not to the English Deists and Whigs but to the Church and her divisions and intolerance, the unbelieving spirit that threatened both Church and State. It was conventionally understood on the Continent that 1688 had been an uprising of Nonconformists, and a Whig was assumed to be a Presbyterian down to the death of Anne. It was easy to infer that a more violent theological conflict would lead to a more violent convulsion. As early as 1743 his terrible foresight discerns that the State is going to pieces, and its doom was so certain that he began to think of a refuge under other masters. He would have deposed the noble, the priest, and the lawyer, and given their power to the masses. Although the science of politics was in its infancy, he relied on the dawning enlightenment to establish rational liberty, and the equality between classes and religions which is the perfection of politics. The world ought to be governed not by parchment and vested rights, but by plain reason, which proceeds from the complex to the simple, and will sweep away all that interposes between the State and the democracy, giving to each part of the nation the management of its own affairs. He is eager to change everything, except the monarchy which alone can change all else. A deliberative assembly does not rise above the level of its average members. It is neither very foolish nor very wise. All might be well if the king made himself the irresistible instrument of philosophy and justice, and wrought the reform. But his king was Lewis XV. D'Argenson saw so little that was worthy to be preserved that he did not shrink from sweeping judgments and abstract propositions. By his rationalism, and his indifference to the prejudice of custom and the claim of posession; by his maxim that every man may be presumed to understand the things in which his own interest and responsibility are involved; by his zeal for democracy, equality, and simplicity, and his dislike of intermediate authorities, he belongs to a generation later than his own. He heralded events without preparing them, for the best of all he wrote only became known in our time.

Whilst Montesquieu, at the height of his fame as the foremost of living writers, was content to contemplate the past, there was a student in the Paris seminary who taught men to fix hope and endeavour on the future, and led the world at twenty-three. Turgot, when he proclaimed that upward growth and progress is the law of human life was studying to become a priest. To us, in an age of science, it has become difficult to imagine Christianity without the attribute of development and the faculty of improving society as well as souls. But the idea was acquired slowly. Under the burden of sin, men accustomed themselves to the consciousness of degeneracy; each generation confessed that they were unworthy children of their parents, and awaited with impatience the approaching end. From Lucretius and Seneca to Pascal and Leibniz we encounter a few dispersed and unsupported passages, suggesting advance towards perfection, and the flame that brightens as it moves from hand to hand; but they were without mastery or radiance.

Turgot at once made the idea habitual and familiar, and it became a pervading force in thoughtful minds, whilst the new sciences arose to confirm it. He imparted a deeper significance to history, giving it unity of tendency and direction, constancy where there had been motion, and development instead of change. The progress he meant was moral as much as intellectual; and as he professed to think that the rogues of his day would have seemed sanctified models to an earlier century, he made his calculations without counting the wickedness of men. His analysis left unfathomed depths for future explorers, for Lessing and still more for Hegel; but he taught mankind to expect that the future would be unlike the past, that it would be better, and that the experience of ages may instruct and warn, but cannot guide or control. He is eminently a benefactor to historical study; but he forged a weapon charged with power to abolish the product of history and the existing order. By the hypothesis of progress, the new is always gaining on the old; history is the embodiment of imperfection, and escape from history became the watchword of the coming day. Condorcet, the master's pupil, thought that the world might be emancipated by burning its records.

Turgot was too discreet for such an excess, and he looked to history for the demonstration of his law. He had come upon it in his theological studies. He renounced them soon after, saying that he could not wear a mask. When Guizot called Lamennais a malefactor, because he threw off his cassock and became a freethinker, Scherer, whose course had been some way parallel, observed: "He little knows how much it costs." The abrupt transition seems to have been accomplished by Turgot without a struggle. The *Encyclopaedia*, which was the largest undertaking since the invention of printing, came out at that time, and Turgot wrote for it. But he broke off, refusing to be connected with a party professedly hostile to revealed religion; and he rejected the declamatory paradoxes of Diderot and Raynal. He found his home among the Physiocrats, of all the groups the one that possessed the most compact body of consistent views, and who already knew most of the accepted doctrines of political economy, although they ended by making way for Adam Smith. They are of supreme importance to us, because they founded political science on the economic science which was coming into existence. Harrington, a century before, had seen that the art of government can be reduced to system; but the French economists precede all men in this, that holding a vast collection of combined and verified truths on matters contiguous to politics and belonging to their domain, they extended it to the whole, and governed the constitution by the same fixed principles that governed the purse. They said: A man's most sacred property is his labour. It is anterior even to the right of property, for it is the possession of those who own nothing else. Therefore he must be free to make the best use of it he can. The interference of one man with another, of society with its members, of the state with the subject, must be brought down to the lowest dimension. Power intervenes only to restrict intervention, to guard the individual from oppression, that is from regulation in an interest not his own. Free labour and its derivative free trade are the first conditions of legitimate government. Let things fall into their natural order, let society govern itself, and the sovereign function of the State will be to protect nature in the execution of her own law. Government must not be arbitrary, but it must be powerful enough to repress arbitrary action in others. If the supreme power is needlessly limited, the secondary powers will run riot and oppress. Its supremacy will bear no check. The problem is to enlighten the ruler, not to restrain him; and one man is more easily enlightened than many. Government by opposition, by balance and control, is contrary to principle; whereas absolutism might be requisite to the attainment of their higher purpose. Nothing less than concentrated power could overcome the obstacles to such beneficent reforms as they meditated. Men who sought only the general good must wound every distinct and separate interest of class, and would be mad to break up the only force that they could count upon, and thus to throw away the means of preventing the evils that must follow if things were left to the working of opinion and the feeling of masses. They had no love for absolute power in itself, but they computed that, if they had the use of it for five years, France would be free. They distinguished an arbitrary monarch and the irresistible but impersonal state.

It was the era of repentant monarchy. Kings had become the first of public servants, executing, for the good of the people, what the people were unable to do for themselves; and there was a reforming movement on foot which led to many instances of prosperous and intelligent administration. To men who knew what unutterable suffering and wrong was inflicted by bad laws, and who lived in terror of the uneducated and inorganic masses, the idea of reform from above seemed preferable to parliamentary government managed by Newcastle and North, in the interest of the British landlord. The economists are outwardly and avowedly less liberal than Montesquieu, because they are incomparably more impressed by the evils of the time, and the need of immense and fundamental changes. They prepared to undo the work of absolutism by the hand of absolutism. They were not its opponents, but its advisers, and hoped to convert it by their advice. The indispensable liberties are those which constitute the wealth of nations; the rest will follow. The disease had lasted too long for the sufferer to heal himself: the relief must come from the author of his sufferings. The power that had done the wrong was still efficient to undo the wrong. Transformation, infinitely more difficult in itself than preservation, was not more formidable to the economists because it consisted mainly in revoking the godless work of a darker age. They deemed it their mission not to devise new laws, for that is a task which God has not committed to man, but only to declare the inherent laws of the existence of society and enable them to prevail.

The defects of the social and political organisation were as distinctly pointed out by the economists as by the electors of the National Assembly, twenty years later, and in nearly all things they proposed the remedy. But they were persuaded that the only thing to regenerate France was a convulsion which the national character would make a dreadful one. They desired a large scheme of popular education, because commands take no root in soil that is not prepared. Political truths can be made so evident that the opinion of an instructed public will be invincible, and will banish the abuse of power. To resist oppression is to make a league with heaven, and all things are oppressive that resist the natural order of freedom. For society secures rights; it neither bestows nor restricts them. They are the direct consequence of duties. As truth can only convince by the exposure of errors and the defeat of objections, liberty is the essential guard of truth. Society is founded, not on the will of man, but on the nature of man and the will of God; and conformity to the divinely appointed order is followed by inevitable reward. Relief of those who suffer is the duty of all men, and the affair of all.

Such was the spirit of that remarkable group of men, especially of Mercier de la Rivière, of whom Diderot said that he alone possessed the true and everlasting secret of the security and the happiness of empires. Turgot indeed had failed in office; but his reputation was not diminished, and the power of his name exeeded all others at the outbreak of the Revolution. His policy of employing the Crown to reform the State was at once rejected in favour of other counsels; but his influence may be traced in many acts of the Assembly, and on two very memorable occasions it was not auspicious. It was a central dogma of the party that land is the true source of wealth, or, as Asgill said, that man deals in nothing but earth. When a great part of France became national property, men were the more easily persuaded that land can serve as the basis of public credit and of unlimited *assignats*. According to a weighty opinion which we shall have to consider before long, the parting of the ways in the Revolution was on the day when, rejecting the example both of England and America, the French resolved to institute a single undivided legislature. It was the Pennsylvania model; and Voltaire had pronounced Pennsylvania the best government in the world. Franklin gave the sanction of an oracle to the constitution of his state, and Turgot was its vehement protagonist in Europe.

A king ruling over a level democracy, and a democracy ruling itself through the agency of a king, were long contending notions in the first Assembly. One was monarchy according to Turgot, the other was monarchy adapted to Rousseau; and the latter, for a time, prevailed. Rousseau was the citizen of a small republic, consisting of a single town, and he professed to have applied its example to the government of the world. It was Geneva, not as he saw it, but as he extracted its essential principle, and as it has since become, Geneva illustrated by the Forest Cantons and the Landesgemeinde more than by its own charters. The idea was that the grown men met in the market-place, like the peasants of Glarus under their trees, to manage their affairs, making and unmaking officials, conferring and revoking powers. They were equal, because every man had exactly the same right to defend his interest by the guarantee of his vote. The welfare of all was safe in the hands of all, for they had not the separate interests that are bred by the egotism of wealth, nor the exclusive views that come from a distorted education. All being equal in power and similar in purpose, there can be no just cause why some should move apart and break into minorities. There is an implied contract that no part shall ever be preferred to the whole, and minorities shall always obey. Clever men are not wanted for the making of laws, because clever men and their laws are at the root of all mischief. Nature is a better guide than civilisation, because nature comes from God, and His works are good; culture from man, whose works are bad in proportion as he is remoter from natural innocence, as his desires increase upon him, as he seeks more refined pleasures, and stores up more superfluity. It promotes inequality, selfishness, and the ruin of public spirit.

By plausible and easy stages the social ideas latent in parts of Switzerland produced the theory that men come innocent from the hands of the Creator, that they are originally equal, that progress from equality to civilisation is the passage from virtue to vice and from freedom to tyranny, that the people are sovereign, and govern by powers given and taken away; that an individual or a class may be mistaken and may desert the common cause and the general interest, but the people, necessarily sincere, and true, and incorrupt, cannot go wrong; that there is a right of resistance to all governments that are fallible, because they are partial, but none against government of the people by the people, because it has no master and no judge, and decides in the last instance and alone; that insurrection is the law of all unpopular societies founded on a false principle and a broken contract, and submission that of the only legitimate societies, based on the popular will; that there is no privilege against the law of nature, and no right against the power of all. By this chain of reasoning, with little infusion of other ingredients, Rousseau applied the sequence of the ideas of pure democracy to the government of nations.

Now the most glaring and familiar fact in history shows that the direct self-government of a town cannot be extended over an empire. It is a plan that scarcely reaches beyond the next parish. Either one district will be governed by another, or both by somebody else chosen for the purpose. Either plan contradicts first principles. Subjection is the direct negation of democracy; representation is the indirect. So that an Englishman underwent bondage to parliament as much as Lausanne to Berne or as America to England if it had submitted to taxation, and by law recovered his liberty but once in seven years. Consequently Rousseau, still faithful to Swiss precedent as well as to the logic of his own theory, was a federalist. In Switzerland, when one half of a canton disagrees with the other, or the country with the town, it is deemed natural that they should break into two, that the general will may not oppress minorities. Thus multiplication of self-governing communities was admitted by Rousseau as a preservative of unanimity on one hand, and of liberty on the other. Helvétius came to his support with the idea that men are not only equal by nature but alike, and that society is the cause of variation; from which it would follow that everything may be done by laws and by education.

Rousseau is the author of the strongest political theory that had appeared amongst men. We cannot say that he reasons well, but he knew how to make his argument seem convincing, satisfying, inevitable, and he wrote with an eloquence and a fervour that had never been seen in prose, even in Bolingbroke or Milton. His books gave the first signal of a universal subversion, and were as fatal to the Republic as to the Monarchy. Although he lives by the social contract and the law of resistance, and owes his influence to what was extreme and systematic, his later writings are loaded with sound political wisdom. He owes nothing to the novelty or the originality of his thoughts. Taken jointly or severally, they are old friends, and you will find them in the school of Wolf that just preceded, in the dogmatists of the Great Rebellion and the Jesuit casuists who were dear to Algernon Sidney, in their Protestant opponents, Duplessis Mornay, and the Scots who had heard the last of our schoolmen, Major of St. Andrews, renew the speculations of the time of schism, which decomposed and dissected the Church and rebuilt it on a model very propitious to political revolution, and even in the early interpreters of the Aristotelian Politics which appeared just at the era of the first parliament.

Rousseau's most advanced point was the doctrine that the people are infallible. Jurieu had taught that they can do no wrong: Rousseau added that they are positively in the right. The idea, like most others, was not new, and goes back to the Middle Ages. When the question arose what security there is for the preservation of traditional truth if the episcopate was divided and the papacy vacant, it was answered that the faith would be safely retained by the masses. The maxim that the voice of the people is the voice of God is as old as Alcuin; it was renewed by some of the greatest writers anterior to democracy, by Hooker and Bossuet, and it was employed in our day by Newman to prop his theory of development. Rousseau applied it to the State.

The sovereignty of public opinion was just then coming in through the rise of national debts and the increasing importance of the public creditor. It meant more than the noble savage and the blameless South Sea islander, and distinguished the instinct that guides large masses of men from the calculating wisdom of the few. It was destined to prove the most serious of all obstacles to representative government. Equality of power readily suggests equality of property; but the movement of Socialism began earlier, and was not assisted by Rousseau. There were solemn theorists, such as Mably and Morelly, who were sometimes quoted in the Revolution, but the change in the distribution of property was independent of them.

A more effective influence was imported from Italy; for the Italians, through Vico, Giannone, Genovesi, had an eighteenth century of their own. Sardinia preceded France in solving the problem of feudalism. Arthur Young affirms that the measures of the Grand Duke Leopold had, in ten years, doubled the produce of Tuscany; at Milan, Count Firmian was accounted one of the best administrators in Europe. It was a Milanese, Beccaria, who, by his reform of criminal law, became a leader of French opinion. Continental jurisprudence had long been overshadowed by two ideas: that torture is the surest method of discovering truth, and that punishment deters not by its justice, its celerity, or its certainty, but in proportion to its severity. Even in the eighteenth century the penal system of Maria Theresa and Joseph II. was barbarous. Therefore no attack was more surely aimed at the heart of established usage than that which dealt with courts of justice. It forced men to conclude that authority was odiously stupid and still more odiously ferocious, that existing governments were accursed, that the guardians and ministers of law, divine and human, were more guilty than their culprits. The past was branded as the reign of infernal powers, and charged with long arrears of unpunished wrong. As there was no sanctity left in law, there was no mercy for its merciless defenders; and if they fell into avenging hands, their doom would not exceed their desert. Men afterwards conspicious by their violence, Brissot and Marat, were engaged in this campaign of humanity, which raised a demand for authorities that were not vitiated by the accumulation of infamy, for new laws, new powers, a new dynasty.

As religion was associated with cruelty, it is at this point that the movement of new ideas became a crusade against Christianity. A book by the Curé Meslier, partially known at that time, but first printed by Strauss in 1864, is the clarion of vindictive unbelief; and another abbé, Raynal, hoped that the clergy would be crushed beneath the ruins of their altars.

Thus the movement which began, in Fénelon's time, with warnings and remonstrance and the zealous endeavour to preserve, which produced one great scheme of change by the Crown and another at the expense of the Crown, ended in the wild cry for vengeance and a passionate appeal to fire and sword. So many lines of thought converging on destruction explain the agreement that existed when the States-General began, and the explosion that followed the reforms of '89 and the ruins of '93. No conflict can be more irreconcilable than that between a constitution and an enlightened absolutism, between abrogation of old laws and multiplication of new, between representation and direct democracy, the people controlling and the people governing, kings by contract and kings by mandate.

Yet all these fractions of opinion were called Liberal: Montesquieu, because he was an intelligent Tory; Voltaire, because he attacked the clergy; Turgot, as a reformer; Rousseau, as a democrat; Diderot, as a freethinker. The one thing common to them all is the disregard for liberty.

XII

The Influence of America

The several structures of political thought that arose in France, and clashed in the process of revolution, were not directly responsible for the outbreak. The doctrines hung like a cloud upon the heights, and at critical moments in the reign of Lewis XV. men felt that a catastrophe was impending. It befell when there was less provocation, under his successor; and the spark that changed thought into action was supplied by the Declaration of American Independence. It was the system of an international extra-territorial universal Whig, far transcending the English model by its simplicity and rigour. It surpassed in force all the speculation of Paris and Geneva, for it had undergone the test of experiment, and its triumph was the most memorable thing that had been seen by men.

The expectation that the American colonies would separate was an old one. A century before, Harrington had written: "They are yet babes, that cannot live without sucking the breasts of their mother-cities; but such as I mistake if, when they come of age, they do not wean themselves; which causes me to wonder at princes that like to be exhausted in that way." When, in 1759, the elder Mirabeau announced it, he meant that the conquest of Canada involved the loss of America, as the colonists would cling to England as long as the French were behind them, and no longer. He came very near to the truth, for the war in Canada gave the signal. The English colonies had meditated the annexation of the French, and they resented that

Reprinted from Acton, *Lectures on the French Revolution* (London: Macmillan, 1925).

the king's government undertook the expedition, to deprive them of the opportunity for united action. Fifty years later President Adams said that the treatment of American officers by the British made his blood boil.

The agitation began in 1761, and by the innovating ideas which it flung abroad it is as important as the Declaration itself, or the great constitutional debate. The colonies were more advanced than Great Britain in the way of free institutions, and existed only that they might escape the vices of the mother country. They had no remnants of feudalism to cherish or resist. They possessed written constitutions, some of them remarkably original, fit roots of an immense development. George III. thought it strange that he should be the sovereign of a democracy like Rhode Island, where all power reverted annually to the people, and the authorities had to be elected anew. Connecticut received from the Stuarts so liberal a charter, and worked out so finished a scheme of local self-government, that it served as a basis for the federal constitution. The Quakers had a plan founded on equality of power, without oppression, or privilege, or intolerance, or slavery. They declared that their holy experiment would not have been worth attempting if it did not offer some very real advantage over England. It was to enjoy freedom, liberty of conscience, and the right to tax themselves, that they went into the desert. There were points on which these men anticipated the doctrines of a more unrestrained democracy, for they established their government not on conventions, but on divine right, and they claimed to be infallible. A Connecticut preacher said in 1638: "The choice of public magistrates belongs unto the people, by God's own allowance. They who have the power to appoint officers and magistrates, it is in their power, also, to set the bounds and limitations of the power and place unto which they call them." The following words, written in 1736, appear in the works of Franklin: "The judgment of a whole people, especially of a free people, is looked upon to be infallible. And this is universally true, while they remain in their proper sphere, unbiassed by faction, undeluded by the tricks of designing men. A body of people thus circumstanced cannot be supposed to judge amiss on any essential points; for if they decide in favour of themselves, which is extremely natural, their decision is just, inasmuch as whatever contributes to their benefit is a general benefit, and advances the real public good." A commentator adds that this notion of the infallible perception by the people of their true interest, and their unerring pursuit of it, was very prevalent in the provinces, and for a time in the States after the establishment of American independence.

In spite of their democratic spirit, these communities consented to have their trade regulated and restricted, to their own detriment and the advantage of English merchants. They had protested, but they had ended by yielding. Now Adam Smith says that to prohibit a great people from making all they can of every part of their own produce, or from employing their stock and industry in the way that they judge most advantageous for themselves, is a manifest violation of the most sacred rights of mankind. There was a latent sense of injury which broke out when, in addition to interference with the freedom of trade, England exercised the right of taxation. An American lately wrote: "The real foundation of the discontent which led to the Revolution was the effort of Great Britain, beginning in 1750, to prevent diversity of occupation, to attack the growth of manufactures and the mechanic arts, and the final cause before the attempt to tax without representation was the effort to enforce the navigation laws." When England argued that the hardship of regulation might be greater than the hardship of taxation, and that those who submitted to the one submitted, in principle, to the other, Franklin replied that the Americans had not taken that view, but that, when it was put before them, they would be willing to reject both one and the other. He knew, however, that the ground taken up by his countrymen was too narrow. He wrote to the French economist, Morellet: "Nothing can be better expressed than your sentiments are on this point, where you prefer liberty of trading, cultivating, manufacturing, etc., even to civil liberty, this being affected but rarely, the other every hour."

These early authors of American independence were generally enthusiasts for the British Constitution, and preceded Burke in the tendency to canonise it, and to magnify it as an ideal exemplar for nations. John Adams said, in 1766: "Here lies the difference between the British Constitution and other forms of government, namely, that liberty is its end, its use, its designation, drift and scope, as much as grinding corn is the use of a mill." Another celebrated Bostonian identified the Constitution with the law of Nature, as Montesquieu called the Civil Law, written Reason. He said: "It is the glory of the British prince and the happiness of all his subjects, that their constitution hath its foundation in the immutable laws of Nature; and as the supreme legislative, as well as the supreme executive, derives its authority from that constitution, it should seem that no laws can be made or executed that are repugnant to any essential law in Nature." The writer of these words, James Otis, is the founder of the revolutionary doctrine. Describing one of his pamphlets, the second President says: "Look over the declaration of rights and wrongs issued by Congress in 1774; look into the declaration of independence in 1776; look into the writings of Dr. Price and Dr. Priestley; look into all the French constitutions of government; and, to cap the climax, look into Mr. Thomas Paine's *Common Sense, Crisis,* and *Rights of Man.* What can you find that is not to be found in solid substance in this 'Vindication of the House of Representatives'?" When these men found that the appeal to the law and to the constitution did not avail them, that the king, by bribing the people's representatives with the people's money, was able to enforce his will, they sought a higher tribunal, and turned from the law of England to the law of Nature, and from the king of England to the King of kings. Otis, in 1762, 1764 and 1765, says: "Most governments are, in fact, arbitrary, and consequently the curse and scandal of human nature; yet none are of right arbitrary. By the laws of God and nature, government must not raise taxes on the property of the people without the consent of the people or their deputies. There can be no prescription old enough to supersede the law of Nature and the grant of God

Almighty, who has given all men a right to be free. If a man has but little property to protect and defend, yet his life and liberty are things of some importance." About the same time Gadsden wrote: "A confirmation of our essential and common rights as Englishmen may be pleaded from charters clearly enough; but any further dependence on them may be fatal. We should stand upon the broad common ground of those natural rights that we all feel and know as men and as descendants of Englishmen."

The primitive fathers of the United States began by preferring abstract moral principle to the letter of the law and the spirit of the Constitution. But they went farther. Not only was their grievance difficult to substantiate at law, but it was trivial in extent. The claim of England was not evidently disproved, and even if it was unjust, the injustice practically was not hard to bear. The suffering that would be caused by submission was immeasurably less than the suffering that must follow resistance, and it was more uncertain and remote. The utilitarian argument was loud in favour of obedience and loyalty. But if interest was on one side, there was a manifest principle on the other—a principle so sacred and so clear as imperatively to demand the sacrifice of men's lives, of their families and their fortune. They resolved to give up everything, not to escape from actual oppression, but to honour a precept of unwritten law. That was the transatlantic discovery in the theory of political duty, the light that came over the ocean. It represented liberty not as a comparative release from tyranny, but as a thing so divine that the existence of society must be staked to prevent even the least constructive infraction of its sovereign right. "A free people," said Dickinson, "can never be too quick in observing nor too firm in opposing the beginnings of alteration either in form or reality, respecting institutions formed for their security. The first kind of alteration leads to the last. As violations of the rights of the governed are commonly not only specious, but small at the beginning, they spread over the multitude in such a manner as to touch individuals but slightly. Every free state should incessantly watch, and instantly take alarm at any addition being made to the power exercised over them." Who are a free people? Not those over whom government is reasonably and equitably exercised; but those who live under a government so constitutionally checked and controlled that proper provision is made against its being otherwise exercised. The contest was plainly a contest of principle, and was conducted entirely on principle by both parties. "The amount of taxes proposed to be raised," said Marshall, the greatest of constitutional lawyers, "was too inconsiderable to interest the people of either country." I will add the words of Daniel Webster, the great expounder of the Constitution, who is the most eloquent of the Americans, and stands, in politics, next to Burke: "The Parliament of Great Britain asserted a right to tax the Colonies in all cases whatsoever; and it was precisely on this question that they made the Revolution turn. The amount of taxation was trifling, but the claim itself was inconsistent with liberty, and that was in their eyes enough. It was against the recital of an act of Parliament, rather than against any suffering under its enactment, that they took up arms. They went to war against a preamble. They fought seven years against a declaration. They saw in the claim of the British Parliament a seminal principle of mischief, the germ of unjust power."

The object of these men was liberty, not independence. Their feeling was expressed by Jay in his address to the people of Great Britain: "Permit us to be as free as yourselves, and we shall ever esteem a union with you to be our greatest glory and our greatest happiness." Before 1775 there was no question of separation. During all the Revolution Adams declared that he would have given everything to restore things as before with security; and both Jefferson and Madison admitted in the presence of the English minister that a few seats in both Houses would have set at rest the whole question.

In their appeal to the higher law the Americans professed the purest Whiggism, and they claimed that their resistance to the House of Commons and the jurisprudence of Westminster only carried forward the eternal conflict between Whig and Tory. By their closer analysis, and their fearlessness of logical consequences, they transformed the doctrine and modified the party. The uprooted Whig, detached from his parchments and precedents, his leading families and historic conditions, exhibited new qualities; and the era of compromise made way for an era of principle. Whilst French diplomacy traced the long hand of the English opposition in the tea riots at Boston, Chatham and Camden were feeling the influence of Dickinson and Otis, without recognising the difference. It appears in a passage of one of Chatham's speeches, in 1775:

> The universal opposition to your arbitrary system of taxation might have been foreseen. It was obvious from the nature of things, and from the nature of man, and, above all, from the confirmed habits of thinking, from the spirit of Whiggism flourishing in America. The spirit which now pervades America is the same which formerly opposed loans, benevolences, and ship-money in this country, is the same spirit which roused all England to action at the Revolution, and which established at a remote era your liberties, on the basis of that grand fundamental maxim of the Constitution, that no subject of England shall be taxed but by his own consent. To maintain this principle is the common cause of the Whigs on the other side of the Atlantic, and on this. It is the alliance of God and Nature, immutable, eternal, fixed as the firmament of heaven. Resistance to your acts was necessary as it was just; and your vain declarations of the omnipotence of parliament, and your imperious doctrines of the necessity of submission will be found equally impotent to convince or enslave your fellow-subjects in America.

The most significant instance of the action of America on Europe is Edmund Burke. We think of him as a man who, in early life, rejected all generalities and abstract propositions, and who became the most strenuous and violent of conservatives. But there is an interval when, as the quarrel with the Colonies went on, Burke was as revolutionary as Washington. The inconsistency is not as flagrant as it seems. He had been brought forward by the party of measured propriety and imperative moderation, of compromise and unfinished thought, who claimed the right of taxing, but refused to employ it. When he urged the differences in every situation and every problem, and shrank from the common denominator and the underlying principle, he fell into step with his friends. As an Irishman, who had married into an Irish Catholic family, it was desirable that he should adopt no theories in America which would unsettle Ireland. He had learnt to teach government by party as an almost sacred dogma, and party forbids revolt as a breach of the laws of the game. His scruples and his protests, and his defiance of theory, were the policy and the precaution of a man conscious of restraints, and not entirely free in the exertion of powers that lifted him far above his tamer surroundings. As the strife sharpened and the Americans made way, Burke was carried along, and developed views which he never utterly abandoned, but which are difficult to reconcile with much that he wrote when the Revolution had spread to France.

In his address to the Colonists he says:

We do not know how to qualify millions of our countrymen, contending with one heart for an admission to privileges which we have ever thought our own happiness and honour, by odious and unworthy names. On the contrary, we highly revere the principles on which you act. We had much rather see you totally independent of this crown and kingdom, than joined to it by so unnatural a conjunction as that of freedom and servitude. We view the establishment of the English Colonies on principles of liberty, as that which is to render this kingdom venerable to future ages. In comparison of this, we regard all the victories and conquests of our warlike ancestors, or of our own times, as barbarous, vulgar distinctions, in which many nations, whom we look upon with little respect or value, have equalled, if not far exceeded us. Those who have and who hold to that foundation of common liberty, whether on this or on your side of the ocean, we consider as the true and the only true Englishmen. Those who depart from it, whether there or here, are attainted, corrupted in blood and wholly fallen from their original rank and value. They are the real rebels to the fair constitution and just supremacy of England. A long course of war with the administration of this country may be but a prelude to a series of wars and contentions among yourselves, to end at length (as such scenes have too often ended) in a species of humiliating repose, which nothing but the preceding calamities would reconcile to the dispirited few who survived them. We allow that even this evil is worth the risk to men of honour when rational liberty is at stake, as in the present case we confess and lament that it is.

At other times he spoke as follows:—

Nothing less than a convulsion that will shake the globe to its centre can ever restore the European nations to that liberty by which they were once so much distinguished. The Western world was the seat of freedom until another, more Western, was discovered; and that other will probably be its asylum when it is hunted down in every other part. Happy it is that the worst of times may have one refuge still left for humanity. If the Irish resisted King William, they resisted him on the very same principle that the English and Scotch resisted King James. The Irish Catholics must have been the very worst and the most truly unnatural of rebels, if they had not supported a prince whom they had seen attacked, not for any designs against their religion or their liberties, but for an extreme partiality for their sect. Princes otherwise meritorious have violated the liberties of the people, and have been lawfully deposed for such violation. I know no human being exempt from the law. I consider Parliament as the proper judge of kings, and it is necessary that they should be amenable to it. There is no such thing as governing the whole body of the people contrary to their inclination. Whenever they have a feeling they commonly are in the right. Christ appeared in sympathy with the lowest of the people, and thereby made it a firm and ruling principle that their welfare was the object of all government.

In all forms of government the people is the true legislator. The remote and efficient cause is the consent of the people, either actual or implied, and such consent is absolutely essential to its validity. Whiggism did not consist in the support of the power of Parliament or of any other power, but of the rights of the people. If Parliament should become an instrument in invading them, it was no better in any respect, and much worse in some, than any other instrument of arbitrary power. They who call upon you to belong wholly to the people are those who wish you to belong to your proper home, to the sphere of your duty, to the post of your honour. Let the Commons in Parliament assembled be one and the same thing with the Commons at large. I see no other way for the preservation of a decent attention to public interest in the representatives, but the interposition of the body of the people itself, whenever it shall appear by some flagrant and notorious act, by some capital innovation, that those representatives are going to overleap the fences of the law and to introduce an arbitrary power. This interposition is a most unpleasant remedy; but if it be a legal remedy, it is intended on some occasion to be used—to be used then only when it is evident that nothing else can hold the Constitution to its true principles. It is not in Parliament alone that the remedy for parliamentary disorders can be completed; hardly, indeed, can it begin there. A popular origin cannot therefore be the characteristic distinction of a popular representative. This belongs equally to all parts of government, and in all forms. The virtue, spirit, and essence of a House of Commons consists in its being the express image of the feelings of the nation. It was not instituted to be a control upon the people. It was designed as a control for the people. Privilege of the crown and privilege of Parliament are only privilege so long as they are exercised for the benefit of the people. The voice of the people is a voice that is to be heard, and not the votes and resolutions of the House of Commons. He would preserve thoroughly every privilege of the people, because it is a privilege known and written in the law of the land; and he would support it, not against the crown or the aristocratic party only, but against the representatives of the people themselves. This was not a government of balances. It would be a strange thing if two hundred peers should have it in their power to defeat by their negative what had been done by the people of England. I have taken my part in political connections and political quarrels for the purpose of advancing justice and the dominion of reason, and I hope I shall never prefer the means, or any feelings growing out of the use of those means, to the great and substantial end itself. Legislators can do what lawyers can not, for they have no other rules to bind them but the great principles of reason and equity and the general sense of mankind. All human laws are, properly speaking, only declaratory; they may alter the mode and application, but have no power over the substance, of original justice. A conservation and secure enjoyment of our natural rights is the great and ultimate purpose of civil society.

The great inlet by which a colour for oppression has entered into the world is by one man's pretending to determine concerning the happiness of another. I would give a full civil protection, in which I include an immunity from all disturbance of their public religious worship, and a power of teaching in schools as well as temples, to Jews, Mahometans, and even

387

Pagans. The Christian religion itself arose without establishment, it arose even without toleration, and whilst its own principles were not tolerated, it conquered all the powers of darkness, it conquered all the powers of the world. The moment it began to depart from these principles, it converted the establishment into tyranny, it subverted its foundation from that very hour. It is the power of government to prevent much evil; it can do very little positive good in this, or perhaps in anything else. It is not only so of the State and statesman, but of all the classes and descriptions of the rich: they are the pensioners of the poor, and are maintained by their superfluity. They are under an absolute, hereditary, and indefeasible dependence on those who labour and are miscalled the poor. That class of dependent pensioners called the rich is so extremely small, that if all their throats were cut, and a distribution made of all they consume in a year, it would not give a bit of bread and cheese for one night's supper to those who labour, and who in reality feed both the pensioners and themselves. It is not in breaking the laws of commerce, which are the laws of nature and consequently the laws of God, that we are to place our hope of softening the divine displeasure. It is the law of nature, which is the law of God.

I cannot resist the inference from these passages that Burke, after 1770, underwent other influences than those of his reputed masters, the Whigs of 1688. And if we find that strain of unwonted thought in a man who afterwards gilded the old order of things and wavered as to toleration and the slave trade, we may expect that the same causes would operate in France.

When the *Letters of a Pennsylvanian Farmer* became known in Europe, Diderot said that it was madness to allow Frenchmen to read such things, as they could not do it without becoming intoxicated and changed into different men. But France was impressed by the event more than by the literature that accompanied it. America had made herself independent under less provocation than had ever been a motive of revolt, and the French Government had acknowledged that her cause was righteous and had gone to war for it. If the king was right in America, he was utterly wrong at home, and if the Americans acted rightly, the argument was stronger, the cause was a hundredfold better, in France itself. All that justified their independence condemned the Government of their French allies. By the principle that taxation without representation is robbery, there was no authority so illegitimate as that of Lewis XVI. The force of that demonstration was irresistible, and it produced its effect where the example of England failed. The English doctrine was repelled at the very earliest stage of the Revolution, and the American was adopted. What the French took from the Americans was their theory of revolution, not their theory of government—their cutting, not their sewing. Many French nobles served in the war, and came home republicans and even democrats by conviction. It was America that converted the aristocracy to the reforming policy, and gave leaders to the Revolution. "The American Revolution," says Washington, "or the peculiar light of the age, seems to have opened the eyes of almost every nation in Europe, and a spirit of equal liberty appears fast to be gaining ground everywhere." When the French officers were leaving, Cooper, of Boston, addressed them in the language of warning: "Do not let your hopes be inflamed by our triumphs on this virgin soil. You will carry our sentiments with you, but if you try to plant them in a country that has been corrupt for centuries, you will encounter obstacles more formidable than ours. Our liberty has been won with blood; you will have to shed it in torrents before liberty can take root in the old world." Adams, after he had been President of the United States, bitterly regretted the Revolution which made them independent, because it had given the example to the French; although he also believed that they had not a single principle in common.

Nothing, on the contrary, is more certain than that American principles profoundly influenced France, and determined the course of the Revolution. It is from America that Lafayette derived the saying that created a commotion at the time, that resistance is the most sacred of duties. There also was the theory that political power comes from those over whom it is exercised, and depends upon their will; that every authority not so constituted is illegitimate and precarious; that the past is more a warning than an example; that the earth belongs to those who are upon it, not to those who are underneath. These are characteristics common to both Revolutions.

At one time also the French adopted and acclaimed the American notion that the end of government is liberty, not happiness, or prosperity, or power, or the preservation of an historic inheritance, or the adaptation of national law to national character, or the progress of enlightenment and the promotion of virtue; that the private individual should not feel the pressure of public authority, and should direct his life by the influences that are within him, not around him.

And there was another political doctrine which the Americans transmitted to the French. In old colonial days the executive and the judicial powers were derived from a foreign source, and the common purpose was to diminish them. The assemblies were popular in origin and character, and everything that added to their power seemed to add security to rights. James Wilson, one of the authors and commentators of the constitution, informs us that "at the Revolution the same fond predilection, and the same jealous dislike, existed and prevailed. The executive, and the judicial as well as the legislative authority, was now the child of the people, but to the two former the people behaved like stepmothers. The legislature was still discriminated by excessive partiality." This preference, historic but irrational, led up naturally to a single chamber. The people of America and their delegates in Congress were of the opinion that a single Assembly was every way adequate to the management of their federal concerns, and when the Senate was invented, Franklin strongly objected. "As to the two chambers," he wrote, "I am of your opinion that one alone would be better; but my dear friend, nothing in human affairs and schemes is perfect, and perhaps this is the case of our opinions."

Alexander Hamilton was the ablest as well as the most conservative of the American statesmen. He longed for monarchy, and he desired to establish a national government and to annihilate state rights. The American spirit, as it penetrated France, cannot well be described better than it was by him: "I consider civil liberty, in a genuine, unadulterated sense, as the greatest of terrestrial blessings. I am convinced that the whole human race is entitled to it, and that it can be wrested from no part of them without the blackest and most aggravated guilt. The sacred rights of mankind are not to be rummaged for among old parchments or musty records. They are written, as with a sunbeam, in the whole volume of human nature, by the hand of the Divinity itself, and can never be erased or obscured by mortal power."

But when we speak in the gross of the American Revolution we combine different and discordant things. From the first agitation in 1761 to the Declaration of Independence, and then to the end of the war in 1782, the Americans were aggressive, violent in their language, fond of abstractions, prolific of doctrines universally applicable and universally destructive. It is the ideas of those earlier days that roused the attention of France, and were imported by Lafayette, Noailles, Lameth, and the leaders of the future revolution who had beheld the lowering of the British flag at Yorktown. The America of their experience was the America of James Otis, of Jefferson, of *The Rights of Man.*

A change followed in 1787, when the Convention drew up the Constitution. It was a period of construction, and every effort was made, every scheme was invented, to curb the inevitable democracy. The members of that assembly were, on the whole, eminently cautious and sensible men. They were not men of extraordinary parts, and the genius of Hamilton failed absolutely to impress them. Some of their most memorable contrivances proceeded from no design, but were merely half measures and mutual concessions. Seward has pointed out this distinction between the revolutionary epoch and the constituent epoch that succeeded: "The rights asserted by our forefathers were not peculiar to themselves. They were the common rights of mankind. The basis of the Constitution was laid broader by far than the superstructure which the conflicting interests and prejudices of the day suffered to be erected. The Constitution and laws of the Federal Government did not practically extend those principles throughout the new system of government; but they were plainly promulgated in the Declaration of Independence."

Now, although France was deeply touched by the American Revolution, it was not affected by the American Constitution. It underwent the disturbing influence, not the conservative.

The Constitution, framed in the summer of 1787, came into operation in March 1789, and nobody knew how it worked, when the crisis came in France. The debates, which explain every intention and combination, remained long hidden from the world. Moreover, the Constitution has become something more than the original printed paper. Besides amendments, it has been interpreted by the courts, modified by opinion, developed in some directions, and tacitly altered in others. Some of its most valued provisions have been acquired in this way, and were not yet visible when the French so greatly needed the guiding lessons of other men's experience. Some of the restrictions on the governing power were not fully established at first.

The most important of these is the action of the Supreme Court in annulling unconstitutional laws. The Duke of Wellington said to Bunsen that by this institution alone the United States made up for all the defects of their government. Since Chief Justice Marshall, the judiciary undoubtedly obtained immense authority, which Jefferson, and others besides, believed to be unconstitutional; for the Constitution itself gives no such power. The idea had grown up in the States, chiefly, I think, in Virginia. At Richmond, in 1782, Judge Wythe said: "Tyranny has been sapped, the departments kept within their own spheres, the citizens protected, and general liberty promoted. But this beneficial result attains to higher perfection when, those who hold the purse and the sword differing as to the powers which each may exercise, the tribunals, who hold neither, are called upon to declare the law impartially between them. If the whole legislature—an event to be deprecated—should attempt to overleap the boundaries prescribed to them by the people, I, in administering the justice of the country, will

meet the united powers at my seat in this tribunal, and, point-
ing to the Constitution, will say to them: 'Here is the limit of
your authority; hither shall you go, but no further.'" The Virginian legislature gave way, and repealed the act.

After the Federal Constitution was drawn up, Hamilton, in
the seventy-eighth number of the *Federalist*, argued that the
power belonged to the judiciary; but it was not constitutionally
recognised until 1801. "This," said Madison, "makes the judiciary department paramount, in fact, to the legislature, which
was never intended, and can never be proper. In a government
whose vital principle is responsibility, it never will be allowed
that the legislative and executive departments should be completely subjected to the judiciary, in which that characteristic
feature is so faintly seen." Wilson, on the other hand, justified
the practice on the principle of the higher law: "Parliament may,
unquestionably, be controlled by natural or revealed law, proceeding from divine authority. Is not this superior authority
binding upon the courts of justice? When the courts of justice
obey the superior authority, it cannot be said with propriety
that they control the inferior one; they only declare, as it is
their duty to declare, that this inferior one is controlled by the
other, which is superior. They do not repeal an act of Parliament; they pronounce it void, because contrary to an overruling
law." Thus the function of the judiciary to be a barrier against
democracy, which, according to Tocqueville, it is destined to
be, was not apparent. In the same manner religious liberty,
which has become so much identified with the United States, is
a thing which grew by degrees, and was not to be found
imposed by the letter of the law.

The true natural check on absolute democracy is the federal
system, which limits the central government by the powers
reserved, and the state governments by the powers they have
ceded. It is the one immortal tribute of America to political
science, for state rights are at the same time the consummation
and the guard of democracy. So much so that an officer wrote, a
few months before Bull Run: "The people in the south are

evidently unanimous in the opinion that slavery is endangered by the current of events, and it is useless to attempt to alter that opinion. As our government is founded on the will of the people, when that will is fixed our government is powerless." Those are the words of Sherman, the man who, by his march through Georgia, cut the Confederacy into two. Lincoln himself wrote, at the same time: "I declare that the maintenance inviolate of the rights of the states, and especially the right of each state to order and control its own domestic institutions according to its own judgment exclusively, is essential to that balance of powers on which the perfection and endurance of our political fabric depend." Such was the force with which state rights held the minds of abolitionists on the eve of the war that bore them down.

At the Revolution there were many Frenchmen who saw in federalism the only way to reconcile liberty and democracy, to establish government on contract, and to rescue the country from the crushing preponderance of Paris and the Parisian populace. I do not mean the Girondins, but men of opinions different from theirs, and, above all, Mirabeau. He planned to save the throne by detaching the provinces from the frenzy of the capital, and he declared that the federal system is alone capable of preserving freedom in any great empire. The idea did not grow up under American influence; for no man was more opposed to it than Lafayette; and the American witness of the Revolution, Morris, denounced federalism as a danger to France.

Apart from the Constitution, the political thought of America influenced the French next to their own. And it was not all speculation, but a system for which men died, which had proved entirely practical, and strong enough to conquer all resistance, with the sanction and encouragement of Europe. It displayed to France a finished model of revolution, both in thought and action, and showed that what seemed extreme and subversive in the old world, was compatible with good and wise government, with respect for social order, and the preservation of national character and custom. The ideas which captured and convulsed the French people were mostly ready-made for them, and much that is familiar to you now, much of that which I have put before you from other than French sources, will meet us again next week with the old faces, when we come to the States-General.

XIII

Letter to Contributors to the Cambridge Modern History

THE following letter was sent out to the contributors to the Cambridge History. It will interest many, as giving characteristic expression to Acton's ideals as a historian. The paragraphs are left as in the original.

[*From the Editor of the Cambridge Modern History.*]

1. Our purpose is to obtain the best history of modern times that the published or unpublished sources of information admit.

The production of material has so far exceeded the use of it in literature that very much more is known to students than can be found in historians, and no compilation at second hand from the best works would meet the scientific demand for completeness and certainty.

In our own time, within the last few years, most of the official collections in Europe have been made public, and nearly all the evidence that will ever appear is accessible now.

As archives are meant to be explored, and are not meant to be printed, we approach the final stage in the conditions of historical learning.

The long conspiracy against the knowledge of truth has been

Reprinted from Gertrude Himmelfarb, *Lord Acton: A Study in Conscience and Politics* (Chicago: University of Chicago Press, 1952).

Letter to Contributors to the Cambridge Modern History

practically abandoned, and competing scholars all over the civilised world are taking advantage of the change.

By dividing our matter among more than one hundred writers we hope to make the enlarged opportunities of research avail for the main range of modern history.

Froude spoke of 100,000 papers consulted by him in manuscript, abroad and at home; and that is still the price to be paid for mastery, beyond the narrow area of effective occupation.

We will endeavour to procure transcripts of any specified documents which contributors require from places out of reach.

2. It is intended that the narrative shall be such as will serve all readers, that it shall be without notes, and without quotations in foreign languages.

In order to authenticate the text and to assist further research, it is proposed that a selected list of original and auxiliary authorities shall be supplied in each volume, for every chapter or group of chapters dealing with one subject.

Such a bibliography of modern history might be of the utmost utility to students, and would serve as a substitute for the excluded references.

We shall be glad if each contributor will send us, as early as he finds it convenient, a preliminary catalogue of the works on which he would rely; and we enclose a specimen, to explain our plan, and to show how we conceive that books and documents might be classified.

3. Our scheme requires that nothing shall reveal the country, the religion, or the party to which the writers belong.

It is essential not only on the ground that impartiality is the character of legitimate history, but because the work is carried on by men acting together for no other object than the increase of accurate knowledge.

The disclosure of personal views would lead to such confusion that all unity of design would disappear.

4. Some extracts from the editor's Report to the Syndics will show the principles on which the Cambridge History has been undertaken.

"The entire bulk of new matter which the last forty years

have supplied amounts to many thousands of volumes. The honest student finds himself continually deserted, retarded, misled by the classics of historical literature, and has to hew his own way through multitudinous transactions, periodicals, and official publications, where it is difficult to sweep the horizon or to keep abreast. By the judicious division of labour we should be able to do it, and to bring home to every man the last document, and the ripest conclusions of international research. . . .

"All this does not apply to our own time, and the last volumes will be concerned with secrets that cannot be learned from books, but from men. . . .

"The recent Past contains the key to the present time. All forms of thought that influence it come before us in their turn, and we have to describe the ruling currents, to interpret the sovereign forces, that still govern and divide the world. . . .

"By Universal History I understand that which is distinct from the combined history of all countries, which is not a rope of sand, but a continuous development, and is not a burden on the memory, but an illumination of the soul. It moves in a succession to which the nations are subsidiary. Their story will be told, not for their own sake, but in reference and subordination to a higher series, according to the time and the degree in which they contribute to the common fortunes of mankind. . . .

"If we treat History as a progressive science, and lean specially on that side of it, the question will arise, how we justify our departure from ancient ways, and how we satisfy the world that there is reason and method in our innovations. . . .

"To meet this difficulty we must provide a copious, accurate, and well-digested catalogue of authorities. . . .

"Our principle would be to supply help to students, not material to historians. But in critical places we must indicate minutely the sources we follow, and must refer not only to the important books, but to articles in periodical works, and even to original documents, and to transcripts in libraries. The result would amount to an ordinary volume, presenting a conspectus of historical literature, and enumerating all the better books, the newly acquired sources, and the last discoveries. It would exhibit in the clearest light the vast difference between history, original and authentic, and history, antiquated and lower than the high-water mark of present learning. . . .

"We shall avoid the needless utterance of opinion, and the service of a cause.

"Contributors will understand that we are established, not under the Meridian of Greenwich, but in Long. 30° W.; that our Waterloo must be one that satisfies French and English, Germans and Dutch alike; that nobody can tell, without examining the list of authors, where the Bishop of Oxford laid down the pen, and whether Fairbairn or Gasquet, Liebermann or Harrison took it up."

CAMBRIDGE
March 12, 1898

XIV

Beginning of the Modern State

MODERN History tells how the last four hundred years have modified the medieval conditions of life and thought. In comparison with them, the Middle Ages were the domain of stability, and continuity, and instinctive evolution, seldom interrupted by such originators as Gregory VII. or St. Francis of Assisi. Ignorant of History, they allowed themselves to be governed by the unknown Past; ignorant of Science, they never believed in hidden forces working onwards to a happier future. The sense of decay was upon them; and each generation seemed so inferior to the last, in ancient wisdom and ancestral virtue, that they found comfort in the assurance that the end of the world was at hand.

Yet the most profound and penetrating of the causes that have transformed society is a medieval inheritance. It was late in the thirteenth century that the psychology of Conscience was closely studied for the first time, and men began to speak of it as the audible voice of God, that never misleads or fails, and that ought to be obeyed always, whether enlightened or darkened, right or wrong. The notion was restrained, on its appearance, by the practice of regarding opposition to Church power as equivalent to specific heresy, which depressed the secret monitor below the public and visible authority. With the decline of coercion the claim of Conscience rose, and the ground abandoned by the inquisitor was gained by the individual.

Reprinted from Acton, *Lectures on Modern History* (London: Macmillan, 1906).

There was less reason then for men to be cast of the same type; there was a more vigorous growth of independent character, and a conscious control over its formation. The knowledge of good and evil was not an exclusive and sublime prerogative assigned to states, or nations, or majorities. When it had been defined and recognised as something divine in human nature, its action was to limit power by causing the sovereign voice within to be heard above the expressed will and settled custom of surrounding men. By that hypothesis, the soul became more sacred than the state, because it receives light from above, as well as because its concerns are eternal, and out of all proportion with the common interests of government. That is the root from which liberty of Conscience was developed, and all other liberty needed to confine the sphere of power, in order that it may not challenge the supremacy of that which is highest and best in man.

The securities by which this purpose has been attempted compose the problem of all later history, and centuries were spent in ascertaining and constructing them. If in the main the direction has been upward, the movement has been tardy, the conflict intense, the balance often uncertain. The passion for power over others can never cease to threaten mankind, and is always sure of finding new and unforeseen allies in continuing its martyrology. Therefore, the method of modern progress was revolution. By a series of violent shocks the nations in succession have struggled to shake off the Past, to reverse the action of Time and the verdict of success, and to rescue the world from the reign of the dead. They have been due less to provocation by actual wrong than to the attraction of ideal right, and the claims that inspired them were universal and detached. Progress has imposed increasing sacrifices on society, in behalf of those who can make no return, from whose welfare it derives no equivalent benefit, whose existence is a burden, an evil, eventually a peril to the community. The mean duration of life, the compendious test of improvement, is prolonged by all the chief agents of civilisation, moral and material, religious and scientific, working together, and depends on preserving, at infinite cost, which is infinite loss, the crippled child and the victim of accident, the idiot and the madman, the pauper and the culprit, the old and infirm, curable and incurable. This growing dominion of disinterested motive, this liberality towards the weak, in social life, corresponds to that respect for the minority, in political life, which is the essence of freedom. It is an application of the same principle of self-denial, and of the higher law.

Taking long periods, we perceive the advance of moral over material influence, the triumph of general ideas, the gradual amendment. The line of march will prove, on the whole, to have been from force and cruelty to consent and association, to humanity, rational persuasion, and the persistent appeal to common, simple, and evident maxims. We have dethroned necessity, in the shape both of hunger and of fear, by extending the scene from Western Europe to the whole world, so that all shall contribute to the treasure of civilisation, and by taking into partnership in the enjoyment of its rewards those who are far off as well as those who are below. We shall give our attention to much that has failed and passed away, as well as to the phenomena of progress, which help to build up the world in which we live. For History must be our deliverer not only from the undue influence of other times, but from the undue influence of our own, from the tyranny of environment and the pressure of the air we breathe. It requires all historic forces to produce their record and submit to judgment, and it promotes the faculty of resistance to contemporary surroundings by familiarity with other ages and other orbits of thought.

In these latter days the sum of differences in international character has been appreciably bound down by the constant process of adaptation and adjustment, and by exposure to like influences. The people of various countries are swayed by identical interests, they are absorbed in the same problems, and thrill with the same emotions; their classics are interchangeable, authorities in science are nearly alike for all, and they readily combine to make experiments and researches in common. Towards 1500, European nations, having been fashioned and composed out of simple elements during the thousand years between the fall of the Roman Empire and that of its successor in the East, had reached full measure of differentiation. They were estranged from each other, and were inclined to treat the foreigner as the foe. Ancient links were loosened, the Pope was no longer an accepted peacemaker; and the idea of an international code, overriding the will of nations and the authority of sovereigns, had not dawned upon philosophy. Between the old order that was changing and the new that was unborn, Europe had an inorganic interval to go through.

Modern History begins under stress of the Ottoman Conquest. Constantinople fell, after an attempt to negotiate for help, by the union of the Greek and Latin Churches. The agreement come to at Florence was not ratified at home; the attempt was resented, and led to an explosion of feeling that made even subjugation by the Turk seem for the moment less intolerable, and that hastened the catastrophe by making Western Christians slow to sacrifice themselves for their implacable brethren in the East. Offers of help were made, conditional on acceptance of the Florentine decree, and were rejected with patriotic and theological disdain. A small force of papal and Genoese mercenaries shared the fate of the defenders, and the end could not have been long averted, even by the restoration of religious unity. The Powers that held back were not restrained by dogmatic arguments only. The dread of Latin intolerance was the most favourable circumstance encountered by the Turks in the Eastern Empire, and they at once offered protection and immunities to the patriarch and his prelates. The conquest of the entire peninsula, with the islands, occupied a generation, and it was good policy meanwhile to do nothing that would diminish the advantage or awaken alarm of persecution. Their system required the increase rather than the conversion of Christian subjects, for the tribute of gold as well as the tribute of blood. The Janissaries were selected among the sons of Christian parents, who became renegades, and who, having neither home nor family, no life but in camp, no employment but arms, became not only the best professional soldiers in the world, but a force constantly active to undo the work of pacific statesmen and to find fresh occasion for war. There were occasional outbreaks of blind ferocity, and at all times there was the incapacity of an uncivilised race to understand the character and the interest of alien subjects more cultivated than themselves. But there was not at first the sense of unmitigated tyranny that arose later; and there was not so great a contrast with life as it was under Italian despots as to make Christians under the Sultan passionately long for deliverance.

From the perjury of Varna, in 1446, when the Christians broke the treaty just concluded at Sregedin, it was understood that they could never be trusted to keep engagements entered into with people of another religion. It seemed a weak-minded exaggeration of hypocrisy to abstain from preying on men so furiously divided, so full of hatred, so incapable of combining in defense of their altars and their homes, so eager in soliciting aid and intervention from the infidel in their own disputes. The several principalities of the circumference, Servia, Bosnia, Wallachia, the Morea, and the islands, varying in nationality and in religion, were attacked separately, and made no joint defence. In Epirus, Scanderbeg, once a renegade, then in communion with Rome, drawing his supplies from the opposite coast of Apulia, which his sentinels on Cape Linguetta could see at sunrise, maintained himself for many years victoriously, knowing that his country would perish with him. John Hunyadi had defended Christendom on the Hungarian frontier so well that the monarchy of his son stemmed the tide of invasion for seventy years. While the Turkish outposts kept watch on the Danube, Mahomet seized Otranto, and all the way upwards to the Alps there was no force capable of resisting him. Just then, he died, Otranto was lost, and the enterprise was not renewed. His people were a nation of soldiers, not a nation of sailors. For operations beyond sea they relied on the seamen of the Aegean, generally Christians, as they had required the help of Genoese ships to ferry them over the Hellespont.

Under Bajazet, the successor, there was some rest for Europe.

404

His brother, who was a dangerous competitor, as the crown went to the one who survived, fled for safety to the Christians, and was detained as a hostage, beyond the possibility of ransom, by the Knights of St. John, and then by the Pope. The Sultan paid, that he might be kept quiet.

For years the Turks were busy in the East. Selim conquered Syria and part of Persia. He conquered Arabia, and was acknowledged by the Sheriff of Mecca caliph and protector of the holy shrine. He conquered Egypt and assumed the prerogative of the Imaum, which had been a shadow at Cairo, but became, at Constantinople, the supreme authority in Islam. Gathering up the concentrated resources of the Levant, Solyman the Magnificent turned, at last, against the enemy who guarded the gates of civilised Europe. Having taken Belgrade, he undertook, in 1526, the crowning campaign of Turkish history. At the battle of Mohacs Hungary lost her independence. The Turks found a Transylvanian magnate who was willing to receive the crown from them; and the broad valley of the Danube continued to be their battlefield until the days of Sobieski and Eugene. But the legitimate heir of King Ladislas, who fell at Mohacs, was Ferdinand, only brother of Charles V.; and Hungary, with the vast region then belonging to the Bohemian crown, passing to the same hands as the ancient inheritance of the Habsburgs, constituted the great Austrian monarchy which extended from the Adriatic to the far Sarmatian plain, and Solyman's victory brought him face to face with the first Power able to arrest his progress. The Turks were repulsed at Vienna in 1529, at Malta in 1564. This was their limit in Western Europe; and after Lepanto, in 1571, their only expansion was at the expense of Poland at Muscovy. They still wielded almost boundless resources; the entire seaboard from Cattaro all round by the Euxine to the Atlantic was Mahometan, and all but one-fourth of the Mediterranean was a Turkish lake. It was long before they knew that it was not their destiny to be masters of the Western as well as of the Eastern world.

While this heavy cloud overhung the Adriatic and the Danube, and the countries within reach of the Turk were in peril of extinction, the nations farther west were consolidating rapidly into unity and power. By the marriage of Ferdinand and Isabella, by their conquest of Granada and the rise of a new hemisphere at their command, Spain for the first time became a great Power; while France, having expelled the English, having instituted a permanent army, acquired vast frontier provinces, and crushed the centrifugal forces of feudalism, was more directly formidable and more easily aggressive. These newly created Powers portended danger in one direction. Their increase was not in comparison with England or with Portugal, so much as in contrast with Italy. England, by the Tudors, had achieved internal tranquillity; and Portugal was already at the head of Europe in making the ocean tributary to trade. But Italy was divided, unwarlike, poor in the civic virtues that made Switzerland impregnable, rich in the tempting luxuries of civilisation, an inexhaustible treasure-house of much that the neighbours gratly needed and could never find elsewhere. The best writers and scholars and teachers, the most consummate artists, the ablest commanders by land and sea, the deepest explorers of the mystery of State that have been known before or since, all the splendours of the Renaissance, and the fruits of a whole century of progress were there, ready to be appropriated and employed for its own benefit by a paramount Power.

It was obvious that the countries newly strengthened, the countries growing in unity and concentration and superfluous forces, should encroach upon those that were demoralised and weakened. By strict reason of State, this was not the policy of France; for the French frontiers were assigned by nature everywhere but in the northeast. There the country was open, the enemy's territory approached the capital; and the true line of expansion was towards Antwerp, or Liège, or Strasburg. But the French were invited into Italy with promise of welcome, because the Angevin claim to Naples, defeated in 1462, had passed to the King of France. The Aragonese, who had been successful in resisting it, was not legitimate, and had been compelled again to struggle for existence by the Rising of the Barons. The rising was suppressed; the discontented Neapoli-

tans went into exile; and they were now in France, prophesying
easy triumphs if Charles VIII. would extend his hand to take
the greatness that belonged to the heir of the house of Anjou.
They were followed by the most important of the Italian Cardinals, Della Rovere, nephew of a former Pope, himself afterwards the most famous pontiff who had appeared for centuries.
Armed with the secrets of the Conclave, the Cardinal insisted
that Alexander VI. should be deposed, on the ground that he
had paid for the papacy in ascertainable sums of money and
money's worth; whereas spiritual office obtained in that way
was *ipso facto* void.

The advent of the French, heralded by the passionate eloquence of Savonarola, was also hailed by Florence and its
dependencies, in their impatience of the Medicean rule, now
that it had dropped from the hands of the illustrious Lorenzo,
into those of his less competent son. Lodovico Sforza, the Re-
gent of Milan, was also among those who called in the French,
as he had a family quarrel with Naples. His father, Francesco,
the most successful of the Condottieri, who acquired the Milanese by marriage with a Visconti, is known by that significant
saying: "May God defend me from my friends. From my enemies I can defend myself." As the Duke of Orléans also descended from the Visconti, Lodovico wished to divert the
French to the more alluring prospect of Naples.

In September 1494 Charles VIII. invaded Italy by the Mont
Genèvre, with an army equal to his immediate purpose. His
horsemen still displayed the medieval armour, wrought by the
artistic craftsmen of the Renaissance. They were followed by
artillery, the newer arm which, in another generation, swept the
steel-clad knight away. French infantry was not thought so well
of. But the Swiss had become, in their wars with Burgundy, the
most renowned of all foot-soldiers. They were unskilled in
manoeuvres; but their pikemen, charging in dense masses, proved
irresistible on many Italian fields; until it was discovered that
they would serve for money on either side, and that when
opposed to their countrymen they refused to fight. At Pavia
they were cut down by the Spaniards and their fame began to

wane. They were Germans, hating Austria, and their fidelity to the golden lilies is one of the constant facts of French history, until the Swiss guard and the white flag vanished together, in July 1830.

Charles reached Naples early in 1495, having had no resistance to overcome, but having accomplished nothing, and having manifested no distinct purpose on his way, when he found himself, for a moment, master of Florence and of Rome. The deliverance of Constantinople was an idea that occurred inevitably to a man of enterprise who was in possession of Southern Italy. It was the advanced post of Europe against the East, of Christendom against Islam; the proper rendezvous of Crusaders; the source of supplies; the refuge of squadrons needing to refit. The Sultan was not an overwhelming warrior, like his father; he had not, like Selim, his successor, control of the entire East, and he was held in check by the existence of his brother, whom Charles took with him, on leaving Rome, with a view to ulterior service, but whom he lost soon after.

Charles VIII. was not a man ripened by experience of great affairs, and he had assumed the title of King of Jerusalem, as a sign of his crusading purpose. But he also called himself King of Sicily, as representing the Anjous, and this was not a disused and neglected derelict. For the island belonged to the King of Aragon, the most politic and capable of European monarchs. Before starting for Italy, Charles had made terms with him, and Ferdinand, in consideration of a rectified frontier, had engaged, by the treaty of Barcelona, to take no unfriendly advantage of his neighbour's absence. The basis of this agreement was shattered by the immediate unexpected and overwhelming success of the French arms. From his stronghold in the South it would be easy for Charles to make himself master of Rome, of Florence, of all Italy, until he came in sight of the lion of St. Mark. So vast and sudden a superiority was a serious danger. A latent jealousy of Spain underlay the whole expedition. The realm of the Catholic kings was expanding, and an indistinct empire, larger, in reality, than that of Rome, was rising out of the Atlantic. By a very simple calculation of approaching contingencies, Ferdinand might be suspected of designs upon Naples. Now that the helplessness of the Neapolitans had been revealed, it was apparent that he had made a false reckoning when he allowed the French to occupy what he might have taken more easily himself, by crossing the Straits of Messina. Ferdinand joined the Italians of the North in declaring against the invader, and his envoy Fonseca tore up the Treaty of Barcelona before the face of the French king.

Having been crowned in the Cathedral, and having garrisoned his fortresses, Charles set out for France, at the head of a small army. As he came over the Apennines into Lombardy, at Fornovo he was met by a larger force, chiefly provided by Venice, and had to fight his way through. A fortnight after his departure the Spaniards, under Gonsalvo of Cordova, landed in Calabria, as auxiliaries of the dethroned king. The throne was once more occupied by the fallen family, and Charles retained nothing of his easy and inglorious conquests when he died in 1498.

His successor, Lewis XII., was the Duke of Orléans, who descended from the Visconti, and he at once prepared to enforce his claim on Milan. He allied himself against his rival, Sforza, with Venice, and with Pope Alexander. That he might marry the widowed queen, and preserve her duchy of Brittany for the Crown, he required that his own childless marriage should be annulled. Upon the Legate who brought the necessary documents the grateful king bestowed a principality, a bride of almost royal rank, and an army wherewith to reconquer the lost possessions of the Church in Central Italy. For the Legate was the Cardinal of Valencia, who became thenceforward Duke of Valentinois, and is better known as Caesar Borgia. The rich Lombard plain, the garden of Italy, was conquered as easily as Naples had been in the first expedition. Sforza said to the Venetians: "I have been the dinner; you will be the supper"; and went up into the Alps to look for Swiss levies. At Novara, in 1500, his mercenaries betrayed him and he ended his days in a French prison. On their way home from the scene of their treachery, the Swiss crowned their evil repute by seizing

Bellinzona and the valley of the Ticino, which has remained one of their cantons.

Lewis, undisputed master of Milan and Genoa, assured of the Roman and the Venetian alliance, was in a better position than his predecessor to renew the claim on the throne of Naples. But now, behind Frederic of Naples, there was Ferdinand of Aragon and Sicily, who was not likely to allow the king for whom he had fought to be deposed without resistance. Therefore it was a welcome suggestion when Ferdinand proposed that they should combine to expel Frederic and to divide his kingdom. As it was Ferdinand who had just reinstated him, this was an adaptation to the affairs of Christendom of the methods which passed for justice in the treatment of unbelievers, and were applied without scruple by the foremost men of the age, Albuquerque and Cortez. Frederic turned for aid to the Sultan, and this felonious act was put forward as the justification of his aggressors. The Pope sanctioned the Treaty of Partition, and as the Crown of Naples was technically in his gift, he deprived the king on the ground stated by the allies. The exquisite significance of the plea was that the Pope himself had invited Turkish intervention in Italy, and now declared it a cause of forfeiture. In 1501 French and Spaniards occupied their allotted portions, and then quarrelled over the distribution of the spoil. For a time Gonsalvo, "the great Captain," was driven to bay at Barletta on the Adriatic; but at the end of 1503 he won a decisive victory, and the defeated French, under Bayard, withdrew from the Garigliano to the Po. Naples remained a dependency of Spain, for all purposes, in modern history.

In the midst of foreign armies, and of new combinations disturbing the established balance of Italian Powers, the lesser potentates were exposed to destruction; and there were forces about sufficient, under capable guidance, to remodel the chaotic centre of Italy, where no strong government had ever been constituted. Caesar Borgia recognised the opportunity as soon as the French were at Milan; the Pope was growing old and was clay in his terrible hands. His sister just then became Duchess of Ferrara, on the border of the defenceless region which he coveted; and the dominions of the King of France, his patron and ally, extended to the Adda and the Po. Never had such advantages been united in such a man. For Caesar's talents were of the imperial kind. He was fearless of difficulties, of dangers, and of consequences; and having no preference for right or wrong, he weighed with an equal and dispassionate mind whether it was better to spare a man or to cut his throat. As he did not attempt more than he could perform, his rapid success awakened aspirations for a possible future. He was odious to Venice, but a Venetian, who watched his meteoric course, wonders, in his secret diary, whether this unerring schemer was to be the appointed deliverer. He was a terror to Florence, yet the Florentine secretary, to whom he confided his thoughts in certain critical hours, wrote of him as men have written of Napoleon, and erected a monument to his memory that has secretly fascinated half the politicians in the world.

With his double equipment as a lieutenant of the French king and as a *condottiere* of the Pope, he began by reviving the dormant authority of Rome, where nominal feudatories held vicarious sway. In the place of many despots struggling not for objects of policy, but for their own existence, there appeared a single state, reaching from sea to sea, from the Campagna to the salt-marshes by the delta of the Po, under a papal prince and *gonfaloniere,* invested with rights and prerogatives to protect the Holy See, and with power to control it. Rome would have become a dependency of the reigning house of Borgia, as it had been of less capable vassals, and the system might have lasted as long as the brain that devised it. Lorenzo de' Medici once said that his buildings were the only works that would outlast him; and it is common in the secular characters of that epoch, unlike the priesthood, not to believe in those things that are abiding, and not to regard organisations that are humble and obscure at first and bloom by slow degrees for the use of another age.

Caesar's enterprise was not determined or limited by the claims of the Vatican. He served both Pope and king, and his French alliance carried farther than the recovery of the

Romagna. Florence became tributary by taking him into pay. Bologna bought him off with a heavy ransom. Venice inscribed his name in the illustrious record of its nobility. None could tell where his ambition or his resources would end, how his inventive genius would employ the rivalry of the invaders, what uses he would devise for the Emperor and the Turk. The era of petty tyranny was closed by the apparition of one superior national tyrant, who could be no worse than twenty, for though his crimes would be as theirs, they would not be useless to the nation, but were thoughtfully designed and executed for the sake of power, the accepted object of politics in a country where the right was known by the result. Caesar was not an unpopular master, and his subjects were true to him in his falling fortunes. The death of Alexander and the decline of the French cause in the South cut short his work in the autumn of 1503. Della Rovere, Cardinal Vincula, whose title came from the Church of St. Peter in Chains, the inflexible enemy of the Borgias, was now Julius II.; and after a brief interval he was strong enough to drive Caesar out of the country; while the Venetians, entering the Romagna under ill omens for the Republic, occupied the remnant of his many conquests.

Julius had resisted Alexander, as a man unfit for his function, and it soon appeared that this was not a private feud, but a total reversal of ideas and policy. The change was not felt in religious reform or in patronage of learning, but first in the notion of territorial politics. Caesar had rebuilt the duchy of Romagna in the service of the papacy; and it was the essence of the schemes of Julius that it should be secured for the Holy See, together with all else that could be claimed by right, or acquired by policy and war. The Borgias had prevailed by arms, and Julius would not consent to be their inferior and to condemn his whole career. He must draw the sword; but, unlike them, he would draw it in the direct interest of the Church. He had overthrown the conqueror, not that the conquests might be dissolved, or might go to Venice, but in order that he himself and his successors might have power in Italy, and through Italians, over the world. Upon this foundation he instituted the temporal power, as it subsisted for three centuries. The jealous municipal spirit of the Middle Ages had dissolved society into units, and nothing but force could reverse the tradition and weld the fragments into great communities. Borgia had shown that this could be done; but also that no victorious *condottiere,* were he even his own son, could be trusted by a Pope. Julius undertook to command his army himself, and to fight at the head of his troops. Letting his white beard grow, putting on armour, and proudly riding his war-horse under fire, he exhibited the most picturesque and romantic figure of his time.

The Venetians, commanding the seaboard with their galleys, were not easy to dislodge from the towns they occupied. Essentially a maritime and commercial Power, their centre of gravity lay so far east that it was once proposed to move the capital from the Lagoons to the Bosphorus. When the advancing Turk damaged their trade and threatened their Colonial empire, they took advantage of Italian disintegration to become a continental state, and the general insecurity and oppression of miniature potentates made it a happy fate to be subject to the serene and politic government, whose three thousand ships still held the sea, flying the Christian flag. Renouncing non-intervention on the mainland, they set power above prosperity, and the interest of the State above the welfare and safety of a thousand patrician houses. Wherever there were troubled waters, the fisher was Venice. All down the Eastern Coast, and along the Alpine slopes to the passes which were the trade route to Northern Europe, and still farther, at the expense of Milan and Naples, the patriarch of Aquileia and the Duke of Ferrara, the Emperor and the Pope, the Queen of the Adriatic extended her intelligent sway. It was under the long administration of the Doge Foscari, Byron's hero, that it dawned upon the Venetians that it might be their mission to supersede the frail and helpless governments of the Peninsula; and their famous politician and historian, Paruta, believed that it was in their power to do what Rome had done. Their ambition was evident to their neighbours, and those whom they had despoiled, under every plausible pretext, awaited the opportunity of retribution.

Julius, taking counsel with Machiavelli, found it easy to form a league composed of their enemies. As it was not the interest of the empire, France and Spain, to spite Venice by strengthening each other, the Venetians imagined they could safely hold their ground, leaving the dependent cities to make their own terms with the enemy. Padua held out victoriously against Maximilian, but the battle of Agnadello was lost against the French in the same year 1509, in which, fighting under the Crescent in the Indian Ocean, the Venetians were defeated by the Portuguese, and lost their Eastern trade. They soon obtained their revenge. Having gained his ends by employing France against Venice in the League of Cambray, Julius now allied himself with the Venetians to expel the French from Milan. He had recovered the papal possessions, he had broken the Venetian power, and in this his third effort to reconstitute Italy, he still succeeded, because he had the support of the Venetians and the Swiss. The French gave battle to the Spaniards at Ravenna and to the Swiss at Novara, and then they evacuated the Milanese.

Lewis XII. swore that he would wreak vengeance on the papacy, and, in conjunction with the Emperor, opened a Council at Pisa, which was attended by a minority of cardinals. Julius met the attack by calling a general Council to meet at the Lateran, which was the first since the great reforming Council, and was still sitting when Julius died in 1513. Like the Council at Pisa, it was regarded at Rome as a move in the great game of Politics, and it made no serious attempt to heal the long-standing and acknowledged wounds of the Church. Its action spread the belief that the reigning diseases were known, but that the remedy was refused, and that reforms that might help religion were not to be expected from Church or State. Julius II. died without having expelled the barbarians, as he had promised. The French were gone, but the Spaniards remained unshaken, and were still the pivot of the operations of the Holy See. The investiture of Naples was granted to Ferdinand of Aragon, and the fairest region in Europe bound Spain irrevocably to the Popes.

Although the Italian scheme of Julius was left halfway, his

Roman scheme was completed; the intermittent suzerainty of the Middle Ages was straitened out into effective sovereignty over the half of Central Italy, where anarchy used to reign, and the temporal power was fixed on foundations solid enough to bear the coming diminution of spiritual power. The added splendours of modern royalty, round which cardinals of reigning houses—Medici, Este, Farnese, Gonzaga—displayed the pomp and ceremony of semi-regal state, in palaces built by Bramante and Michael Angelo, with the ambassadors and protectors of the Powers, and the heads of princely families that had worn the tiara, made Rome the magnetic pole of aristocratic society. As the capital of an absolute monarchy, as others were, it became associated with principles which, in the Middle Ages, it resisted with spiritual and secular weapons; and the magnitude of the change was apparent when Leo X., by the Concordat of Bologna, conceded to Francis I. the choice of bishops and the higher patronage of the Church of France. For Francis on his accession sent an army into Italy, the last work of Julius II. was overthrown at Marignano, and France again was master of the Milanese.

The final struggle was to come at the vacancy of the Imperial throne. Ferdinand of Aragon was dead, and Naples passed to the King of undivided Spain. It was the unswerving policy of Rome that it should not be united with the Empire, and against that fixed axiom the strongest dynasty of emperors went to pieces. The Reformation had just begun in Germany, and Leo wished one of the Northern Electors to be chosen as Maximilian's successor. In conformity with the political situation, he would have preferred Frederic of Saxony, the protector of Luther. The election of Charles, in 1519, was a defiance of the Balance of Power, a thing not to the taste of the Middle Ages, but becoming familiar in those days. France, unable formerly to keep Naples against Spain, had now to defend Lombardy against Spain, supported by Germany, Naples, and the Netherlands. Francis maintained the unequal struggle for four years, although his most powerful vassal, Bourbon, brought the enemy to the gates of Marseilles. The decisive action of the long Italian war was fought at Pavia in June 1525, where Francis was taken prisoner, and was compelled to purchase his release by cruel sacrifices.

The years that followed are only a phase in the permanent subjugation of Italy, but they are memorable in another connection. For the triumph of Pavia brought the suppression of the Lutherans within the range of practical politics. The Peasants' War had damaged their position; the Emperor was able now to execute the Imperial decree of Worms, and there were some in Germany who desired it. He made it a condition of his prisoners' deliverance that he should assist in destroying them; and Francis readily offered to do it by coming in person, and bearing half the charge. Charles proposed to take him at his word, when he learnt that the Pope was at the head of a great alliance against him. Pope Clement was advised by the best ecclesiastic in his court, the *Datario* Giberti, to try one more struggle before the chains were riveted, and before he became, as they said, a Spanish chaplain. It is a war, said Giberti, not for power or dominion, but for the redemption of Italy from perpetual bondage; and he placed his master, for the moment, at the head of the nation. Clement concluded a treaty with the Emperor's enemies at Cognac, released Francis from his oath to observe the Treaty of Madrid, and endeavoured to make Pescara, the victor of Pavia, turn traitor by the prospect of the throne of Naples.

In this way Charles was compelled to turn his arms against Rome. He protested that he would risk all his crowns for the sake of revenge, and appealed to Germany, with its Lutherans, for support. Tell them, he wrote, that they are wanted against the Turk. They will know what Turk we mean. They knew it so well that the landsknechts came provided with silken nooses for the necks of cardinals, besides a gold-thread one for the Pope. He issued a detailed manifesto against him, the work of Valdes, one of the rare Lutherans of Spain; and those who were in the secret expected that the shrift would be short. Francis had intended from the first moment to break his word, and to execute no conditions injurious to France, but he came too late.

A large body of Germans poured over the Alps and joined the Spaniards in Lombardy. It was observed afterwards that the Spaniards were the most vindictive, but it was the Germans who made the push for Rome; and Bourbon, on the plea of economy, as he could not pay them, led them through the passes of the Apennines, overthrowing the Medici at Florence on the way. Rome was taken almost without resistance, and Clement shut himself up in St. Angelo, while the city was given over to unmerciful pillage, the prelates were held to ransom, and all the secret treasure was got at by torture. That month of May 1527, with its awful experience, was an end to the pride and the hope and the gladness of the pagan revival; a severe and penitential spirit came over society, preparing to meet the Reformation by reform, and to avert change in doctrine by a change in morality. The sack of Rome, said Cardinal Cajetan, was a just judgment on the sufferers. The city was now the Emperor's, by right of conquest, to bestow as he chose, and the Romans were not unwilling that it should be his capital. Some said that the abolition of the temporal power would secure peace among the Powers, whilst others thought that the consequence would be a patriarch in France, if not in England as well. The last effort of the French being spent, and Doria having gone over to the Emperor, taking with him Genoa, the key of French influence, the chain of transactions which began with the Neapolitan expedition of 1494, concluded in 1530 with the siege of Florence. Charles made peace with France at Cambray, and with the Pope at Barcelona, and received the Imperial crown at Bologna.

This was the consummation of the Italian wars, by which the main conditions of modern politics were determined. The conflicts which had lasted for a generation, and the disorder and violence which were older still, were at an end; Italy obtained repose from her master, and spent for centuries her intellect in his service. Pescara, Ferrante Gonzaga, Philibert Emanuel, Spinola, were the men who made Spain the first of military powers. And Parma's invincible legions, which created Belgium, wrested Antwerp from the Dutch, delivered Paris against Henry IV., and watched the signals of the Armada that they might subdue England, were thronged with Italian infantry. Excepting Venice, strong in her navy and her unapproachable lagoon, Spain dominated thenceforward over Italy, and became, by her ascendency in both Sicilies, a bulwark against the Turks.

Italy passed out of general politics, and was a force in Europe only through Rome. The Conclave, and the creation of cardinals to compose the Conclave, made it a constant school of negotiation and intrigue for the best diplomacy in the world. By favour of the Habsburgs, the papacy obtained a fixed dominion, secure against all comers, requiring no military defence, no wasting and profitless expenditure, nothing to dissolve the mirage of an ideal government, under spiritual and converted men. The pontificates became steadily longer, averaging six years in the sixteenth century, eight in the seventeenth, twelve in the eighteenth, sixteen in the nineteenth, and by the original and characteristic institution which is technically known as nepotism, the selection of a Prime Minister, not from the College of the ecclesiastical aristocracy, but from the family of the reigning sovereign, the tonsured statesmen introduced a dynastic infusion into the fluctuations of elective monarchy.

The triumph and coronation of the Emperor Charles V., when he was superior to all that Europe had beheld since Charlemagne, revived the ancient belief in a supreme authority elevated on alliance with the priesthood, at the expense of the independence and the equipoise of nations. The exploits of Magellan and Cortez, upsetting all habits of perspective, called up vain dreams of the coming immensity of Spain, and roused the phantom of universal empire. The motive of domination became a reigning force in Europe; for it was an idea which monarchy would not willingly let fall after it had received a religious and an international consecration. For centuries it was constantly asserted as a claim of necessity and of right. It was the supreme manifestation of the modern state, according to the image which Machiavelli had set up, the state that suffers neither limit nor equality, and is bound by no duty to nations or to men, that thrives on destruction, and sanctifies whatever things contributed to increase of power.

This law of the modern world, that power tends to expand indefinitely, and will transcend all barriers, abroad and at home, until met by superior forces, produces the rhythmic movement of History. Neither race, nor religion, nor political theory has been in the same degree an incentive to the perpetuation of universal enmity and national strife. The threatened interests were compelled to unite for the self-government of nations, the toleration of religions, and the rights of men. And it is by the combined efforts of the weak, made under compulsion, to resist the reign of force and constant wrong, that, in the rapid change but slow progress of four hundred years, liberty has been preserved, and secured, and extended, and finally understood.

Index